AGORANOMIA
STUDIES IN MONEY AND EXCHANGE
PRESENTED TO JOHN H. KROLL

Chris Williams

JOHN H. KROLL

Agoranomia

Studies in Money and Exchange
Presented to John H. Kroll

EDITED BY
PETER G. VAN ALFEN

THE AMERICAN NUMISMATIC SOCIETY
NEW YORK
2006

ISBN 10: 0-89722-298-9
ISBN 13: 978-0-89722-298-3

Library of Congress Cataloging-in-Publication Data
Agoranomia : studies in money and exchange presented to John
H. Kroll / edited by Peter G. van Alfen.
      p. cm.
  Essays in English and French.
  Includes bibliographical references and index.
  ISBN-13: 978-0-89722-298-3
  ISBN-10: 0-89722-298-9
  1. Coins, Greek--History. 2. Coinage--Greece--History.
3. Numismatics, Greek. 4. Greece--Antiquities. 5. Money--
Greece--History. 6. Exchange--Greece--History. 7. Greece--
Commerce--History. I. Kroll, John H. II. Van Alfen, Peter G.
  CJ335.A45 2006
  737.4938--dc22

                                              2006018073

Printed in China

Contents

Preface

Friends, students, and colleagues have joined together to produce this volume of studies for Professor John ("Jack") H. Kroll on his retirement from the University of Texas at Austin in May 2006. Jack Kroll joined the faculty of the Classics Department in 1973 and over the course of more than three decades distinguished himself as a well-loved mentor and colleague. Prior to his position in Texas, and after completing his Ph.D. at Harvard in 1968, he served as the numismatist for the excavations of the Athenian Agora conducted by the American School of Classical Studies at Athens. Although his published work has covered a broad range of topics, including Athenian bronze allotment plates, architectural sculpture, and epigraphy (see the following bibliography), it is in the field of numismatics and ancient money that Kroll has made his greatest contributions, and where his writing has been most eloquent. Because of this extended interest in Kroll's own work, we have limited the focus of this volume to studies in money and exchange.

Kroll's first serious introduction to numismatics, like many students in the United States, was through the American Numismatic Society's (ANS) graduate summer seminar, which he attended in 1963. Encouraged by his advisors to "get a hoard," that is to complete an all encompassing, technical study of a single hoard of coins as the best possible means of delving into numismatics, he began work on a late Hellenistic hoard of tetrobols from Kos, which had been donated to the ANS in1960. The resulting study, his first numismatic publication, appeared the following year in the ANS' *Museum Notes*. In arguing that the magisterial legends found on the coins represented not political officers but rather individuals who had privately funded the state's coinage, Kroll already demonstrated a preference for looking beyond the often-favored political interpretations of coinage to those more grounded in its practical, monetary aspects. This functional approach to coinage and money has been a hallmark of his work since.

With his appointment as the numismatist for the American School's excavations in the Athenian Agora, Kroll began his far-reaching work on the coinages of Athens. In a dozen articles, a *Sylloge Nummorum Graecorum* volume, and his monograph on the coins from the Agora excavations, Kroll has become the recognized authority on Athenian coinage, from the first silver issues in the sixth century BC to the Roman Imperial bronze issues of the second and third centuries AD. Among his several important contributions to the study of Athenian coinage, Kroll revisited the evolution of the late-sixth-century Athenian issues, arguing that the change in coin types, from the so-called *Wappenmünzen* to the *gorgoneion* tetradrachms and finally to the famed owl types, reflected not the political upheavals in Archaic Athens, but rather fundamental changes in Athenian monetary policy. With the increased production of Laurion silver, the Athenians found they had a desirable surplus commodity and sought a stable form in which to export it: thus the development of the large denomination tetradrachm and constant symbols to place on the coins that were representative of the city itself and its authority rather than of private moneyers. Kroll's conclusion was to suggest that the adoption of the owl types was not politically motivated as generally thought, that is somehow anti-tyrannical or pro-democratic in intent, but was motivated by wholly economic considerations under the direction of the last Athenian tyrant, Hippias.

Kroll's work on the Classical period coinages of Athens has touched on other controversial topics. Although silver-plated, bronze-cored coins are almost universally recognized as the work of ancient counterfeiters, Kroll has shown that the Athenians, in the final desperate months of the Peloponnesian War in 406/5 BC, issued an official plated coinage, an argument that is supported not only by coin finds, but textual evidence as well. The Athenians peculiar relationship with their popular coinage, Kroll argued, necessitated an emergency coinage approximating its normal issues, at least in appearance, and not simple bronze or other base metal issues of the kinds issued by other states in duress. This same Athenian response to base metal coinage plays a role in Kroll's study of the earliest issue of Athenian fractional bronze coinage. Compared to other communities, the Athenians were quite late in producing bronze fractions. Many *poleis* had already begun production in the fifth century; the Athenians studiously avoided bronze issues until, as Kroll suggests, the innovative financial reforms of Eubulos in the mid-fourth century perhaps required such unprecedented measures. Most recently, Kroll has begun work on the question of Athens' post-Peloponnesian War coinage, tentatively identifying an owl issue of the 390s where one was previously thought not to exist.

It is, however, in his cataloguing and studying nearly 17,000 coins from the Athenian Agora excavations that Kroll has demonstrated his intellectual rigor and stamina. The publication of his Agora study in 1993 was a milestone in archaeological numismatics, one that will not see an equal for years, if not decades, not only because of the thoroughness of its conspectus (see de Callataÿ this volume), but also due to its solid presentation of the material and honest interpretation. The volume also stands as a useful summary of his previous work on the various series of Athenian coinage.

While Kroll has made essential contributions to the study of Athenian and other coinages, his current work focuses on the beginnings of coinage in general. In recent years, as the debate over the social, historical, and economic origin of coinage in the western world has become ever larger and more complex, Kroll has kept the debate well-grounded in the realities of monetary function and the material evidence. Kroll's service in this regard has partly been as a relentless reviewer of the several recent books and chapters offered by (cultural) historians that touch on coinage's origins and its use in Archaic societies. Kroll's reviews, particularly those of books by Kurke, Schaps, and von Reden, have shown the fallacies of approaches to early coinage that do not show sufficient consideration to the material evidence and the work of generations of numismatists. While certainly not adverse to the symbolic, ideological, or political dimensions of coinage, Kroll has found it necessary to stress repeatedly that these are aspects wholly secondary to its utilitarian, fiscal purposes, and so finds serious fault with studies that unduly emphasize or distort the abstract over the concrete. In order to highlight the fact that the introduction of coinage was not as momentous an invention as some (e.g., Kurke, Schaps) have insisted, simply because eastern Mediterranean societies were already monetized well before the arrival of coinage, Kroll has offered a series of innovative articles and chapters on the early monetary use of Hacksilber and other types of bullion in the Aegean. As for the reasons behind the introduction of coinage per se, Kroll, like several others, sees it merely as an isolated, official response to problems associated with the monetary use of electrum in Lydia, where there was a natural abundance of the alloy. The obvious benefits of using in various types of transactions small ingots of precious metals, which had been stamped by an authority thus guaranteeing weight and metal quality, appealed to the neighboring Greek communities, who soon picked up the concept and effectively ran with it. The transformative effect of coinage, as can be seen in Kroll's work, was primarily in lowering transaction costs and other pragmatic economic concerns, not in the social or political ramifications of monetization.

Jack Kroll's influence in numismatics extends well beyond his publications. For over forty years he has maintained close ties with the ANS, first as a student in the graduate summer seminar, and subsequently as Fellow, Trustee, and now Second Vice President of the Board of Trustees. Through his vision and adherence to principle, he has helped to guide the ANS through its recent transformations, and so has helped to set the course for numismatics as a discipline into the new century. For his dedication his fellow Trustees and the staff at the ANS are deeply grateful.

This volume would not have been possible without the talent and dedication of the ANS' editorial staff, Müşerref Yetim and David Yoon, to whom I express my fullest appreciation. Also deserving thanks are Ute Wartenberg Kagan, Executive Director of the ANS, for her unwavering support, and Robert Fellman, Stephen O'Connor, Joanne Isaac, and Alan Roche for their assistance. It is our hope, and that of the contributors, that this volume reflects the diligence and care that Jack has put into his own work, and therefore rightly honors the man and his contributions to the discipline.

Peter G. van Alfen

John H. Kroll
Bibliography to Date

Books

1972. *Athenian bronze allotment plates.* Harvard: Harvard University Press.

1993. *The Athenian Agora XXVI. The Greek coins.* Princeton: The American School of Classical Studies at Athens.

2002. *Sylloge Numorum Graecorum Deutschland, Staatliche Münzsammlung München,* vol. 14: *Attika, Megaris, Aigina.* Munich: Hirmer Verlag.

Articles

1964. The late Hellenistic tetrobols of Kos. *American Numismatic Society Museum Notes* 11: 81–117, pls. 18–24.

1967. Dikasts' pinakia from the Fauvel collection and the Paris forger of dikasts' pinakia. *Bulletin de correspondance hellénique* 91: 379–400.

1967. Three Corinthian vases in the Fogg art museum. *Antike Kunst* 11: 17–22, pls. 9–10.

1971. Three inscribed Greek bronze weights. In: *Studies presented to George M.A. Hanfmann,* pp. 87–93, pl. 28. Mainz.

1972. Two hoards of Athenian bronze coins of the first century BC. *Αρχαιολογικόν Δελτίον* 27: 86–120, pls. 34–40

with G. Miles, and S. G. Miller. 1973. An early Byzantine and a late Turkish coin hoard from the Athenian Agora. *Hesperia* 42: 301–311, pls. 59–60.

1973. The Eleusis hoard of Athenian imperial coins and some deposits from the Athenian Agora. *Hesperia* 42: 312–333.

1974. Numismatic appendix to V. R. Grace, revisions in early Hellenistic chronology. *Athenische Mitteilungen* 89: 201–203.

1976. Aristophanes' *ponēra chalkia:* a reply. *Greek, Roman and Byzantine Studies* 18: 329–341.

1977. An archive of the Athenian cavalry. *Hesperia* 46: 121–46, pls. 33–39.

1977. Some Athenian armor tokens. *Hesperia* 46: 141–46, pl. 40.

1979. A chronology of early Athenian bronze coinage, ca. 350–250 BC. In: O. Mørkholm and N. Waggoner, eds., *Greek numismatics and archaeology, essays in honor of Margaret Thompson,* pp. 39–154, pls. 16–17. Wetteren, Belgium.

1979. The Parthenon Frieze as a votive relief. *American Journal of Archaeology* 83: 349–352, pl. 56.

1979. Coins. In: C. Houser, ed., *Dionysos and his circle, ancient through modern,* pp. 45–52. Cambridge, Mass.

with F. Mitchel. 1980. Clay tokens stamped with the names of Athenian military commanders. *Hesperia* 49: 86–96, pls. 13–14.

1981. From Wappenmünzen to gorgoneia to owls. *American Numismatic Society Museum Notes* 26: 1–32, pls. 1–2.

1982. A spurious Athenian bronze coin. *Gazette numismatiquie suisse* 32: 59–60.

1982. The ancient image of Athena polias. In: *Studies in Athenian architecture sculpture and topography presented to Homer A. Thompson. Hesperia*: Supplement 20: 65–76, pl. 11.

1984. More Athenian bronze allotment plates. In: *Studies presented to Sterling Dow on his eightieth birthday,* Greek, Roman, and Byzantine Monograph 10, pp. 165–171, pls. 10–11. Durham.

with N. Waggoner. 1984. Dating the earliest coins of Athens, Corinth, and Aegina. *American Journal of Archaeology* 88: 325–340.

with H. Nicolet-Pierre. 1990. Athenian tetradrachm coinage in the third century BC. *American Journal of Numismatics* 2: 1–35, pls. 1–6.

1996. The Piraeus 1902 hoard of plated drachms and tetradrachms. In: *XAPAKTHP: Αφιέρωμα στη Μάντω Οικονομίδου*, pp. 139–146. Athens.

1996. Hemiobols to assaria: the bronze coinage of Roman Aigion. *Numismatic Chronicle* 156: 49–78, pls. 15–19.

1997. Traditionalism vs. Romanization in bronze coinages of Greece. 42–31 BC. *Topoi, Orient-Occident* 7: 123–136.

1997. Coinage as an index of Romanization. In: M. Hoff and S. Rotroff, eds., *The Romanization of Athens*, pp. 134–150. Oxford: Oxford University Press.

1997. The Athenian imperials: results of recent study. In: *Nomismata, Historisch-numismatische Forschungen* I: 61–69, pls. III–IV.

1998. Silver in Solon's laws. In: R. Ashton and S. Hurter, eds., *Studies in Greek numismatics in memory of Martin Price*, pp. 225–232. London: Spink.

2001. The Greek inscriptions of the Sardis synagogue. *Harvard Theological Review* 94: 5–136.

2001. Observations on monetary instruments in pre-coinage Greece. In: M. S. Balmuth, ed., *Hacksilber to coinage: new insights into the monetary history of the Near East and Greece, a collection of eight papers presented at the 99th annual meeting of the Archaeological Institute of America*, pp. 77–91. New York: American Numismatic Society.

2001. A small find of silver bullion from Egypt. *American Journal of Numismatics* 13: 1–20.

2002. The British Museum lot of silver from the Taranto 1911 hoard. Electronic publication at http://www.numismatics.org/publications/taranto1911/index.

2003. The evidence of Athenian coins. In: O. Palagia and S. Tracy, eds., *The Macedonians in Athens, 323–229 BC*, pp. 206–212. Oxford: Oxford University Press.

2003. Weights, bullion currency, coinage. In: V. Karageorghis and N. Stampolidis, eds., *Sea routes: interconnections in the Mediterranean 16th–6th c. BC, proceedings of the international symposium held at Rethymnon, Crete, September 29–October 2, 2002*, pp. 313–320. Athens.

with N. Cahill. 2005. New Archaic coin finds at Sardis. *American Journal of Archaeology* 109: 589–617.

Forthcoming. Athenian tetradrachms recently recovered in the Athenian Agora. *Revue numismatique.*

Forthcoming. The emergence of ruler portraiture on early Hellenistic coins: the importance of being divine. In: P. Schultz and R. von den Hoff, eds., *Early Hellenistic portraiture.* Cambridge: Cambridge University Press.

Forthcoming. The monetary use of weighed bullion in Archaic Greece. In: W. V. Harris, ed., *The nature of ancient money.* Oxford: Oxford University Press.

Reviews

1976. Review of P. Tyler, *The Persian wars of the 3rd century* AD *and Roman Imperial monetary policy,* AD *253–68, Historia Einzelschriften,* Heft 23. In: *American Journal of Philology* 97: 420–421.

1979. Review of M. Price and N. Waggoner, *Archaic Greek silver coinage: the Asyut hoard.* In: *American Journal of Archaeology* 83: 359–360.

1986. Review of T. Buttrey et al., *Greek, Roman, and Islamic coins from Sardis.* In: *American Journal of Archaeology* 90: 117–118.

1990. Review of J. Casey and R. Reece, eds., *Coins and the archaeologist.* In: *American Journal of Numismatics* 2: 181–183.

1993–94. Review of A. Burnett, M. Amandry, and P. P. Ripolles, *Roman provincial coinage,* I, *from the death of Caesar to the death of Vitellius (44* BC–AD *69).* In: *American Journal of Numismatics* 5–6: 241–248.

1997. Review of S. von Reden, *Exchange in ancient Greece.* In: *American Journal of Archaeology* 101: 175–176.

1998. Review of K. Hitzel, *Die Gewichte griechishen Zeit aus Olympia: Ein Studie zu den vorhellenistischen Gewichtssystemen in Griechenland.* In: *American Journal of Archaeology* 102: 632–633.

2000. Review of L. Kurke, *Coins, bodies, games, and gold: the politics of meaning in Archaic Greece.* In: *Classical Journal* 96: 85–90.

2001. Review of G. Le Rider, *La naissance de la monnaie.* In: *Revue suisse de numismatique* 80: 199–206

2002. Review of A. Meadows and K. Shipton, eds. *Money and its uses in the ancient Greek world.* In: *Bryn Mawr Classical Review* 2002.07.24. http://ccat.sas.upenn.edu/bmcr/ 2002-07-24 .html.

2004. Review of H. Nicolet-Pierre, *Numismatique grecque.* In: *American Numismatic Society Magazine* 3.1: 61–62.

2005. Review of D. M. Schaps, *The invention of coinage and the monetization of ancient Greece.* In: *The Classical Review* 55: 344–346.

Agoranomia: Studies in Money and Exchange Presented to John H. Kroll, pp. 1–20
© 2006 The American Numismatic Society

Les Talents d'Homère

HÉLÈNE NICOLET-PIERRE[*]

Notre mot "talent", dont l'étymologie, via le *talentum* latin, est indéniablement le vocable grec τάλαντον, en est venu à signifier,[1] dans la langue courante, un ensemble de capacités, plutôt artistiques ou littéraires, sortant de l'ordinaire. Homère ne manquait pas de ce ou ces talents-là, certes. Mais puisque le même terme permet, dans le français des numismates, un innocent jeu de mots, nous avions un prétexte attirant pour relire quelques pages du corpus homérique,[2] qui ne sauraient laisser tout à fait indifférent le chercheur curieux, comme Jack Kroll, de tout ce qui touche aux origines très lointaines de la monnaie.

Dans la prose grecque classique, un talent, comme chacun sait, désigne tantôt l'unité de mesure la plus élevée d'un système métrologique particulier (le talent babylonien pèse 70 mines attiques, explique Hérodote 3.89), tantôt un certain poids de métal (un talent d'or, un talent d'argent) conforme à cette unité. Essayons de mettre de côté ces notions pour aborder sans aucun à priori la magie d'Homère. Que dit le poète qui use du terme τάλαντον dans différents contextes de l'*Iliade* et de l'*Odyssée*?

---

*Directeur honoraire du Cabinet des médailles, Bibliothèque nationale de France, Paris.

1. Glissement de sens qui provient, disent les lexicographes, de la "parabole des talents" dans l'*Evangile selon Saint Mathieu* 25.14: au sens premier, ces talents sont les sommes d'argent confiées par le maître, dont il espère qu'elles fructifieront.

2. Le nom d' "Homère" est employé souvent, dans notre texte, par commodité, mais nous ne pensons pas pour autant que la "question homérique" soit définitivement réglée au bénéfice d'un auteur unique datable du VIIIe s. avant notre ère. Cf. la si utile synthèse récente de Carlier (1999: 113) en particulier.

Les emplois du mot "talent" dans l'*Iliade*[3]

On trouve les *talanta* dans deux contextes bien différents: dans les mains de personnages en train de peser, ils désignent sans conteste la balance. Ailleurs, ils figurent parmi les prix proposés lors d'une compétition, ou bien parmi des cadeaux de haute valeur, et ils sont, là, le résultat d'une pesée, ainsi qu'il est dit (parfois) dans la formulation du texte lui-même.

Scène de pesée dans la vie quotidienne

Une comparaison assez développée, au Chant 12 (433–435) nous peint une scène de pesée avec la description précise des gestes accomplis:

> ...ὧς τε τάλαντα γυνὴ χερνῆτις ἀληθής, ἥ τε σταθμὸν ἔχουσα καὶ εἴριον ἀμφὶς ἀνέλκει ἰσάζουσα... ("On dirait quelque soigneuse ouvrière qui, une balance (τάλαντα) à la main, ayant d'un côté un poids (σταθμός), de l'autre de la laine, cherche, en la soulevant, à équilibrer les deux...")

Il s'agit d'une balance à deux plateaux suspendus à un fléau. Lorsque celui-ci, tenu par le milieu, revient à l'horizontale, l'équilibre est parfait. Notre terme français "balance" signifie à lui seul "à deux plateaux" (*bi-lanx*). On comprend aisément le pluriel d'Homère, *talanta*, qui nomme les deux plateaux constituant la balance.

Le recours à cette comparaison, destinée à rendre imaginable la bataille indécise, l'équilibre entre des combattants également acharnés, s'explique bien, la tâche accomplie par la femme étant, depuis la haute antiquité, très familière à tous—ainsi que le type de balance suggéré par l'auteur. L'ancienneté de ce type est également bien connue des archéologues d'aujourd'hui, comme nous le verrons plus loin.

Les pesées effectuées par Zeus

Trois passages de l'*Iliade* décrivent la scène célèbre de Zeus réglant par une pesée le sort des héros:

(1) Après une longue scène de bataille entre Troyens et Achéens, Zeus intervient: "Mais l'heure vient où le soleil a franchi le milieu du ciel; alors le Père des dieux déploie sa balance d'or; il y place les deux déesses du trépas douloureux, celui des Troyens..., celui des Achéens...; puis, la prenant par le milieu, il la soulève, et c'est le jour fatal des Achéens qui penche..." (...χρύσεια πατὴρ ἐτίταινε τάλαντα...ἕλκε δὲ μέσσα λαβών...[8.69–72])

(2) Il intervient de même au Chant 22, alors qu'Achille poursuit Hector autour des murs de Troie sans pouvoir l'atteindre (22.209): "Mais les voici qui reviennent aux fontaines [les sources du Scamandre] pour la quatrième fois. Cette fois, le Père des dieux déploie sa balance d'or; il y place les deux déesses du trépas douloureux, celle d'Achille, celle d'Hector...

---

3. Nous citons pour l'*Iliade* les excellentes traductions de Paul Mazon dans l'édition des Belles Lettres.

Puis, la prenant par le milieu, il la soulève, et c'est le jour fatal d'Hector qui, par son poids, l'emporte et disparaît dans l'Hadès". On retrouve les formules mêmes du passage précédent: seul le contenu des plateaux a changé.

(3) Dans la mort des combattants, de façon plus générale, le poète, non sans mélancolie, voit et décrit toujours le geste de Zeus: "L'homme a vite assez du combat: le bronze y verse à terre trop de paille pour peu de grain, à l'heure où Zeus fait pencher la balance, Zeus seul arbitre de tous les combats humains… (…ἐπὴν κλίνῃσι τάλαντα Ζευς…[19.221–224])".

LA BALANCE DE ZEUS, MÉTAPHORE DU DESTIN

Si dans les passages précédents nous pouvions remarquer l'usage de termes très précis associés à l'usage de la balance, y reconnaître un objet portatif, que l'on déploie, que l'on soulève, dont tel ou tel plateau penche, en 16.658 la mention de la "balance de Zeus" (avec un seul déterminant: "sacrée") prend une signification différente. Elle n'est autre qu'une métaphore, la pure transposition d'une idée abstraite: "Hector monte sur son char et se tourne vers la fuite, en même temps qu'il crie aux autres Troyens de fuir. Il a reconnu la balance sacrée de Zeus!" (γνῶ γὰρ Διὸς ἱρὰ τάλαντα [16.657–658]).

Auparavant, Homère avait décrit la perplexité de Zeus quant au sort immédiat de Patrocle. Zeus décide enfin que le combat continuera quelque temps encore et, donnant pour un moment l'avantage aux Grecs, affaiblit Hector. C'est ce dernier qui dans sa lâcheté soudaine "reconnaît" l'intervention divine, celle du Zeus arbitre décrite en 19.223, et l'identifie sans hésiter à la balance, image du destin.

DES TALENTS COMME PRIX EN COMPETITION

(1) Une récompense d'un demi-talent d'or est promise par Achille dans la course à pied en l'honneur de Patrocle mort. C'est le troisième et dernier prix: ἡμιτάλαντον δὲ χρυσοῦ λοισθήϊ' ἔθηκε (23.751).

Le premier prix est un cratère en argent façonné (par des ciseleurs de Sidon), le deuxième un bœuf "énorme et lourd de graisse". Au demi-talent gagné par Antiloque, Achille en ajoute un autre, car Antiloque a su le flatter: τοι ἡμιτάλαντον ἐγὼ χρυσοῦ ἐπιθήσω (23. 796).

Il lui met dans les mains ce demi-talent, comme n'importe quel objet: ὣς εἰπὼν ἐν χερσὶ τίθει, ὁ δ᾽ἐδέξατο χαίρων (23.797).

Notons que ce dernier vers est un vers formulaire, déjà utilisé par exemple en 23.624, lorsque le vieux Nestor reçoit l'urne du 5e prix non décerné et manifeste son contentement.

(2) Deux talents d'or étaient annoncés, plus haut dans le Chant 23, comme quatrième prix de la course de chars (23.269).[4] En tête viennent une captive et un trépied-chaudron à anses de 22 mesures. Le deuxième prix est une jument pleine, le troisième "un bassin tout brillant

---

4. τῷ δὲ τετάρτῳ θῆκε δύω χρυσοῖο τάλαντα.

neuf, de 4 mesures". Puis arrivent les deux talents d'or, et enfin une "urne à deux poignées", neuve. A l'issue de la course, "Mérion de son côté enlève les deux talents d'or, le quatrième, puisque c'est son rang d'arrivée" (ἀνάειρε δύω χρυσοῖο τάλαντα [23.614]).

Dans les deux passages analysés ci-dessus, la liste des récompenses est relativement longue. Elles sont forcément de valeur inégale. Pour tenter de les comparer, on doit admettre que leur hiérarchisation est "normale" et plaisante à la fois pour le poète et pour l'imaginaire de son auditoire. On constate que la récompense en talents d'or vient après d'autres prix plus enviables, appartenant (comme ailleurs les cadeaux) à des catégories de biens consommables: femmes, animaux domestiques, ustensiles utiles. Mais la qualité propre de chacun de ces prix est exceptionnelle, indiquée par une profusion de qualificatifs qui en fait des dons prestigieux, et qui souligne comme il se doit la munificence d'Achille lorsqu'il s'agit d'honorer Patrocle. Deux talents d'or, préférables à l'urne à deux poignées, neuve[5] (dont on ne nous indique pas le métal, mais on peut l'imaginer de bronze), ne sont pas un simple prix de consolation: ils doivent aussi représenter un prix digne d'Achille et de Patrocle. La place de ces talents dans la liste nous permet-elle d'entrevoir la valeur exacte que leur accorderait le poète? Nous chercherons quelque réponse à cette question plus loin. Peut-être nous renseigne-t-elle tout d'abord sur l'intention de l'aède, certainement désireux de nous éblouir.

(3) Au Chant 18 on rencontre encore une autre récompense de deux talents d'or, dans une compétition, mais qui est de nature toute différente, puisque ce prix est le seul prévu: il ira au meilleur "juge". Sur le bouclier qu'Héphaistos a forgé pour Achille, dans la cité paisible une scène de médiation[6] est représentée:

> Les anciens sont assis sur des pierres polies, dans un cercle sacré. Ils ont dans les mains le bâton des hérauts sonores, et c'est bâton en main qu'ils se lèvent et prononcent, chacun à son tour. Au milieu d'eux, à terre, sont deux talents d'or;[7] ils iront à celui qui, parmi eux, dira l'arrêt le plus droit (18.503–508).

Ces deux talents d'or ne sont certainement pas un salaire (cf. Brown 1998),[8] mais une haute récompense, puisqu'elle est unique et intervient dans un contexte très solennel, chacun des orateurs revêtant la majesté du héraut lorsqu'il parle à son tour. A se demander s'il n'y aurait pas là quelque souvenir des deux plateaux d'or de Zeus, l'arbitre par excellence.

---

5. L'urne est ἀπύρωτον (23.270), elle n'a pas connu le feu. Il ne peut guère s'agir d'une coupe à boire.

6. La cause a déjà été jugée, mais le plaignant nie avoir reçu la compensation ("le prix du sang") que son adversaire affirme avoir déjà donnée (18.497–502).

7. 18.507: κεῖτο δ᾽ ἄρ᾽ ἐν μέσσοισι δύω χρυσοῖο τάλαντα. On notera que le mot *talanta*, toujours complément dans les autres occurrences de la même formule dans l'*Iliade*, se trouve employé ici au nominatif pluriel. Ce menu détail est peut-être à ajouter à la liste de tous ceux qui font de la description du bouclier d'Achille un morceau à part dans l'épopée.

8. L'auteur estime que deux interprétations sont possibles et complémentaires pour ce passage. Vu le contexte, nous préférons de beaucoup retenir la première, et insister sur la valeur honorifique de la récompense.

DIX TALENTS PARMI DES PRÉSENTS MAGNIFIQUES

Des cadeaux de dix talents sont mentionnés dans deux circonstances particulièrement drama-tiques, chaque fois au milieu d'une longue énumération de présents exceptionnels, à la mesure de l'enjeu et des partenaires. Il s'agit des cadeaux d'Agamemnon à Achille, plus tard de Priam à Achille. Dans les deux cas il fallait fléchir la redoutable colère du héros grec, fils d'une déesse: afin qu'il revienne combattre avec les siens—les sauver d'un désastre (Chants 9 et 19); pour finir, qu'il rende aux Troyens le corps d'Hector, le noble adversaire qu'il a le plus haï (Chant 24).

(1) "Devant vous tous ici j'énumérerai mes illustres présents, proclame Agamemnon: sept trépieds encore ignorants de la flamme, dix talents d'or (δέκα δὲ χρυσοῖο τάλαντα [9.122]), vingt bassins resplendissants, douze chevaux solides, taillés pour la victoire (123–124)… Je lui donnerai encore sept femmes habiles aux travaux impeccables (128)…(avec elles, Briséis qu'il a respectée: 9.132–133)". Le roi de Mycènes promet encore une part énorme du butin espéré, et une de ses filles en mariage, bien dotée. Ulysse en messager exact reprend mot pour mot (9. 264) les promesses d'Agamemnon.

   Plus loin, au Chant 19, Homère nous peint la préparation et la remise des cadeaux:

   De la baraque ils emportent les sept trépieds promis, les vingt bassins resplendissants, les douze chevaux. Ils emmènent aussi, sans tarder, sept femmes habiles…et pour huitième, la jolie Briséis. Ulysse pèse[9] un total de dix talents d'or, puis il se met en tête des jeunes Achéens, et ceux-ci, sur ses pas, apportent les présents (243–248)….

(2) Le vieux roi de Troie Priam prépare des cadeaux somptueux pour Achille, qu'il va sup-plier de lui remettre le corps d'Hector son fils (Chant 24):

   Il retire [de ses coffres] douze robes splendides, douze manteaux simples, autant de couvertures, autant de pièces de lin blanc, autant de tuniques enfin. Il pèse et emporte un total de dix talents d'or, deux trépieds luisants, quatre bassins, enfin une coupe splendide…(χρυσοῦ δὲ στήσας ἔφερεν δέκα πάντα τάλαντα [24.229–234]).

Dans les seuls cas où nous trouvions mentionnés un total de dix talents (ci-dessus), la remise de cadeaux est associée à une sorte de transaction: *captatio benevolentiae* grâce à laquelle un échange pourra se faire. Agamemnon "rachète" sa conduite passée, Priam ap-porte la rançon d'Hector. Mais l'efficacité de ces dons va de pair avec la décision des dieux (24.112–119, et *passim*): il est impossible de les dissocier sans trahir Homère.

   Au niveau des affaires humaines, ces dix talents nous paraissent une valeur importante, mais on ne peut la ranger de façon précise en relation avec la valeur des autres objets ap-portés. Les énumérations du poète ici ne semblent pas ordonnées du plus au moins, ni à l'inverse. L'intérêt et l'utilité littéraires de ces passages tient à l'effet d'accumulation plus qu'à l'importance intrinsèque de tel ou tel élément, de toute façon un présent splendide. Ce n'est

---

9. 19.247: χρυσοῦ δὲ στήσας Ὀδυσεὺς δέκα πάντα τάλαντα….

pas d'eux que nous pouvons espérer déduire quelque valeur exacte, même relative, pour ces talents. Mais on note qu'il faut les peser (στήσας du verbe ἵστημι): un talent apparaît ainsi comme un poids défini à l'avance.

Les emplois du mot "talent" dans l'*Odyssée*[10]

Le nombre d'emplois est beaucoup plus réduit: 12 occurrences dans l'*Iliade* et 5 seulement pour les 24 chants de l'*Odyssée*, avec *talenton* une fois au singulier. Dans quatre des cinq cas, le contexte est une énumération de cadeaux. Comme dans l'*Iliade*, les talents sont toujours d'or.

(1) Cadeaux pour Ulysse, chez Alkinoos: "Que chacun [des douze rois] fasse donc apporter une écharpe tout fraîchement lavée, une robe, un talent de son or le plus fin…" (καὶ χρυσοῖο τάλαντον ἐνείκατε τιμήεντος [8.393])

(2) Cadeaux (de Polybe, un habitant de la Thèbes d'Egypte, la ville où les maisons regorgent de richesses) à Ménélas: "deux baignoires d'argent et deux trépieds en or, avec dix talents d'or…" (δέκα δὲ χρυσοῖο τάλαντα [4.129]) (même formule dans l'*Iliade,* ci-dessus, 9.122 et 264, cadeaux d'Agamemnon).

(3) Cadeaux magnifiques reçus autrefois par Ulysse d'un ennemi, prêtre d'Apollon, qu'il a épargné: "sept talents d'or travaillé, un cratère où tout était d'argent, un lot de douze amphores de vin de liqueur…" (χρυσοῦ μέν μοι δῶκ᾽ εὐεργέος ἑπτὰ τάλαντα [9.202]).

(4) Cadeaux encore plus magnifiques d'un homme riche à un hôte: "sept talents de bel or ouvré, un cratère à fleurs tout en argent, douze robes, autant de manteaux non doublés, quatre femmes fines travailleuses…" (χρυσοῦ μέν οἱ δῶκ᾽ εὐεργέος ἑπτὰ τάλαντα [24.274–279]). La seule modification par rapport à 9.202 ci-dessus est le pronom personnel; l'adjectif grec qualifiant l'or est le même.

Impossible de discerner une hiérarchisation dans les présents qu'énumèrent les vers cités. Les treize,[11] les dix, les sept talents d'or font partie chaque fois d'un ensemble de cadeaux somptueux, témoignages de reconnaissance ou de générosité envers l'hôte, qui n'appellent pas de retour immédiat (cf. Hooker 1996).[12] Mais qu'est au juste cet or "bien travaillé"? Un tel qualificatif ne se rencontrait pas dans l'*Iliade*, où au contraire apparaissait la mention d'une pesée préalable à la remise du présent. Sous quelle forme se présente-t-il? Le qualificatif fait-il allusion à la qualité de l'or converti en simples lingots, ou à l'apparence d'objets en or ayant une forme élaborée à l'avance, tels des éléments d'ornementation ou de parure? Dans un cas comme dans l'autre, une intervention humaine a été nécessaire. Il ne faut sans doute pas surinterpréter cet adjectif attaché à l'or, qui pourrait bien faire partie du stock de formules reposantes où puise l'aède selon les besoins du rythme.

---

10. Traductions de Victor Bérard, édition des Belles Lettres.

11. Ulysse doit recevoir en tout treize talents, car Alkinoos lui donnera les mêmes présents que ses vassaux.

12. L'auteur y critique à juste titre, semble-t-il, l'application sans nuances aux textes homériques de la théorie des anthropologues relative au don et au contre-don.

(5) Un dernier passage reprend la formule deux talents d'or pour la rétribution par Egisthe du veilleur qui toute l'année devait guetter le retour d'Agamemnon. "Deux talents d'or étaient le salaire promis" (ὑπὸ δ᾽ ἔσχετο μισθὸν χρυσοῦ δοιὰ τάλαντα [4.525–526]).

C'est là le seul passage des deux poèmes homériques où de l'or est associé au terme *misthos*. Ailleurs, soit on n'a aucune précision relative aux salaires (*Il.* 12.435, 21.441–457; *Od.* 10.84), soit le *misthos* est la récompense—aristocratique—promise pour une mission dangereuse (*Il.* 10.304, "le prix de sa peine", traduit P. Mazon, et elle consiste en un char et deux bons chevaux) ou, au contraire, la rétribution en nature pour un ouvrier agricole (*Od.* 18.358: nourriture, vêtements, chaussures).

Ce qui nous frappe d'emblée, à l'examen minutieux des vers où est employé le terme "talent", est la différence entre les deux épopées homériques (cf. Rutherford 1993). Le mot est plutôt rare. Mais en dépit du petit nombre d'emplois, on constate qu'à une riche palette de significations dans l'*Iliade* s'oppose la monotonie, pour ne pas dire la platitude, des emplois dans l'*Odyssée*. A travers notre mince étude de vocabulaire se révèlent deux mondes assez profondément étrangers l'un à l'autre. Celui de l'*Iliade* est certainement le plus intéressant pour notre sujet. Car il semble qu'il nous permette une exploration plus lointaine des origines du *talanton*. Nous ferons un détour par le grec mycénien, qui a chance d'être éclairant quand il s'agit d'entrer dans le monde de l'épopée la plus ancienne.

PESÉE DE LA LAINE, *TALASIA* ET *TALENTON*

Le mot par lequel l'auteur de l'*Iliade* désigne l'instrument servant à peser est étroitement apparenté à un terme déchiffré dans les tablettes mycéniennes du palais de Pylos.

En prose grecque classique, ταλασία désigne le travail de la laine (Platon, *Politique* 282a: ἡ ταλασιουργική, l'art de la ταλασία, qui comprend le cardage, la filature et la fabrication du vêtement; cf. Duhoux 1976: 109 et suiv.). Dans le grec mycénien du XIIIᵉ siècle, on a découvert que le terme *ta-ra-si-ja* peut avoir le sens de "quantité de laine allouée" à une ouvrière (Palmer 1969: 292; Duhoux 1976: 110; cf. Aura Jurro 1993: s.v.; Chantraine 1999: s.v.), de même qu'il désigne dans une série homogène d'une cinquantaine de tablettes le poids de bronze confié pour transformation à des forgerons (Lejeune 1961). La continuité du geste de la pesée de la laine à travers toute l'antiquité ne fait pas de doute (fig. 1). On sait que le latin dispose du mot *lanipendens* (f.) pour désigner "celle qui pèse la laine". Le terme classique *talasia* viendrait directement du mycénien, selon Y. Duhoux, avec une évolution sémantique "analogue à celle de *pensum* latin, dont le sens étymologique, quantité pesée, a évolué en poids de laine à filer distribué aux servantes" (et, de là, a fini par signifier "tâche à faire"). La parenté de racine entre *ta-ra-si-ja*/*talasia* et le nom ancien de la balance (tel du moins que l'atteste l'*Iliade*) paraît certaine, même s'il est impossible, selon Ventris et Chadwick (1973: 508) de voir dans *talasia* un dérivé direct de *talanton*, par un *talansia* provenant d'un *talant-ia* comme l'avaient suggéré M. Lejeune et L. R. Palmer.

FIGURE 1. Pesée de la laine, une des scènes représentées sur un petit lécythe attribué par Beazley au peintre Amasis. H. 17,1 cm. Vers 560–550 BC. Je remercie vivement Michèle Daumas et Agnès Rouveret qui ont l'une et l'autre attiré mon attention sur l'intérêt documentaire exceptionnel de ce vase, où sont figurées diverses étapes du travail de la laine. Cf. surtout Karouzou (1956: 43–44), et von Bothmer (1984: 185–187) (New York, Metropolitan Museum 31.11.10. Fletcher Fund, 1931).

LE TALENT, PLATEAU DE BALANCE

Les *talanta* de Zeus désignent sans conteste, nous l'avons vu, les deux plateaux d'une balance, qui se trouve être l'instrument d'une pesée un peu particulière puisqu'elle est divine et que du résultat dépendra la vie ou la mort des héros.

Cette pesée a été diversement interprétée. On y a vu une pesée des âmes, une "psychostasie" comparable sinon identique au jugement des morts de la religion égyptienne. G. Björck (1945) a refusé à juste titre cette interprétation, approuvant les critiques et la conclusion formulées dès 1845 par J. de Witte: "Autre chose est la psychostasie homérique, autre chose la psychostasie chez les Egyptiens". En outre le terme d' "âme" (qui traduirait ψυχή) est impropre: il s'agit plus précisément d'une "kèrostasie", de la pesée des κῆρες des combattants, de leur sort mauvais respectif. Les pesées dramatiques de Zeus ne prennent en compte ni les fautes ni les mérites des hommes, dont la mort dépend simplement d'un arbitraire supérieur que nous appelons Destin. "Rien n'annonce une rémunération ou des peines réservées à une autre vie", ajoutait J. de Witte. Sans référence aux actes des vivants, la balance dans l'*Iliade* ne symbolise pas un jugement équitable mais bien plutôt la soumission au destin.

Après l'Homère de l'*Iliade*,[13] *talanta* au sens de "plateaux de balance" semble n'être employé que par des poètes. Deux exemples très clairs de la survie de cette signification

---

13. N.B. Ni *talanta* ni *talanton* ne figure dans les œuvres conservées d'Hésiode.

particulière doivent être mentionnés. Nous trouvons les *talanta* de Diké dans l'*Hymne homérique à Hermès*, que J. Humbert (1951) datait du dernier tiers du VIᵉ siècle: "Ils parvinrent rapidement, les beaux enfants de Zeus (Apollon et le petit Hermès, qui a volé les vaches d'Apollon!) sur la cîme de l'Olympe odorant, et allèrent trouver le Cronide, leur père: c'est là que les attendaient les plateaux de Justice:" κεῖθι γὰρ ἀμφοιτέροισι δίκης κατέκειτο τάλαντα (v. 324).

Le contexte, avec Zeus pour arbitre, rappelle bien sûr les pesées effectuées par le dieu dans l'épopée homérique. Mais la valeur du recours à la balance est totalement différente, puisqu'il s'agit ici, au contraire de l'*Iliade*, de dire le droit, et que Zeus y semble devenu "juste".

Au contraire, dans *Les Perses*, Eschyle se montre bien plus fidèle à l'esprit de l'*Iliade* lorsqu'il reprend l'idée d'un destin incompréhensible, qui a donné la victoire à l'armée la plus faible, en alourdissant les plateaux d'une chance mal partagée: τάλαντα βρίσας οὐκ ἰσορρόπῳ τύχη (v. 346).[14]

On note aussi que, dès le VIᵉ siècle, est attesté l'emploi du singulier *talanton* pour désigner la balance entière, dans un texte poétique (Théognis de Mégare 1.157, vers 540?), mais aussi en prose dans une inscription archaïque: un décret de Cyzique (Jeffery 1961: n° 51)[15] mentionne des taxes parmi lesquelles nous remarquons tout particulièrement le τάλαντον, que les éditeurs des *Nomima* traduisent "le droit pour le poids public". La stèle regravée au premier s. avant notre ère reproduit une inscription du VIᵉ s. que L. H. Jeffery datait "c. 525–500" d'après les deux lignes conservées de la gravure d'origine.

L'IDÉOGRAMME "BALANCE" ET LE TALENT

Les travaux des linguistes dans la seconde moitié du XXᵉ s. nous montrent qu'à l'époque mycénienne déjà existait une équivalence entre l'instrument de pesée et un certain poids: elle est bien antérieure à la version écrite de l'*Iliade*, où nous avons constaté ces deux sens pour τάλαντα.

En effet un idéogramme "balance" est employé par les scribes grecs mycéniens dans l'écriture dite "linéaire B"(Vandenabeele et Olivier 1979: 154–160, 290–291) (fig. 2). Déjà sur 24 documents inscrits en linéaire A on rencontre le dessin d'une balance à deux plateaux pendus à un fléau pourvu d'un crochet de suspension (fig. 3). C'est le signe commun aux deux écritures qui porte le n° AB 118 dans Godard et Olivier (1976–1985). La balance décrite par Homère appartient à la catégorie dépourvue de support vertical. Un objet de ce genre, tenu dans la main par un personnage masculin, est figuré sur le célèbre cratère d'Enkomi (Chypre) (fig. 4) datable du début du XIVᵉ siècle (HR III A 1, Vandenabeele et Olivier 1979: 292).

14. "C'est un dieu dès lors qui nous a détruit notre armée, en faisant de la chance des parts trop inégales dans les plateaux de la balance!" (v. 345–6, tr. Mazon).
15. Citée en entier par van Effenterre et Ruzé (1994: n° 32).

Dans les tablettes mycéniennes déchiffrées, ce signe représente l'unité supérieure dans un système de mesure des poids (Lejeune 1971: 175). D'où la "traduction" courante du métrogramme balance par le mot TALENT en conformité avec la langue de l'*Iliade*, en conformité d'autre part avec l'habitude de l'époque classique où le talent est le poids le plus lourd. Rien apparemment ne nous indique de façon indubitable la prononciation correspondant à un signe emprunté aux Minoens. Mais il est logique de supposer que les Grecs mycéniens donnaient aux plateaux de balance un nom très proche du nom trouvé dans l'*Iliade*, puisque, nous l'avons vu plus haut, la même racine est à l'origine du mot qui dans les tablettes correspond à une certaine quantité de matériau pesé (*ta-ra-si-ja*).

Ce détour par le grec mycénien peut-il être éclairant quant à la valeur absolue d'un talent-poids dans les poèmes homériques?

Depuis le début du XXᵉ siècle, on connaît un lourd poids de pierre, orné de deux poulpes en relief, qui fut découvert par Arthur Evans[16] dans un magasin du palais de Cnossos. Il pèse 29 kg et Evans n'a pas manqué d'y voir le poids-étalon minoen d'un talent ("a light talent of a peculiarly Egyptian type", "a somewhat low version of the Babylonian talent"), peut-être un ancêtre oriental de l'unité de poids grecque d'époque classique. D'autant que dix-neuf lingots de cuivre trouvés peu après (en 1903) par les archéologues italiens à Haghia Triada (Crète) offraient un poids moyen semblable (29,1316 kg) (Evans 1935: 652).

Après le déchiffrement du linéaire B, on a admis couramment[17] que le métrogramme "balance" indiquait dans les documents en grec mycénien un poids du même ordre, voisin de 30 kg. Mais on notera avec intérêt l'avertissement donné par M. Lejeune (1971: 175):

> Les valeurs relatives des diverses unités de poids sont établies de façon certaine… Les valeurs absolues des unités de poids ne sauraient, en revanche, être définies avec certitude. C'est un ensemble de présomptions, de caractère archéologique, qui a amené à supposer que l'unité supérieure (TALENT) correspondait, environ, à une trentaine de kilogrammes; mais on ne dépasse pas, ici, le stade des probabilités, et si l'on propose des équivalences en kilogrammes et en grammes des données de nos tablettes, il convient toujours d'en marquer, par un point d'interrogation, le caractère incertain.

Si pour la pesée du bronze une unité supérieure d'un peu moins de 30 kg, impliquant l'usage d'une balance accrochée à (ou reposant sur) un support solide, n'est pas invraisemblable, si elle a été d'autant mieux admise que pour l'attribution de laine ou la pesée d'autres denrées on trouve seulement les unités divisionnaires, dans les textes homériques le talent est toujours un poids d'or: il est évident qu'il ne peut pas s'agir de la même unité, qui nous entraînerait vers des résultats absurdes. On reste libre d'imaginer un rapport de valeur entre un talent de bronze d'une trentaine de kilos et un talent d'or mycénien dont nous ignorerions le poids.

---

16. Fig. 635 dans Evans (1906: 342, fig. 1); et (1935: 650 et suiv.).
17. Par exemple Palmer (1969: 15).

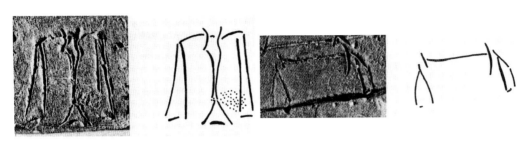

FIGURE 2. Représentations de balances en linéaire B. D'après Vandenabeele et Olivier 1979: pl. 93, 2 et pl. 96, 3.
La première repose sur un support vertical, la deuxième en est dépourvue.

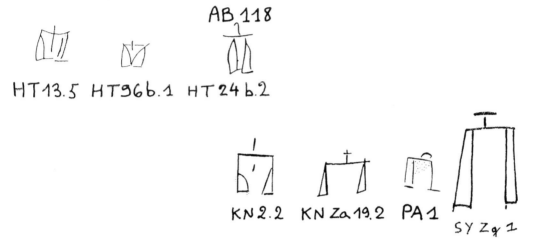

FIGURE 3. Variantes du signe AB 118 en linéaire A (balance suspendue). D'après Godart et Olivier (1986 5. 43).

FIGURE 4. Cratère mycénien d'Enkomi (Chypre). A droite, Zeus tenant une balance.
(Nicosie, Musée archéologique)

Mais aucun document mycénien ni homérique ne laisse entrevoir un tel rapport, bien que l'or ne soit pas absent des tablettes et qu'à Pylos un inventaire de gens de métiers mentionne quatre orfèvres (Lejeune 1971: 169–170).

Les balances d'or de l'*Iliade* et l'archéologie

Parmi les nombreux objets d'or exhumés par Schliemann (1879) à Mycènes, on n'a pas manqué de remarquer l'exceptionnelle (et toujours unique) découverte de petites balances d'or, qui se trouvent aujourd'hui au Musée Archéologique National d'Athènes (fig. 5).[18] Elles proviennent de la tombe à fosse III du cercle A, datable d'après la science actuelle de l'HR I, c'est-à dire à peu près de la période 1550–1500.[19]

Il vaut la peine de revenir à la présentation qu'en fait Schliemann (1879: 276–277) lui-même, et qui a nourri bien des commentaires:

> Toujours dans le même tombeau, j'ai recueilli deux paires [*sic*][20] de balances en or; mais il n'y en a qu'une paire dont j'aie pu photographier le fléau; celui de l'autre paire était écrasé et n'avait plus de forme. Les deux fléaux sont des tubes formés de plaques d'or très minces, qui étaient sans aucun doute traversés d'un morceau de bois destiné à leur donner de la consistance; j'ai même retrouvé des débris de bois carbonisé dans plusieurs parties des tubes d'or. Les plateaux étaient reliés aux fléaux par de longs rubans d'or très minces. Deux des plateaux sont ornés de fleurs, les deux autres de papillons bien dessinés. Il est évident que ces balances n'ont jamais pu servir; elles ont été faites exprès pour accompagner les corps des trois princesses dans leur tombeau et doivent avoir, par conséquent, un sens symbolique. J'appelle l'attention du lecteur sur les balances que l'on trouve dans les peintures murales des tombeaux égyptiens, et où sont pesées les bonnes et les mauvaises actions des morts. Dans tous les cas, ces balances rappellent tout de suite à notre souvenir le beau passage d'Homère (*Iliade* 22: 209–213) où Jupiter [*sic*] prend ses balances d'or et pèse les destinées d'Hector et d'Achille"… (tr. J. Girardin).

Sur un éventuel sens symbolique des balances d'or dans leur contexte funéraire mycénien, il semble que nous ne soyons pas plus avancés que Schliemann en 1879. Les plateaux d'une seule des trois balances sont ornés de papillons aux ailes déployées. Cette image a suffi pour qu'A. Evans reprenne la vieille idée d'une "pesée des âmes".[21] Nous avons vu plus haut qu'elle n'est pas du tout corroborée par les textes homériques concernant les "pesées de Zeus". Pourtant le rapprochement des balances d'or avec les scènes de l'*Iliade* est quasiment inévitable. En quel sens est-il justifié?

18. Deux balances ont été identifiées et illustrées par Schliemann, une troisième a été reconstituée plus tard par Valérios Stais, cf. Karo (1930–33: n° 70, ill.13, et n° 81–82, pl. 34).

19. D'après Touchais (1989: 326), le cercle A est "traditionnellement daté entre 1600 et 1500". La tombe III ferait partie des plus récentes.

20. *A pair of scales* signifie en fait *une* balance.

21. Evans fait allusion au "sepulchral type of gold scales for the weighting of the butterfly soul from the 3rd Shaft Grave at Mycenae"(1935: 661).

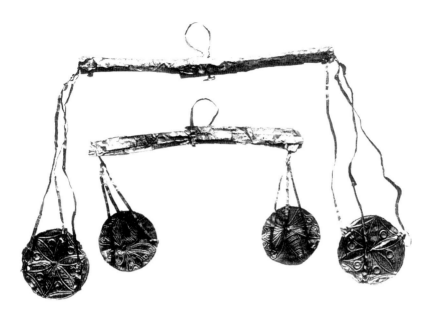

FIGURE 5. Deux balances d'or de Mycènes (tombe III du "Cercle A"). Karo 81: Longueur du fléau, 23 cm; diamètre des plateaux, 6,2 cm. Karo 82: Longueur du fléau, 21 cm; diamètre des plateaux, 5.2–5.3 cm. La troisième balance (Karo 1930–33: 70–91) serait plus petite (fléau 16 cm) et les plateaux (diam. 5.5 cm) sans décor.

On pourrait penser que l'Homère du VIIIᵉ siècle a composé des épisodes tels que *Il.* 8.69–70 et 22.209 en transposant simplement dans le monde des dieux une scène de la vie quotidienne de son temps. Mais l'usage des balances y prolonge les époques précédentes, et les balances mycéniennes sont aujourd'hui bien connues. Elles sont de bronze, comme le montrent les trouvailles assez nombreuses (dans maisons ou tombes) cataloguées par F. Vandenabeele et J.-P. Olivier (1979: 154–160; 290–291), trouvailles de petites balances à peu près complètes (avec fléau et chaînettes) et plus souvent de plateaux présentant des trous de suspension. La balance suspendue existe déjà dans la civilisation minoenne, comme l'atteste l'utilisation du signe dans l'écriture (la sténographie, disent L. Godard et J.-P. Olivier) des scribes de Cnossos, d'Haghia Triada et d'autres sites crétois.

Les *talenta* de l'*Iliade* ont deux caractéristiques: nous l'avons vu, elles sont d'or, et elles sont tenues par Zeus. Aussi faut-il examiner séparément les deux questions qui leur sont attachées: Homère peut-il avoir recueilli quelque souvenir de balances d'or, qui auraient eu une fonction particulière? Est-il le créateur du mythe d'un dieu "peseur de sorts", ou le trouve-t-il dans la tradition des aèdes qui l'ont précédé?

On ne peut exclure aussi radicalement que le faisait Schliemann, que ces petites balances aient pu servir dans le concret, par exemple à peser des produits rares, fards, parfums, épices, ou même de la poudre d'or? Une balance, de bronze il est vrai, porte un reste de métal fondu.[22] La balance d'or pourrait bien être le souvenir, élaboré par les créateurs de l'épopée homérique, d'une réalité mycénienne, l'offrande funéraire d'un objet d'usage, beaucoup plus luxueux naturellement dans une tombe royale ou princière, offrande comparable à celle des tasses ou gobelets d'or ou d'argent que l'on y a recueillis.

Sommes-nous victime, ce-disant, du "mirage mycénien"? En dépit de la tendance récente à "lire" les poèmes homériques dans leur contexte d'actualité (IXe–VIIIe siècles?), jusqu'à y rechercher l'émergence de la cité grecque par l'analyse de certains comportements communautaires,[23] il nous paraît impossible de nier la forme de continuité avec le passé mycénien que représente la présence dans nos épopées de tant d'éléments dont l'ancienneté, d'abord prouvée par des données archéologiques,[24] l'est maintenant aussi par la linguistique. C'est ainsi que sa connaissance approfondie des dialectes grecs et de la langue homérique incite C. J. Ruijgh à faire remonter à l'époque mycénienne la naissance de la tradition épique grecque, dans sa forme orale et formulaire. Et l'adaptation du dialecte mycénien aux règles de l'hexamètre dactylique pourrait même indiquer un emprunt du vers héroïque au monde minoen (Ruijgh 1989).[25]

Quant au thème de la pesée des destinées, le grand spécialiste de la religion grecque M. P. Nilsson n'hésitait pas à le déclarer transmis du monde mycénien à Homère, bien avant qu'il soit possible de comprendre le linéaire B. Le vase chypro-mycénien d'Enkomi (fig. 4) suffisait à le confirmer à ses yeux: il y reconnaît Zeus (Nilsson 1933: 266).[26] Or on sait maintenant qu'à peu près tous les dieux du panthéon homérique (dont Zeus bien sûr: *di-we*, à Cnossos et à Pylos) sont attestés dans les tablettes (cf. Chadwick et Baumbach 1963), et l'interprétation de Nilsson nous semble en prendre une force nouvelle.

Présents et récompenses dans les poèmes homériques: des talents "symboliques"?

Est-il possible, est-il nécessaire de définir selon des unités de mesure classiques les talents d'or offerts dans l'épopée? Depuis Aristote, la question intrigue les lecteurs érudits d'Homère.

---

22. Vandenabeele et Olivier : "le caractère utilitaire a été prouvé par la découverte dans la chambre Delta 16 de Théra, où une grande tache de métal fondu -peut-être de l'argent- se trouve sur l'un des plateaux" (1979: 159).

23. Nous empruntons ces formules à Baslez (2003: 30).

24. Hooker en a rappelé assez récemment la liste (1988).

25. Voici comment il reconstitue (573–574) la transmission de cet héritage, sous son double aspect de reproduction et de création continue: "Il est donc permis de supposer que la tradition épique est née, en dialecte proto-achéen, dans les centres de la civilisation mycénienne. Après leur destruction vers la fin du XIIIe siècle, cette tradition a été continuée par les Eoliens dans le nord-est de la Grèce. Ceux-ci l'ont ensuite apportée en Asie Mineure au début du Ier millénaire. Là, elle a été empruntée par les Ioniens (vers 900?), pour recevoir sa forme linguistique définitive dans l'épopée d'Homère".

26. Même idée développée dans Nilsson (1950: 34–36). Le vase d'Enkomi est l'un des cinq vases que commente Karageorgis (1958: 383–387, pl. 98–101).

Dans le long article "Talent" du *Dictionnaire des Antiquités grecques et romaines* (Daremberg et Saglio 1929),[27] Ernest Babelon fait le point de la bibliographie ancienne, où aucune solution ne lui paraît définitivement établie (en dépit de la tentative, par exemple, de P. Bortolotti 1877).[28] Aussi en vient-il à écrire: "Les petites balances d'or des [*sic*] tombes de Mycènes ne peuvent être que des balances symboliques; les disques d'or, si légers, seraient aussi des talents symboliques, image de la richesse du défunt, mais non des talents réels". Les disques d'or en question sont ceux que trouva Schliemann à Mycènes, dans la tombe III où il découvrit aussi les balances d'or (Schliemann 1879: 245–247, fig. 239–242), disques que J. N. Svoronos a considérés[29] comme les véritables talents dont pouvait parler Homère. Il est sensible en effet à la grande ressemblance (par leurs dimensions et leurs décors) de ces disques avec les *talanta* des balances. Ceux qu'illustre Schliemann, sur les 701 qu'il dit avoir recueillis, sont ornés de motifs au repoussé, très stylisés, aussi élégants que variés (poulpe, papillon, feuille, rosace, jeux de spirales…) (fig. 6). Leurs diamètres, indiquait Svoronos, varient entre 5 et 7 cm, leurs poids entre 1,5 et 3 g. Ces irrégularités lui paraissent tout à fait en accord avec des expressions tirées d'un fragment d'Aristote (fr. 164, Rose), selon lesquelles le talent dans Homère ne serait pas une mesure bien définie. Cet argument est indirect[30] et peu solide.

Néanmoins l'interprétation de Svoronos ne manque pas d'intérêt, puisqu'elle attire notre attention sur des objets remarquables et rarement commentés. Cet or-là est bien réel. Grâce au catalogue précis de G. H. Karo (1930–33), on dénombre par exemple 116 disques ornés d'une feuille de palmier, 60 ornés d'une rosace, 121 d'un papillon, 67 d'un poulpe, 131 de divers jeux de spirales, 147 de "vagues". D'autres plaques rondes très ornées ont été trouvées ailleurs par Schliemann, sans parler des nombreux bijoux ou éléments décoratifs dont il reproduit quelques-uns dans sa publication (Schliemann 1879: 269, 275 [tombe III], 401, 405, 407 [tombe I]). Une telle profusion d'or, ainsi que la maîtrise artisanale et artistique dont témoignent ces objets, à l'apogée mycénienne, n'ont pu manquer de frapper tous les spectateurs du luxe palatial, de s'inscrire dans la mémoire collective et d'entrer aisément dans la légende. Les talents que des héros d'Homère tirent de leurs réserves pour les mettre en jeu ou les offrir, associés à d'autres objets non moins précieux, ont-ils une fonction autre qu'ostentatoire? Il ne semble pas (cf. Hooker 1996), et peu importe alors leur poids exact d'or, si leur nom suffit à rappeler les disques d'or de jadis, grands comme des plateaux de balance et réservés aux maîtres des palais. La fonction pratique de ces disques ("plaques",

27. Les *Tables* ont paru en 1929.

28. S'aidant surtout de comparaisons avec des passages bibliques, l'auteur arrive à conclure que le talent d'or des présents, dans Homère, devait avoir à peu près le poids d'un *shekel* ou encore d'un statère lourd de Crésus (environ 10 g).

29. Svoronos, où sont illustrés douze disques et les deux balances (1906). Cf. *Revue belge de numismatique* (1908): 433–445 et pl. 8–9.

30. Le scholiaste qui cite Aristote à propos de *Iliade* 2.69 cherche en fait une explication pour l'adjectif *atalantos*—égal, semblable à—et croit y trouver l'idée opposée à celle d' "inégalité" qui serait attachée à *talanton*.

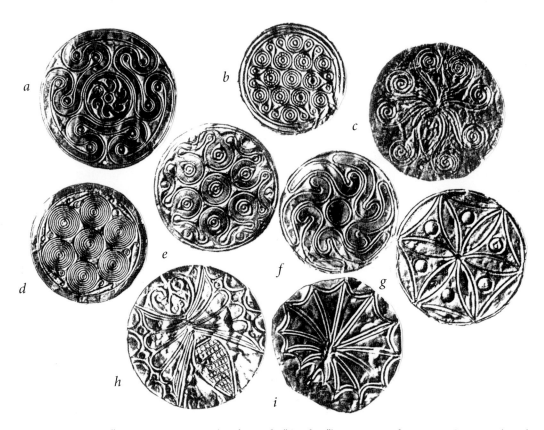

Figure 6. Disques d'or trouvés à Mycènes (tombe III du "Cercle A"): *a*, Karo 16, dia. 6,8 cm, Svoronos (1906) pl. 7,3; *b*, Karo 11, dia. 6 cm, Svoronos (1906) pl. 7,2; *c*, Karo 18, dia. 6,2 cm, Svoronos (1906) pl. 7,4; *d*, Karo 10, dia. 5,6 cm, Svoronos (1906), pl. 6,5; *e*, Karo (1930–33) 14, dia. 6,4 cm, Svoronos (1906), pl. 6,6; *f*, Karo 12, dia. 6,1 cm, Svoronos (1906), pl. 6,3; *g*, Karo 20, dia. 6,2 cm, Svoronos (1906), pl. 7,1; *h*, Karo 2, dia. probable 6,6 cm, Svoronos (1906), pl. 6,1; *i*, cf. Karo 8, dia. 6,5 cm, cf. Svoronos (1906), pl.7, 5–6. On note évidemment que les disques *g* et *h* présentent un décor semblable à celui des balances 81 et 82 (fig. 5).

"plaquettes", "rondelles") reste très difficile à définir. Ils étaient de dimensions telles et en nombre si grand dans la tombe III du cercle A de Mycènes qu'on hésite à y voir simplement l'ornementation de vêtements ou de linceuls. Mieux que le "symbole" de la richesse royale comme l'écrivait Ernest Babelon, ils ont pu être, du vivant de leurs possesseurs, une manière de stocker une partie de cette richesse elle-même, sous une forme destinée, parmi d'autres, aux usages sociaux dont nous trouvons l'écho dans les poèmes homériques. Beaucoup d'autres objets précieux les accompagnent. Les contextes funéraires[31] seuls nous permettent d'avoir une idée de cette richesse. Les disques d'or n'en sont certainement pas la seule

31. On lira par exemple l'énumération du contenu de la tombe IV du cercle A de Mycènes dans Treuil et al. (1989: 327).

mesure, comme les modernes ont eu tendance à le penser, influencés sans doute par la place privilégiée donnée ultérieurement à l'or dans l'économie des échanges. Chez Homère, l'or à lui seul n'achète rien.[32] Son rôle n'est pas médiocre pour autant, car il semble bien, comme la γέρας, la part de choix, enrichir aussi ou surtout d'honneur le vainqueur ou l'hôte qui le reçoit. Des talents d'or, comme les produits de luxe, grands vases, tissus, témoignent du statut social de qui les possède et peut en disposer: c'est en ce sens, nous semble-t-il, qu'on est en droit de les dire symboliques. Peut-être aurions-nous là l'explication de la récompense étonnante promise par l'usurpateur Egisthe à un serviteur zélé (*Od.* 4.526)?

Le texte homérique signale parfois que l'on pèse des talents avant de les donner (*Il.* 19.247; 24.232). L'or "précieux", "bien travaillé" (τιμήεις, εὐεργής), doit vraisemblablement être imaginé par le poète sous une forme matérielle proche des magnifiques plaquettes d'or mycéniennes. En même temps, la rédaction du texte indique qu'il faut recourir à la balance pour qu'un talent, deux talents, etc. existent: le talent apparaît alors, fondamentalement, comme un certain poids d'or et pas un objet particulier. Sans doute les aèdes savent bien que dans la vie réelle, à l'âge du fer (ou même avant?), les métaux sont une marchandise à peser, et susceptible d'avoir une valeur d'échange. Mais cette dernière est largement occultée dans l'épopée héroïque. Le talent y est un poids, comme dans les tablettes mycéniennes, mais ne joue pas pour autant un rôle d'unité monétaire ou pré-monétaire.

Aussi paraît-il vain de tenter de définir en grammes ces talents "de poète" transmis dans des formules dont l'ancienneté est elle-même si difficile à apprécier. On peut tout au plus, dans quelques rares cas où des récompenses sont hiérarchisées, les comparer à d'autres biens qui sont présentés par le conteur comme extrêmement désirables. Nous pouvons revenir sur les deux épisodes du Chant 23 de l'*Iliade*, où la liste des prix mis au concours par Achille jette une lueur sur la valeur psychologique accordée par le poète et son auditoire à tel ou tel bien. Prenons au sérieux les données de 23.269 et 751, et un peu d'arithmétique homérique nous amènera à penser que: si un bœuf bien gras est plus désirable qu'un demi-talent d'or, deux bœufs gras seraient plus désirables qu'un talent. Ainsi un talent pourrait être à peu près l'équivalent d'une paire de bœufs ordinaires. Si une jument pleine est largement plus désirable que deux talents, un cheval pourrait être à peu près comparable à un talent.

On arrivera ainsi à proposer de mettre au même niveau de richesse honorable à con-quérir une paire de bœufs, un cheval, un talent d'or.[33] Mais nulle part dans l'*Iliade* il n'est dit ni suggéré qu'échanger un talent permettrait de se procurer aisément bœufs ou cheval. L'or, propriété aristocratique, n'apparaît pas comme un produit négociable.

Au VIe siècle où les poèmes homériques ont été fixés par écrit à Athènes, la situation est toute différente dans la vie réelle. A l'époque de Pisistrate, en Lydie et en Ionie l'électrum puis l'or et l'argent ont déjà donné naissance à des monnaies dont on ne peut nier, entre

---

32. Et nous constatons que les évaluations "sérieuses" des biens y sont faites en bovins. Cf. *Od.* 1.429–431 (Euryclée achetée toute jeune "pour le prix de 20 bœufs").

33. Dans l'estimation d'Euryclée à "20 bœufs" (*Od.* 1.429–431) nous retrouverions *grosso modo* les 10 talents d'or des présents magnifiques de l'*Iliade*.

autres fonctions peut-être, le rôle commercial. Mais les poèmes d'Homère continuent à transporter leurs lecteurs ou leurs auditeurs dans le monde des héros, monde archaïsant modelé et remodelé en une tradition probablement ininterrompue.

Symboliques ou non, les balances et les disques d'or exhumés par Schliemann existent et sont à ce jour un des plus éloquents témoignages sur la richesse en or de Mycènes. Nous pensons qu'à propos des *talenta* J. N. Svoronos (1906) s'approcha plus que d'autres de la "vérité" (du rêve?) d'Homère, même si son interprétation ne peut pas être adoptée dans tous ses détails. Les fabuleux objets d'or accompagnant certains morts à Mycènes ne pouvaient être totalement oubliés lorsque prit forme l'épopée héroïque,[34] pas plus que n'étaient oubliés les magnifiques ustensiles de bronze ou les casques recouverts d'ivoire de sanglier et les cuirasses des Achéens χαλκοχίθωνες. Sur tous ces souvenirs de luxe et de gloire guerrière les aèdes ont rêvé et brodé à l'envie. Du plus doué d'entre eux sans doute, celui que nous percevons à travers l'*Iliade*, il nous reste aujourd'hui encore pas mal de choses à apprendre —et une grande oeuvre à savourer.

BIBLIOGRAPHIE

Aura Jorro, F. 1993 (1999). *Diccionario micénico* (Diccionario griego-espanol. Anejo II). Madrid: CSIC.

Baslez, M.-F. 2003. *Les sources littéraires de l'histoire grecque*. Paris: Armand Colin.

Björck, G. 1945. Die Schicksalswaage. *Eranos* 43: 58–66.

Bortolotti, P. 1877. Del talento Omerico. In: *Commentationes philologae in honorem Theodori Mommseni scripservnt amici. Adiecta est tabvla*, pp. 282–290. Berlin: Weidmannos.

Brown, A. 1998. Homeric talents and the ethics of exchange. *Journal of Hellenic Studies* 118: 165–172.

Carlier, P. 1999. *Homère*. Paris: Fayard.

Chadwick, J., et L. Baumbach. 1963. The Mycenaean Greek vocabulary. *Glotta* 41: 157–271.

Chantraine, P. 1999. *Dictionnaire étymologique de la langue grecque, histoire des mots*. Avec un supplément sous la direction de A. Blanc, Ch. de Lamberterie, et J.-L. Perpillou. Paris: Klincksieck.

Daremberg, C., et E. Saglio. 1929 [1969]. *Dictionnaire des antiquités grecques et romaines*. Graz: Akademische Druck- u. Verlaganstalt.

De Witte, J. 1844/45. Scènes de la psychostasie homérique. *Revue archéologique* 1: 645–656.

Duhoux, Y. 1976. *Aspects du vocabulaire économique mycénien: cadastre, artisanat, fiscalité*. Amsterdam: A. M. Hakkert.

Evans, A. 1906. Minoan weights and mediums of currency. In: G. F. Hill, ed., *Corolla numismatica, numismatic essays in honour of Barclay V. Head*, pp. 336–367. London: H. Frowde.

---

34. C'est la découverte par Schliemann, dans la tombe V, d'un grand canthare d'or aux anses ornées d'oiseaux (Karo 1930–33: n° 412) qui a permis de mieux comprendre la description par Homère du vase à boire de Nestor, roi de Pylos, dans l'*Iliade* (11.632–635).

———. 1935. *The Palace of Minos at Cnossos*, vol. IV, part II. London: MacMillan and Co.

Godard, L., et J.-P. Olivier. 1976–1985. *GORILA: Recueil des inscriptions en linéaire A*, 5 vols. Ecole française d'Athènes, Etudes Crétoises 21. Paris: P. Geuthner.

Hooker. J. T. 1988. From Mycenae to Homer. In: J. H. Betts, J. T. Hooker and J. R. Green,eds., *Studies in Honour of T. B. L.Webster*, vol. 2, pp. 57–64. Bristol: Bristol Classical Press.

———. 1996. Gifts in Homer. In: F. Amory, P. Considine, et S. Hooker, eds. *Scripta minora. Selected essays in Minoan, Mycenaean, Homeric and Classical Greek subjects*, pp. 539–550. Amsterdam: Hakkert.

Humbert, J., ed. et trad. 1951. *Homère.* Paris: Les Belles Lettres.

Jeffery, L. H. 1961. *The local scripts of archaic Greece: a study of the origin of the Greek alphabet and its development from the eight to the fifth centuries B.C.* Oxford: Clarendon Press.

Karageorgis, V. 1958. Myth and epic in Mycenaean vase painting. *American Journal of Archaeology* 62: 383–387.

Karo, G. H. 1930–33. *Die Schachtgräber von Mykenai*, 2 vols. Munich: Bruckmann.

Karouzou, S. 1956. *The Amasis painter.* Oxford: Clarendon Press.

Lejeune, M. 1961. Les Forgerons de Pylos. *Historia* 10: 409–434.

Nilsson, M. P. 1933. *Homer and Mycenae.* London: Methuen and Co.

———. 1950. *The Minoan-Mycenaean religion and its survival in Greek Religion*, 2nd ed. Lund: C. W. K. Gleerup.

Palmer, L. R. 1969. *The interpretation of Mycenaean Greek texts.* Oxford: Clarendon Press.

Ruijgh, C. 1989. L'héritage mycénien. La langue et l'écriture. In: R. Treuil, P. Darcque, J.-C. Poursat, and G. Touchais, *Les Civilisations égéennes du Néolithique et de l'Age du Bronze*, pp. 569–584. Paris: Presses universitaires de France.

Rutherford, R. B. 1993. From the *Iliad* to the *Odyssey. Bulletin of the Institute of Classical Studies* 38: 37–54.

Schliemann, H. 1879. *Mycènes, récit de recherches et découvertes faites à Mycènes et à Tirynthe,* avec une préface de M. Gladstone…traduit de l'anglais par J. Girardin. Paris: Hachette.

Svoronos, J. N. 1906. Τὰ Ὁμηρικὰ "χρυσοῖο τάλαντα". *Journal international d'archéologie numismatique* 9: 181–189.

Touchais, G. 1989. Le début du Bronze Récent hors de Crète. In: R. Treuil, P. Darcque, J.-C. Poursat, and G. Touchais, *Les Civilisations égéennes du Néolithique et de l'Age du Bronze*, pp. 325–351. Paris: Presses universitaires de France.

Van Effenterre, H., et F. Ruzé. 1994. *Nomima: recueil d'inscriptions politiques et juridiques de l'archaïsme grec*, vol. 1. Collection de l'Ecole française de Rome 188. Rome: Ecole française de Rome.

Vandenabeele, F., et J.-P. Olivier. 1979. *Les idéogrammes archéologiques du linéaire B*, Ecole française d'Athènes, Etudes Crétoises 24. Paris: P. Geuthner.

Ventris, M., et J. Chadwick. 1973. *Documents in Mycenaean Greek*, 2nd ed. Cambridge: Cambridge University Press.

Von Bothmer, D. 1984. *The Amasis painter and his world: vase-painting in sixth-century B.C. Athens*. Malibu, Calif.: J. Paul Getty Museum; New York: Thames and Hudson.

Agoranomia: Studies in Money and Exchange Presented to John H. Kroll, pp. 21–36

Argyrōnetos: Les transformations de l'échange dans la Grèce archaïque

Raymond Descat*

Mon point de départ est un passage d'Athénée, citant Théopompe de Chios au livre 6 de son *Banquet des Sophistes* (265 b–c), dont Pierre Vidal-Naquet (1973: 25) écrivait qu'il "a été au cœur de la discussion de ces dernières années sur l'esclavage". Il a été en particulier à l'origine de la fameuse formule de M. I. Finley (1959: 164) "one aspect of Greek history, in short, is the advance, hand in hand, of freedom and slavery".

> Les premiers Grecs à utiliser des esclaves achetés avec de l'argent (*argyrōnetois doulois*) furent les Chiotes comme le dit Théopompe au dix-septième livre de ses *Histoires*. Les Chiotes furent les premiers Grecs après les Thessaliens et les Lacédémoniens à utiliser des esclaves, mais ils n'en firent pas l'acquisition de la même manière que ces derniers. En effet, Lacédémoniens et Thessaliens ont, comme on le verra, constitué leur catégorie servile à partir de Grecs qui habitaient avant eux le pays qu'ils occupent maintenant: les premiers à partir des Achéens, les Thessaliens à partir des Perrhèbes et des Magnètes. Les uns ont nommé les peuples réduits en esclavage *hilotes* et les autres *pénestes*. Quant aux Chiotes, ce sont des barbares dont ils ont fait leurs esclaves, et ils l'ont fait en payant pour cela un prix.

Ce texte a donc été considéré comme une approche historique de l'esclavage-marchandise dont il resterait à préciser la date de formation. Y. Garlan conclut ainsi pour "une date non déterminée, mais certainement postérieure aux invasions doriennes de la fin du second millénaire" (Garlan 1982: 52). Mais l'intérêt qu'y a trouvé Finley vient du lien qu'il établit avec

*Institut Ausonius, Université Michel-de-Montaigne Bordeaux.
J'ai le plaisir de dédier cette étude à J. Kroll, qui sait si bien ce que monnaie veut dire.

un texte épigraphique daté du VIe s. et attribué généralement à Chios, appelé souvent "loi constitutionnelle", qui mentionne l'existence d'une *boulē dēmosiē* interprétée comme une des plus anciennes, sinon la plus ancienne, instance démocratique dans la cité grecque.[1] Dans ce cadre politique le développement de l'esclavage est associé, comme à Athènes à l'époque des lois de Solon, à la disparition des dépendances traditionnelles. Dans cette conception, l'esclavage de Chios daterait donc plutôt du VIe s. Le fait nouveau qu'évoquerait le passage de Théopompe ne serait pas en lui-même l'acquisition des esclaves, car cette pratique existait auparavant (on achète des esclaves dans les tablettes mycéniennes et dans Homère) mais la mise en marche simultanée du processus de démocratisation dans la cité et du développement de l'esclavage-marchandise. Même s'il faut remarquer que Théopompe ne dit rien de tel dans le fragment conservé, cette interprétation avait l'avantage, comme pour Athènes, de donner une explication forte à un phénomène social caractéristique de la cité.

Or l'on sait depuis plusieurs années que la vision d'une cité de Chios qui se "démocratise" à l'époque archaïque à la lumière de l'inscription est aujourd'hui un leurre et que la *boulē dēmosiē* a le sens probable d'un conseil national pour toute la cité, ce qui est une étape certes essentielle de l'histoire politique mais qui ne suppose pas l'existence d'une démocratie. Chios est au Ve s. une aristocratie et la réflexion de Théopompe ne s'appuie pas sur un lien avec une démocratisation du pouvoir à l'époque archaïque.

On peut donc se demander pourquoi Théopompe fait cette remarque dont P. Vidal-Naquet (1973: 39) rappelle qu'elle n'avait aucun précédent. Les textes grecs qui évoquent les débuts de l'esclavage parlent seulement d'un temps avant l'esclavage comme d'une période très ancienne et donc pauvre où il n'y avait pas encore d'esclaves (Hdt. 6.137). Thucydide dans l'*Archéologie* du premier livre de son histoire ne fait même pas mention d'un tel début de l'esclavage. L'explication de la vision *historique* de Théopompe serait donc selon P. Vidal-Naquet, à rechercher dans la crise de la dépendance de type hilotique à son époque. On ne peut douter qu'un tel fait ait joué au IVe s. un rôle important dans la prise de conscience historique et donc temporaire de cette forme de servitude, mais il ne faut pas y voir la seule raison puisque Théopompe parle aussi du système des Pénestes en Thessalie qu'on ne peut considérer alors en disparition (Ducat 1994: 103–104). Au moins dans "une réflexion sur l'autre forme de l'esclavage", une comparaison avec Sparte a certainement joué. On se prend donc à penser que cette comparaison avec Sparte est le cœur de la réflexion de Théopompe.

Chios est en effet renommée dans les textes antérieurs à Théopompe non pas seulement pour avoir des esclaves, mais pour en avoir beaucoup, *comme Sparte*. Thucydide (8.40) le dit clairement: "aucune cité, celle de Lacédémone exceptée, ne possédait plus d'esclaves que Chios; leur multitude nécessitait à leur égard un système de répression sévère". Cette abondance d'esclaves est le trait distinctif que veut retenir Athénée dans ses citations; il va en effet montrer après le texte de Théopompe des témoignages, critiques sur les Chiotes, portant sur

---

1. Sur ce texte, voir le commentaire de Van Effenterre et Ruzé (1994 vol. 1: 262–267).

cet excès d'esclaves (Athén. 6.265–266). Théopompe défend au contraire cette situation en soulignant le premier une différence dans l'origine des esclaves avec Sparte, ce qui explique sans doute que cette domination n'est pas remise en cause, à la différence de celle des Spartiates sur les hilotes. L'abondance des esclaves à Chios n'est donc pas le fait du guerrier, mais du marchand. Mais le fait le plus curieux, c'est qu'ils en ont acheté beaucoup.

Le sens d'*argyrōnetos*

Je voudrais donc poser la question suivante: est-ce que ce passage, associé étroitement par Athénée au mot *argyrōnetos*, n'est pas un révélateur important pour l'évolution des pratiques d'échanges en Grèce? Le mot n'est pas en soi un synonyme parfait d'esclave—marchandise, puisque ce dernier n'existe pas en grec. Les Grecs emploient toujours les mêmes termes génériques, comme *doulos*, que ce soit pour la dépendance ou pour ce que les historiens modernes appellent esclavage—marchandise ou esclavage tout court. Ce que dit Athénée suivant Théopompe est autre chose: il dit que les gens de Chios sont les premiers à acheter "avec de l'argent" des esclaves. Je pense que l'expression "acheté avec de l'argent" ne veut pas dire seulement "en payant un prix" (expression sur laquelle je reviendrai), mais bien avec de "l'argent". Que cela ne soit pas l'équivalent passe—partout d'un mot comme esclave—marchandise est rendu plus clair par deux faits au moins.

Le premier c'est qu'il existe de manière courante le mot *ōnetos* ("acheté"), qui est le plus générique et qui est antérieur à Théopompe puisqu'on le rencontre dans un passage homérique "mon père était fort riche…mais ma mère n'était qu'une concubine achetée (*ōnetē pallakis*)" (*Od.* 14.202). Dans Aristophane, nous notons ainsi la présence des esclaves "nouvellement achetés", *neōnetoi* (*Cav.* 2 et aussi *Pl.* 769: "je rentre chercher des dons de bienvenue pour les yeux comme on fait pour des esclaves nouvellement achetés").

Le second c'est qu'il y a au moins deux autres manières d'acheter des esclaves dans le vocabulaire grec: *alōnetos* "acheté avec du sel" en Thrace (Hesychios, *Souda*, etc. s.v.) et *chrysōnetos* "acheté avec de l'or" en Crète (Athén. 6.263e). On peut donc proposer l'idée que ce terme *argyrōnetos* n'est pas à l'origine un terme banal qui serait le simple équivalent d'esclave acheté, mais bien un fait spécifique auquel renvoie Théopompe et qui est passé inaperçu de ce point de vue. Nous partirons donc de ce simple constat: la nouveauté n'est pas ici d'acheter des esclaves, on le fait depuis longtemps en Grèce, mais de les "acheter avec de l'argent".

Il n'est donc pas étonnant que l'usage du terme *argyrōnetos* n'apparaisse qu'à l'époque classique (première mention en 458 dans l'*Agamemnon* d'Eschyle v. 949) et qu'il soit alors relativement peu utilisé par les auteurs. Son usage est lié pour l'essentiel à deux aspects qu'il exprime tout particulièrement. D'un côté une étape historique dans l'esclavage, dans la perspective et peut-être l'influence de Théopompe qui a très certainement utilisé le mot; c'est en effet le terme qui définit le mieux la période qui connaît l'esclavage par rapport à la période où il n'y avait pas d'esclaves (par exemple Timée dans Athénée 6.264c ou Diod. Sic. 1.70). De l'autre il est employé dans des énumérations pour accentuer l'écart entre les catégories, les hommes libres (Dém. *Tr. Alex.* 3) et autres esclaves comme les prisonniers de guerre (Diod. Sic. 33.14). Il est probable que, s'il n'est pas plus utilisé, c'est parce qu'il fait double emploi avec la simple idée d'acheter des esclaves qui se fait usuellement avec de la monnaie d'argent. Mais à un certain moment la construction du syntagme "acheté avec de l'argent" n'a pas été une opération sans signification.[2]

Il ne doit pas paraître surprenant qu'un mot comme *argyrōnetos* ait un sens ancré dans une période historique déterminée. Il n'est pas le seul dans le domaine de l'économie et de l'échange. Ces mots ont connu un bouleversement considérable qui n'a d'égal que celui du vocabulaire politique, mais si la disparition de l'*anax* ou la transformation du *basileus* ont été longuement étudiés par les hellénistes, il n'en est pas de même du sens à donner à la transformation des termes de l'échange, et en particulier de l'achat et de la vente. Une étude comparable doit être faite et c'est ce que je propose d'aborder dans ces lignes. *Argyrōnetos* en témoigne doublement parce qu'il est un composé d'*argyros* "argent" mais aussi de la famille d'*ōneisthai* "acheter" et que sur ces deux points (*acheté* avec de l'argent et acheté *avec de l'argent*) il exprime une nouveauté historique.

L'ÉCHANGE AU DÉBUT DE L'ARCHAÏSME: VALEUR ET PAIEMENT

Pour comprendre ces points, il faut se défaire de nos habitudes. Pour nous, la relation marchande est perçue comme une unité, constituée de deux phases mêlées étroitement l'une avec l'autre, l'achat et la vente. Dans le monde grec le plus ancien que nous puissions comprendre de ce point de vue, soit celui du début de l'archaïsme, avec les textes d'Homère et d'Hésiode, les choses ne se présentent pas ainsi. L'échange marchand ne constitue pas un acte unique et homogène. Chaque opération qui forme ce que nous appelons la relation marchande a au contraire son unité et sa logique qui se reflètent dans l'usage des mots. E. Benvéniste l'a montré d'une manière saisissante (1969 I: 125–129). *Ōneisthai* qui veut dire "acheter" dans le grec classique ne s'utilise pas en forme verbale. Pour "acheter" Homère emploie le verbe *priasthai* utilisé avec un complément: *priasthai ktēassi* ("acheter avec des biens") est la formule courante. Or il ne s'agit pas d'une quelconque variante stylistique, cela touche au contraire le sens profond de l'opération. En effet le substantif *ōnos* est employé,[3] mais il n'est pas lié à un échange matériel, il désigne la transaction et l'accord qui est établi à cette occasion alors que *priasthai* désigne le paiement. Quand il s'agit d'un esclave par exemple, le participe *ōnētē* existe et définit un cadre social (*Od.* 14.202), mais quand le Chrysès, le prêtre d'Apollon, réclame sa fille capturée par Agamemnon, il la veut *apriatē* (*Il.* 1.99), parce qu'il ne veut rien payer *réellement* pour la récupérer. Que désigne exactement *ōnos*? C'est l'opération qui termine la discussion de l'échange, c'est-à-dire le fait de

---

2. On retrouve encore un emploi lié à un achat fait explicitement en argent dans certains textes, comme un contrat sur un parchemin d'époque parthe (Minns 1915: 28).

3. Voir aussi l'analyse de E. Scheid-Tissinier (1994: 78–82).

"donner un prix" ou de "rapporter un prix" selon que l'on se place du côté de l'acheteur ou du vendeur, exactement donner la valeur de la contrepartie de l'objet échangé (*Od.* 15.445) "hâtez-vous d'amener la contrepartie de ce que vous transportez" (trad. Scheid-Tissinier 1994: 82). Du point de vue de l'échange la meilleure traduction en serait l'idée de *valeur* établie à l'occasion de la transaction. Il n'est pas surprenant que ce terme soit souvent accompagné d'une forme verbale, *alphanō* qui le précise, forme elle aussi spécifique du texte homérique, et qui disparaît de la même façon dans l'usage classique. On dira donc d'un bien qui est échangé (en l'occurrence d'un esclave) qu'il "vaut une grande valeur *murion ōnon alphoi*" (*Od.* 15.453) ou qu'il "vaut cent bœufs [*hekatomboion ēlphon*]" (*Il.* 21.79). On voit le composé *alphesiboios* utilisé pour l'estimation des jeunes filles qui "valent des bœufs" (*Il.* 18.593) et qui renvoie à tous les composés bien connus en nombre de bœufs qui constituent l'étalon de valeur homérique.

La question est donc maintenant la suivante: pourquoi le paiement est-il, dans cette conception archaïque de l'échange, séparé de la transaction qui estime la valeur? Pour deux raisons majeures. En premier lieu le paiement ne s'effectue pas avec les biens qui servent d'unités de valeur (en l'occurrence le bœuf) ou du moins pas de manière systématique et obligée. En second lieu le paiement ne termine pas nécessairement toutes les transactions; il existe des cas, qui sont habituellement présentés comme des pratiques de *dons*, où l'échange est suivi d'un paiement différé. Reprenons successivement ces points.

BIENS D'ÉCHANGE, SPHÈRES D'ÉCHANGE

Dans le monde homérique, si la valeur est estimée en bœufs, ce n'est pas en bœufs que l'on paye habituellement. La seule expression générale qui existe est la suivante: on paie *avec des biens (ktēassi)*. Il n'y a pas au fond de spécification catégorielle: tous les biens peuvent servir de biens d'échange. Dans le seul exemple de transaction complète de l'*Iliade*, l'achat de vin ne se dit pas *acheter* du vin mais *acheter du vin* en un seul mot (*oinizō*), c'est-à-dire que d'un côté il y a les vendeurs du vin (des Lemniens), de l'autre les acheteurs Achéens qui apportent en contrepartie du bronze, du fer, des peaux, des bœufs et des esclaves (*Il.* 7.472–475). La tradition voudrait qu'on parle dans ce cas de *troc*, mais ce mot est à récuser car il est profondément inexact. Je ne reviens pas sur ce point plus en détail car il a été discuté ailleurs (Descat 2001). Le troc a été créé dans l'imaginaire occidental pour désigner les échanges des peuples qui n'ont pas de monnaie (Servet 2001), mais l'échange homérique ne fonctionne pas sans monnaie, c'est une économie à "monnaie multiple",[4] où un ensemble large d'objets peut être à la fois, et selon les cas, produit et moyen d'échange sans que ces aspects soient exclusifs ou contradictoires. Cette habitude disparaîtra ensuite dans le monde grec et le mot *ktēar* avec elle. C'est en effet à partir de la période post-homérique que l'on paie avec des *chrēmata* comme l'entérine ensuite la science *oikonomique*, le logos *oikonomikos*, à l'époque classique qui distingue entre les biens que l'on possède pour produire (les *ktēmata*) et ceux

4. Expression de G. Condominas (1989).

qui servent à l'utilisation et aux dépenses (*chrēmata*), comme le dit l'auteur sophiste du *Discours à Démonicos* attribué à Isocrate (1.28):

> Efforce-toi d'organiser ta fortune tant en biens à dépenser (*chrēmata*) qu'en biens de possession (*ktēmata*); il faut savoir faire du profit pour avoir des *chrēmata* et être capable d'acquérir pour avoir des *ktēmata*.

Or nous n'en sommes pas là dans le texte homérique où le sens de *chrēmata* n'est pas encore celui de biens spécialisés dans l'échange. La notion de *chrēmata* reste liée à l'idée de biens que l'on utilise d'abord en les consommant, comme Télémaque qui se plaint de ses productions qui disparaissent (*Od.* 2.78, 16.315) ou les prétendants qui s'en glorifient (*Od.* 16.389). Mais il faut noter que l'évolution est rapide et que la langue témoigne d'une période charnière. Dans l'épopée l'on demande au navigateur qui arrive les raisons de son voyage (le sens précis sera développé un peu plus bas): "mes hôtes, votre nom? d'où-nous arrivez-vous sur la route des ondes? faites-vous le commerce (*prexis*)? n'êtes-vous que pirates qui, follement, courez et croisez sur les flots et, risquant votre vie, vous en allez piller les côtes étrangères ?" (*Od.* 3.70–74). Dans le texte plus tardif de l'*Hymne à Apollon* au vers 397 on ajoute maintenant à *prexis* pour en préciser le sens *chrēmata* "pour leur commerce et pour des biens, ils voguaient sur un vaisseau noir vers Pylos". L'évolution est déjà sensible dans Hésiode *Trav.* 68 et dans *Od.* 19.284. Les historiens se sont intéressés de près à la question de savoir quand *chrēmata* pouvait désigner la monnaie frappée[5] (et il faut noter que le passage est en quelque sorte difficilement repérable) mais ont accordé peu d'importance à l'émergence du mot comme type de bien spécialisé comme moyen d'échange. On doit considérer cependant qu'il s'agit d'une étape décisive dans l'évolution des échanges.

Si la langue ne connaît pas de biens spécialisés comme moyens d'échange, c'est l'indice en revanche que tous les biens ne circulent pas de la même façon.[6] L'économie homérique est tout à fait semblable aux économies non marchandes (Morris 1986) que l'anthropologue P. Bohannan définissait comme "multicentrées": "dans une économie multicentrée, il existe plusieurs sphères de transactions différentes. Chaque sphère est caractérisée par différents items de biens et de services et souvent par des principes d'échanges et de valeurs morales différentes" (Bohannan 1968: 227). Le vocabulaire témoigne d'une première séparation générale faite entre les biens qui ne bougent pas, les *keimelia* et ceux qui bougent, les *probata*. Dans cette dernière catégorie, il y a effectivement des sphères distinctes. Elles sont décrites au moins une fois en *Iliade* 9.400. Achille y souligne l'idée que par rapport à la vie qui, une fois perdue ne se rattrape plus, les richesses s'échangent, s'en vont et reviennent mais de façons différentes "on enlève bœufs, gras moutons; on acquiert trépieds et chevaux aux crins blonds", les premiers sont appelés des biens *lēistoi* et les seconds des biens *ktētoi*. Que veut dire cette distinction? Elle n'est certainement pas, comme il semble au premier abord,

---

5. Un bon état de la question dans Faraguna (2003: 110–112).
6. La différence des formes de transaction est parfaitement soulignée par R. Seaford (2004: 23–26).

à prendre au pied de la lettre car on peut razzier sans nul doute des chevaux et des trépieds. Elle évoque en réalité deux pratiques sociales d'échange, dont l'une (celle des biens *leistoi*) est bizarrement définie par des traits qui en apparence sont un refus de l'échange mais qui se retrouve ailleurs dans l'épopée et en particulier dans la fameuse interrogation devant un étranger qui arrive, que je viens d'évoquer et que je précise maintenant: "mes hôtes, votre nom? d'où-nous arrivez-vous sur la route des ondes? faites-vous le commerce (*prexis*)? N'êtes-vous que pirates (*lēistēres*) qui, follement, courez et croisez sur les flots et, risquant votre vie, vous en allez piller les côtes étrangères?" (*Od.* 3.70–74).

L'interprétation traditionnelle est d'y reconnaître des différences de catégories sociales, voire professionnelles, à la suite d'A. Mele (1979) qui distingue la *prexis* qui serait le fait traditionnel des aristocraties des autres formes qui seraient issues de nouvelles couches sociales. Mais le texte ne dit pas cela (Morris 1986: 5); il décrit une typologie des formes d'échanges qui n'est pas clairement réductible à une catégorie sociale particulière. La *prexis*, qui est le fait des *prekteres* (*Od.* 8.161–164), est une action d'échange socialement *efficace* parce qu'on dispose de partenaires et que l'échange, étant l'effet des amitiés et des relations durables, fonctionne donc dans un cadre établi.[7] L'autre forme, qui est celle des *lēistēres* est un échange qui s'établit sans relations sociales préalables, contact de personnes qui sont des "étrangers" les uns aux autres, qui vont en quelque sorte à "l'aventure" sociale, où il n'y a pas de certitude de résultat, d'où l'insistance dans le passage du vocabulaire du vain, de l'inefficace (*mapsidiōs*, Descat 1986: 282–285) et qui peut déboucher soit sur une relation d'échange soit sur une opposition et un rapport de force comme l'évoque la traduction par piraterie.

On reconnaît donc dans la Grèce homérique deux grandes sphères d'échange où l'on retrouve les principaux traits décrits par ailleurs dans les études anthropologiques:

1. L'échange avec des partenaires clairement établis et reconnus comme tels, ce qui veut dire que le règlement de la transaction n'en est pas nécessairement immédiat, même s'il peut l'être, ou bien que la valeur ne s'épuise pas lors d'un seul échange et qu'il peut y avoir un paiement différé, étant donnée la confiance liée au cadre social. Ce type d'échange peut être donc rapproché dans certains cas de la catégorie du don ou du crédit social. A l'intérieur de ce cadre qui existe dans tous les milieux sociaux, il faut introduire la différence entre les biens échangés. Le milieu de l'aristocratie homérique auquel Achille renvoie, lui qui ne prétend pas faire une ethnographie sociale différenciée mais traiter de son cadre personnel, montre que cette hiérarchie des valeurs est respectée puisque les biens *ktētoi* (les chevaux et les trépieds) acquis par des canaux sociaux récurrents sont supérieurs en valeur dans l'exemple aux biens *leistoi*: le seul trépied évalué dans l'épopée vaut 12 bœufs (*Il.* 23.703) et

---

7. Ce rôle d'efficacité de la *prexis* dans les échanges se retrouve dans les rites. On connaît à Mégare un culte ancien d'une Aphrodite *Praxis* (Paus. 1.43.6), qui renvoie à l'efficacité d'Aphrodite dans les échanges et en particulier dans les échanges sur l'agora (Pirenne-Delforge 1994: 91).

les chevaux sont plus chers que bœufs et moutons. Mais ce contexte aristocratique n'épuise pas la portée de ce type d'échange que M. Sahlins (1976: 247) appelait la "réciprocité généralisée"; il existe aussi chez le propriétaire des *Travaux et Jours* d'Hésiode en rapport avec ses voisins, et dans ce contexte il n'est pas lié aux biens de prestige seulement.

2. Les échanges qui ne sont pas liés à l'existence d'hôtes traditionnels, de type plus varié (selon les toutes les formes de besoin), où le règlement de la transaction du fait de la non-existence de liens antérieurs doit être plus immédiat ou bien n'être qu'immédiat. Ce cadre aussi peut être ouvert à toutes les situations sociales, au contact avec un "étranger social" avant que des liens ne se tissent. Ce peut être un élément de rupture d'anciennes relations ou d'explorations de nouvelles et en partie ce que M. Sahlins (1976: 248–249) appellerait la "réciprocité équilibrée ou négative" selon les cas. Nous n'en savons pas beaucoup dans les textes sur l'échange des biens de subsistance quand il existe en dehors des relations de servitude ou de dépendance tributaire. On doit noter qu'ils se retrouvent dans les deux types d'échange.

Un dernier point doit être précisé. Plus le type d'échange fonctionne sur un cadre social reconnu avec des partenaires définis socialement, plus la confiance sociale règne entre eux en quelque sorte (plus le paiement peut être différé de la transaction), plus ces derniers sont prêts à admettre la polyvalence de certains biens.[8] Ceux-ci ont alors une valeur symbolique immédiatement acceptée, comme les trépieds de la phrase d'Achille et les autres objets qui peuvent avoir le rôle de monnaies: chaudrons, doubles haches, phiales, coupes, broches, pièces de vêtement, etc.

Dans ce cadre, la valeur des objets, dont on a vu qu'elle était un aspect essentiel de la transaction, n'est pas déterminé par un "prix de marché", prix qui serait à la fois totalement indifférent aux partenaires et aux conditions de l'échange et comparable de ce fait sur une même échelle de valeur à tous les autres produits. Puisque les objets circulent dans des sphères d'échanges séparées les unes des autres, chacune correspondant à différents types de biens et de prestations. Il n'y a aucune raison pour que des biens que l'on offre pour "payer" une fiancée soient équivalents de ceux utilisés pour acheter des biens de subsistance. Ce qu'on appelle la valeur d'un bien est l'expression de la hiérarchie de ces sphères qui regroupent différents produits de même équivalence de valeur, mais non le niveau individuel de chaque article pris séparément.

Prenons l'exemple de l'or, qui sera un élément de base des futures valeurs monétaires. L'or se situe dans les circuits d'échange au niveau moyen de 100 bœufs, quels que soient la forme et le poids exact de l'objet. Entre Glaukos et Diomède (*Il.* 6.234–236), le poète intervient en quelque sorte lui-même pour noter une apparente absurdité puisque Glaukos "échange de l'or contre du bronze, soit la valeur de 100 bœufs contre celle de 9". C'est aussi

---

8. D'où le rôle déterminant du rituel pour donner une valeur symbolique à un objet (Seaford 2004: 39–67).

à 100 bœufs qu'est estimée chaque frange d'or de l'égide d'Athéna (*Il.* 2.449), de même que les 9 bœufs du bronze représentent une valeur moyenne de ce métal (de 12 bœufs pour un grand trépied [*Il.* 23.703] à 1 bœuf pour un chaudron [*Il.* 23.885]). La valeur de 100 bœufs est donc le niveau des objets d'or placés dans un circuit de biens et de prestations de prestige. Cent bœufs est parallèlement le niveau des prestations offertes à l'occasion des mariages dans l'aristocratie (*Il.* 11.244) comme la valeur du noble capturé, en l'occurrence Lycaon (*Il.* 21.79–80). Cette conception des prix permet de comprendre que la valeur des objets d'argent est du même ordre que celle de l'or, contrairement aux critères de la "valeur march-ande" des métaux, puisque le cratère d'argent "de six mesures" fabriqué par les Sidoniens est l'objet qui a permis l'achat de Lycaon (*Il.* 23.741) et qu'il vaut donc aussi 100 bœufs. Ce qui compte est la valeur des sphères d'échange et non pas de l'objet en tant que tel.

Ce système d'échange est-il stable? Comme le montre aussi l'anthropologie économique, ces sphères d'échange ne restent pas immuables, elles connaissent des perturbations plus ou moins fortuites et qui peuvent ou non avoir des conséquences de plus ou moins d'importance. Ce qui amène des modifications, ce sont les faits de conversion (au sens de Bohannan) d'une sphère à l'autre, qui peuvent modifier des prix qui s'appuient sur la con-naissance d'un ordre social. Dans ce cadre, le rapport avec l'étranger, par définition inédit, est un bouleversement potentiel. Il existe dans l'épopée un exemple de conversion brutale, signalé comme une anomalie, c'est la célèbre transaction, évoquée plus haut, qui scelle le pacte de *xēnia* entre Glaukos et Diomède (*Il.* 6.234–236), où Homère note que Glaukos "échange de l'or contre du bronze, soit la valeur de 100 bœufs contre celle de 9".[9] Le pre-mier prix que nous connaissons pour l'or en Grèce le placerait donc dans un rapport de $11^{1}/_{9}$ à 1 face au bronze si l'on devait l'exprimer dans un rapport de type monétaire, ce qui fait de l'or vu sous cet angle un métal exceptionnellement peu cher. L'explication se situe dans la confusion de deux sphères d'échange, due à l'inexpérience de Glaukos. Diomède propose un échange équilibré, *amoibos*, au terme immédiat alors que Glaukos se situe dans les relations d'hospitalité patrimoniales et offre, comme son aïeul, de l'or, qui est pour lui, un "crédit" pour l'avenir et non un paiement dans l'immédiat. Dans ce cas la modification est une simple péripétie qui ne touche pas la valeur générale de l'or. Dans d'autres situa-tions et lors d'échanges restreints entre deux groupes, cela peut avoir plus de conséquences. On peut citer un exemple ethnologique de modification brutale rapporté par M. Godelier (1973: 286) chez les Baruyas de Nouvelle-Guinée où une tribu qui fabriquait des barres de sel se met à les échanger pour avoir des haches d'acier (au prix de trois barres de sel la hache d'acier) avec des partenaires commerciaux qui étaient de redoutables guerriers can-nibales. Un jour, le jeune Baruya (la jeunesse est un signe d'inexpérience comme Glaukos par rapport à Diomède), qui arrive dans la clairière où se faisaient traditionnellement les

---

9. Von Reden (1995: 26) évoque la difficulté de compréhension de ce passage (et voir la bibliographie rassem-blée à sa note 70). Sur ce passage aussi Scheid-Tissinier (1994: 160–162).

échanges, est paniqué à l'idée de rencontrer les cannibales et s'enfuit après avoir déposé dans sa précipitation quatre barres et non plus trois. Ce fut désormais le nouveau "prix" du sel au détriment des producteurs.

Dans un système d'échange qui est donc ouvert à des évolutions, on doit penser que la transformation que montre le fait linguistique "d'acheter avec de l'argent" est très profonde. Comment les pratiques ont évolué? il est certes plus facile de constater le résultat que de comprendre le détail des évolutions qui touchent par répercussion toute la société de la Grèce archaïque.

ARGYRŌNETOS: LES PERTURBATIONS DE L'ÉCHANGE ARCHAÏQUE

Dans le mot *argyrōnetos* il y a deux aspects nouveaux qui correspondent aux points que l'on vient d'évoquer dans notre présentation de l'échange archaïque: le fait que l'action d'*ōneisthai* soit maintenant en rapport direct avec le paiement et la place de l'argent comme bien d'échange. Il n'y a plus de différence entre la transaction et le paiement—*on achète avec de l'argent*; la valeur et le prix ne forment plus qu'une seule action qui est caractéristique de l'évolution vers ce qu'on peut appeler, avec précaution mais pour simplifier, le rapport marchand tel qu'on le comprend aujourd'hui. On doit donc supposer que la modification s'est faite autour du rôle de l'argent, qui est à la fois l'indice et le moteur de la transformation de la structure même de l'échange. Mais là aussi il faut se défier d'un schéma trop facile qui est pourtant constamment présent dans les études historiques, je veux dire l'obstination à trouver dans l'époque archaïque grecque la naissance du comportement marchand associé très souvent autour d'une autre idée toute faite, la naissance de la monnaie (en dernier lieu Schaps 2003), sous-entendue comme étant la monnaie frappée, qui est pourtant une innovation sans nom. La relation de type marchand (marquée par un gain immédiat qui est un objectif central) existe déjà dans une économie multicentrée comme l'est l'économie homérique et de la même façon les économies voisines du monde grec qui n'utilisent pas la monnaie frappée, mais une monnaie pesée, la connaissent. Il s'agit d'être au plus près des réalités documentaires, rappelons-le extrêmement rares pour cette période, de ne pas chercher une matrice originelle qui serait la naissance du marchand mais de discerner dans la pratique matérielle des échanges des évolutions qui sont accompagnées par des contextes idéologiques.[10] C'est en ce sens seulement qu'une histoire économique et qu'une histoire culturelle de l'échange aboutiront à une vraie complémentarité.

La "grande transformation" (en paraphrasant un titre célèbre de l'anthropologie économique), c'est l'utilisation de l'argent (et accessoirement de l'or) comme bien d'échange (Kroll 1998; Descat 2001). Je n'exclus pas l'idée que les métaux les plus précieux, l'or et

---

10. C'est pourquoi je ne reprendrais pas une formule trop téléologique comme celle qu'utilise R. Seaford (2004: 39), qui parle d'une "final crisis of the reciprocity" pour résumer les échanges homériques. Je reconnais toutefois que compte tenu de la rareté de nos sources (d'où une raison supplémentaire de les analyser toujours plus), la téléologie nous emporte souvent.

l'argent, sous forme d'anneaux, de bagues ou de boucles d'oreilles, puissent remplir une fonction de biens d'échange dans certains cas à l'époque homérique mais il faut noter une chose importante: l'argent et l'or ont essentiellement un rôle de stockage des richesses, mais ne sont habituellement ni un moyen d'échange ni un étalon de valeur. L'argent et l'or sont bien sûr une réalité de la société homérique, dont ils constituent un des fondements du luxe, composant certains des objets de prix qui font le prestige de l'aristocratie, biens déposés (*keimēlia*) dans les trésors (*thesauroi*) des palais, mais ce sont des valeurs "dormantes" pour l'essentiel qui ne jouent pas de rôle actif dans les échanges courants. Ils n'interviennent pas habituellement dans ce qu'on doit appeler les échanges à paiement immédiat: on a vu que les Achéens achètent du vin aux Lemniens avec du bronze, du fer, des peaux, des bœufs et des esclaves, mais pas avec de l'argent (*Il.* 7.472–475).

Or l'argent pesé devient l'étalon de référence des échanges entre les VIIe et VIe s. Ce n'est pas un fait purement endogène au monde grec. Le point commun des premiers emplois d'*argyrōnetos*, quand une origine est précisée, c'est un lien avec le fait oriental ou "barbare". Dans l'*Alceste* d'Euripide, le lien avec une origine en Asie Mineure est explicite "mon fils, qui te flattes-tu de poursuivre de tes injures? Un Lydien ou un Phrygien payé de ton argent?" (v. 675–676). Le témoignage le plus ancien, celui de l'*Agamemnon* d'Eschyle qui date de 458, présente un aspect particulier puisqu'il n'évoque pas l'esclave contrairement à la plupart des autres occurrences mais le fait oriental reste bien présent. Agamemnon refuse de marcher sur le tapis de pourpre "c'est une grande honte en gâchant sous ses pas un tel luxe d'étoffes achetées à *prix d'or*" (v. 948–949). J'ai laissé la traduction française de P. Mazon dans la *CUF*: dans l'esprit du traducteur, c'est l'idée du luxe qui est exprimé pour lui par le métal de la plus haute valeur, l'or. Cette idée existe dans le texte certes, mais elle est plus connotée de manière plus précise par l'argent, comme au Proche-Orient. Ce qu'Agamemnon reproche à sa femme dans cet accueil et dans le tapis de pourpre qui le symbolise, c'est trop d'Orient, trop d'habitudes de barbare: "ne m'entoure pas, à la manière d'une femme, d'un faste amollissant; ne m'accueille pas, ainsi qu'un barbare, genoux ployés, bouche hurlante; ne jonche pas le sol d'étoffes, pour me faire un chemin qui éveille l'envie" (v. 918–921). C'est bien à ce monde que le mot renvoie.[11] Ce n'est pas le fait du hasard.

Chios est bien connue pour ses liens avec l'Asie Mineure voisine. Les esclaves de Chios sont achetés en Asie Mineure. L'archéologie (en particulier la céramique) montre que les Chiotes sont très présents à Gordion (Lawall 1997), et probablement à une certaine époque les plus présents des Grecs, ce qui signifie clairement des autorisations de commercer qui leur sont accordées par les autorités de Phrygie et de Lydie. Et l'on sait que les Chiotes sont très attentifs à ne pas perdre leurs positions commerciales. On peut noter à ce propos comment ils se sont opposés aux Phocéens, en 546, pour la défense de l'*emporion* (la place

---

11. Ce n'est pas sur l'aspect commercial sur lequel insiste en revanche von Reden (1995: 161–165; 1998: 260–261).

de commerce) des îles Oinoussa (Hdt. 1.165) qui est importante dans le commerce avec la Lydie. Le premier marchand d'esclaves dont nous connaissons l'existence dans la tradition littéraire est un certain Panionios de Chios, qui, à la fin du VIᵉ siècle, achetait des esclaves en Carie pour les revendre, après les avoir castrés, à Ephèse ou à Sardes (Hdt. 8.104). D'autres anecdotes confirment ce rôle comme l'histoire d'un certain Dionysos (Elien fr. 71) qui vend à Chios comme esclave une personne qu'il avait reçu dans le Pont de pirates et dont il avait accepté de la famille une rançon.

L'aspect en quelque sorte régional du commerce avec l'Asie et l'utilisation de l'argent se confirme quand on compare ce mot à d'autres "régionalismes", comme on l'a noté plus haut, *alōnetos* "acheté avec du sel" quand on commerce en Thrace et plus curieusement en Crète: "les Crétois appellent leurs esclaves qui sont dans les villes 'achetés avec de l'or'" (Athénée 6.263e) mais cela renvoie aussi à des pratiques, puisque la rareté de l'argent en Crète archaïque est manifeste (Stéfanakis 1999).

L'utilisation de l'argent pesé dans le monde grec est une orientalisation des pratiques d'échange qui ne doit pas remonter plus haut que le VIIᵉ siècle. Le témoignage de Théopompe se date donc très logiquement, même s'il reste une incertitude qu'on ne peut réduire. Il ne fait guère de doute, et je ne développe pas ce point ici, que l'argent est, en Grèce, plus utilisé au VIIᵉ s. qu'avant et qu'il est aussi très demandé, de plus en plus, au Proche-Orient. S'il bouge c'est que sa valeur, au moment où les échanges se développent de plus en plus, n'est pas du tout la même dans les deux zones et du même coup les prix.[12] Que cette situation puisse stimuler les échanges dans certains lieux entre les zones est très probable mais, c'est cela qui nous intéresse ici, elle va entraîner aussi des modifications sur les modalités d'échange. Cette orientalisation des pratiques n'est pas un simple fait de mode, elle entraîne des perturbations considérables.

La perturbation essentielle est un phénomène qui est décrit dans la littérature anthropologique comme un fait de conversion d'une sphère d'échange à l'autre (Meunier 1976: 124–125). Son importance et son irréversibilité entraînent une suppression à terme des sphères d'échanges. Comme on le voit dans le cas des Chiotes, l'utilisation de l'argent s'est faite d'abord avec des étrangers d'Asie Mineure, donc qui n'étaient pas au départ des partenaires sociaux traditionnels. Dans ce cas la pratique dominante est celle du paiement immédiat. Comme ces rapports n'ont fait que s'étendre entre les deux groupes, l'influence a été constante et durable. La différence entre les sphères d'échanges a été bouleversée par l'utilisation comme moyen d'échange d'un objet qui n'avait de signification jusque-là que dans un cadre social différent. L'utilisation de l'argent comme moyen de paiement est en effet aux antipodes de son utilisation, quand elle existait, dans le monde homérique, puisqu'il était réservé au contexte aristocratique et très associé aux circuits de paiements différés. On

---

12. A la même époque, au VIᵉ s., un sicle d'argent (soit l'équivalent en poids de deux drachmes) en Babylonie permet d'acheter 180 l. d'orge (je remercie F. Joannès de cette information), à Athènes sous Solon (Plut. *Sol.* 23) une drachme permet d'acheter un médimne soit environ 45 l. L'argent vaut deux fois moins cher à Athènes qu'à Babylone.

peut noter ainsi un exemple où *ōnos* est associé à un paiement. Il est fait mention d'un *don*, *edōke ōnon* (*Il.* 23.746), et l'on a précisément un objet d'argent. Il s'agit du rachat d'un noble capturé, opération de la plus haute valeur sociale. Or c'est ce métal qui signifiait la plus haute valeur des sphères au point qu'il en était exclu des échanges qui va devenir le bien "circulant" par excellence et moyen d'échange des paiements courants.[13] Il n'y pas bouleversement plus fort envisageable. Valeur et prix vont donc être identifiés et mêlés dans la même opération. Cela explique que le "prix" et le "paiement" soient désormais incarnés particulièrement par le mot *timē*. La *timē* était dans le monde homérique absente des relations d'échange. C'est le signe de la valeur de la hiérarchie la plus haute, associée à la royauté (Benvéniste 1969 2.43–55), mais de ce fait le terme avait aussi une valeur spécifique de compensation *immédiate* à l'occasion d'une décision qui concernait le rang social (Redfield 1975: 32–34) c'est-à-dire de caractère juridique, comme l'exprime par exemple un passage de l'*Odyss.* 22.57: "nous allons t'apaiser, trouver dans le pays, soit en or, soit en bronze, de quoi te rembourser tout ce qu'on a pu boire et dévorer chez toi, en t'amenant chacun l'amende de vingt bœufs". Dans ce contexte tout à fait particulier des relations, le métal précieux pouvait apparaître. Or les échanges avec les étrangers sont des échanges à paiement immédiat et avec utilisation de l'argent, d'où la nouveauté capitale que représente la *conversion* du mot *timē* dans ce cadre marchand et qui reproduit la *conversion* des sphères d'échange. Le texte de Théopompe, il faut le souligner, reflète très fidèlement dans les mots choisis cette innovation: il parle au sens littéral des gens de Chios qui acquièrent les esclaves *timēn kataballontes* dont la traduction la plus juste serait "en déposant un paiement". Valeur et prix sont confondus, l'échange homérique a vécu.

Les perturbations sont d'autant plus importantes que parmi les produits qui sont les plus échangés entre la Grèce et l'Orient, il y a l'esclave, étant donné que cela concerne au départ des produits à valeur élevée pour une clientèle aristocratique ce qui est le cas de l'esclave, où l'argent on l'a vu jouait déjà à la marge un certain rôle. Les premières conséquences portent sur une hausse considérable de l'approvisionnement par rapport aux "anciennes" pratiques de la guerre: la première cité, Chios, qui achète des esclaves, on le voit, en achète *beaucoup*. On ne peut mieux résumer le contraste avec les opérations guerrières, d'autant plus que ce commerce est en Asie Mineure renforcé par un marché traditionnel de mise en servitude familial pour endettement. La plupart des premiers *argyrōnetoi* furent donc sans aucun doute des esclaves. On peut rapprocher de cela le fait que dans la plus ancienne exemption de taxes que l'on connaisse dans le monde grec, à Cyzique au milieu du VIe siècle (*Syll.*³ 4 lignes 5–6), on notera que la cité exclut de ce privilège précisément la vente des esclaves et des chevaux, autre produit aristocratique et comme on l'a vu plus haut lié aussi aux transactions les plus élevés.

---

13. Ce qui aboutit à la phrase d'Héraclite sur le métal précieux comme équivalent général (fr. 90): "au prix du feu toute chose est échangée et le feu au prix de toutes ensemble, comme on échange avec l'or les marchandises (*chrēmata*) et avec les marchandises l'or" (trad. Bollack et Wismann 1972: 264). L'or ici est au sommet de la valeur marchande des métaux précieux, pleinement le "chef" de l'argent (Hipponax fr. 38).

Les conséquences de l'arrivée plus nombreuse d'esclaves sur la structure sociale ont été importantes. Ce n'est pas le but de mon propos, mais j'en dirai juste un mot puisque cela a été la perspective de Finley. Il faut considérer les choses de manière différente. Finley pensait que c'était la crise de la dépendance dans certaines cités qui précédait l'arrivée de l'esclavage, ce dernier étant une solution de remplacement du travail dépendant. C'est très probablement l'inverse: l'achat d'esclaves précède et provoque la crise des dépendances (Mactoux 1988; Morris 2002). Pour Finley c'est la démocratisation et la lutte politique, comme à Athènes, qui pousse vers l'esclavage, en fait la démocratisation n'existe pas dans la cité grecque archaïque de manière homogène. Par contre ce qu'on voit c'est l'achat d'abord et le texte d'Athénée renvoie bien à l'idée que l'esclavage acheté n'est pas perçu par les Grecs comme un besoin mais comme un luxe de la vie. Les Chiotes sont punis par la suite de leur *truphē*.

Les conséquences de la disparition des sphères d'échanges homériques se déclinent désormais dans toutes les nouveautés que connaît l'échange. La valeur n'est plus liée aux différences établies entre les sphères mais à la valeur d'échange du métal, ce qui entraîne de nouvelles façons d'exprimer la hiérarchie sociale (Kurke 1999). Le plus significatif va être l'établissement de systèmes d'étalons de poids et mesures, associé dès la tradition classique à la fois dans le mythe (Palamède) et dans le domaine historique (Phidon d'Argos) (plus tard Pline *HN* 7.198 attribue cette invention aux deux) (Grimaudo 1998: 15–35). Dans le cadre des sphères d'échanges, la coutume sociale tenait lieu de référence.[14] Les choses ont évolué sur deux points essentiels, le métal précieux devient moyen d'échange (d'où l'importance de la pesée) et l'échange se détermine le plus souvent par un paiement effectif. C'est la communauté politique qui va jouer le rôle nécessaire de garant dans les pratiques (étalons) et dans les lieux (organisation de l'espace de l'agora). Pour en terminer par un dernier retour à Finley et installer à côté de sa formule sur l'esclavage l'autre plateau de la balance, on peut dire *in short*, qu'avec l'*argyrōnetos*, nous assistons à la marche "main dans la main" du contrôle de la cité et de la liberté de l'échange.

BIBLIOGRAPHIE

Benvéniste, E. 1969. *Le vocabulaire des institutions indo-européennes.* Paris: Éditions de Minuit.

Bohannan, P. 1968. *Tiv economy.* Evanston, Ill.: Northwestern University Press.

Bollack, J., et H. Wismann. 1972. *Héraclite ou la séparation.* Paris: Éditions de Minuit.

Condominas, G. 1989. De la monnaie multiple. In: *L'Argent*, pp. 95–119, Communications 50. Paris: École des hautes études en sciences sociales.

---

14. Ce qui ne veut pas dire qu'il n'y a pas de lois sur certains aspects des échanges, mais plutôt que l'échange n'occupe pas la même position que dans la période ultérieure par rapport aux préoccupations d'ensemble de la communauté.

Descat, R. 1986. L'Acte et l'effort. *Une idéologie du travail en Grèce ancienne (VIIIème–Vème s.).* Paris: Belles Lettres.

———. 2001. Monnaie multiple et monnaie frappée en Grèce archaïque. *Revue numismatique* 157: 69–82.

Ducat, J. 1994. *Les Pénestes de Thessalie.* Paris: Belles Lettres.

Faraguna, M. 2003. 'Nomisma' e 'polis'. Aspetti della riflessione greca antica sul ruolo della moneta nella società. In: *Moneta mercanti banchieri: i precedenti greci e romani dell'euro: atti del convegno internazionale, Cividale del Friuli, 26-28 settembre 2002, Milan*, pp. 109–135. Pisa: ETS.

Finley, M. I. 1959. Was Greek civilization based on slave labour? *Historia* 8: 145–164.

Garlan, Y. 1982. *Les esclaves en grèce ancienne.* Paris.

Godelier, M. 1973. *Horizon, trajets marxistes en anthropologie.* Paris: F. Maspero.

Griamudo, S. 1998. *Misurare e pesare nella Grecia antica: teorie, storia, ideologie.* Palerme: L'Epos.

Kroll, J. H. 1996. Silver in Solon's laws. In: R. Ashton and S. Hurter, eds., *Studies in Greek numismatics in memory of Martin Jessop Price*, pp. 224–232. London: Spink.

Kurke, L. 1999. *Coins, bodies, games and gold. The politics of meaning in Archaic Greece.* Princeton: Princeton University Press.

Lawall, M. 1997. Greek transport amphoras at Gordion. *Anatolica* 23: 21–23.

Mactoux, M. M. 1988. Lois de Solon sur les esclaves et formation d'une société esclavagiste. In: T. Yuge et M. Doi, eds., *Forms of control and subordination in antiquity*, pp. 331–354. Leiden: Brill.

Mele, A. 1979. *Il commercio greco arcaico: prexis ed emporie.* Naples: Institut français de Naples.

Meunier, R. 1976. Formes de la circulation. In: F. Pouillon, ed., *L'Anthropologie économique: courants et problèmes*, pp. 117–145. Paris: F. Maspero.

Minns, E. 1915. Parchments of the Parthian period from Avroman in Kurdistan. *Journal of Hellenic Studies* 35: 22–65.

Morris, I. 1986. Gift and commodity in archaic Greece. *Man* 21: 1–17.

———. 2002. Hard surfaces. In: P. Cartledge, E. Cohen, and L. Foxhall, eds., *Money, labour, and land: approaches to the economies of ancient Greece*, pp. 8–43. London: Routledge.

Pirenne-Delforge, V. 1994. *L'Aphrodite grecque: contribution à l'étude de ses cultes et de sa personnalité dans le panthéon archaïque et classique.* Liège: Centre international d'étude de la religion grecque antique.

Redfield, J. R. 1975. *Nature and culture in the* Iliad: *the tragedy of Hector.* Chicago: University of Chicago Press.

Sahlins, M. 1976. *Age de pierre, âge d'abondance. L'Économie des sociétés primitives,* trad. franç. Paris.

Schaps, D. 2003. *The invention of coinage and the monetization of ancient Greece.* Ann Arbor: University of Michigan Press.

Scheid-Tissinier E. 1994. *Les usages du don chez Homère. Vocabulaire et pratiques.* Nancy: Presses universitaires.

Seaford, R. 2004. *Money and the early Greek mind: Homer, philosophy, tragedy.* Cambridge: Cambridge University Press.

Servet, J. M. 2001. Le troc primitif, un mythe fondateur d'une approche économiste de la monnaie. *Revue numismatique* 157: 15–32.

Stefanakis, M. I. 1999. The introduction of coinage in Crete and the beginning of local minting. In: A. Chaniotis, ed., *From Minoan farmers to Roman traders: sidelights on the economy of ancient Crete*, pp. 247–268. Stuttgart: F. Steiner.

Syll.[3]: W. Dittenberger. 1915–24. *Sylloge inscriptionum graecarum.* 3rd edition. Leipzig: S. Hirzelium.

Van Effenterre, H., et F. Ruze. 1994. *Nomima: recueil d'inscriptions politiques et juridiques de l'archaïsme grec.* Collection de l'Ecole française de Rome 188. Rome: Ecole française de Rome.

Vidal-Naquet, P. 1973. Réflexions sur l'historiographie grecque de l'esclavage. In: *Actes du colloque 1971 sur l'esclavage*, pp. 25–44. Besançon-Paris.

Von Reden, S. 1995. *Exchange in ancient Greece.* London: Duckworth.

———. 1998. The commodification of symbols: reciprocity and its perversions in Menander. In: C. Gill, N. Postlethwaite, and R. Seaford, eds., *Reciprocity in ancient Greece*, pp. 255–278. Oxford: Oxford University Press.

Agoranomia: Studies in Money and Exchange Presented to John H. Kroll, pp. 37–48
© 2006 The American Numismatic Society

KUKALIM, WALWET, and the Artemision Deposit:
Problems in Early Anatolian Electrum Coinage

PLATE 1

ROBERT W. WALLACE*

Nearly twenty years ago, with much trepidation, I sent Jack Kroll a copy of an article just published (Wallace 1987) on the origin of electrum coinage. Jack's enthusiastic response to the hypotheses of an unknown and junior scholar—his letter lies before me today—he has several times repeated in print, encouraging me in all sorts of ways. In anticipation of fresh progress from our ongoing analysis of the metallic content of these earliest coins, I am pleased to dedicate to Jack further thoughts on five problems posed by Anatolian electrum.[1]

In 1966 and 1968 respectively, Margaret Thompson and Colin Kraay published two electrum sixths of the Lydian lion-head type, reverse punch-linked, and inscribed with letters including KALI (Weidauer 1975: nos. 114, 115; see plate 1 nos. 1–2). Thompson wrote that preceding K on the American Numismatic Society sixth was an uncertain letter "consisting of a vertical stroke and *perhaps* a diagonal to the right".[2] Kraay's Ashmolean sixth confirms that this letter is U. In 1992, Numismatic Fine Arts (NFA) published the first known third of this type, inscribed UKALLI (plate 1 no. 3); as Gusmani (1982: 71) has indicated, *-lli-* for *-li-* is attested elsewhere in Lydian.[3] Finally, in 2000, Harlan Berk published a

---

*Department of Classics, Northwestern University.

1. See most recently Jack's thoughtful discussion of the origin of electrum coinage in his review of Le Rider's *La Naissance de la monnaie* (Kroll 2001). For our metallurgical analysis (in which Peter van Alfen and Paul Keyser are collaborating), see van Alfen (2005). I am grateful to Henry Kim, Aaron Berk, and Peter van Alfen for digital photographs of the four KUKALIM coins, and to Ed Waddell for a digital photograph of the WALWET series "a" third. Thanks also to Roberto Gusmani, Craig Melchert, and Calvert Watkins for their e-mail communications.

2. Browne incorrectly reports that both K and U are visible on this coin (2000: 178–179). For the virtually uncontested attribution of these lion-head coins to the Lydian royal mint, see Le Rider (2001: 47–48) and Wallace (1988: 203–204), an article updated and supplemented in the following paragraphs.

3. Numismatic Fine Arts International, Inc., Auction 30 (8 December 1992) no. 95. In his catalogue for April

second third of this type, obverse die-linked with the NFA third (plate 1 no. 4). On this coin, Gerald Browne (2000) read the letters KUKALIM.[4] As plate 1 no. 4 shows, the letters KU- are clear. The final letter remains incomplete and uncertain. However, the standard legend on Lydian seals ends in -L- and the suffix -IM, either from the Lydian verb "to be" (cf. Gk. *eimi*): "I am of x" (Gusmani) or a dative/reflexive -(i)*m*: "x to me", that is, "[I belong] to x" (Melchert).[5] Gusmani himself had restored the coin legend ṚKALI(M), "I am of Ṛkas". The seal represented a coin's original owner and thus source. An Ionian stater with grazing deer (Weidauer 1975: no. 39) records "I am the seal [*sēma*] of Phanes". As the new third does not clarify the final letter, it should be dotted: thus, KUKALIṂ. If M is correct, this legend should mean "I am of Kukaś", or "I belong to Kukaś".

Who was Kukaś? Browne (2000) concludes that he "is probably none other than Gyges (Greek: Gugēs), king of Lydia c. 680–644 BC", and therefore the Lydians were already strik- ing coins in the first half of the seventh century. This conclusion is of a piece with Browne's (1996: 49–52) earlier revival of J. P. Six's 1890 hypothesis that the legend WALWE. on some thirty-nine Lydian lion-head coins refers to Alyattes, the king of Lydia, believed to have ruled between 610 and 560.[6] In support of that hypothesis, Browne published a twelfth with the legend [WA]LWET. Also favoring Alyattes, one year earlier, Karwiese (1995: 123 n. 480) noted that the final letter on coin no. 63 in Numismatics Fine Arts auction 27 of 4–5 December 1991 is consistent with T, not L (see plate 1 no. 5). Finally, the uncertain final letter on Weidauer nos. 91, 92, and 95—and for Browne, many more specimens in Weidau- er—also seems more consistent with T. To be sure, the alternative reading WALWEL would be consistent with KUKALIM; as Gusmani (1972: 49, 51) noted, some smaller Lydian seals omit the final -IM. Nonetheless, Weidauer nos. 91, 92, and 95, Browne's twelfth, and NFA 27/63 are most consistent with WALWET. As for the identity of this person, Calvert Wat- kins confirms to me that "WALWET = Aluattes is quite a good suggestion", the initial W disappearing in Ionian just as Persian Vindafarna became Greek Intaphernes (Hdt. 3.70).[7]

Is then Kukaś Gyges? Gusmani and Watkins both agree that Lydian "Kukaś" could well be Greek "Gugēs". Watkins, however, suggested to me several alternative directions where I might look—and further investigation uncovered two problems. First, and less seriously, Hanfmann (1983: 57, with figs. 109–110) identified as the name GuGu a monogram oc-

1986 no. 111, Busso Peus published a fairly worn third that he believed bore traces of the -KALIL- legend. This cannot be confirmed from his photograph; the lion head facing right on this coin is of a more conventional Lyd- ian style than on other -KALI- coins, there is no trace of an opposing lion head, and finally, the reverse punches seem not to be linked with other -KALI- coins.

4. Harlan J. Berk, Buy or Bid Sale no. 112, closing 13 January 2000, coin no. 2.

5. Gusmani (1971: 1–7; 1972: 47–51; 1982: 58, s.v. "-im"); Melchert (1994: 340, 376).

6. For a history of the different readings of these letters, see Wallace (1988). Robinson (1951: 163) and (less consistently) Karwiese (1991: 11–13, but cf. 8–9) also identified WALWET as Alyattes. Some thirty-nine WAL- WET coins were known to Karwiese (1995: 121).

7. If, as I have argued (and see Melchert 1994: 340), *walwe-* is the Lydian word for "lion", it is an obvious sug- gestion that Walwetes (*vel sim.*)—"Leo-"—was named after that royal beast.

curring irregularly twenty-five times on the stone blocks of a retaining wall inside Gyges'
tomb. As Hanfmann noted, however, Gusmani read these same letters as VeVe—a reading
certainly consistent with Hanfmann's photograph—and the monogram could be a mason's
mark. Second and more seriously, Gyges' name appears in the forms GU-UG-GU or GU-
GU in the records of Assyrian Ashurbanipal (668–626 BC), as an ally against the Cimmeri-
ans.[8] Similarity with Greek Gugēs may suggest that Gyges' Lydian name was something like
Gug-, although as Melchert writes to me, Lydian did not consistently contrast voiceless and
voiced stops, and *ku-ka* may have been pronounced or heard as *gu-ga*.

The coins themselves pose a further serious difficulty for Browne's identification.
Already in publishing the first of the -KALI- *hektai*, Thompson noted that this coin was
reverse punch-linked with a WALWET coin. That same punch was used on both Kraay's
-KALI- *hektē* and on a second WALWET coin (see Weidauer 1975: 111). Furthermore, according to Weidauer (1975: 62; see also Karwiese 1991: 11), the edge of the punch on both
-KALI- *hektai* is damaged. It is improbable that a single punch was used in Gyges' era and
three generations later, after the reigns of Ardys and Sadyattes. It is impossible that a punch
would have deteriorated on what Browne considers the earlier coins. Their common but
deteriorating reverse punch indicates that WALWET and KUKALIM coins were more or
less contemporary and that at least some WALWET coins were produced before our -KALI-
hektai.[9] Croesus succeeded Alyattes, traditionally ruling from 560 to 546, although I hope
elsewhere to challenge the earlier of those dates.[10]

What is the date of these coins? A growing consensus now assigns many different early
electrum issues to a fairly short period of time, possibly starting as late as the early sixth
century.[11] The Austrian excavators have argued that the celebrated Central Basis deposit
of the Artemision at Ephesos may not have been laid down until the first half of the sixth
century, possibly not until the time of Croesus, and that the ninety-three different coins
it contained (including six WALWET coins) derive from a more or less coherent period
(Bammer 1984: 165–183; 1983–84: 91–108; 1991: 63–64). Just so, Spier (1998: 328–331)
describes several early hoards of electrum coins of quite varied composition. However,
this consensus position should be modified in one significant respect. Robinson (1951:
161), Karwiese (1995: 126), and, seemingly independently, Spier (1998) argued from the
Artemision and other hoard evidence that Weidauer Group XV (Lydian lion head right
with "four rayed nose wart": 17 at the Artemision) preceded her Group XVI (Lydian lion

---

8. *Reallexikon der Assyriologie* (Berlin: 1971), 3: 720, s.v. "Gyges". See also Cogan and Tadmor (1977).

9. Le Rider (2001: 56): "Les monnaies qui portent ces legends sont proches les unes des autres dans le temps".

10. A central problem lies in the formulaic quality of our single source for the length of Croesus' reign, Hdt.
1.86: "In this way Sardis was captured by the Persians and Croesus taken prisoner, after a reign of fourteen years
and a siege of fourteen days … Cyrus chained Croesus and placed him with fourteen Lydian boys on a great
pyre". Various Eastern documents confirm that Croesus was overthrown in 546. I am quite sure that at least two
of Herodotos' three fourteens were invented.

11. See Karwiese (1991: 5–6, with references); Spier (1998: 327–334), citing similar views of Price; and Le
Rider (2001: 59–67).

head right with "many rayed nose wart": none at the Artemision). Although that conclusion might not hold if many fewer Group XVI coins were struck than Group XV coins, or if Group XVI coins came from a mint that did not circulate along the coast, in fact, Group XVI coins vastly outnumber Group XV coins[12] and may therefore be expected to have circulated widely. If we accept this conclusion, the very large issue of Weidauer Group XVI coins was struck between the time of the Artemision deposit and Croesus' introduction of bimetallic coinage.[13]

How do these considerations affect the WALWET (Group XVII) and KUKALIṂ (Group XVIII) series? One series of WALWET coins (Weidauer 1975: nos. 103–110, her series "a" [see pp. 104–105], but cf. below; see also plate 1 no. 6) is of the Group XV "four rayed nose wart" type, and numerous punch links (Weidauer 1975: 111) connect coins of this series with Group XV coins that, according to Weidauer (and I agree), never bore the name WALWET (e.g., Weidauer 1975: nos. 74, 75, 78). Non-WALWET sixths 76 and 77 share both reverse punches with WALWET sixths 106 and 108, applied on the same sides of the coin reverses and in the same order. Non-WALWET sixth 78 shares one punch with four WALWET sixths (105, 106, 108, and 109), applied on the same side of the reverse and in the same order. It is therefore clear that the same mint was striking series "a" WALWET sixths and Group XV non-WALWET sixths at the very same time. Although all of Weidauer's series "a" WALWET coins are sixths, an (at the time unique) third from this series is illustrated on plate 1 no. 6, which was sold on the Internet by the Maryland coin dealer Ed Waddell in 2001. Two further thirds of this type were illustrated and sold by Harlan Berk in 2005.

In the light of these observations, it is important to note that Weidauer no. 104, the single coin from Gordion alleged to bear the legend WALWET, in fact does not. Weidauer's claim is based only on her own queried and (to judge from the photograph) not compelling identification of obverse 103 with obverse 104, where, however, the "Legende [ist] nicht mehr auf dem Schrötling" (Weidauer 1975: 26). Weidauer no. 104 shares both reverse punches with Weidauer no. 103, a WALWET coin, but not apparently its obverse die. In publishing the Gordion hoard, Bellinger (1968) says nothing of WALWET. Weidauer no. 104 should therefore be renumbered to follow 76–78. The Gordion hoard included no WALWET coin.

Similarly, among her other WALWET series "a" coins (nos. 105–110), Weidauer reports that sixths 106 and 107 have no legend. Sixth 106 is linked with 76, 77, 78, and 105 only by common reverse punches; only reverse punches link 107 with 103 and 104. As Weidauer

---

12. So Karwiese (1995: 142). Of 27 anepigraphic Lydian lion-head coins Berk has published over the last decade, 24 or 25 belong to Group XVI, and two or three to Group XV. In Berk's photo file of other dealers, which goes back decades, 37 coins belong to Group XVI and six to Group XV. All eight coins of this type on the Classical Numismatic Group website at the time of writing belong to Group XVI. At CoinArchives.com, 32 coins are of Group XVI and seven are of Group XV. Finally, of 45 Lydian coins in the Gordion hoard, all but one or two belong to Group XVI (Bellinger 1968: 10 n. 2).

13. For Croesus' coinage, see Ramage and Craddock (2000: 18).

herself notes that WALWET coins shared punches with non-WALWET coins of the same lion type, 106 and 107 should also be renumbered to follow 76–78. Of the eight WALWET *hektai* and five WALWET thirds in the Berk photo file that are not included in Weidauer, all are of series "b".[14] Series "a" WALWET coins have suddenly become quite scarce.

Furthermore, it has never been observed that just like the Group XV non-WALWET lion-head coins, series "a" WALWET obverses did not depict two facing lions with legend in between. All of the coins in Group XV and WALWET series "a" had only a single lion head facing right. Only WALWET series "b" coins feature opposing lion heads. These coins are of a more primitive and rustic style (cf. plate 1 no. 5). In addition, the series "a" die cutter did not bother to make the legend especially legible on the coin flan (cf. plate 1 no. 6). On WALWET series "b" and the four KUKALIM coins, the legend is far more legible and centered. Coins of series "b" share many die links among them, and two links with KUKALIM coins, also marked by opposing lion heads. None of these coins is linked to WALWET series "a" or Group XV coins.

Accordingly, Weidauer Group XV should be revised to include two parts: series "a" WALWET coins and the similar non-WALWET coins, with single lion head facing right and often punch-linked with series "a" WALWET coins. Group XVII may retain the series "b" WALWET coins with opposing lion heads. These coins should be juxtaposed with Group XVIII KUKALIM coins, which were struck at the same mint.

Thus, WALWET series "a" coins and non-WALWET Group XV coins, with very similar obverses and reverses and sometimes punch-linked, were struck simultaneously, at the same mint, and before the date of the Artemision deposit. The many punch links among WALWET series "a" coins and among WALWET series "b" coins show that both issues were small.

Were WALWET series "b" coins struck at a different time or at a different mint from WALWET series "a" and Group XV coins? Without adducing any argument, Karwiese (e.g., 1995: 141) believes that series "b" coins were struck later than series "a" coins, apparently at the same mint. Two arguments may support the alternative hypothesis that these two series were struck in the same period but at different mints. First, both series were struck before the Artemision deposit, and so at any rate have a common *terminus ante*. Second, there are no punch links between series "a" and series "b". It may seem hard to explain why a single mint would issue one small series of WALWET coins and later issue a second small series, after an interval long enough to require a completely new set of reverse punches but short enough so that Group XV and series "b" coins were both included in the Artemision deposit.

14. The Berk WALW. sixth (Buy or Bid Sale closing 16 January 1997, no. 1 and plate 1) and the Classical Numismatic Group WAL? sixth (Mail Bid Sale 51, 15 September 1999, no. 441) are also series "b". Classical Numismatic Group Mail Bid Sale 55, 13 September 2000, claims to add another sixth of series "a" (no. 542) and another sixth of series "b" (no. 544), but the legends are at best very faint.

In this connection, one further problem requires discussion. The Artemision deposit of 93 coins included 32 "lion paw" fractions, many of them punch-linked, out of 96 known specimens of the type (Karwiese 1995: plate 1). Karwiese illustrates that a significant number of these "lion paw" fractions are punch-linked with three WALWET coins (Weidauer 1975: nos. 99, 103, 105) and one series "a" non-WALWET coin (Weidauer 1975: no. 78); punch wear shows that these issues were struck simultaneously.[15] Weidauer nos. 103, 105, and 78 are all series "a" WALWET or Group XV coins. Thus, the mint striking these coins was also striking "lion paw" fractions. However, Weidauer no. 99 is series "b"—the single series "b" WALWET coin at the Artemision. According to Karwiese, this coin is punch-linked with one "lion paw" (no. 91), which in turn shares an obverse die with one other "lion paw" (no. 89). If Karwiese is right, these links could support the hypothesis that the "lion paws" were struck at the same mint as both WALWET series "a" and WALWET series "b" coins. That is, a single mint at a single time struck series "a" and series "b" WALWET coins. However, it is equally possible that a separate mint striking series "b" WALWET coins also struck "lion paws". One of its WALWETs and two of its "lion paws" made it into the Artemision deposit. I add that Karwiese's photograph of the reverse punch in question does not decisively link Weidauer no. 99 with a "lion paw."

If series "a" and series "b" WALWET coins were struck by two separate mints, it is easy to assign series "b" coins to a provincial or branch mint, as the artistry on series "b" is in every way inferior to that of series "a". Although series "b" WALWET coins are not punch-linked with other lion-head types, Karwiese (1991: 9–10) and following him Le Rider (2001: 49–50) both concluded on the basis of photographs that three series "b" coins are punch-linked with a pictureless specimen now in commerce.[16] The KUKALIM coins (punch-linked to WALWET series "b" but with a more savage and toothier lion) were struck at this same mint, either later during the issue of the WALWET series "b" coins or else shortly afterward, as their common punch had somewhat deteriorated. As the two KUKALIM sixths are punch-linked and the two KUKALIM thirds are obverse die-linked, it is apparent that the Kukaś issue also was small.

In a different way, Karwiese (1991: 12–17; 1995: 133–135) himself hypothesized Lydian royal coin production by more than one mint, concluding from the large number of very often punch-linked "lion paw" fractions in the Artemision that these fractions were struck at Ephesos' citadel Koressos.[17] As he identifies WALWET with Alyattes and accepts that WALWET coins were struck at Sardis (1991: 8–9), he concludes that the four punches these

15. Karwiese (1995: 133–142). Cf. *IGCH* 1156 (now dispersed), containing 30 lion-head coins, 26 "lion paw" coins, and four AR coins with a man's head.

16. I question the standard inference that the striated obverse die used on some electrum coins was intended to keep a flan from slipping when struck. Such slippage is entirely hypothetical. The presence of striations on some coins with figures confirms that striations were a design. No die study has yet determined if these coins were struck at the same mint.

17. Karwiese (1991: 11–17; 1995: 118–123). On Karwiese (1995), see especially Wartenberg (1997).

coins have in common were transferred from Sardis to Ephesos. Le Rider (2001: 52–53) was surely right to doubt this last conclusion, even if a sister of Croesus married Melas, the tyrant of Ephesos (Ael. *VH* 3.26). I therefore propose a simple and obvious alternative explanation: At least most of the often die-linked Lydian coins in the Artemision temple deposit were struck at Sardis and constitute a single dedication at that temple by Alyattes or more likely by Croesus, who I shall argue was already on the throne c. 580 (see note 10, above). Herodotos elaborates Croesus' many gold offerings at shrines (1.50–55, 69; see also 87.1), including "the golden cows and most of the columns at Ephesos" (1.92) and a treasure at Branchidai near Miletos (5.36, 1.92). An extant column base of the Artemision temple is inscribed KR BA AN = *Kroisos basileus anethēke*: "King Croesus dedicated" (Bammer and Muss 1996: 46–47). Pindar (1 *Pyth.* 94) and Bacchylides (3.35–48, 61–62) mention Croesus' rich dedications at Delphi. Lydian kings were famous for dedicating at Greek shrines. Gyges sent fabulous gold and silver treasures to Delphi (Hdt. 1.14). According to Herodotos (1.22), Alyattes built two temples to Athena near Miletos. The Artemision deposit contained four of the rarer series "a" WALWET or Group XV coins and only one series "b" WALWET coin.

If this dedication hypothesis is right, all or most of the "lion paw" fractions, the series "a" WALWET coins, and Group XV coins were struck at Sardis and brought to Ephesos probably under Croesus. This dating is consistent with the archaeological evidence (Karwiese 1995: 126).

A reverse punch shared by WALWET series "b" and KUKALIM coins, the many reverse punch links indicating small issues, and the unusual use of names all indicate that the WALWET and KUKALIM coins reflect an experiment of perhaps two mints during one brief period. The series "a" mint (at Sardis?) was striking many more non-WALWET coins than WALWET coins at the same time. Of the 96 extant "lion paw" fractions, Karwiese (1995: 138–142) has tentatively identified 28 obverse dies and 44 reverse punches. This was a very large issue. On the current consensus, these coins will have been struck not before the late seventh century and more likely in the early years of the sixth century. The apparent date of the Artemision "pot hoard" pot, 650–625 (Williams 1991–93), must therefore be considered anomalous.[18]

Kukaś cannot have been the first king of Lydia. On the other hand, the lion head was the symbol and seal of the Lydian king, something presumably not available to nonroyals,

---

18. Although still cited by Browne (2000: 179), Weidauer's iconographic parallels for dating these Lydian coins to the third quarter of the seventh century (1975: 99–107) also have been judged unconvincing. See Price (1976) and above all Akurgal (1983). As for the typeless quite gold-looking stater of 10.73 g shown to me by Harlan Berk in 1997 (Wallace 2001: 130), Berk published this coin as electrum (Buy or Bid Sales, closing 29 January 1998 and closing 27 May 1998: no. 1 and plate 1). If so, its weight was not derived from the later "Croesids" of c. 10.7 g gold or silver, but reflects a unique use (for electrum) of a more generally diffused Mediterranean weight standard (Wallace 2001). An electrum standard of 14+ g was equivalent to 10.7 g gold, given a common natural electrum alloy of c. 75% gold.

and these coins were struck at the same mint that struck coins for Alyattes. It is an obvious suggestion that Kukaś (Gugaś?) was a member of the royal family, striking coins with his family's lion-head seal. If these coins were struck at a provincial mint, Kukaś may have been the governor of that province, just as Croesus was the governor of Adramyttion in the Troad before he became king (Nic. Dam. *FGrH* 90 F 65). The issues by Kukaś did not motivate the Alyattes issues, as I once had suggested (Wallace 1988: 207). Punch deterioration on the KUKALIM coins shows that the WALWET coins were struck first.

Finally, Spier (1998: 331–333) has assembled the coins of an electrum series of opposing boar's heads with apparently Lydian letters resembling -LATE- between them.[19] Subsequently, a boar's head twenty-fourth of the series, without legend, was published as no. 400 in the Triton VI sale, closing 13 January 2003. This series is punch-linked with two staters (Weidauer nos. 57, 58) and a sixth (Triton VI sale, also no. 400) showing the forepart of a lion facing left. Weidauer (1975: 66–67), Karwiese (1991: 12), and Le Rider (2001: 53) all contend that coins of the latter type are royal, and so therefore were the boar's heads. I am less confident. Many variants of the lion motif were current in archaic Asia Minor, and in Lydia the boar was a symbol of evil, according to Hanfmann (1983: 95, with references in n. 68). Although the script on these coins is not Lycian, it is worth noting that different Lycian dynasts used boar's head types from c. 520 (on the standard dating), and the Lycians had never been subject to Lydia (Hdt. 1.28).

It may be helpful to summarize my main conclusions so far:

1. One Lydian lion-head coin legend reads WALWET and is Alyattes.

2. A second coin legend reads KUKALIM and refers to a royal person of Alyattes' period.

3. A third series of coins, marked -LATE-, need not be royal or struck at the same mint.

4. Of the two series of WALWET coins, series "a" had only a single lion head facing right. These coins are a subsection of Weidauer Group XV, they were struck at the same time as Group XV coins and many "lion paw" fractions, and both series "a" and Group XV coins are much more rare than Group XVI and series "b" WALWET coins with opposing lion heads.

5. Group XV coins, series "a" WALWET coins, and many "lion paw" fractions appear to have been struck at Sardis. Series "b" WALWET coins were possibly struck at a branch mint.

6. Both WALWET issues and the KUKALIM issue were small.

7. The often die-linked Lydian coins in the Artemision deposit were quite possibly a dedication by Alyattes or more likely by Croesus during the early years of his reign.

---

19. For future attempts to decipher the boar's head legend, I note that the legend on all WALWET coins goes from up downward, while the legend on all KUKALIM coins goes from down upward.

8. The Gordion hoard did not contain a WALWET sixth but a punch-linked Group XV sixth.

Finally, in addition to legends, issues, and dates, we may be able to make progress on two smaller problems presented by our lion-head coins. First, none of the 436 coins of the Lydian lion-head type known to Karwiese (1991: 8 n. 27) is larger than a third. Dies for the KUKALIM and series "b" WALWET coins were incised with two opposing lion heads and a legend in between. However, the designs on these dies were always much larger than the planchets: whether on the right or the left, only traces of the second lion appear on the coins. Why did the mint not cut dies that fit the planchet? The standard view that the dies were engraved to strike a larger denomination[20] is untenable. With 436 Lydian lion-head coins, none larger than a third and punch-linked with some 96 "lion paw" fractions, we can ever more confidently say that no such lion-head denomination existed. Even if the Lydians did strike some lion-head staters, the extensive issues of thirds, sixths, and twelfths would certainly have justified purpose-cut dies. The design on these different denominations is each made to scale, thus proving that the dies were purpose-cut, in every case fully reproducing only one lion head.

How may we explain why this (possibly provincial?) mint designed dies much larger than the coin flans? Any or all of three speculations may be suggested. First, if the stamp on these coins was derived from a king's seal showing opposing lion heads (cf. the Croesids), that seal itself would have been larger than a third. The die reproduced the seal to scale. Second, the partial stamp may have signaled fractional size. Third, if both lion heads were to appear on the flan, they would be quite small in relation to it. Until Croesus conceived of producing oblong flans, the (Sardis?) mint adopted the more impressive solution of fully reproducing only one lion head facing right. The (branch?) mint tried the less successful experiment of reproducing fragments of both lions.

Our last problem derives from these coins' reverse incuse punches. A number of scholars have argued that these punches, cutting deeply and irregularly into the coin flans, were designed to show that these early lumps of electrum were not plated.[21] However, it is curious that on every Lydian lion-head coin with two reverse punches the striker never used the same punch twice. In every case, he put down the first punch and picked up a second, usually of a different size. Why? If in fact the purpose of these deep punches was to show that a coin was not plated, the presence of different and often contrasting punch marks on a coin may reproduce and therefore be explained by the widespread custom of test punching. Multiple test punches on any piece of precious metal or coin must inevitably have looked

20. See, e.g., Kraay (1976: 24), Spier (1998: 332), Jenkins (1972: 29): "It is typical of the primitive technique of these coins that the whole design is not preserved complete.... Probably the die was made for a stater".

21. See Karwiese (1991: 8 n. 27, 20–21). Earlier, Karwiese (1987) goes so far as to call the obverse type a "secondary phenomenon". See also Robinson (1951: 164) and Kraay (1976: 21). Notwithstanding Le Rider (2001: 50–51), the existence of plated specimens does not discredit but may confirm this hypothesis.

different. The mints copied this look. This conceit was retained on most Ionian electrum issues, the size difference between punches being most extreme on the coins of Phokaia (Kraay 1976: 27 and plate 70). Already perhaps from 580–570, the earliest Greek silver coins, Aeginetan turtles, were also issued with varying series of irregular reverse punches, copying eastern practice.[22] As Kraay (1976: 34) suggested, long after Phokaia had ceased striking electrum, the Aeginetans may have helped to spread this style to Caria, on a series of early silver staters struck on the Aeginetan silver standard but on the Phokaic electrum model, with large and small incuse punches and a wide variety of obverse types.[23]

BIBLIOGRAPHY

Akurgal, E. 1983. Zur Datierung der ältesten ionischen Münzen mit Löwenkopfdarstellungen. In: R. M. von Boehmer and H. Hauptmann, eds., *Beiträge zur Altertumskunde Kleinasiens (Festschrift für K. Bittel)*, pp. 1–11. Mainz: von Zabern.

Ashton, R., and S. Hurter, eds. 1998. *Studies in Greek numismatics in memory of Martin Jessop Price*. London: Spink.

Bammer, A. 1983–84. Chronologische und stratigraphische Probleme der archaischen Kultanlagen von Ephesos. *Hephaistos* 5–6: 91–108.

———. 1984. *Das Heiligtum der Artemis von Ephesos*. Graz: Akad. Druck- & Verl.-Anst.

———. 1991. Les sanctuaries des VIIIe et VIIe siècles à l'Artemision d'Ephèse. *Rossiiskaia Arkheologiia*: 63–64.

Bammer, A., and U. Muss. 1996. *Das Artemision von Ephesos*. Mainz: von Zabern.

Bellinger, A. R. 1968. Electrum coins from Gordion. In: C. M. Kraay and G. K. Jenkins, eds., *Essays in Greek coinage presented to Stanley Robinson*, pp. 10–15. Oxford.

Browne, G. M. 1996. Notes on two Lydian texts. *Kadmos* 35: 49–52.

———. 2000. A new Lydian text. *Kadmos* 39: 178–179.

Cogan, M., and H. Tadmor. 1977. Gyges and Ashurbanipal. A study in literary transmission. *Orientalia* 46: 65–85.

FGrH: F. Jacoby. 1923–1958. *Die Fragmente der griechischen Historiker*. Leiden.

Gusmani, R. 1971. Lydisch -*im* "ich bin"? *Die Sprache* 17: 1–7.

———. 1972. Lydische Siegelabschriften und Verbum Substantivum. *Kadmos* 11: 47–54.

———. 1982. *Lydisches Wörterbuch*. Ergänzungsband 2. Heidelberg: Winter.

Hanfmann, G. 1983. *Sardis from prehistoric to Roman times*. Cambridge, Mass.: Harvard University Press.

IGCH: M. Thompson, O. Mørkholm, and C. M. Kraay, eds. 1973. *An inventory of Greek coin hoards*. New York: American Numismatic Society.

22. So Jenkins (1972: 42). For the types, see Kraay (1976: 44). For the date of the inception of Aeginetan coinage, see Kroll and Waggoner (1984: 336–339).
23. For a possible alternative attribution of this series to Lycia, see Sheedy (1998: 324–325).

Jenkins, G. K. 1972. *Ancient Greek coins*. New York: Putnam.

Karwiese, S. 1987. Zwischen Punze und Amboss. *Litterae Numismaticae Vindobonenses* 3: 5–23.

———. 1991. The Artemisium coin hoard and the first coins of Ephesus. *Revue belge de numismatique et de sigillographie* 137: 1–28.

———. 1995. *Die Münzprägung von Ephesos*, vol. 1, *Die Anfänge: Die ältesten Prägungen und der Beginn der Münzprägung überhaupt*. Vienna and Cologne: Böhlau.

Kraay, C. M. 1968. *Report of the visitors [of the] Ashmolean Museum,* pp. 43–44.

———. 1976. *Archaic and classical Greek coins*. Berkeley: University of California Press.

Kroll, J. H. 2001. Review of Le Rider 2001. *Schweizerische Numismatische Rundschau (Revue suisse de numismatique)* 80: 199–206.

Kroll, J. H., and N. M. Waggoner. 1984. Dating the earliest coins of Athens, Corinth, and Aegina. *American Journal of Archaeology* 88: 325–340.

Le Rider, G. 2001. *La naissance de la monnaie*. Paris: Presses Universitaires de France.

Melchert, H. C. 1994. *Anatolian historical phonology*. Amsterdam and Atlanta: Rodopi.

Price, M. J. 1976. Review of Weidauer 1975. *Numismatic Chronicle* 15: 273–275.

Ramage, A., and P. Craddock. 2000. *King Croesus' gold: excavations at Sardis and the history of gold refining*. Cambridge, Mass.: Harvard University Art Museums.

Robinson, E. S. G. 1951. The coins from the Ephesian Artemision reconsidered. *Journal of Hellenic Studies* 71: 156–167.

Sheedy, K. A. 1998. The dolphins, the crab, the sphinx, and "Aphrodite". In: R. Ashton and S. Hurter, eds., *Studies in Greek numismatics in memory of Martin Jessop Price,* pp. 321–326. London: Spink.

Spier, J. 1998. Notes on early electrum coinage and a die-linked issue from Lydia. In: R. Ashton and S. Hurter, eds., *Studies in Greek numismatics in memory of Martin Jessop Price,* pp. 327–334. London: Spink.

Thompson, M. 1966. Some noteworthy Greek accessions. *American Numismatic Society Museum Notes* 12: 1–4.

van Alfen, P. 2005. The early electrum project. *American Numismatic Society Magazine* 4, no. 1: 32–33.

Wallace, R. W. 1987. The origin of electrum coinage. *American Journal of Archaeology* 91: 385–397.

———. 1988. WALWE. and .KALI. *Journal of Hellenic Studies* 108: 203–207.

———. 2001. Remarks on the value and standards of early electrum coins. In: M. Balmuth, ed., *Hacksilber to coinage: new insights into the monetary history of the Near East and Greece*, pp. 127–134. New York: American Numismatic Society.

Wartenberg, U. 1997. Review of Karwiese 1995. *Schweizerische Numismatische Rundschau (Revue suisse de numismatique)* 76: 263–267.

Weidauer, L. 1975. *Probleme der frühen Elektronprägung*. Fribourg: Typos I.

Williams, D. 1991–93. The "pot hoard" pot from the archaic Artemision at Ephesus. *Bulletin of the Institute of Classical Studies* 38: 98–104.

Agoranomia: Studies in Money and Exhange Presented to John H. Kroll, pp. 49–60
© 2006 The American Numismatic Society

Small Change and the Beginning of Coinage at Abdera

PLATE 2   JONATHAN H. KAGAN[*]

Professor Jack Kroll has done much to expand our knowledge of the early monetization of Greece and the beginning of silver coinage (Kroll and Waggoner 1984; Kroll 2001; 2005). For this reason, I am both pleased and honored to offer him this essay analyzing an early hoard of coins from Abdera that provides pertinent information on both these subjects.

The hoard first appeared on the London market in 2000. Thirty-one coins have so far been identified.[1] There is no way to know whether this is the entire find. Of the thirty-one coins, two are tetradrachms and all the others are of a lower denomination. Eighteen are, remarkably, hemiobols, whose existence was unknown prior to this discovery. Unlike bullion hoards from the Near East, the coins are in outstanding condition. The absence of issues from any other mint and the preponderance of small change make it possible that the find spot was close to Abdera itself. All of the coins are from the first period of Abdera's coinage, placing the hoard clearly in the sixth century BC. As such, it is exceedingly rare. Only one other comparable hoard of small change exists from central and northern Greece, *CH* 8.20, which contained sixty-five obols of Aegina (Kim 1994). A majority of coins have been recovered from the marketplace and will be presented in Professor Kroll's honor to the National Numismatic Museum in Athens so that they will be available for further study.

---

[*]New York, NY.

1. The author only reassembled the hoard after it was dispersed. It is possible that some of the identified coins are not from the find.

CATALOGUE[2]

Tetradrachm

>   *Obv.:* Seated griffin l. front legs on ground; smooth breast, feathered wing.
>   *Rev.:* Quadripartite incuse square.

>   1. 14.83 g. *Obv.* Same die as May 17? (CNG Triton IV 5 Dec. 2000 no. 185)
>   2. 14.84 g. *Obv.* Same die as 1. (Zhuyuetang Collection no. 67)

Didrachms

>   *Obv.:* Seated griffin l. one front leg raised.

>   *3. 7.36 g. *Obv.* Feathered breast and wing.
>   *Rev.* Incuse square diagonally divided into 8 triangles.
>   4. 7.36 g. *Obv.* Feathered breast and wing. Trace of symbol under raised leg.
>   *Rev.* Quadripartite incuse square. (CNG Triton IV, 5 Dec. 2000 no. 186)
>   *5. 7.54 g. *Obv.* Smooth breast; feathered wing. Same die as May 18. (ex Sakha hoard)
>   *Rev.* Quadripartite incuse square.
>   6. 7.40 g. *Obv.* Feathered breast; smooth wing.
>   *Rev.* Quadripartite incuse square. (CNG Mail Bid 55, 13 Dec. 2000, 257)
>   *7. 7.50 g. *Obv.* Same die as 6.
>   *Rev.* Same die as 6.

Drachms

>   *Obv.:* Seated griffin l. one front leg raised.
>   *Rev.:* Quadripartite incuse square.

>   *8. 3.68 g. *Obv.* Feathered breast and wing. May 20. (same die?)
>   9. 3.63 g. *Obv.* Same die as 8.
>   *Rev.* Die of May 20? (CNG Mail Bid 55, 13 Dec. 2000, no. 258)

Hemidrachms

>   *Obv.:* Seated griffin l. one front leg raised.
>   *Rev.:* Quadripartite incuse square.

>   *10. 1.80 g. *Obv.* Worn, maybe feathered breast; feathered wing.
>   *Rev.* One box of quadripartite square diagonally divided.
>   11. 1.82 g. *Obv.* Feathered breast and wing. (CNG Triton IV, 5 Dec. 2000 no. 187)[3]

---

2. Type references from May (1966). Asterisked coins are illustrated on plate 2.
3. One other hemidrachm exists that might also be part of the hoard, although the metal is not of the same quality. It was recently in the inventory of CNG no. 750358. It weighs 1.80 g and appears to come from another obverse die.

Obols

> *Obv.*: Seated griffin l.
> *Rev.*: Quadripartite incuse square.

*12. 0.65 g. *Obv.* Right foreleg raised.
*13. 0.58 g. *Obv.* Both forelegs on ground.

Hemiobols

> *Obv.*: Griffin head l.
> *Rev.*: Quadripartite incuse square.

> O1

*14. 0.11 g. Thin flan cracked with part of coin missing.
*15. 0.29 g. Probably same die as 14.

> O2

*16. 0.36 g.

> O3

*17. 0.34 g.

> O4

*18. 0.32 g.
*19. 0.36 g. Shares same reverse die with 18.

> O5

*20. 0.30 g.
*21. 0.33 g.
 22. 0.33 g. (CNG Mail Bid 55, 13 Dec. 2000, lot. 260)
 23. 0.31 g. (CNG Mail Bid 55, 13 Dec. 2000, lot. 260)
*24. 0.35 g.
*25. 0.33 g. Same reverse die as 24.
 26. 0.33 g. Same reverse die as 24. (CNG Mail Bid 55, 13 Dec. 2000, lot. 259)
*27. 0.30 g. Same reverse die as 24.
*28. 0.33 g. Same reverse die as 24.
*29. 0.31 g. Same reverse die as 24.

> O6

*30. 0.30 g. Same reverse die as 24.
*31. 0.32 g.

Despite its small size, this hoard, when compared to what was known to May at the time of his die study, materially increases the number of surviving coins of lower denominations:

Denomination	Specimens known to May	Examples in hoard	Obverse dies known to May	New obverse dies in hoard
Didrachm	3	5	1	3
Drachm	2	2	1	0
Hemidrachm	0	2	0	2
Obol	3	2	3	2
Hemiobol	0	18	0	6

Purpose of Coinage

Abdera is one of the best-attested mints in mixed sixth-century Greek hoards. Coins of Abdera were found in the two earliest Greek finds containing groups from northern Greece: Ras Shamra and *IGCH* 1185. A tetradrachm was buried in the Persepolis deposit, and coins from Abdera show up in the Egyptian hoards from Sakha and Demanhur. An Abdera tetradrachm is the only coin from Northern Greece found in the Selinus hoard. In part for this reason, the mint has played an important role in the debates about the purpose of Greek silver coinage and its chronology.

Kraay used Abdera as an example of a mint whose limited amount of small change made it unlikely that the original purpose of its coining would be to facilitate local trade. Kraay (1964: 87) believed silver coinage was developed primarily to enhance the ability of the state to make payments. Kim (1994: 66), studying the wealth of newly discovered fractions, challenged Kraay's view. As one of his test cases, he chose to reexamine the Archaic and Classical obols of Abdera. Two-thirds of the available specimens only appeared in recent years. Kim recorded 95 examples from 46 dies, while May had only 31 obols from 16 dies. For the very earliest obols (Kim Groups A to C), Kim's study added 7 obverse dies from 15 new examples. The two obols from this hoard are both from new dies, indicating the possibility of a much larger population—a point Kim anticipated (1994: 54).

This is not the place to summarize the different theories concerning the origin of coinage—that has been admirably done by Seaford (2004: 131ff). What one can stress, however, is the importance to the debate of the discovery of the large group of hemiobols. The only hemiobols previously known come from May's Period II and have a scallop-shell reverse (May 1966: 198–199). This situation, combined with the inability to tie Mende's early small fractions to the start of its tetradrachms and the absence of fractions accompanying the earliest issues of Acanthus (Kim 1994: 38, 55), might have given the impression that large denominations developed first, at least in northern Greece. Such a view is now untenable, and any theory of the Greek adoption of silver coinage in this region must account for an extensive denominational system at its outset.

Metrology and Fiduciarity

Crucial to understanding the purpose of coinage is answering the question: To what extent did early Greek silver coinage have an element of fiduciarity? At the simplest level, we need to know whether, at their introduction, coins were to be counted or weighed when used locally.[4] Metrology is an important tool to help determine this, and the new Abdera hoard provides fertile material for testing theories. The eighteen hemiobols are in excellent condition, in contrast to so many northern Greek fractions that are isolated surface finds and are often, therefore, very porous. Moreover, the hoard context gives us evidence that they represent a circulating sample.

Upon first examination, what is striking is the variation in weight. One should discount no. 14 because it is broken. (Nevertheless, its very presence is not without interest. While thin, the flan of the remaining part of the coin is comparable to the other specimens. Was it still good tender or at least good enough to fool someone? We cannot know for sure, but at least we know that its prior owner held on to it.) The other examples range from 0.29 g to 0.36 g. Such variation, when extrapolated to a large denomination like the octodrachm one finds at Abdera, becomes significant. At the low end, it produces an octodrachm of 27.84 g, and at the high end, 34.56 g. Excluding no. 14, the average weight is 0.324 g, and the median is 0.33 g. This provides octodrachm values of 31.1 g and 31.7 g. May considered the octodrachm to have been on a standard of 29.80 g. The fractions indicate a higher value.

At the time when most of the weight standards we now take for granted were assigned, the purpose of early Greek coinage was largely thought to be for foreign trade. It followed that coins were unlikely to have been struck light to standard if they were to find international acceptance. This type of thinking has led to serious errors. For instance, the earliest coinage of Larissa, for which the drachms range up to 5.87 g, was assigned to the Persian standard of 5.3 g (then thought to be 5.6 g). As with Abdera, new denominations have been discovered, including hemiobols, and the purpose of Larissa's coinage has to be reexamined. Once internal monetization rather than foreign trade is considered, then the standard is quickly seen to be Aeginetan, and the coinage suddenly makes more sense historically (see Kagan 2004).

Likewise at Abdera, foreign trade, especially with the East, was seen as the driving force behind the coinage then thought to be dominated by large denominations. The 29.8-g standard for the octodrachm (14.9 g for the tetradrachm) made sense to May because it allowed for an "easy" conversion to gold (popular as a monetary metal in the East): 7.5 tetradrachms to one gold unit of 8.35 g (May 1966: 16–17). Why a city should want to export silver as coin rather than bullion to people who then treat it as bullion is a question scholars of this school never adequately answered.[5] The moment one contemplates that the Abderites would have

---

4. The best discussion of this subject can now be found in Seaford (2004: 136ff).

5. The late sixth-century coin hoard found in Myt Rahineh in Egypt (*IGCH* 1636) should have provided some caution in this regard. In addition to a mere twenty-three cut-up coins, 73 kg of uncoined silver was discovered.

used their coins locally and would have wanted to maintain an adequate supply of them, the picture changes.

To be fair to May, he lacked much of the information available today. Many of the early coins he had access to probably derived from eastern hoards and suffered the ravages of circulation. In contrast, the Decadrachm hoard (*CH* 8.48) consisted of coins likely taken from a treasury showing little wear. Of the four octodrachms in the hoard, the lightest was 29.8 g and the heaviest 30.21 g. There were fourteen tetradrachms, of which eight weighed over 15 g, the heaviest at 15.29 g. The lightest was 14.89 g. The two heaviest of the didrachms in the above catalogue would produce tetradrachms of 15.00 g and 15.08 g, respectively. The heavier obol at 0.65 g would yield a 31.2 g octodrachm. Greek mints may not have been accurate to a hundredth of a gram, but certainly to a tenth. Given the added value of coinage, one should expect large denominations to be lighter than standard, especially examples that have survived 2,500 years. For this reason, we should consider slightly above 31 g to be the standard for the octodrachm, not 29.8 g. This, perhaps not coincidently, is equal to five Aeginetan drachms; fourteen octodrachms would equate to a 436 g mina.

To return to our hemiobols, in looking at both the variation in weight and at the average and median, it seems likely that we are looking at some sort of batch process. A set amount of silver is turned into a fixed number of coins.[6] The impact of this is that the coinage would have integrity when taken as a whole, but any given example could be seriously off standard. Clearly, with such a system, the coins were intended to be counted and could no doubt be freely exchanged for larger denominations, but would have had little appeal to residents of other areas. Absent an official value, the coins would have been as burdensome as bullion given the extent of the weight variation.

There is no doubt a relationship between this ability of a Greek *polis* to have a limited amount of fiduciarity and the popularity and rapid spread of silver coinage in the Greek world. It is rewarding to see this phenomenon at work in the opening phase of Abdera's coinage.

CHRONOLOGY

In general, a hoard comprising coins of a single mint does not offer much in the way of chronological insights. In this case that is largely true, but to the extent that it helps us relate the weight system at Abdera to the Aeginetan, there might be historical implications. Abdera was a colony of Teos founded by refugees fleeing Persian rule around 545. Its coinage parallels the types of Teos; however, at Abdera, the griffin always faces left while at Teos it looks right. Teos' Archaic and Classical coins were all thought to be on the Aeginetan standard until twenty years ago, when Hurter (1984: 118) published a well-preserved stater of

---

By the time we see carefully weighed Athenian coins in great quantity in the East effectively acting as bullion, coinage was already a much more accepted and widespread phenomenon in that region.

6. Kim (1994: 79) comes to a similar conclusion for the obols of Abdera.

13.96 g, which is on the Milesian standard. The coin was found in the Antilibanon hoard, a deposit that represented an accumulation over many years, providing no *terminus post quem* for the coin. Hurter suggested that Teos, like other western Asia Minor mints, notably Cnidus and Samos, began on the Milesian standard and then switched (as was the case at Cnidus) to the Aeginetan standard.

While no more Milesian staters of Teos have turned up, numerous fractions that should be associated with this early phase of coinage have emerged. Matzke (2002) has usefully collected these, but inexplicably does not connect them with the stater. He publishes two drachms with weights of 6.77 and 6.22 g, and eight hemidrachms, the heaviest of which are 3.49 and 3.36 g. He suggests a light Samian standard (13.1 g) for the fractions and an "Abderite" standard for the Antilibanon stater. This flies in face of the recorded weights and the well-documented experience of other mints. Matzke (2002: 36 n. 34), in fact, seems to associate the early Teian fractions with the Samian coins listed by Barron (1966: 21, 168ff). In this he is right, but he seems not to realize that these are on the Milesian 14 g standard, not the light Samian.

Chronologically speaking, the important point is that it is reasonable to assume that the coinage at Abdera, with its link to the Aeginetan standard, began at about the same time Teos adopted the standard. Hence the Milesian-weight coins of Teos are likely to be earlier than any issues of Abdera. A similar conclusion was also reached by Matzke (2002: 41), who also saw a weight relationship, but arrived there by lowering the standard at Teos to a reduced Aeginetan of 11.8 g, rather than raising May's standard at Abdera. A quick look at Balcer's (1968) catalogue shows several examples at or above 12 g. Allowing for wear and the unlikelihood of finding large denominations over theoretical weight, there is no need to create a new standard for Teos.

In his article, Matzke also proposed a reordering of May's Period 1, with the implication that Abdera's coinage would begin around 540. While this hoard provides no help with absolute dates, it does not support Matzke's groupings. Matzke criticizes the Anglo-Saxon school of "downdating", pointing out some likely errors in the publication of the Asyut hoard, particularly in the dates used for the Persepolis deposit (Matzke 2002). Having made some valid criticisms, Matzke seems to discard any value to comparative hoard analysis and creates for himself a *tabula rasa*, in which he can rearrange Abdera issues in a way that allows May 4, the type that was found in the Persepolis deposit, to fall at the end of Period I. This approach represents a step backwards in numismatic methodology. It is especially ironic in that it has been shown that the mistakes in the dating of the Persepolis deposit were due not to overreliance on the closing dates of hoards, but in allowing erroneous stylistic judgments with respect to the Cypriot coins to outweigh the very evidence provided by the hoards themselves (Kagan 1994: 36–41).

The relative chronology and sequence of Abdera's early coinage has been worked out based on close comparison of the different elements contained in each of the recorded deposits (Kagan 1992: 22). The earliest find is Ras Shamra, followed by *IGCH* 1185, Sakha, Demanhur, and Selinus. Matzke (2002: 50) ignores this and assigns the tetradrachm from Ras Shamra not to his first group but to his second group, and associates it with no. 4 from this hoard. He is likely correct in this association, but he was unaware of no. 3, the obverse of which is virtually identical to no. 4. No. 3 has a reverse unique to Abdera in that it resembles that found on early Aeginetan coins. It seems all but certain that this coin must be put at the start of Abdera's coinage, confirming the primacy of the Ras Shamra deposit. It is interesting that a similar phenomenon occurred at other mints, such as Mende and Thasos. Thasos' earliest coins, which are only known from *IGCH* 1185, have diagonally divided reverses, predating the quadripartite square.

Matzke places no. 1 from our hoard in his earliest group, which he has predate Ras Shamra. This coin likely shares the obverse die of the poorly preserved May 17 and is very close to the obverse die of May 15–16. Matzke also includes these coins in this group. A die duplicate of May 15 is contained in *IGCH* 1185, which also has an example of May 9, the coin from Ras Shamra. *IGCH* 1185, while close in date to Ras Shamra, has consistently later coins. In addition to these coins, Matzke's first group contains the tetradrachms May 22 and 23 (from May's Group X), the latter coin coming from the Demanhur find. That in itself is not a problem because the coins in that hoard were collected over a reasonable period. However, the well-preserved tetradrachm of Abdera found in the Selinus hoard has been associated with just this issue (Arnold-Biucchi 1988: 14).[7] Where there is an overlap of mints between the Selinus and Demanhur hoards, the coins in the Selinus deposit are more recent. Specifically, one finds Type 3 Aegina staters and Ravel 2 (Pegasus / Athena head) staters of Corinth in Selinus but not in Demanhur. The Selinus hoard, unlike some of the eastern hoards, appears to contain coins taken from circulation at a point in time rather than collected over time. There are certainly coins in the find that are considerably older than the burial date, but generally they show wear. The Abdera coin is particularly fresh, with high points of detail still visible. While at the end of the day a single coin in a hoard can never be dispositive, absent better evidence (including stylistic judgment), it is hard to place that coin at the start of Abdera's coinage. May 23, given what we know today, should be considered the last issue of Abdera in Demanhur and certainly later than the type of May 4, which was found in both Demanhur and Persepolis.[8]

Given current judgments about the Persepolis deposit and the other hoard evidence, it is rash to date the beginning of Abdera's coinage later than 520. How much earlier it should

---

7. The authors date the find to the last decade of the sixth century.

8. Matzke's stylistic argument for placing May 4 at the end of Period I is based on the smooth wing and breast of the griffin. This forces him, however, to also put May 1 (a coin with no hoard context) at the end as well. This die depicts a striding griffin most similar to that found on May 9 from Ras Shamra. While it is true that smooth breast and wing seem to become standard in Period II, there may be exceptions. The octodrachm with the legend ΑΠΟΛ and negro head symbol has a feathered breast and wing. This issue, unknown to May but found in the Decadrachm hoard (Fried 1987: pl. I.7) and the Zhuyuetang Collection (no. 68), must be later than any of May's Period I issues.

start is still uncertain. Matzke's date of 540 is possible, but we need different evidence to support it. Since the publication of May's die study, we have learned that there was no break in the mint in 449 because of the Coinage Decree. The Decadrachm hoard also lowered the dates of Group III by ten to twenty years (Kagan 1987). This means that we must extend the life of May's Group I if we are to maintain the 540 starting date. The hoard under study here demonstrates that Abdera's early coinage was more extensive than we thought, perhaps supporting the high chronology. At the same time, we find together in this hoard coins in good condition, associated with the Ras Shamra find, die-linked to the Sakha hoard, and related to Demanhur, leaving open the possibility that coinage at Abdera, once it began, was an explosive phenomenon.

We know from the only recently reconstructed Second Paean of Pindar that the early colonists did not have an easy time of it (Graham 1991; 1992: 48–50). Pindar records a three-part conflict with the local Paeonians: an early success followed by defeat and then a decisive victory at the Battle of Melamphyllon. No dates are given, but the events must predate the Persian conquest of Thrace (Graham 1992: 51). In the absence of any break in the early coinage (a point reinforced by the new hoard), it would seem logical to have all three phases take place prior to the initiation of coinage and hence at the early foundation of the city.

Inscriptions point to a uniquely close relationship between mother and colony (Graham 1992: 53–54). The weight relationship (established above) and the coordination of type make it more than likely that the earliest coins from Abdera and the Aeginetan-weight coins of Teos are roughly contemporary. It strikes the author as unlikely that Teos would be ready, immediately after conquest by the Persians and the exodus of many of its citizens, to begin abundantly producing Aeginetan-weight coinage. Even if they began preconquest, the Milesian coins, with the emphasis on small denominations, are what one would expect to find at a depleted Teos in the decade or so following the arrival of the Persians. Finally, in the Second Paean there is the tantalizing evidence that there was a refoundation of Teos by Abderans. There is no fixed date for this, and Graham (1991: 177) feels it is likely to be either after the Ionian Revolt or before the Persian incursion into Thrace. If the latter (especially if c. 530), it is tempting to accept the suggestion of Chryssanthaki (2001: 394–397) that it was this event that led to the introduction of the Teian Aeginetan-weight coinage. It would certainly explain the newfound wealth at Teos.[9]

Numismatically and historically, the author prefers a starting date for Abdera around 530. This is consistent with the new fixed point we have in sixth-century numismatic chronology (Cahill and Kroll 2005) that allows us to safely call "croesids" Croesids. Unfortunately, the reality remains, as Kroll notes (Cahill and Kroll 2005: 609), that "reliable

9. Chryssanthaki would start the Abdera coinage first, just before the refoundation. One looks forward to the publication of her thesis on the monetary history of Abdera, which I have not been able to consult in manuscript.

chronological pegs for anchoring the development of Archaic coinage in Western Asia Minor and Greece are far more limited than is often realized". Absent such pegs, there remains a margin of error of plus or minus as much as ten years. Nevertheless, this contribution, hopefully, has done something to clarify the picture that, thanks in large part to the efforts of Jack Kroll, has been coming more and more into focus.

Bibliography

Arnold-Biucchi, C., L. Beer-Tobey, and N. Waggoner. 1988. A Greek Archaic silver hoard from Selinus. *American Numismatic Society Museum Notes* 33: 1–35.

Balcer, J. M. 1968. The early silver coinage of Teos. *Schweizerische Numismatische Rundschau (Revue suisse de numismatique)* 47: 5–50.

Cahill, N. and J.H. Kroll. 2005. New archaic coin finds at Sardis. *American Journal of Archaeology* 109, no. 4: 589–617.

CH: Coin Hoards. 1975–. London: Royal Numismatic Society.

Chryssanthaki, K. 2001. Les trois foundations d'Abdère. *Revue des Études Grécques* 114: 383–406.

Barron, J. P. 1966. *The silver coins of Samos.* London: Athlon Press.

Fried, S. 1987. The Decadrachm hoard: an introduction. In: I. Carradice, ed., *Coinage and administration in the Athenian and Persian empires*, pp. 21–28. Oxford: British Archaeological Reports.

Graham, A. J. 1991. 'Adopted Teians': a passage in the new inscription of public imprecations from Teos. *Journal of Hellenic Studies* 111: 176–178.

———. 1992. Abdera and Teos. *Journal of Hellenic Studies* 112: 44–73.

Hurter, S., and E. Pászthory. 1984. Archaischer Silberfund aus dem Antilibanon. In: A. Houghton, S. Hurter, et al., eds., *Studies in honor of Leo Mildenberg: numismatics, art history, archaeology*, pp. 111–125. Wetteren: Cultura Press.

IGCH: M. Thompson, O. Mørkholm, and C. M. Kraay, eds. 1973. *An inventory of Greek coin hoards.* New York: American Numismatic Society.

Kagan, J. H. 1987. The Decadrachm hoard: chronology and consequences. In: I. Carradice, ed., *Coinage and administration in the Athenian and Persian empires*, pp. 21–28. Oxford: British Archaeological Reports.

———. 1992. IGCH 1185 reconsidered. *Revue belge de numismatique et de sigillographie* 138: 1–24.

———. 1994. An Archaic Greek coin hoard from the eastern Mediterranean and early Cypriot coinage. *Numismatic Chronicle* 154: 17–52.

———. 2004. The so-called Persian weight coinage of Larissa. Ὀβολός 7: 79–86.

Kim, H. 1994. *Greek fractional silver coinage: a reassessment of the inception, development, prevalence, and functions of small change during the late Archaic and early Classical period.* M. Phil. thesis, Oxford University.

Kraay, C. 1964. Hoards, small change, and the origin of coinage. *Journal of Hellenic Studies* 84: 76–91.

Kroll, J. H. 2001. Observations on monetary instruments in pre-coinage Greece. In: M. Balmuth, ed., *Hacksilber to coinage: new insights into the monetary history of the Near East and Greece*, pp. 77–91. New York: American Numismatic Society.

Kroll, J. H., and N. Waggoner. 1984. Dating the earliest coins of Athens, Corinth, and Aegina. *American Journal of Archaeology* 88, no. 3: 325–340.

Matzke, M. 2002. Die frühe Münzprägung von Teos in Ionien. Chronologische und metrologische Untersuchungen um die Frühzeit der Silbermünzpägung. *Jahrbuch für Numismatik und Geldgeschicte* 50: 21–53.

May, J. M. F. 1966. *The coinage of Abdera (540–345 BC)*. London: Royal Numismatic Society.

Meadows, A., and R. W. C. Kan. 2004. *History re-stored: ancient Greek coins from the Zhuyuetang Collection*. Hong Kong: Zhuyuetang Ltd.

Seaford, R. 2004. *Money and the early Greek mind: Homer, philosophy, tragedy*. Cambridge: Cambridge University Press.

Agoranomia: Studies in Money and Exchange Presented to John H. Kroll, pp. 61–86
© 2006 The American Numismatic Society

The "Lete" Coinage Reconsidered

PLATES 3–4   SELENE PSOMA*

The "Lete" coinage has received a good deal of attention to date (Head 1911: 198; Svoronos 1919: 76–83; Gaebler 1935: 67–72, pl. XIV nos. 17–33, XV nos. 1–2, 7; Stucky 1984; Smith 2000) and is without doubt one of the earliest—if not the earliest—in northern Greece (Price-Waggoner 1975: 34–35). The approximately 10-g staters bear the dancing maenad and satyr scene on the obverse and an incuse square on the reverse (plate 3 nos. 1–4) (Gaebler 1935: pl. XIV nos. 17–33, pl. XV nos. 1–2, 7; Smith 2000: 217). Smaller denominations bear either the same obverse type (plate 3 nos. 5–7) or a "veretrum tenens" satyr (plate 3 nos. 8–12) (Gaebler 1935: pl. XIV 32 [half-stater], pl. XV nos. 3–6 [*hēmiekta*]).

As is the case with most of the early uninscribed Archaic coinages of the Thraco-Macedonian district, the attribution of the so-called Lete coinage is problematic (Picard 1996: 1073; Psoma 2003a: esp. 227–228). The city of Lete was proposed by B. V. Head (*BMC Macedonia* 79: no. 19–21, pl. VIII no. 25; Head 1911: 198) as the minting authority of these coins, and this attribution was based on the reading ΛΕΤΑΙΟΝ/ΛΕΤΕΙΟΝ believed to be found on a few specimens of one of the latest issues of that mint. Many scholars, including the late N. G. L. Hammond (1979: 77, 83), followed Head. However, doubts about this reading were formulated by von Sallet (1889: 92). This same inscription was read as a retrograde ΣΙΡΙΝΟΝ by J. N. Svoronos (1919: 76), who proposed attributing this coinage to Sirrai, a city of a tribe of the interior situated northwest of the Pangaion. Dressel and Regling (1927) doubted Svoronos' reading, but apparently thought that the coinage should be attributed to

*Center for Greek and Roman Antiquity, The National Hellenic Research Foundation, Athens, Greece.

the wider Pangaion area,[1] as did C. M. Kraay (1976: 148). In a most illuminating article, Michael Smith (2000: 217) rightly pointed out that this inscription was "nothing more than the product of wear and breakage over time on that particular die itself", and also attributed this coinage to Thrace. In his doctoral thesis, he proposed an attribution to Eion (Smith 1999). I would like to carry this discussion forward in this article, which I would like to dedicate to Jack Kroll, the distinguished specialist on Archaic Greece and eminent numismatist from whose writings on early coinages I have learned so much.

ICONOGRAPHY

As regards the city of Lete, its most important deity seems to have been Artemis, daughter of Leto.[2] Many offerings from a sanctuary of Demeter and the Kale Thea were also found in old excavations of the city (Hatzopoulos 1994: 123–127). We know nothing of the history and the cults of the city of Sirrai in this early period.[3]

Dionysos and his companions were very important in the region known today as Eastern Macedonia, which was in antiquity the central part of the wider geographical area of Thrace.[4] Herodotus (8.138) speaks of an important old sanctuary of the god in the Pangaion,[5] and we know that vineyards had been cultivated in the area since the Neolithic age (Pilhofer 1995: 100–105; Pikoulas 2001a: 200–201). According to Hesychios (s.v. Δατός), Datos means "vintage" or "harvest", and a city of this name existed in that area (Picard 1994; Counillon 1998). Dionysos and Herakles are the most important divinities of the city of Thasos. Thasos, Galepsos (Psoma 2003a), Pergamos,[6] and a number of cities and tribes under Thasian influence adopted types connected with the cult of Dionysos.[7] Although we reject Svoronos' reading ΣΙΡΙΝΟΝ, the attribution of this coinage to this area is reasonable, as Sirrai is to be placed in the wider geographic area of Thasian influence.

THE WEIGHT STANDARD

As M. Smith, following Svoronos, noted, these coins were struck on the "Thasian" version of the "Thraco-Macedonian" standard (Table 1). In fact, staters of approximately 10 g were struck by the city of Thasos itself as well as by Neapolis and Galepsos, cities of the Thasian Peraia and colonies of Thasos (Papaevangelou 2000).[8] Staters of this weight and types

1. Dressel and Regling note (1927: 42): "Die allgemeine Lokalisation der ganzen Gruppe übrigens in das Bergwerksgebiet wird von niemand bestritten, es mögen verschiedene Stämme und Orte an deren Prägung teilhaben".
2. See also the philological evidence on the existence of a sanctuary of Leto close to the homonymous city (Theagenes *FGrH* 774 F 6 [= Steph. Byz. s.v.]; Ael. Herod. *De pros. cathol.* 3.1.342; see also Smith 1999: 16–17).
3. On the early literary evidence on the city of Sirrai, see Papazoglou (1988: 379 n. 9–12) and Smith (1999: 23).
4. Svoronos and Smith use the term "Thrace". On the limits between Macedonia and Thrace and on the special significance of these terms, see Zahrnt (1997).
5. On the sanctuary of Dionysos, see Pikoulas (2001a: 200–201).
6. On the attribution to Pergamon of Gaebler (1935: 141, pl. XXVII no. 11), see Psoma (2000–03: 233–243, pl. 57–58).
7. On these coinages, see Picard (2000a). A different opinion is adopted by Smith (1999: 40–43).
8. On the goats of Aigai attributed to Galepsos, cf. Psoma (2003).

TABLE 1. From Strymon to the Nestos

	Berge	Thasos	Neapolis	Galepsos	Pergamos	Ennea Odoi	"Eion"
Staters	satyr and maenad dancing	satyr-maenad	Gorgoneion	goat		cow and calf	
Hemistaters	satyr and maenad dancing	satyr-maenad				cow and calf	2 birds
Tritai		satyr-maenad					
Hektai					half-goat		
Hēmiekta	veretrum tenens satyr	satyr	Gorgoneion	goat	head of goat		2 birds
Half *Hēmiekta*		2 dolphins		half-goat			
Fourth *Hēmiekta*	head of satyr	dolphin					bird

similar to those of Thasos (plate 3 no. 13) bearing the centaur-maenad couple were put into circulation by other minting authorities in contact with Thasos, such as the Orrescii (plate 3 no. 14) and the Laiaioi[9] as well as by the Ichnaioi (Picard 2000: 244–245) and three other minting authorities: the first group bears a cow and calf on the obverse (Ennea Odoi?: plate 3 no. 15; Svoronos 1919: pl. XVIII nos. 1, 3–24),[10] the second, a running centaur (Svoronos 1919: pl. VI nos. 1, 4), and the third, which is slightly lighter, a mysterious running figure, which may be Dionysus holding a double thyrsos (Svoronos 1919: pl. XVII nos. 1–10). An early group of coins issued by the city of Dicaea by Abdera were also staters and double staters on the "Thasian" version of the "Thraco-Macedonian" standard (May 1965: 8; Schoenert-Geiss 1975: 16, 21).

The rare "Lete" half-staters of approximately 5 g (plate 3 nos. 5–7) belong to the very early groups (Smith 1999: 65–67; 2000: 220). This denomination was struck by Thasos, "Eion", and in a limited number by the Orrescii,[11] as Smith pointed out, and also by the same minting authority of the cow and calf staters (Ennea Odoi?).[12] Although extremely

9. The silver staters with a centaur-maenad couple bear the legend ΛΑΕΙΤΙΚΟΝ. On these coins, see Price and Waggoner (1975: 33–34, no. 94). The Laiaioi are referred to by Thucydides (2.96.3, 2.97.2) as a tribe living on the western frontier of the Odrysian kingdom. See also Archibald (1998: 107–109, 127).

10. See also note 12, below.

11. Smith (2000: 220) is referring to Svoronos (1919: 58, pl. V no. 23).

12. According to Smith (2000: 220), who follows Svoronos (1919: 136–139, pl. XVIII nos. 1–24), the Bottiaeans also struck hemistaters. The coins he refers to, with cow and calf on the obverse, were not struck by the Bottiaeans (Smith 220 n. 40: *SNG ANS* 925); they are also issues on the Thasian version of the Thraco-Macedonian standard, whose attribution remains uncertain. However, their weight standard, staters of approximately 10 g and later 8 g and hemistaters of 5 g, point to their attribution to the same general area of what we call "Thasian

limited, this 5 g fraction corresponds to the contemporary, if not earlier, coins from the Gerakini/Chalkidike hoard (*CH* 8.37).[13]

An interesting point concerning the "Lete" coinage and noted by Smith is the significant number of c. 0.90 g coins (*hēmiekta*) that this minting authority put into circulation (plate 3 nos. 8–12) (Gaebler 1935: pl. XV nos. 3–6; Smith 1999: 67–72; 2000: 220). This denomination, which is mentioned in Thasian inscriptions, was also struck by Thasos (plate 4 no. 16) as well as by Galepsos (plate 4 no. 17), Pergamos (plate 4 no. 18), and "Eion" (plate 4 no. 19), the western "Thasian" colony at the mouth of the Strymon (Koukouli-Chryssanthaki 2000: 366 n. 126–127; 2002: 38–39). With their weight of approximately 0.90 g, *hēmiekta* remained the most popular fraction in the area of the Thasian Peraia and well to the north of it. An important number of hoards of the fifth and fourth centuries BC buried in the area also contained *hēmiekta*: (1) the Pontolivado hoard (*CH* 8.16), with 27 *hēmiekta* from Thasos and four from Neapolis (Oeconomides 1990: 533–540); (2) the small Drama hoard (*CH* 8.75), with *hēmiekta* from "Eion"[14] and Thasos; and (3) the Bulgaria 1977/78 hoard (*CH* 7.25), buried around 400 BC (?), with two Thasian staters and *hēmiekta* (two "diobols"). Other hoards buried later, in the fourth century BC, also bear that same fraction: (4) *IGCH* 720 from Skrevatno (400 or 350 BC);[15] (5) *CH* 7.46 from Potamoi, Drama (346 BC) (Poulios 1998); (6) *CH* 9.18 (400 BC or even later); and (7) *CH* 9.61 (360/350 BC) (Psoma 2002). The last two hoards (6 and 7) were buried in the cemetery of ancient Gazoros. *Hēmiekta* with the forepart of a goat that we have already attributed to Galepsos as well as others of "Eion" circulated further west (Petrova 1996). In the excavations of Thasos, Amphipolis, and Galepsos, *hēmiekta* of Galepsos were also found (Picard 1996). *Hēmiekta* from "Lete" were also present in the excavations of the classical cemetery of Galepsos.[16] A smaller fraction, known by only five specimens, weighing from 0.12 g to 0.37 g (half-*hēmiekton*?), with a head of a satyr on the obverse, was attributed to "Lete" by Smith (1999: 72–74).

CIRCULATION PATTERNS AND CHRONOLOGY

Unlike *hēmiekta*, "Lete" staters did not circulate locally. Only three "Lete" staters have been found in Greece. The first comes from Stagira (Sismanidis 1995 [1998]: 390) and the second from Neos Skopos (Valla 2003: 118). A third one, at the Museum of Cavala, is of uncertain

influence". The letters EN on the obverse of the final issue, struck from a single pair of dies, refer probably to Ennea Odoi (Kraay 1976: 151). On the settlement at Ennea Odoi, see Koukouli-Chryssanthaki (2002: 40–41). The "significant change in the society of the settlement at the end of the seventh century and the beginning of the sixth century BC" probably refers to the foundation of a Parian colony at Ennea Odoi. In that case, this Parian colony could be the issuing authority of the cow and calf staters and hemistaters.

13. See the 19+ persic dr. (crab/incuse) of 5.30 g, like the 6508 Alpha Bank Numismatic Collection (ex coll. Ath. Ghertsos) in the Gerakini hoard, according to *CH* 8.37.

14. *Hēmiekta* of "Eion" were also part of *IGCH* 364 (ancient Tragilos: 8 coins), *CH* 8.75 (Drama, 1983, 400 BC: 15 coins, 3 "diobols" and 1 obol of Thasos, 1 triobol of Neapolis): *Αρχαιολογικό Έργο στη Μακεδονία και τη Θράκη* 9, 1995 (1998): 411–422, esp. 413–414.

15. See Psoma (2002: 215), with the previous bibliography.

16. As Mr. V. Poulios kindly informed me.

provenance. As is the case with other North Greek coinages, the "Lete" staters were part of some of the earliest hoards buried in Egypt and the East, and they are also present in a hoard buried in the North Balkan area.

The North

An interesting point is the presence of an early fifth-century hoard of "Lete" staters in Nevrokop, Bulgaria (*IGCH* 693, Nevrokop 1946, 500–475 BC), the site of the later Roman Nicopolis ad Nestum.[17] Another hoard from the same place contains early Thasian staters (*IGCH* 692, *BIAB* 13 [1939] 344, Nevrokop 1939, 500–475 BC: Orrescii, 1 stater [Gaebler 1935 pl. 18 no. 10]; staters of Thasos). Two[18] other hoards with Thasian Group I staters (460–450) were also buried in Bulgaria (Picard 1999: 334–336): the first one in Venkovec, sixty kilometers east of Sofia (*IGCH* 691, *BIAB* 26 [1963] 257, 500–475 BC: Thasos: 4+ staters [Archaic style]) and the second one in Krusevo, 32 kilometers east of Plovdid (*IGCH* 695, 475 BC: Thasos, 51 stater; Athens, 1 tetradrachm; Parium 101 drachms [incuse rev.]).

Thasian fractions circulated also in that same area: a *trite* (cf. plate 4 no. 20) was part of a hoard buried in Kostenec,[19] situated together with Nevrokop and Venkovec in the western Thracian plain. Thasian fractions, as well as *hemiekta* of "Eion" on the same standard, were found in the excavations of Koprivlen, an important *emporion* some kilometers south of Nevrokop in the Middle Nestos and on the same trade route connecting (via the Western Rhodopes) the Aegean coast with the upper Hebros valley (Bozkova et al. 2002: 475). As Picard (1999: 341) has already pointed out, staters of this first Thasian group were part of hoards buried "à l'Ouest de la Bulgarie" and this area "correspond en gros à l'itinéraire permettant aux Thasiens de se rendre à Pistiros, en empruntant la vallée de Strymon".

The East

For the relative chronology of the "Lete" coinage, its presence in early hoards is decisive. In these hoards, the "Lete" staters were buried together with coins of other minting authorities of the Thraco-Macedonian district. Staters of "Lete" were part of the Ras Shamra 1936 (*IGCH* 1478, 525–520, 510–500 BC: 12 staters—Schaeffer 1939; Stucky 1984; cf. Price and Waggoner 1975: 17, 34–35), the Mit Rahineh 1860 (*IGCH* 1636: 500 BC [Price], 525 BC [Kraay], 525–500 BC [Kagan]: 1 stater—Price 1977: 6–8; Kraay 1977; Kagan 1994), the Demanhur 1900/1901 (*IGCH* 1637, Hermopolis Parva, 500 BC: 17 staters),[20] the Adana 1971 (*CH* 1.4, South Anatolia, 500 BC: 1 stater—Robinson 1973: pl. XXV),[21] the Asia Mi-

---

17. On coin finds of pre-Macedonian times in Thrace, see Archibald (1998: 126–135). On this hoard, see Smith (1999: 104–105).

18. According to Picard (1999: 342), "des monnaies du premier groupe sont présentes dans quatre trésors". The fourth one, of Kostenec (Picard 1999: 342 n. 32), contained only one *trite* of the earliest group. All other Thasian coins belonged to the second group.

19. See note 18, above.

20. Kagan (1994: 20) notes: "Demanhur had coins with the slightly later vertical folds".

21. On the "Lete" specimen, see Robinson (1973: 233).

nor? 1989 (*CH* 8.19, 500 BC: 3 staters),[22] the "Rhodes 1880" (*IGCH* 1185, 450 BC [*IGCH*], cf. also *CH* 8.21, 500 BC: 3 staters—Kagan 1992: pl. I–V),[23] and the Sakha 1897 (*IGCH* 1639, 500–490 BC: 4 staters) hoards. All these hoards were buried before 500 BC, and the "Lete" specimens included are stylistically distinguished by the curved parallel folds of the nymph's skirt (Kraay 1976: 148; Price and Waggoner 1975: 34). These folds become vertical on the Demanhur "Lete" staters (Kraay 1976: 149; Price and Waggoner 1975: 34) and at about 500 BC, they broaden. The figures on the obverse are now larger, and we find a "Union Jack" pattern on the reverse, as in the Benha el Asl 1929 "Lete" stater (*IGCH* 1640, 500 BC, 490–485 [Robinson]: 10 or 6 staters, cf. plate 4 no. 21) (Kraay 1976: 149; Price and Waggoner 1975: 34–35). Some "Lete" specimens of the style also occurred in hoards buried in the early fifth century BC: Taras 1911 (*IGCH* 1874: 508 BC [*IGCH*], 500–490 [Kagan]: 18 staters),[24] Delta (*IGCH* 1638, 490–485: 1 stater), Antilibanon 1976 (*CH* 6.4, 5: 475 BC; cf. *CH* 7.12: 480 [Price]: 1 stater—Hurter and Paszthory 1984: pl. 14–17), Jordan 1967 (*IGCH* 1482: Hauran, near Bostra, 445 BC: 2 staters—Kraay and Moorey 1968: 182), and Balkh 1966 (*IGCH* 1820, 390–380 BC: 1 stater—Troxell and Spengler 1969). The latest issues of the "Lete" mint present an interesting development in the design of the reverse: the old diagonally divided reverse punch is now replaced by one with rectilinear division (Kraay 1976: 149; Price and Waggoner 1975: 34). A specimen with such an arrangement of the reverse is part of the Balkh hoard.

Chronology and General Attribution

Staters of this first Thasian group were also part of the earliest hoards that contained "Lete" specimens.[25] The editors of the Asyut hoard state that "the earliest coins of Thasos, not present in this hoard [sc. Asyut], share the fabric and style of the earlier examples of the 'Lete' second group, i.e. during the last quarter of the 6th century" (Price and Waggoner 1975: 35; Kraay 1976: 149; Smith 1999: 80). Further comparison with the coinage of Neapolis clearly

22. Kagan (1994: pl. 1–9, esp. 20) notes "characterized by small dumpy flans, curved parallel folds in the nymph's skirt and rough incuses. Such coins were found exclusively in the following hoards: Adana, Mit Rahineh, Ras Shamra, Sakha and *IGCH* 1185".

23. On the "Lete" specimens, see especially Kagan (1992: 6–7).

24. Kagan (1994: 20) notes: "…while the Taranto already contained the more developed wider flans with squatter figures".

25. Egypt 1971/72, *CH* 2.10, 500 BC: 1; Demanhur 1900/01, *IGCH* 1637, 500 BC: 12; Asia Minor? 1989, *CH* 8.19, 500 BC: 4; Taras 1911, *IGCH* 1874, 508 BC, 500–490 BC: 11; Sakha 1897, *IGCH* 1639, 500–490 BC: 1; Benha el Asl 1929, *IGCH* 1640, 500 BC, 490–485 BC: 2; Delta, *IGCH* 1638, 490–485 BC: 1; Nevrokop 1939, *IGCH* 692, 500–475 BC: "staters"; Antilibanon 1976, *CH* 6.4, 5 and 7.12, 475 BC or 480 BC (Hurter): 1; Pontolivado 1972, *CH* 1.11, 475 BC: 10 st, 29 fr.; Near East, 1980, *CH* 7.16, 38-39 (Kraay) 475 BC: 1; Zagazig 1901, *IGCH* 1645, 470 or post-470 BC: 1; South Asia Minor, *CH* 8.48, 465 BC: 9; Asyut 1968/69, *IGCH* 1644, 475 BC: 27; West Asia Minor 1963, *IGCH* 1182, 460 BC: 1; Rhodes 1880, *IGCH* 1185, *CH* 8.21, 500 or 450 BC: 8; Jordan 1967, *IGCH* 1482, 445 BC: 1; Massyaf 1961 (near ancient Baetocaece), *IGCH* 1483, 425–420 BC: 1 fragment; Bulgaria 1977/78, *CH* 7.25, 400 BC: 2 staters, 2 diobols; Cabul 1933 (anc. Cabura, Paropamisadae), *IGCH* 1830, 380 BC: 1 fragment. See also Smith's interesting and illuminating analysis on the arrival of Greek coins in Egypt and the Levant (1999: 138–166).

shows that the beginning of minting at "Lete" preceded that of the Gorgoneia. As for the end of the "Lete" coinage, the stylistic development of the obverse as well as the form of its reverse and the absence of "Lete" specimens from the Asyut hoard (*IGCH* 1644) buried c. 475 BC (Price and Waggoner 1975: 117–125; Kraay 1977: 193; Kagan 1987: 22) and the important Decadrachm hoard (*CH* 8.48) buried c. 460 BC (Kagan 1987: 23) place the end of the "Lete" coinage around the Persian Wars. It was almost at the same period that both Neapolis and Galepsos ceased coining such staters.[26]

Although style and typology reveal that the first "Lete" staters were earlier than the very early Thasian staters (Price and Waggoner 1975: 34–35),[27] weight standard, iconography, and technique suggest strong ties with Thasos and cities of the Thasian Peraia (see Table 1). The suggestion that the "Lete" coinage mint was located in the so-called Thasian Peraia, the mainland opposite Thasos, seems more than convincing. The "Lete" mint produced quite an important output "in a fairly short period of time, as suggested by the hoard evidence" (Smith 2000: 221). These observations support the view that the mint was located in the so-called mining district, opposite Thasos (Smith 1999: 78; 2000: 221). Babelon (1932: 1115), Svoronos (1919: 76–77), Dressel and Regling (1927: 42), Schaeffer (1939: 469), Smith (2000: 218), and Kraay (1976)[28] have all proposed attributing this coinage to this area.

The Mining District

Evidence for the rich gold- and silver-producing region of Thrace is often reported by ancient authors (Th. 4.105.1; Str. 7a.134.1–4; Thphr. *HP* 9.13.46; [Aris.] *Mir.* 832b 28; D.S. 31.8.7; Arr. *An.* 7.9.3; Lucian *Sacr.* 11). The available philological evidence clearly distinguishes four main precious metal-producing areas in Thrace, namely the island of Thasos (Hdt. 6.46–47; D.S. 11.70.1; Arr. *FGrH* 156 F 68; Zen. *Epitome* 3.11.2 [= 4.34.4]) and, on the mainland (Hdt. 6.46–47; Th. 1.100.2; Th. 1.101.3), Skapte Hyle (Hdt. 6.46–47; Thphr. *Lapid.* 17.2; Marcell. Biogr., *Thuc.* 14.3 and 19.2; Constant. Porphyr. *De virtutibus et vitiis* 2.30.7), the area of Datos-Crenides (Hdt. 9.75, cf. D.S. 11.70.5; Str. 7a.1.33; Zen. *Epitome* 3.11.2 [= 4.34.4]; D.S. 16.8.6) (later Philippi: Arist. *Mir.* 833a 28 = *Fragm. varia* 6.37.255), the Pangaion (Aeschyl. frg. 10b 84.25 and 27; Ath. 2.16.4; Lucianus *Hypernephelos* 18; Polyb. 22.18.2–6; Euseb. *Praep. Ev.* 10.6.7; Hdt. 5.17, 7.112), and the general region of the river Strymon (Hdt. 5.23; Paus. *Att. verb. coll.* 18.4 [Suid. s.v. χρυσός κολοφώνιος]; Str. 7.7.4 C 323; Nonn. *Dionys.* 43.417).

Gold specifically is reported in Thrace by Thucydides (4.105), Strabo (7a.134.1 and 4), and Lucian (*Sacr.* 11.10). According to the literary evidence, gold was also found in Thasos (Hdt. 6.46–47; Arr. *FGrH* 156 F 68; Zenobius *Epitome* 3.11.2 [= 4.34.4]) and the Skapte Hyle (Hdt. 6.46–47; Zenobius *Epitome* 3.11.2 [= 4.34.4];

---

26. On Galepsos and Neapolis, see Psoma (2003a: 233, 240). For "Aegae," see Lorber (2000: pl. 14, esp. 117). For Neapolis, see Papaevangelou (2000).

27. On these very early Thasos staters, see Picard (1999: 343–344).

28. Kraay proposed attributing this coinage to the *ethnos* of Satrai (1976: 148).

Marcell. *Thuc.* 14.3), in the area of Datos (Hdt. 9.75; Str. 7a.133.19; Zenobius *Epitome* 3.11.2 [= 4.34.4])[29] and Philippi ([Aris.] *Mir.* 833a 28; D.S. 16.8.6–7) as well as in the Pangaion (Hdt. 7.112; Eus. 10.6.7) and the wider Strymon area (Paus. *Att. verb.*, ξηι' 18.4 [= Suid. s.v. χρυσός κολοφώνιος]). Silver was available in the Pangaion (Hdt. 7.112; 5.15) and the Strymon (Hdt. 5.23).

The most important precious-metal mints are to be located between the Strymon and the Nestos, and it is in this area that the "Lete" coinage minting authority was most probably located. The literary evidence also indicates control of the mints by Thasos and local *ethnē* (Satrai, Odomantai, and Pieres), according to Herodotus (7.112), some of which also minted coins.[30]

The "Lete" Coinage Again

Although Head is certainly wrong in attributing our coinage to Lete, and Svoronos is equally incorrect in attributing it to Sirrai, the fact that they attribute this coinage to cities is not without importance. It is highly unlikely that the "Lete" coinage is to be attributed to a local tribe, for three reasons: (1) First, as we have already suggested in a previous publication, fractions were normally struck by cities. The coinage of what we might call "tribes", in an attempt to translate the ancient term *ethnē*, was limited mostly to heavy denominations (Psoma 2003: 237). "Lete" struck a large number of *hēmiekta* absent from the "oriental" hoards. These *hēmiekta* were mostly destined for local circulation. *Hēmiekta* were also struck in important numbers by Thasos, Neapolis, Galepsos, and "Eion". Thasos, Galepsos, and "Eion", on a more limited scale, struck also *tritēmora*.[31] The presence of fractions may possibly be an important argument in favor of attributing this coinage to a civic mint. The Orrescians and the Ichnaioi put also *hēmiekta* and *tritēmora* (Orrescii) in circulation, albeit in very limited quantities. (2) Second, the style, iconography, and technique also suggest a civic character to this coinage. (3) Finally, the absence of legends from the "Lete" coinage, despite making its attribution problematic, may also point the way to a correct attribution. Early Archaic silver coinages of Greek cities situated on the Thracian coast are anepigraphic. Examples are Thasian silver issues of the first and the second period (plate 3–4 nos. 13, 16, 20; Picard 2000b); coins from Galepsos depicting goats except the city's last issues (plate 4 no. 17) (Lorber 2000: pl. 14; Psoma 2003a: 234–237); early issues of the Thracian Dikaia and from Abdera itself, which display only the initials of magistrates;[32] "Chalcidean"-weight staters[33] from Argilos (Liampi 1994), Potidaea (Wartenberg 1998: 367 n. 22);

---

29. See also Koukouli (2000: 368 n. 139). This evidence is discussed by Hammond (1983).

30. This evidence is discussed by Hammond (1983).

31. On the coinages of Thasos, see Picard (1999; 2000b: 303); of Neapolis, see Papaevangelou (2000); and of Galepsos, see Psoma (2003: 232).

32. On the coinage of Abdera, see Chryssanthaki (2000: 150–157 [Période I, 520–500], 157–164 [Période II, 500–480], 64–72 [Période III, 475–450]).

33. On the use of the term *stater* for these Attic-weight tetradrachms, cf. Psoma (2001).

and Sermylia (Psoma 2001); and early Euboean-weight staters (Attic-Euboïc tetradrachms) from Akanthos, Mende, Potidaea, Skione, and Torone (Gaebler 1935: 23–25 [Akanthos], 72–73 nos. 1–3 [Mende], 103–104 nos. 1–4 [Potidaea], 108 no. 1; Price and Waggoner 1975: 192–193 [Skione]; Gaebler 1935: 114 no. 1–3; Hardwick 1998: pl. 29 [Torone]). Inscriptions were later put on issues of the cities in question: names of magistrates (Torone and Abdera),[34] the ethnic or simply part of it on the obverse (Abdera,[35] Mende, Potidaea, Skione, Sermylia) (Price 1987: 44–46), while later silver issues (after 460 BC) of some of these cities bear the ethnic in a developed form on the reverse (Price 1987: 44). These legends allow us to attribute these coinages to our cities. Olivier Picard summarizes this *locus communis* (at least among numismatists) in a most valuable phrase.[36] He underlines the point that the numismatic habits of the Greek cities of the North do not differ at all from those of the Classical Greek world south of the Haliakmon: "dans la Grèce classique, le type frappé sur la monnaie (qu'il soit accompagné ou non de l'ethnique, qui ne joue qu'un rôle secondaire) permet d'identifier la cité émettrice et donc de savoir où la pièce a cours légal" (Picard 2000a: 245). These habits can be further illustrated by the coins produced by a number of Greek cities in the Chalkidike that struck Euboean staters bearing similar obverse types displaying "Tierkämpfe".[37] From Akanthos comes a fight between a lion and a bull; from Mende, between a lion and a donkey; from Skione, between a lion and a deer; and from Stageira, between a lion and a boar. The presence of the distinctive emblems of various cities representing animals such as bulls, donkeys, deer, and boars fighting against odds allow one to attribute the coins to their minting authorities without problems.

Things are very different with some "Thraco-Macedonian" coinages struck on the Thasian version of the so-called Thraco-Macedonian standard. These coinages bear the same obverse types and different ethnics (Picard 2000a: 243–244). Furthermore, all the minting authorities issuing these types changed them simultaneously. Picard (2000a: 245) concluded "le rapport entre l'image monétaire et le pouvoir émetteur n'est pas le même que pour les cités. Dans notre région, un même type est couramment associé à de noms différents… et le même nom se retrouve dans des séries distinctes… le type monétaire ne renvoie pas à l'autorité émettrice".

---

34. On Torone, see Hardwick (1998: pl. 29).

35. According to Price (1987: 45), the beginning of period IV is absent from the Decadrachm hoard buried c. 465/60 BC; Chryssanthaki (2000: 72ff): beginning of period IV, c. 450 BC.

36. Picard (1995: 1071): "l'étude de l'origine de ces monnaies au bouc présente les mêmes difficultés que toutes les séries monétaires archaïques anonymes qui n'ont pas été suivies d'émissions plus récentes où le type monétaire, qu'il soit identique ou qu'il ait quelque peu évolué, se présente désormais accompagné d'un ethnique qui assure l'identité de l'atelier émetteur".

37. See also Picard (2000a: 242). The city of Mende is not included in his table on p. 242. On Mende's coins of that type included in the Asyut hoard (*IGCH* 1644: Price and Waggoner 1975: pl. XI no. 192), see also Tselekas (2000)—an unknown mint according to Tselekas—and Mende according to Psoma (2003b: 43). The second specimen of Mende was part of the Asyut hoard (Price and Waggoner 1975: 40 no. 166).

Picard would seem to be almost correct in regard to these "Thraco-Macedonian" coinages. The fact that he includes the "Lete" coinage and the "goats of Aigai" among these coinages is, however, slightly surprising, because their types are not to be found on other coinages. We have already attributed elsewhere (Psoma 2003a: 239) to the city of Galepsos the early fifth-century "goats of Aigai", a coinage on the same Thasian version of the "Thraco-Macedonian" standard, including staters (plate 4 no. 22) and an important number of fractions, *hēmiekta*, and *tritēmora*, on the grounds that Galepsos' fourth-century bronze coins also bear the "Aigai goat" type on their reverse (plate 4 no. 23) while some of the latest fifth-century silver issues of staters and *hēmiekta* have the initials of the ethnic in the Thasian alphabet (ΛΑ=ΓΑ: plate 4 no. 17). The "Aigai goats" types were never shared by another minting authority. This is also the case with the anepigraphic "Lete" types, which, in light of the evidence discussed above, should be connected to a single minting authority, a city situated somewhere in the Thasian Peraia. In view of this, these two coinages should be included in the two tables for the cities in Picard (2000a: 242), and certainly in the first table entitled "Cités à l'Est de Strymon (Maronée, Abdère, Dicaea, Thasos, Argilos)".[38]

The same evidence means that the "Lete" coinage has to be attributed to a civic mint of the so-called mining district. Only a few cities existed in this area at this early period. The Athenian Tribute Lists (*ATL*) and the meager literary evidence give us some information on these Greek settlements.[39] Just west of the Strymon stood Argilos (Liampi 1994), an Andrian colony, while east of the river lay Eion (Isaac 1986: 60–62; Papazoglou 1988: 388–389), which, following Koukouli-Chrysanthaki (2000: 366 n. 126–127; Smith 1999: 35–36), we consider a Thasian settlement. Further east were situated Galepsos (Isaac 1986: 63–64; Psoma 2003a), Apollonia(?), Oisyme, Pistyros, and Neapolis (Isaac 1986: 65–70), all Thasian colonies.[40] A supposed city named Perne is also mentioned by later writers as being a Thasian settlement.[41] The legendary Datos is also to be found in the same area.[42] All these cities, with the exception of Datos, are situated on the coast and are related in one way or another to Thasos.[43] The influence of this Parian colony north of the coastline is revealed by the rich archaeological material excavated at many sites.[44] The literary evidence concerning the mines controlled by the Thasians in the very early fifth century BC and the Thasian presence on the coast in later periods both reveal the existence of what is termed today the

38. Although Argilos is situated west of the river. It is interesting to note that Smith (1999: 25–32) proposed an attribution to a Greek city based on completely different arguments.

39. See also *ATL* 1.232 (Argilos), 426–427 (Tragilos), 373 (Pergamos), 252–253 (Galepsos), 354–355 (Neapolis), 324–325 (Kystiros), 244–245 (Berge); Isaac (1986, 59 [Berge], 60–62 [Eion], 62–63 [Phagres], 63–64 [Galepsos], 64–65 [Oisyme], 65 [Apollonia and Antisara], 66–69 [Neapolis], 70 [Pistyros], 70–71 [Stryme]).

40. See also Isaac (1986: 60–70), and Pébarthe (1999: 136–137).

41. On Perne, see Psoma (2000–03: 242) and the unique British Museum stater of 9 g bearing the centaur-maenad couple and the legend [Π]ΕΡΝΑΙΩΝ (Svoronos 1919: 60, pl. VI no. 13).

42. See note 54 below.

43. Antisara is reported by Stephanos Byzantios (s.v. *Antisara*) to be the *epineion* of Datos.

44. See the remarkable synthesis of all archaeological evidence by Koukouli-Chrysanthaki (2002).

Thasian Peraia (Pébarthe 1999; Funke 1999: 58–60) and is called by ancient literary tradition and inscriptions the ΗΠΕΙΡΟΣ (Picard 1994: 466; Brunet 1997: 229–230 n. 2). Some other cities of the area situated inland, namely Tragilos, Gazoros, and Berge in Bisaltia, as well as Phagres and Pergamos, the last two being cities of the Pieres, are also mentioned by the literary tradition and in some cases also by the Athenian Tribute Lists.

The Athenian Tribute Lists

Of the limited number of cities in this general area mentioned by the literary evidence, we will concentrate our interest on those mentioned by the Athenian Tribute Lists (*ATL* 1.232 [Argilos], 426–427 [Tragilos], 373 [Pergamos], 252–253 [Galepsos], 354–355 [Neapolis], 324–325 [Kystiros], 244–245 [Berge]). This most important document of ancient Greek history reveals a limited number of cities in the area of the Strymon as well as west of the river. Amphipolis, founded by a prominent Athenian in only 437 (Papastavru 1936: 11–13; 1965: 17–19), after years of desperate Athenian efforts (Meiggs 1972: 68ff, 84ff), is never listed as a tribute payer for reasons already discussed in detail by others (Kallet-Marx 1993: 175–176 with previous bibliography).

Argilos

Argilos, an Andrian colony (Isaac 1986: 60–62; Papazoglou 1988: 388–389) situated on the coast some kilometers west of the river mouth, paid one talent tribute to the Athenians from 454/3 until the mid-430s (*IG* I³ 259.4.22; 266.2.30; 267.2.5; 268.3.6; 269.3.21; 270.3.21; 271.2.56; 272.1.50; [274.6.15]), and 1,000 drachms in 433/2 (*IG* I³ 279.2.54), 430/29 (*IG* I³ 281.2.24), and 429/8 (*IG* I³ 282.2.9). Argilos is also mentioned in the 425/4 *taxis phorou* (*IG* I³ 71.3.177). The much-discussed amount of 10.5 talents of 454/3[45] is very probably the result of obscure historical events of the late 450s and a supposed temporary control of mints or trade routes by this city. This same year, 454/3, is considered by some ancient sources as the first year of the reign of Perdiccas II and as the last year of the reign of his father Alexander I.[46]

In the late sixth century BC and later on, Argilos struck silver coins on the "Chalcidic"[47] divergence of the so-called Thraco-Macedonian standard with Pegasus on the obverse. This same type of winged horse also occurs in later issues of Argilos, which makes the attribution of the archaic Pegasi possible (Liampi 1994).

Tragilos

Tragilos, a city in Bisaltia (Isaac 1986: 54; Papazoglou 1988: 361–362), close to the modern

---

45. For the most recent discussion, see Liampi (1994: 23).

46. According to the *Marmor Parium* (*FGrH* 239 A 58 = *IG* XII 5 444.a58) and Nicomedes of Acanthus (*FGrH* 772 F2), Perdiccas II reigned over forty-one years. See Hammond (1979: 103–104).

47. For what I call the "Chalcidic" divergence of the so-called Thraco-Macedonian standard, see Psoma (2003: 230).

Aidhonochori (Koukouli-Chrysanthaki 1968: 358–359; Isaac 1986: 5–6),[48] was assessed at one talent in the famous 425/4 assessment (*IG* I³ 71.4.112) and in 422/1 (*IG* I³ 77.5.25). The city of Tragilos struck coins after the mid-fifth century BC and later on. The types of these issues, ear of corn and bunch of grapes, were clearly inspired by the rich agricultural production of the area. Tragilos' fourth-century bronze issues bear a head of Hermes wearing a *petasos* on the obverse and a rose on the reverse (Papaevangelou 1995).

Phagres

The Pierian city of Phagres (Isaac 1986: 62–63; Papazoglou 1988: 389–390; Loukopoulou 2004: 865), located in modern Orphani (Papazoglou 1998: 390 n. 31), is not explicitly mentioned by the Athenian Tribute Lists. However, in the assessment of 425/4, the Phagresioi are eventually included in the obscure *Pieres para Pergamon* (*IG* I³ 71.4.62–63). During the fourth century BC, Phagres issued bronze coins with a head of Apollo on the obverse and the forepart of a lion on the reverse (Liampi 1991).

Pergamos

The second Pierian *teichos* listed by Herodotus (7.112.1) after Phagres, Pergamos[49] is also mentioned in the assessment of 425/4 BC (*IG* I³ 71.4.64: [Περγ]αμ[οτειχῖται]). A unique coin in the Numismatic Museum in Athens (plate 4 no. 18) has been recently attributed to that small city (Psoma 2000–03: 241–241 n. 41), which must be located in Koules Mousthenis (Pikoulas 2001a: 176–179). The silver *hēmiekton* of the end of the second quarter of the fifth century BC bears the head of a goat on the obverse, two ivy leaves, and the initials ΠΕ on the reverse.

Galepsos

Galepsos (Koukouli-Chrysanthaki 1980: 319–320; Isaac 1986: 63–64; Papazoglou 1988: 398–399; Loukopoulou 2004: 861), a Thasian colony on the mainland (modern Gaïdourokastro), was assessed for the first time in 454/3, at one talent; at 3,000 drachms from 454/3 (*IG* I³ 259.4.15) to 446/5 (*IG* I³ 266.2.14); at 3,000 drachms from 443/2 (*IG* I³ 269.3.3) to 440/39 (*IG* I³ 272.2.57); and at 1,000 drachms from 433/2 (*IG* I³ 279.2.35) to 429/8 (*IG* I³ 282.2.21). Elsewhere I have attributed to Galepsos the famous goat coinage, staters and fractions on the "Thasian" standard with the "Aigai" goat on the obverse (plate 4 nos. 17, 22; Psoma 2003a). These issues date from the first half of the fifth century BC (Psoma 2003a: 233 n. 42) and were also part of various hoards buried in Egypt and the East (Psoma 2003a: 233 n. 43–45). "Aigai" *hēmiekta* found in the excavations of the cemetery of Galepsos strengthen this attribution.[50]

48. Although Isaac does not seem convinced by the identification of the ancient city of Tragilos with the modern village of Aidhonochori, proposed by both Perdrizet (1900) and Koukouli-Chrysanthaki (1968: 359), coins of Tragilos are usually found in excavations of that site.
49. Pikoulas does not mention the 425/4 assessment (2001a: 176). Cf. Loukopoulou (2004: 857).
50. The author is grateful to Mr. V. Poulios for this information.

Neapolis

Neapolis par'Antisaran (the modern Kavala), another Thasian colony on the mainland east of Galepsos and Oisyme, paid 1,000 drachms to the League from 454/3 (*IG* I³ 259.6.9) to 429/8 (*IG* I³ 282.2.19). The Thasian-standard coinage of Neapolis is well known and present in Archaic hoards buried in Egypt and the East.[51] The Gorgoneion on the obverse reveals the importance of the cult of Athena at Neapolis (Gaebler 1935: 79; Kraay 1976: 150).[52]

Kystiros

Kystiros, which, like Pistyros, is mentioned by the literary sources, is another Thasian colony on the mainland (Isaac 1986: 70), and was assessed at the small amount of 300 drachms in 434/3 (*IG* I³ 278.6.37). Coins have not yet been attributed to that city. The archaeological site of Pontolivado, where an important early-fifth-century hoard was found, has been identified with Pistyros.[53]

Datos

The city mentioned by ancient writers as Δατὸς ἀγαθῶν is located inland, in the area of Krenides, close to the site of the later Philippi. Its *chora* is mentioned in a fourth-century inscription from Philippi, and its *epineion* was Antisara, according to Stephanus.[54] A certain Timandros was the *thearodokos* of Asclepius around 360 for the city of Datos (*IG* IV² 1 94.1b.32). Datos is also mentioned in the fifth-century historiographic tradition (Hdt. 9.75), although coins have so far not been attributed to the city.

Eion

An attribution to Eion (Smith 1999: 32–39, 168) seems rather problematic. This strongly fortified (Hdt. 7.107.2; cf. Loukopoulou 2004: 860–861) western "Thasian" colony was a supply base for the Persian army (Hdt. 7.25.2) from 513 to 476/5, under the command of a Persian governor (Hdt. 7.107).

---

51. Neapolis' staters were part of the following hoards: *IGCH* 1185 (Rhodes 1880, 450 BC: 1 stater; cf. *CH* 8.21 [Kagan 1992], Rhodes? before 1880, 500 BC), *IGCH* 1637 (Demanhur 1900/01, 500 BC: 4 staters), *IGCH* 1638 (Delta 1887, 500 BC: 1 stater), *IGCH* 1639 (Sakha 1897, 460 BC, 1 stater), *IGCH* 1640 (Benha el Asl 1929, 485 BC: 1 stater, 1 fragment), *IGCH* 1646 (Fayum 1957, 460 BC: 1 stater), *CH* 2.10 (Egypt 1971/72, 500 BC: 1 stater), *CH* 7.10 (500 BC: 1 stater; cf. *IGCH* 1874), *CH* 7.12 (Syria 1978/79, 480 BC: 1 fragment of stater; cf. *CH* 6.4–5), *CH* 7.16 (Near East 1980, 475 BC: 1 fragment of stater), *CH* 8.44 (part of *IGCH* 1644). For Neapolis' specimens in hoards buried in European ground, see *CH* 8.16 (Pontolivado 1971, 510 BC: 12 staters, 4 *hēmiekta*), *IGCH* 363 (Chalkidike c. 1936, 400–375 BC: 15 drachms, 50 triobols), *IGCH* 364 (Aidhonochori c. 1936, 400–375 BC: 40 drachms, 35 triobols), *CH* 8.75 (Drama 1983: 1 triobol), *CH* 7.46 (Potamoi of Drama 1981, 325 BC: 340 triobols), *CH* 9.61 (Gazoros, eastern Macedonia, 375–350 BC: 1 triobol).

52. See also Loukopoulou (2004: 862–864).

53. On the Pontolivado hoard, see Oeconomides (1990). On the identification with Pistyros, see Koukouli-Chrysanthaki (1980: 322–325), Isaac (1986: 70), Pébarthe (1999: 136–137 n. 59), Loukopoulou (2004, 866-867).

54. See note 43, above. See also Picard (1994), Counillon (1998), and Loukopoulou (2004: 859–860).

Berge

Berge (Papazoglou 1988: 355–359),[55] an inland city,[56] was assessed for the first time in 452/1 at the amount of 2,880 drachms (*IG* I³ 261.4.29).[57] In 447/6, its contribution was raised to 5,400 drachms (*IG* I³ 265.1.93) and in 435/4 was readjusted to 4,200 drachms (*IG* I³ 277.6.30). The same amount occurs also in 433/2 (*IG* I³ 279.2.51) and 432/1 (*IG* I³ 280.2.43). The ethnic of the city is also mentioned in 429/8 (*IG* I³ 282.2.32).

On the basis of an inscription found in the important archaeological site in the vicinity of Neos Skopos, on the east bank of the Strymon, the *editor princeps*, Z. Bonias, and Koukouli-Chrysanthaki have identified the site as Berge. Although a private document, as Matthaiou (2000–03) has shown in masterly fashion, the inscription from Berge of the first half of the fifth century BC reveals a strong Thasian influence. It was written in the Thasian alphabet and the Ionic dialect. The person, who according to the inscription received land by lot from the city of Berge, bore the name Timesikrates, which occurs in Thasos but is extremely rare in mainland Greece.

The strong ties between Berge and Thasos are also relevant for the Classical period silver and bronze coinage of the city (plate 3–4 nos. 8, 9, 24, 25).[58] During the fourth century, Berge struck small bronze coins (*khalkoi*) with the head of a satyr on the obverse and a fish, probably a reference to the alluvial environment, on the reverse (plate 4 no. 24).[59] The fourth-century silver *tritai* (or *drachmai*) of Berge, one of which was part of a small circulation hoard buried in the middle of the fourth century in the cemetery of neighboring Gazoros (*CH* 9.61),[60] follow the Thasian version of the "Thraco-Macedonian" standard and

55. According to Strabo (7 frag. 36), Berge was a *kōmē* situated in the land of the Bisaltai, about 200 *stadia* from Amphipolis. The Ptolemaus manuscript tradition of Ptolemy's *Geography* (3.12.28) reveals that Berge was a city either of the Odomantike or of Bisaltia (cf. Müller, *Ptol.* 510.4 and 514.2; Papazoglou 1988: 358). An inscription of the early third century AD reveals the location of the city in the vicinity of Serres, Hadrianoupolis, Gazoros, and Skimbertos (Edson 1947: 94). Serres and Gazoros (Papazoglou 1988: 379–385) are both situated east of the river. The literary and epigraphic evidence was discussed by Papazoglou (1988: 355–359), who proposed locating the city in Nigrita, west of the river, although she would seem to have believed that Berge might also be located east of the Strymon. Papazoglou rightly pointed out that it was difficult "d'indiquer dans la région comprise entre Amphipolis et Serrès, une localité archéologique susceptible d'être identifiée à Bergè… il ne reste qu'à attendre une découverte épigraphique qui tranchera la question". In recent years, archaeological evidence as well as epigraphic evidence has thrown light on the problem of the location of Berge. Koukouli-Chrysanthaki (2000: 359 nos. 71, 73, 74) and Bonias (2000) gave almost simultaneously a few years ago a description of the important archaeological site of Neos Skopos, whose older remains are dated to the Late Bronze Age. The site was continuously used during the Early Iron Age (c. 600 BC in North Greece), and also has Classical, Hellenistic, and Roman phases (cf. Loukopoulou 2004: 858–859).

56. For Pseudo-Skymnos 654, Berge was situated a long way from the coast.

57. See also *IG* I³ 262.4.24 of 451/0 BC.

58. On the Thasian inspiration for these coins, see Picard (1985; 1987: 159–160). Picard considered the silver *tritai* with the legend BEPΓAIOY as Thasian issues, and the inscription BEPΓAIOY as the name of a magistrate.

59. Psoma (2002: 221), following Picard (1985: 182) and *contra* Peter (1997: 105–106), Archibald (1998: 129–130; 1999: 363), and Fischer-Bossert (1998: 199).

60. For the attribution of these coins to Berge (a *locus communis* among historians but not shared by numismatists), see Psoma (2002).

bear the Thasian type of satyr and maenad on the obverse (plate 4 no. 25). Bergaean fourth-century silver issues and Thasian third-period silver issues[61] differ only in their legends. The Thasian issues and the first issues of Berge bear the legend on the obverse; later on, the legend of the *tritai* of Berge moved to the reverse, in a more developed form.

The Proposed Attribution of the "Lete" Coinage

We saw above the coinages attributed to the cities of the western part of the central Thracian district mentioned in the Athenian Tribute Lists, namely, west of the Strymon, Argilos and Tragilos, and, east of the river and closer to the mountain Pangaion, Phagres, Pergamos, Galepsos, Neapolis, and Berge. Argilos struck pegasi, following a "Chalcidian" weight standard; Galepsos, the "Aigai" goats; and Neapolis, the Gorgoneia, following the "Thasian" standard. Small issues of silver and later bronze coins were struck by Tragilos, Phagres, Pergamos, and Oisyme, a Thasian colony that never appears in the Athenian Tribute Lists (see Isaac 1986: 66). Silver and bronze coins bear types inspired either by the rich agricultural production of the region, as in the case of Tragilos and Pergamos or, in the case of Neapolis, Phagres, Oisyme, and Pergamos, by their own or their prestigious neighbors' and metropolis' religious background (Psoma 2003a: 233–234; 2000–03: 236–237). The Dionysian circle is clearly very important in Thasos (satyr and nymph), Galepsos (goat and head of Apollo/goat), Pergamos (goat/ivy leaves), and Berge (satyr/nymph and head of satyr). If Galepsos and Pergamos chose the Dionysian goat for their coinage, Berge followed Thasos very closely in the first half of the fourth century BC.

To return to the "Lete" coinage: for all the reasons presented above, I am tempted to attribute this coinage to a civic mint of the western part of the central Thracian district. Either Datos or Berge was probably the minting authority of the "Lete" coinage. Coins have never been attributed to the city of Datos. This is not, however, the case with Berge and this, together with the fact that the fourth-century Bergaean coin types display the satyr-maenad couple, are the reasons why we are tempted to attribute the "Lete" coinage to the city of Berge.

The coinage of Berge began some years before the coinage of Thasos, which adopted the Bergaean monetary standard and types similar to those of Berge: the dancing satyr and maenad couple. During the Archaic period, the couple danced in Berge—and went one step further in the coinage of Thasos. These slightly different types indicate the different minting authorities during the Archaic period. During the early fourth century, when after a long period of time Berge struck its new coinage, the satyr-maenad couple was again the obverse type of its silver *tritai* (or *drachmai*), and the legend ΒΕΡΓ, ΒΕΡΓΑΙ on the obverse moved to the reverse and became ΒΕΡΓΑΙΟΥ (νομίσματος). This allowed the user to identify the minting authority as the city of Berge and not to confuse these issues with the almost

61. On the date of Thasian coinage of the third period, see Picard (1999).

contemporary or slightly earlier output of the Thasian mint.[62] The head of the satyr on the obverse of its bronze coins brings additional evidence to the iconographic prototypes and tradition.

Fractions of this Archaic coinage have been found in the greater area.[63] We mentioned above the Nevrokop hoard and the Archaic coinage in question, which circulated together with Thasian coinage in the Thracian hinterland via the same trade routes. We should also note that the 2003 excavations in Neos Skopos uncovered an Archaic "Lete" stater. Attributing this important coinage to the city of Berge has, however, more than one consequence as regards numismatics and the history of the wider area of the so-called Thasian Peraia, which we shall now explore.

The Creation of the "Thasian" Version of the "Thraco-Macedonian" Weight Standard

As Bergaean coinage was earlier than Thasian coinage, it must be the Bergaean weight standard that was adopted by Thasos and her colonies Neapolis and Galepsos, as well as by other coin-issuing entities under the influence of the "Thasian" weight standard and iconography. The weight standard was therefore created by a city in the vicinity of the mining district. As we noted above, inscriptions from Thasos reveal influences from Asia Minor regarding the divisionary system and related onomastic values. The inscriptions mention staters, *hektai*, and *hēmiekta*. Contacts with Asia Minor and the importation of products from there were important for Thasos during the seventh century BC (Pouilloux 1964: 15–17; 1982: 96). At the end of the sixth century, Histiaeus of Miletus, according to Herodotus (5.23), tried to establish his influence in that same region, with temporary support from the Great King (Briant 2002: 155, 320). Finally, Paros, the mother-city of Thasos and probably of Berge as well, "gehört zur Welt Ostioniens", according to Kontoleon (1964: 73); in light of the divisionary system of its colonies in the North, this certainly seems reasonable.

The Inland Area of the "Thasian Peraia"

Attributing this important coinage to Berge requires that we take a different view of the so-called Thasian Peraia.[64] In the late sixth and early fifth centuries, Berge, instead of being a Thracian settlement on the east bank of the Strymon, was an advanced Greek colony, such as coastal Galepsos and Neapolis, and Thasos itself. Athenian taxation of the fifth century

---

62. The adoption of the Thasian type for the fourth-century coinage of Berge is clearly connected with the importance of Thasian coinage, which remains the most important coinage between the Nestos and the Strymon from the beginning of the fifth century to the mid-fourth century BC. After 479 and the gradual end of the coinages of Galepsos and Berge and the staters of Neapolis, the output of the Thasian mint was the only one that supplied the markets from the Aegean coast to north of the Rhodopes. This, together with the similarity of the archaic types of Berge and Thasos, accounts for the fourth-century types of the city of Berge.

63. We owe this information to Mr. V. Poulios.

64. On the Thasian Peraia see also Pouilloux (1954: 34, 46, 48 n. 6, 56, 62, 74, 107, 109, 149), Koukouli (2000, 2002), and Bonias (2000: 235–245).

and information on literary cycles produced in the city during the fourth century convinced Isaac (1986: 59) that "in the fifth and fourth century, Berge really was a Greek town, even though it was rather far inland". Papazoglou (1988: 384 n. 56) also noted the excellent quality of the archaeological remains at the site of Neos Skopos. Close to the mining district and in the vicinity of the river, the position of the city was carefully chosen by the Parians (or the Thasians). It also seems likely that Berge received a Thasian population later in the early fifth century, as the inscription in the Thasian alphabet of Neos Skopos suggests (Matthaiou 2000–03: 231). Strong Thasian influence appears also in the coinage of Pergamos, a Pierian *teichos*, where Thasian pottery has also been found (Psoma 2000–03). On the west coast of the Strymon, at Tragilos, archaeological remains dating from the second quarter of the sixth century reveal Greek influence (Koukouli-Chrysanthaki 1983: 358–359).

Metropolis and *Apoikia*

If Berge was a Thasian colony, it was the *metropolis*, Thasos, that adopted the types and weight standard of the colony. This phenomenon is paralleled by the case of Abdera and Teos (Chryssanthaki 2000: 153). In the case of Berge, this may be partially explained by the city's proximity to the mining district. Another explanation is also possible: Berge, like Thasos itself, was a Parian colony. The early presence of Parians in North Greece and especially in area of the so-called Epirus and the Strymon is clear in contemporary lyric poetry (Pouilloux 1964, 1982, 1990 [= *BE* 1990: 263, 499]), as well as in one of the earliest Thasian inscriptions, as Pouilloux has convincingly showed (*IG* XII Suppl. 412; Pouilloux 1989, 1990 [= *BE* 1990: 263, 499]). This famous late-sixth-century epigram from Amphipolis' north wall concerns Tokes, who mentions the Parians and their struggle for control of the strategic area of Eion ([Ἠι]όνος ἀνφ' ἐρατῆς ὤλεσι βαρνάμενος). Although both Lazarides and Pouilloux considered Tokes, because of his Thracian name, to be the offspring of a mixed Greek-Thracian marriage (like Thucydides' father), one can deduce from Mihailov's (1983 [1986]: 387–388) observations on the name that Tokes was a Greek, and almost certainly a Parian, who fought with other Parians for Eion.

The strong ties of Paros with the north are also relevant in the case of Neapolis and Galepsos. A fourth-century inscription from Paros reveals arbitration on its part between Thasos and Neapolis, *metropolis* and *apoikia* (*IG* XII 5, 109; cf. also Pouilloux 1954: 184–187; Graham 1971: 76–79). A boundary stone of the second half of the sixth century BC (?) found in Galepsos mentions the *hekatompedos* temple of Demeter (*BE* 1994:433 [Hatzopoulos]).[65] A *hekatompedos* temple was certainly one of the city's most important sanctuaries (although *extra muros*),[66] which demonstrates again the importance of the cult

65. See also Bonias (2000: 239 n. 48).
66. Only two *hekatompedoi* are mentioned in the inscriptions, the Archaic temple of Athena on the Athenian Akropolis and our temple at Galepsos. A temple of Hera of this size in Plataea is mentioned by Thucydides (3.68.3).

of Demeter for Greek colonies (Polignac 1984: 112–118; 1990). Demeter seems to be, together with Herakles and Dionysos, one of the most important deities of both Paros[67] and its colony Thasos.[68] Parian coins as well as coins of Galepsos bear a goat on their obverse (Kraay 1976: 45 n. 2),[69] an animal most obviously connected to the cult of Demeter in Paros (Diog. L. 4.45; Hdt. 6.134; Steph. Byz., s.v. Πάρος).

Thasos and the "Thasian Peraia"

The attribution of important Archaic coinages to cities of the "Thasian Peraia"[70] such as Berge and Galepsos, long considered part of the Thasian state, as well as the evidence discussed above, clearly show that what we know of the "Thasian Peraia" needs to be reconsidered. Thasos' immense resources, described by Herodotus and apparent in both the Archaic and Classical archaeological remains of the city, as well as in the thirty talents that the city paid as *phoros* to the Athenians after 446/5,[71] were derived not so much from the control of Neapolis, Galepsos, and probably Berge[72] as from small *emporia* and well-organized control of commerce in the area (Pouilloux 1954: 37ff, 106–134).[73]

Although new powers such as the Bisaltai emerged in northern Greece after the Persian Wars, Thasos seems to have had enough power to reestablish her influence in the area (Psoma 2003: 240). In 465, increasing Athenian interest in the Strymon valley and its multiple resources, as well as Thasian refusal to give up some *emporia* on the mainland, led to a clash.[74] Alexander I arrived later in Bisaltia (Kagan 1987: 24–25; Price 1987: 43–47; Hatzopoulos and Loukopoulou 1992: 17–25),[75] where Thasos probably reestablished her influence around 450. Berge was at that moment (post-452) a member of the Athenian empire, and was assessed down to the early 420s. There is no written information for the city from the last quarter of the fifth century or the beginning of the fourth century (Isaac 1984: 59; Papazoglou 1988: 357–359; Koukouli-Chrysanthaki 2000: 351; Bonias 2000: 236).[76] Later, in the first half of the fourth century, Berge struck its silver and bronze coinages, recalling her long-defunct Archaic issues on the same standard. It was around 360 that the famous

---

67. On Paros, see Kontoleon (1964) and Rubensohn (1949: 1844–45).

68. On Thasos, see Pouilloux (1954: 25, 74, 330, no. 125.). Cf. *IG* XII 8.363 and Pouilloux (1951: 90–96).

69. On the goat of Parian coins see also Diog. L. 4.45. On Galepsos, Pergamos, and the Parian influences on their coinages, see Psoma (2003: 237–241).

70. On the Peraia, see Thuc. 4.107.3; 5.6.1. Cf. Pouilloux (1954: 106–134), Graham (1971: 81–89), Pébarthe (1999: 136), and Brunet (1997: 231, 234–235).

71. See also Picard (1998: 591–598), where the thirty talents are connected with the end of war indemnities that Thasos paid to the Athenians from 464 BC onward. In the view of Pébarthe (1999: 142), Thasos paid these high amounts to the Athenians after reestablishing control of mines on the Peraia.

72. See also Pébarthe (1999: 136). On the terms *emporia* and *apoikiai*, see also Wilson (1997), Casevitz (1993: 20), and Bresson (1993: 226).

73. See also Picard (1998), Pébarthe (1999: 138), and Loukopoulou (1999: 368–371).

74. On these *emporia* on the mainland, see the remarks of Pébarthe (1999: 136–138).

75. See also Faraguna (1998: 369–377): Alexander's mint had to be located at the Pangaion.

76. See also Brunet (1997: 239–241.77).

writer Antiphanes of Berge,[77] who was a student of Plato and was considered the Münch-hausen of the Classical world, received the sacred ambassadors of the Epidaurian Asklepios in his city (*IG* IV² 1 94.1b.19). The city is also mentioned by later writers: by Strabo, who refers to it as a *kōmē*, as well as by Ptolemy, Stephanus of Byzantion, Hierocles, and Constantine Porphyrogenitus.[78] A citizen of Berge is mentioned in an agonistic inscription from Hellenistic Dion (Tataki 1998: 73, no. 2).

Even if the literary tradition is not rich, the archaeological remains and inscription from Neos Skopos, and now its Archaic coinage, reveal the importance of Berge, a Greek city in the land of either the Bisaltai, the Edonoi, or the Odomantai,[79] and a Greek city in Thrace.

Key to Plates 3–4

1. "Lete", stater, ACBNC (Athens) 6109: 9.69 g
2. "Lete", stater, ACBNC (Athens) 6102: 9.89 g
3. "Lete", stater, ACBNC (Athens) 6103: 9.32 g
4. "Lete", stater, ACBNC (Athens) 6104: 9.83 g
5. "Lete", half-stater, ACBNC (Athens) 6107: 4.68 g
6. "Lete", half-stater, ACBNC (Athens) 6108: 4.56 g
7. "Lete", half-stater, ACBNC (Athens) 6112: 4.83 g
8. "Lete", *hēmiekton*, ACBNC (Athens) 6140: 1.14 g
9. "Lete", *hēmiekton*, ACBNC (Athens) 6139: 1.26 g
10. "Lete", *hēmiekton*, ACBNC (Athens) 6118: 0.81 g
11. "Lete", *hēmiekton*, ACBNC (Athens) 6130: 0.95 g
12. "Lete", *hēmiekton*, ACBNC (Athens) 6125: 0.80 g
13. Thasos, stater, ACBNC (Athens) 7110: 9.77 g
14. Orrescii, stater, ACBNC (Athens) 5136: 9.50 g
15. "Ennea Odoi", stater ACBNC (Athens) 6663: 7.76 g
16. Thasos, *hēmiekton*, ACBNC (Athens) 7145: 1.02 g
17. Galepsos, *hēmiekton*, ACBNC (Athens) 5755: 0.89 g
18. Pergamos, *hēmiekton*, NMA (Athens): 0.89 g
19. "Eion", *hēmiekton*, Archaeological Museum of Cavala: 0.628 g
20. Thasos, *trite*, ACBNC (Athens) 4148: 2.38 g
21. "Lete", stater, ACBNC (Athens) 6110: 8.78 g
22. Galepsos, stater, ACBNC (Athens) 5734: 9.56 g
23. Galepsos, *chalkous*, ACBNC (Athens) 10043: 2.33 g
24. Berge, *chalkous*, Imhoof-Blumer coll. (Berlin): 1.18 g
25. Berge, *trite* (or *drachm*), Archaeological Museum of Cavala: 3.128 g

77. On Antiphanes, see the information collected by Psoma (2002: 222).

78. For the literary evidence, see Detschew (1976: 51–52), Koukouli-Chrysanthaki (2000: 351–353), and Bonias (2000: 236–238).

79. Strabo 7 frg. 36 (ἐν τοῖς Βισάλταις) and Ptol. 3.12.28 (τῆς Ὀδομαντικῆς καί Ἠδωνίδος).

BIBLIOGRAPHY

Archibald, Z. 1998. *The Odrysian kingdom of Thrace. Orpheus unmasked.* Oxford Monographs on Classical Archaeology. Oxford: Clarendon Press.

———. 1999. Review of Peter, U., *Die Münzen der thrakischen Dynasten (5.–3. Jahrhundert v. Chr.). Hintergründe ihrer Prägung. Numismatic Chronicle* 159: 362–364.

ATL: B. D. Meritt, H. T. Wade-Gery, and M. F. McGregor, eds. 1939–1953. *The Athenian tribute lists.* 4 vols. Cambridge, Mass.: Harvard University Press.

Babelon, E. 1932. *Traité des monnaies grecques et romaines. Deuxième partie. Description historique.* Paris.

BÉ: *Bulletin Épigraphique*, published in: *Revue des Études Grecques.*

BIAB: *Bulletin de l'Institut Archéologique Bulgare* (Sofia).

BMC Macedonia: Head, B. V. 1879. *A catalogue of Greek coins. The British Museum (BMC) Macedonia.* London.

Bozkova, A., P. Delev, S. Alexander, and D. Vulcheva. 2002. Koprivlen: A Thracian settlement on the Middle Nestos. In: *Thrace and the Aegean. Proceedings of the VIIIth international congress of Thracology, Sofia-Yambol, 25–29 September 2000,* pp. 469–484. Sofia.

Bonias, Z. 2000. Une inscription de l'ancienne Bergè. *Bulletin de correspondance hellénique* 124: 227–246.

Bresson, A. 1993. Les cités grecques et leurs emporia. In: A. Bresson and P. Rouillard, eds., *L'Emporion,* pp. 163–226. Paris: De Boccard.

Briant, P. 2002. *From Cyrus to Alexander: a history of the Persian Empire,* trans. P. T. Daniels. Winona Lake: Eisenbrauns.

Brunet, M. 1997. Thasos et son empire à la fin du V et au début du IV s. avant Jésus-Christ. In: P. Brulé and J. Oulhen, eds., *Esclavage, guerre, économie en Grèce ancienne, Mélanges Y. Garlan,* pp. 229–242. Rennes: Presses Universitaires de Rennes.

Casevitz, M. 1993. Emporion: emplois classiques et histoire du mot. In: A. Bresson and P. Rouillard, eds., *L'Emporion,* pp. 9–22. Paris: De Boccard.

CH: *Coin Hoards.* 1975–. London: Royal Numismatic Society.

Chryssanthaki, K. 2000. *L'Histoire monétaire d'Abdère du VI avant J.-C. au II siècle après J.-C.* Unpublished doctoral thesis.

Counillon, P. 1998. Datos en Thrace et le Périple de Pseudo-Scylax. *Revue des Études Anciennes* 100: 115–124.

Detschew, D. 1976. *Die thrakischen Sprachreste.* Wien.

Dressel, H., and K. Regling. 1927. Zwei ägyptischer Funde altgriechischer Silbermünzen. *Zeitschrift für Numismatik* 37: 1–138.

Edson, Ch. 1947. Notes on the Thracian phoros. *Classical Philology* 42: 88–105.

Faraguna, M. 1998. Aspetti administrativi e finanziari della monarchia macedone tra IV e III secolo A.C. *Athenaeum* 86: 349–395.

Fischer-Bossert W. 1998. Review of Peter, U., *Die Münzen der thrakischen Dynasten (5.–3. Jahrhundert v. Chr.). Hintergründe ihrer Prägung. Schweizerische Numismatische Rundschau (Revue suisse de numismatique)* 77: 195–202.

Funke, P. 1999. Einige Überlegungen zum Festlandbesitz griechischer Inselstaaten. In: V. Gabrielsen et al., eds., *Hellenistic Rhodes: politics, culture, and society. Papers of an international conference held at Friglsang Manor on 29 August–1 September 1994*, pp. 55–75. Aarhus: Aarhus University Press.

Gaebler, H. 1935. *Die Antiken Münzen Nord-Griechenlands,* Band III, *Makedonia und Paionia.* Berlin: Gerog Reimer.

Graham, A. J. 1971. *Colony and mother city in ancient Greece.* New York: Barnes & Noble.

Hammond, N. G. L. 1979. *A history of Macedonia*, vol. 2. Oxford: Clarendon Press.

———. 1983. The lettering and the iconography of Macedonian coinage. In: W. G. Moon, ed., *Ancient Greek art and iconography*, pp. 245–258. Madison: University of Wisconsin Press.

Hardwick, N. 1998. The coinage of Terone from the fifth to the fourth centuries BC. In: R. Ashton and S. Hurter, eds., *Studies in Greek numismatics in memory of Martin Jessop Price*, pp. 119–134. London: Spink.

Hatzopoulos, M. B. 1994. *Cultes et rites de passage en Macédoine.* ΜΕΛΕΤΗΜΑΤΑ 19. Athens.

———, and L. Loukopoulou. 1992. *Recherches sur les marches orientales des Téménides I.* ΜΕΛΕΤΗΜΑΤΑ 11. Athens.

Head, B. V. 1911. *Historia nummorum.* 2nd ed. Oxford: Clarendon Press.

Hurter, S., and E. Paszthory. 1984. Archaïscher Silberfund aus dem Antilibanon. In: A. Houghton et al., eds., *Studies in honor of Leo Mildenberg: numismatics, art history, archaeology*, pp. 111–125. Wetteren: Cultura.

IG: Inscriptiones Graecae. 1873–.

IGCH: M. Thompson, O. Mørkholm, and C. M. Kraay, eds. 1973. *An inventory of Greek coin hoards.* New York: American Numismatic Society.

Isaac, B. D. 1986. *The Greek settlements of Thrace until the Macedonian conquest.* Leiden.

Kagan, J. H. 1987. The decadrachm hoard: chronology and consequences. In: I. Carradice, ed., *Coinage and administration in the Athenian and Persian empires*, pp. 21–28. BAR International Series 343. Oxford: British Archaeological Reports.

———. 1992. *IGCH* 1185 reconsidered. *Revue belge de numismatique et de sigillographie* 138: 1–24.

———. 1994. An Archaic Greek coin hoard. *Numismatic Chronicle* 154: 17–52.

Kallet-Marx, L. 1993. *Money, expense, and naval power in Thucydides History 1–5.24.* Berkeley: University of California Press.

Kontoleon, N. 1964. Archilochos und Paros. In: J. Pouilloux, ed., *Entretiens de la Fondation Hardt pour l'étude de l'Antiquité Classique X "Archiloque"*, pp. 39–86. Genève.

Koukouli-Chrysanthaki, Ch. 1968. ΑΗΔΟΝΟΧΩΡΙΟΝ. *Αρχαιολογικόν Δελτίον* 23.2: 358–59.

———. 1980. Οἱ ἀποικίες τῆς Θάσου στό Βόρειο Αἰγαῖο. Νεώτερα Εὑρήματα. In: *Α Τοπικό Συνέδριο. Ἡ Καβάλα καί ἡ περιοχή της*, pp. 309–325. Θεσσαλονίκη.

———. 1983. Οἱ ἀνασκαφικές ἔρευνες στήν ἀρχαία Τράγιλο. In: *Αρχαία Μακεδονία III: Ανακοινώσεις κατά το τρίτο Διεθνές Συμπόσιο Θεσσαλονίκη, 21-25 Σεπτεμβρίου 1977*, pp. 123–146. Θεσσαλονίκη.

———. 2000. Αρχαία Βέργη. In: *ΜΥΡΤΟΣ. Μνήμη Ιουλίας Βοκοτοπούλου*, pp. 351–375. Θεσσαλονίκη.

———. 2002. The development of the cities in eastern Macedonia. In: *Thrace and the Aegean, proceedings of the VIII international congress of Thracology, Sofia-Yambol, 25–29 September 2000*, pp. 37–58. Sofia.

Kraay, C. M. 1976. *Archaic and classical Greek coins*. Berkeley: University of California Press.

———. 1977. The Asyut hoard: some comments on chronology. *Numismatic Chronicle* 137: 189–198.

———., and P. R. S. Moorey. 1968. Two fifth-century hoards from the Near East. *Revue numismatique* 124: 181–231.

Lazaridis, D. I. 1976. Ἐπίγραμμα Παρίων ἀπὸ τὴν Ἀμφίπολιν. *Αρχαιολογική Εφεμερίς* 115: 164–181.

Liampi, K. 1994. Ἄργιλος. Ιστορία και Νόμισμα. *Νομισμάτικα Χρόνικα* 13: 7–36.

———. 1991. Η νομισματοκοπία του Φάγρητος. *Νομισμάτικα Χρόνικα* 10: 25–31.

Lorber C. C. 2000. The goats of "Aigai". In: S. Mani-Hurter and C. Arnold Biucchi, eds., *Pour Denyse. Divertissements numismatiques*, pp. 113–133. Berne.

Loukopoulou, L. D. 1999. Sur le statut et l'importance de l'emporion de Pistiros. *Bulletin de correspondance hellénique* 123: 359–371.

———. 2004. Thrace from Strymon to the Nestos. In: M. H. Hansen and Th. H. Nielsen, eds., *An inventory of archaic and classical poleis*. Oxford: Oxford University Press.

Matthaiou, A. P. 2000–03. Ἐπιγραφὴ ἐκ Βέργης. *Ηόρος* 14–16: 227–232.

May, J. M. F. 1965. The coinage of Dikaia-by-Abdera c. 540/35–476/5 BC. *Numismatic Chronicle* 5: 1–25.

Meiggs, R. 1972. *The Athenian empire*. Oxford: Clarendon Press.

Mihailov, G. 1986. L'Onomastique dans l'aire thraco-macédonienne. In: *Αρχαία Μακεδονία IV: Ανακοινώσεις κατά το τέταρτο Διεθνές Συμπόσιο Θεσσαλονίκη, 21-25 Σεπτεμβρίου 1983*, pp. 377–392. Θεσσαλονίκη.

Oeconomides, M. 1990. Αρχαϊκός "θησαυρός" αργυρών νομισμάτων από το Ποντολίβαδο (1971). In: *Μνήμη Δ. Λαζαρίδη. Πόλις και Χώρα στην Αρχαία Μακεδονία και Θράκη, Πρακτικά Αρχαιολογικού Συνεδρίου, Καβάλα 9–11 Μαΐου, 1986* pp. 533–540. Θεσσαλονίκη.

Papaevangelou, Cl. 1995. Τράγιλος. Ενα νομισματοκοπείο στη Βισαλτία, Επιστημονικό Συμπόσιο. In: *Η Νιγρίτα- η Βισαλτία δια μέσου της Ιστορίας, Νιγρίτα 27–28 Νοεμβρίου 1993*, pp. 54–58. Θεσσαλονίκη.

———. 2000. *Η Νομισματοκοπία της Νεαπόλεως.* Unpublished doctoral thesis.

Papazoglou, F. 1988. *Les villes de Macédoine à l'époque romaine. Bulletin de correspondance hellénique* Suppl. 16. Athènes-Paris.

Papastavru, J. 1936. *Amphipolis. Geschichte und Prosopographie,* Klio Beiträge zur Alten Geschichte 37.

———. 1965. *RE Suppl.* X, s.v. Amphipolis: 17–19.

Pébarthe, Chr. 1999. Thasos, l'empire d'Athènes et les emporia de Thrace. *Zeitschrift fur Papyrologie und Epigraphik* 126: 131–154.

Perdrizet, P. 1900. Tragilos. In: *Actes du Congrès International de Numismatique de Paris. CIN*, pp. 149–154. Paris.

Peter, U. 1997. *Die Münzen der thrakischen Dynasten (5.-3. Jahrhundert v. Chr.). Hintergründe ihrer Prägung.* Berlin: Akademie Verlag.

Petrova, E. 1996. The 5th-century BC coins from the Museum of Macedon. *Macedonian Numismatic Journal* 2: 7–12.

Picard, O. 1985. La diffusion du classicisme par les monnaies en Thrace, à la fin du V et au début du IV siècle. In: *Actes du XII Congrès international d'archéologie classique, Athènes 1983,* pp. 180–185.

———. 1987. Monnaies et gravure monétaire à Thasos à la fin du Vᵉ siècle. In: *Φίλια ἔπη εἰς Γεώργιον Μυλωνᾶν,* pp. 150–163. Athens.

———. 1994. Les Thasiens du Continent et la fondation de Philippes. In: *Mélanges en l'honneur de Tran Tam Tinh, Coll. Hier pour aujourd'hui,* pp. 459–473. Paris.

———. 1996. Les monnaies au bouc attribuées à Aigai. *Bulletin de la Société française de numismatique* 50.6: 1071–1075.

———. 1998. Thucydide et le tribut de Thasos. *Revue des Études Anciennes* 100: 591–598.

———. 1999. Le commerce de l'argent dans la charte de Pistiros. In: *Dossier: nouvelles perspectives pour l'étude de l'inscription de Pistiros. Bulletin de correspondance hellénique* 123: 334–346.

———. 2000a. Monnayages en Thrace à l'époque achémenide. In: O. Casabonne, ed., *Mécanismes et innovations monétaires dans l'Anatolie achémenide, Numismatique et Histoire, Actes de la Table Ronde Internationale d'Istanbul, 22–23 mai 1997,* pp. 239–252. Paris: Institut français d'études antoliennes d'Istanbul.

———. 2000b. Le monnayage de Thasos aux époques grecque et romaine. In: Y. Grandjean and Fr. Salviat, eds., *Guide de Thasos. Sites et Monuments 3,* pp. 303–306. Athens.

Pikoulas, Y. A. 2001a. *Ἡ Χώρα τῶν Πιέρων. Συμβολὴ στὴν τοπογραφία της.* Αθήνα.

———. 2001b. Τέχνη και Τεχνική στα αμπέλια και τους οινεώνες της Β. Ελλάδας. In: *Θ' τριήμερο εργασίας, Αδριανή Δράμας, 25–27 Ιουνίου 1999,* ΠΤΙΕ, pp. 83–94.

Pilhofer, P. 1995. *Philippi. I. Die erste christliche Gemeinde Europas, Wissenschaftliche Untersuchungen zum neuen Testament 87.* Tübingen: J. C. B. Mohr.

Polignac, Fr. de, 1984. *La naissance de la cité grecque: cultes, espace et société VIIIᵉ–VIIᵉ siècles avant J.-C.* Paris: Découverte.

———. 1990. Déméter ou l'altérité. In: M. Detienne, ed., *Tracés de fondation*, pp. 289–299. Louvain: Peeters.

Pouilloux, J. 1951. Trois notes thasiennes. I. Le sanctuaire de Démeter. *Bulletin de correspondance hellénique* 75: 90–96.

———. 1954. *Recherches sur l'histoire et les cultes de Thasos*. Paris: De Boccard.

———. 1964. Archiloque et Thasos: Histoire et Poésie. In: J. Pouilloux, ed., *Entretiens de la Fondation Hardt pour l'étude de l'Antiquité Classique X "Archiloque"*, pp. 3–36. Genève.

———. 1982. La fondation de Thasos: archéologie, littérature et critiqe historique. In: L. Hadermann-Miguich et al., eds. *Rayonnement grec. Hommages à Ch. Delvoye*, pp. 90–101. Bruxelles.

———. 1989. Akératos de Thasos: poésie et histoire. In: R. Étienne et al., eds., *Architecture et poésie dans le monde grec. Hommage à G. Roux*, pp. 193–204. Lyon: De Boccard.

———. 1990. Pariens et Thasiens dans le nord de la Grèce à l'époque archaïque. In: *Μνήμη Δ. Λαζαρίδη, Πόλις και Χώρα στην Αρχαία Μακεδονία και Θράκη, Πρακτικά Αρχαιολογικού Συνεδρίου, Καβάλα 7–11 Μαΐου 1986*, pp. 479–484. Θεσσαλονίκη.

Poulios, V. 1998. "Θησαυρός" αργυρών νομισμάτων Φιλίππου Β', Θάσου και Νεάπολης από τους Ποταμούς Δράμας. *Αρχαιολογικόν Δελτίον* 53: 187–256.

Price, M. 1977. Mit Rahineh (1860): *IGCH* 1636. *Coin Hoards* 3: 6–8.

———. 1987. The coinages of the northern Aegean. In: I. Carradice, ed., *Coinage and administration in the Athenian and Persian empires: the ninth Oxford Symposium on coinage and monetary history*, pp. 43–47. BAR International Series 343. Oxford: British Archaeological Reports.

———., and N. Waggoner. 1975. *Archaic Greek coinage: The Asyut hoard*. London: V. C. Vecchi.

Psoma, S. 2001. ΣΤΑΤΕΡ ΜΑΧΟΝ. Η ομάδα νομισμάτων της Σερμυλίας. *Νομισμάτικα Χρόνικα* 20: 13–44.

———. 2002. Le trésor de Gazôros et les monnaies aux légendes ΒΕΡΓ, ΒΕΡΓΑΙ, ΒΕΡΓΑΙΟΥ. *Bulletin de correspondance hellénique* 126: 205–229.

———. 2003a. Les boucs de la Grèce du Nord. Problèmes d'attribution. *Revue numismatique* 159: 227–242.

———. 2003b. La Grèce et les Balkans à l'époque archaïque et classique. In: *Survey of Numismatic Research (1996–2001). The XIII International Numismatic Congress*, pp. 39–71. Madrid.

———. 2000–03. Πέργαμος, τεῖχος Πιέρων. *Ηόρος* 16–19: 233–43.

Robinson, E. S. G. 1973. A hoard of Greek coins from southern Anatolia? *Revue numismatique* 128: 229–237.

Rubensohn, O. 1949. *RE* XVIII4. s.v. *Paros*: 1781–1871.

Sallet, A. von. 1889. *Beschreibung der antiken Münzen II*. Berlin.

Schaeffer, F. A. 1939. Une trouvaille de monnaies archaïques grecques à Ras Shamra. In: *Mélanges syriens offerts à M. René Dussaud*, pp. 461–487. Paris.

Sismanidis, K. 1995 [1998]. Η συνέχεια της έρευνας στα αρχαία Στάγειρα το 1995. *Αρχαιολογικό Έργο στη Μακεδονία και τη Θράκη* 9: 383–393.

Smith, M. N. 1999. *The mint of "Lete" and the development of coinage in the north Aegean*. Unpublished doctoral dissertation, Rhode Island, 1999.

———. 2000. The Archaic Coinage of "Lete". In: B. Kluge und B. Weisser, eds., *XII Internationaler Numismatischer Kongress Berlin 1997, Akten-Proceedings-Actes*, pp. 217–221. Berlin: Staatliche Museen zu Berlin.

Schönert-Geiss, E. 1975. *Die Münzprägung von Bisanthe, Dikaia, Selymbria*. Berlin: Akademie der Wissenschaften.

Stucky, R. A. 1984. Zum Münzschatz von Ras Shamra-Ugarit-Leukos Limen (Syrien). *Schweizerische Numismatische Rundschau (Revue suisse de numismatique)* 63: 5–16.

Svoronos, J. N. 1919. *L'Hellénisme primitif de la Macédoine*. Paris.

Tataki, A. B. 1998. *Macedonians abroad. A contribution to the prosopography of ancient Macedonia*. ΜΕΛΕΤΗΜΑΤΑ 26. Athens.

Tzanavari, K. 2002. Μαρμάρινα αγαλμάτια Άρτεμης από την αρχαία Λητή. In: *Αφιέρωμα στη μνήμη του γλύπτη Στέλιου Τριάντη, Μουσείο Μπενάκη, 1ο Παράρτημα*, pp. 241–261. Αθήνα.

———. 2001. Μαρμάρινο αγάλματιο της Μητέρας των Θεών από την αρχαία Λητή. In: *Άγαλμα. Μελέτες για την Αρχαία Πλαστική προς τιμήν του Γ. Δεσπίνη*, pp. 363–375. Αθήνα.

Troxell, H., and W. F. Spengler. 1969. A hoard of Greek coins from Afghanistan. *American Numismatic Society Museum Notes* 15: 1–19.

Tselekas, P. 2000. Λέων και όνος. Η περίπτωση ενός απροσδιόριστου νομισματοκοπείου. *Όβολός* 4: 51–60.

Valla, M. 2003. Παρατηρήσεις για τη χρήση του χώρου στα όρια της αρχαίας πόλης του Νέου Σκοπού Σερρών. *Αρχαιολογικό Έργο στη Μακεδονία και τη Θράκη* 17: 111–125.

Wartenberg, U. 1998. Calymna calymniated. A nineteenth-century misattribution. In: R. Ashton and Silvia Hurter, eds., *Studies in Greek numismatics in memory of Martin Jessop Price*, pp. 363–371. London: Spink.

Wilson, J.-P. 1997. The nature of Greek overseas settlements in the Archaic period: emporion or apoikia. In: L. G. Mitchell and P. J. Rhodes, eds., *The development of the polis in archaic Greece*, pp. 199–207. London and New York: Routledge.

Zahrnt, M. 1997. Πόλις Μακεδονίας-Πόλις Θράκης. In: *Αφιέρωμα στον N.G.L. Hammond, Παράρτημα Μακεδονικών* 7: 543–550. Θεσσαλονίκη.

Agoranomia: Studies in Money and Exchange Presented to John H. Kroll, pp. 87–98
© 2006 The American Numismatic Society

A Legal Fiction: The Athenian Law of Sale

Edward E. Cohen[*]

In 1950, the German legal scholar Fritz Pringsheim promulgated his "Greek Law of Sale". Although other aspects of this book have drawn heavy criticism,[1] there has been virtually universal acceptance of Pringsheim's insistence on a fundamental rule, which "Greek law never abandoned",[2] that a sale attains juridical significance (that is, gives rise to a legal action for claims relating to the transaction) only through simultaneous payment of the purchase price and delivery of the good being purchased (Pringsheim 1950: 86–90, 179–219).[3] This rule renders the sale of goods or services, for legal purposes, an instantaneous transaction: immediately prior to the exchange, neither party has any juridical obligation or right relative to the other. Since a legal relationship, and hence a basis for court enforcement of an obligation between the parties, could thus arise only upon actual performance of services (or delivery of goods) against actual payment of the full purchase price, Greeks could not enter into legally enforceable "executory" (i.e., future) obligations, such as deferred

[*]Department of Classics and Ancient History (adjunct), University of Pennsylvania.

1. For negative evaluations of Pringsheim's intermixture of Homeric allusions and truncated remnants from Roman Egypt, the collection of "texts across time and space" (von Reden 2001: 74), see Finley (1951) and Préaux (1961), cf. Gernet (1951: 221–222). For a challenge to Pringsheim's alleged "modernizing" assumption of a "sophisticated" Greek economy, see Millett (1990: 180–181).

2. Because of Pringsheim's pervasive insistence on the unity of "Greek law", discussion of his views mandates occasional use of the term (1950). But reference to "Greek law" in this paper should be understood as consonant with Foxhall and Lewis' conclusion that "as a coherent entity it does not exist . . . but as variations on a theme [it] does remain analytically useful" (1996: 2–3). Similarly, see Troianos and Vélissaropoulos-Karakostas (1997: 34–35). With only two special exceptions, *The Greek Law of Sale* was the last book published in English with a title implying the unity of "Greek law" (Gagarin 2005).

3. See in accord: Gernet (1954–1960: 1.261), Jones (1956: 227–232), Wolff (1957, 1961), MacDowell (1978: 138–140), Harris (1988: 360), Millett (1990: 174), von Reden (2001: 74), Maffi (2005).

delivery of merchandise or delayed transfer of ownership of commodities being purchased—or into legally enforceable agreements for the future provision of services. Vendors could not provide credit to a buyer, because, under Pringsheim's formulation, the seller had no continuing legal relationship with the buyer prior to receiving payment, and hence would have had no security interest in the good after transfer. Delivery of a good without simultaneous payment was therefore tantamount to a gift of the item to the would-be buyer. Pringsheim's Greek Law of Sale thus eliminates vendor-supplied credit, and hence the creation of debt-related "credit money", as a source of possible increase in a *polis'* money supply, and thereby provides strong support for M. I. Finley's influential assertion that the money supply at Athens was essentially inelastic because of its reliance on "coin" and because of the lack of "machinery for credit". This inelasticity mandated the essentially "primitive" nature of all ancient economies (Finley 1999: 196–197). Reiterated forcefully over the years, this catechism has come to exert a wide influence.[4]

Yet Pringsheim's Greek Law of Sale, despite its striking acceptance by contemporary scholarship, is incompatible with the ancient sources. In this paper, I will first review the relevant (and unusually numerous) testimonia contradicting Pringsheim's thesis. I will then consider how a conclusion so blatantly in conflict with the actual evidence has come to enjoy such rare uniform approval.

Consensual Agreements at Athens

Athenian sources enunciate, with repetitive consistency, a single fundamental principle entirely incompatible with the modern academic Greek Law of Sale: a mere consensual agreement (*homologia*)[5] is "legally binding" (*kyria*)[6] from the moment of mutual consent, even when the *homologia* is clearly anterior to provision of the service, delivery of the good, or payment in full of the anticipated purchase price. Athenian law thus holds "legally binding…whatever arrangements one party might agree upon with another" (Demosthenes

---

4. Cf., for example, Bogaert (1968: 328, 354–355, 374–375), Rougé (1966: chapters 2 and 7), and Humphreys (1978: 153): "the ancient banks lacked the main function of the modern bank, that of creating credit". With increasing dogmatism, Finley insisted on this orthodoxy over several decades: cf. Finley (1953a: 74), with reference specifically to Classical Athens, Finley (1953b: 490–491), and the first edition of *The Ancient Economy* (Finley 1973: 141–143).

5. For *homologia* as "contract" at Athens, see Vélissaropoulos-Karakostas (1993: 163–165; 2002: 131–136). Refuting Wolff's attempt (1957: 53–61) to define *homologia* as "acknowledgement" or "admission" (cf. Mirhady 2004: 58; Thür 1977: 180–185), Kussmaul (1969: 30–37) offers numerous examples where *homologein* conveys future promissory obligations. Cf. Kussmaul (1985). For Hellenistic and Roman usage of *homologia*, see Soden (1973); for Byzantine and later Greek practice, see Papayiannis (1992: esp. 35).

6. When described as *kyrios*, a law (*nomos*) or decree (*psēphisma*) is "in force" or has "legal effect". See Dem. 24.117: τοὺς ἄλλους νόμους ἀκύρους οἴεται δεῖν εἶναι, αὐτὸν δὲ καὶ τὸν αὐτοῦ νόμον κύριον; Dem. 50.1: περὶ τῶν νόμων, πότερα κύριοί εἰσιν ἢ οὔ; Dem. 23.32 (τὸν νόμον κύριον). Cf. Gernet (1955: 219): "valable et efficace (κύρια)". A court that is *kyrios* is one having legal authority: see Dem. 13.16; 26.9; 57.56. *Akyros* (lacking legal authority): Dem. 24.2, 79, 102, 148, 154. Cf. Vélissaropoulos-Karakostas (2002); Carawan (forthcoming).

47.77).[7] Hypereides records that "the law states: whatever arrangements one party might agree upon with another are legally binding".[8] Demosthenes 42 similarly refers to "the law" that "mutual agreements (*homologiai*) are legally binding".[9] Deinarkhos insists that the "law of the *polis*" imposes legal liability on anyone who violates any agreement (*homologēsas*) made with another citizen.[10]

Isokrates cites the Athenian rule that agreements between individuals ("private agreements": *homologiai idiai*) be "publicly" enforceable, and insists on the importance of complying with these consensual arrangements (*hōmologēmena*).[11] In fact, as Pringsheim concedes,[12] some texts even emphasize this mutuality of commitment as essential to the creation of a legally enforceable obligation. Thus Demosthenes 56.2 confirms the binding effect of "whatever arrangements a party might willingly agree upon with another",[13] and Demosthenes 48 cites "the law" governing agreements "which a willing party has agreed upon and covenanted with another willing party".[14] Breach of such agreements is known to have given rise to a legal action entitled "procedure for the violation of agreements" (*dikē synthēkōn parabaseōs*).[15] Scholars in antiquity consistently report that for the Greeks consensual agreements were legally significant: Aristotle in the *Rhetoric* notes that "the laws" deem "legally binding" (*kyria*) whatever the parties agree upon (provided that these private arrangements are consistent with prevailing law),[16] and Roman commentators and teachers held a similar view of Hellenic legal principles (Asconius *Commentary on Cic. In Verrem* 2.1.36 [91]; Gaius 3.154; cf. Mitteis 1891: 459–475). Even Athenian popular discourse recognized the primacy of consensual agreements among willing parties: in a discussion of the demands of erotic love, the acclaimed playwright Agathon alludes to the city laws sanctifying "that which a willing person should agree upon with another willing person".[17]

---

7. τὸν (νόμον) ὃς κελεύει κύρια εἶναι ὅσα ἂν ἕτερος ἑτέρῳ ὁμολογήσῃ. A naked promise by one party was not itself actionable (Wolff 1966: 322; Vélissaropoulos-Karakostas 1993: 165–166).

8. §13: ὁ νόμος λέγει, ὅσα ἂν ἕτερος ἑτέρῳ ὁμολογήσῃ κύρια εἶναι.

9. Dem. 42.12: τὸν (νόμον) κελεύοντα κυρίας εἶναι τὰς πρὸς ἀλλήλους ὁμολογίας.

10. Dein. 3.4: καὶ ὁ μὲν κοινὸς τῆς πόλεως νόμος, ἐάν τις εἰς ἕνα τινὰ τῶν πολιτῶν ὁμολογήσας τι παραβῇ, τοῦτον ἔνοχον εἶναι κελεύει τῷ ἀδικεῖν. The text (Nouhaud 1990) incorporates Lloyd-Jones' emendation (εἰς ἕνα τινὰ) for manuscripts A and N's ἐναντίον.

11. τὰς μὲν ἰδίας ὁμολογίας δημοσίᾳ κυρίας ἀναγκάζετ᾽ εἶναι (18.24); ἀναγκαῖον εἶναι τοῖς ὡμολογημένοις ἐμμένειν (18.25). On enforcement of private agreements through public procedures, see Carawan (forthcoming).

12. "... ἑκών merely emphasizes that contracts depend on consent, whereas delicts do not" (Pringsheim 1950: 36).

13. τοῖς νόμοις τοῖς ὑμετέροις (sc. Ἀθηναίοις) οἳ κελεύουσι, ὅσα ἂν τις ἑκὼν ἕτερος ἑτέρῳ ὁμολογήσῃ κύρια εἶναι. For the effect of fraud or improper influence on requisite volition, see Wolff (1957: 484 n. 3); Maschke (1926: 162); Simonetos (1939: 193ff); Jones (1956: 222). Cf. Plato *Kriton* 52e, *Laws* 220d.

14. §§ 11, 54: τὸν νόμον...καθ᾽ ὃν τὰς συνθήκας ἐγράψαμεν πρὸς ἡμᾶς αὐτούς...ἃ μὲν ὡμολόγησεν καὶ συνέθετο ἑκὼν πρὸς ἑκόντα.

15. Pollux 8.31. On this procedure, see Katzouros (1981).

16. *Rhet.* 1375b9–10, 1376b: ὁ μὲν κελεύει κύρια εἶναι ἅττ᾽ ἂν συνθῶνται, ὁ δ᾽ ἀπαγορεύει μὴ συντίθεσθαι παρὰ τὸν νόμον...αἱ μὲν συνθῆκαι οὐ ποιοῦσι τὸν νόμον κύριον, οἱ δὲ νόμοι τὰς κατὰ νόμους συνθήκας. Cf. Dem. 24.117, 46.24.

17. Plato *Symp.* 196c2–3: ἃ δ᾽ ἂν ἑκὼν ἑκόντι ὁμολογήσῃ, φασὶν οἱ πόλεως βασιλῆς νόμοι δίκαια εἶναι.

Epigraphic evidence also demonstrates the legal significance of executory agreements. The sale of real estate without payment of the full purchase price—impossible under the Pringsheim thesis—is confirmed by a *horos* inscription published some decades after the appearance of *The Greek Law of Sale*,[18] resolving the interpretation of a number of previously disputed examples of seller-financed mortgages (Finley 1985: nos. 3, 112, 113, 114, 115; *SEG* 34 [1984]: 167). Here an unknown debtor has encumbered, to a certain Philon, land, house, and gardens "for the unpaid portion of the purchase price owed on half the land" (literally, "for the price owed on half the land").[19] "The crucial point about this *horos*" is that "the borrower here had not yet paid over the full price to Philon, but was still able to offer the property as security" (Millett 1990: 178).

Discussions of exchange at Athens often focus only on the transfer of goods and ignore the sale of services (cf. Millett 1990: 171 n. 12).[20] But agreements for the provision of labor often involve covenants for future performance. Executory contractual arrangements for sexual services, for example, were commonplace at Athens.[21] In Lysias 3, Theodotos—in order to enjoy the foreign travel and other enticements offered by a new patron—blatantly violates an agreement with an earlier customer to provide future sex for money already paid.[22] In contrast, Diophantos in Aiskhines 1 resorted to legal procedure to collect monies owed for sexual services provided but never paid for.[23]

But the full importance of mere mutual commitments to buy and sell in the future is best illustrated by the dispute between Epikrates and Athenogenes. This case, involving the purchase and sale of assets, is of significant evidentiary importance because it is the only Athenian business "deal" preserved in detail.[24] In a court presentation written by Hypereides, Epikrates claims that Athenogenes conspired with a manipulative female business

---

18. *SEG* 34 (1984): 167 = Millett (1982, no. 12A): ὅρος χωρίου καὶ οἰκίας καὶ κήπων πεπραμένων ἐπὶ λύσει Φιλίωνι Ἁλαιειτιμῆς ἐνοφειλομένης τοῦ ἡμίσεος χωρίου ϟϟϟ.

19. Millett notes the possibility of an alternative interpretation: "the debtor bought the property from an unnamed third party, paying him in full by borrowing the price of half the land from Philon". But Millett correctly concludes that the interpretation offered in the text above is "by far the more plausible and economical explanation of the text" (in Finley 1985, xvii).

20. The only serious (albeit brief and now dated) studies of the sale of labor services at Athens are Fuks (1951) and Mossé (1976).

21. In fact, the phrase "whoring under contract" (*syngraphē*)—a usage popularized by a prominent *politēs* who had worked as a prostitute—had become idiomatic in local discourse (Aiskh. 1.165).

22. αὐτὸς τριακοσίας δραχμὰς ἔδωκε Θεοδότῳ, συνθήκας πρὸς αὐτὸν ποιησάμενος (Lysias 3.22). His opponent denies the existence but not the possibility of any such contractual arrangement: μηδενὸς αὐτῷ συμβολαίου γεγενημένου...φανερός ἐστιν ἐγκαλέσας οὐδέποτ᾽ ἀργύριον οὐδὲ μνείαν περὶ τούτου οὐδεμίαν ποιησάμενος (§26).

23. Aiskh. 1.158: τίς γὰρ ὑμῶν τὸν ὀρφανὸν καλούμενον Διόφαντον οὐκ οἶδεν, ὃς τὸν ξένον πρὸς τὸν ἄρχοντα ἀπήγαγεν...ἐπαιτιασάμενος τέτταρας δραχμὰς αὐτὸν ὑπὲρ τῆς πράξεως ταύτης ἀπεστερηκέναι...

24. The absence from our corpus of other cases involving sales should not suggest that legal disputes relating to property were in fact rare at Athens. Harrison has identified no fewer than fifteen additional forensic presentations whose contents have not been preserved but whose titles suggest that they focused on issues involving property (1968: 200 n. 1).

broker (Antigona) to induce him to assume the ruinous debts of a worthless perfumery business operated by Midas, Athenogenes' slave—when all he wanted was sex with Midas' son! To that end, Antigona had arranged a transaction in which Epikrates was to pay 4,000 drachmas to Athenogenes as consideration for his freeing Midas and both of his sons.[25] But Athenogenes instead persuaded Epikrates to enter into a written contract providing, *inter alia*, that for 4,000 drachmas Athenogenes would sell to Epikrates the assets of the perfumery, including its inventory and its slave employees. Furthermore, Epikrates was to assume the debts of the business, obligations that (he claims to have been assured) would be easily met by the business' inventory.[26] Negating Pringsheim's insistence on sale as an instantaneous transaction that arises only from an actual transfer of assets and the simultaneous payment of the purchase price, Epikrates never suggests that Athenogenes' failure to deliver assets in an amount equal to (or in excess of) the business' liabilities vitiated his obligation to assume these undisclosed obligations. If consensual agreements alone could not create a legal obligation, Athenogenes would arguably have had no right to retain the 4,000 drachmas, and Epikrates, no obligation to pay the business' obligations. Instead, Epikrates acknowledges that, as a matter of law, consensual arrangements are binding (*kyria*), but only if they are "fair" (*dikaia*).[27] As has been often noted (cf. Whitehead 2000: 267–269; MacDowell 1978: 140; Dorjahn 1935: 279), this is a difficult argument (Epikrates is unable to cite any explicit Athenian legal precept supporting his assertion),[28] and is a contention he would not have been forced to advance were Pringsheim's interpretation of the "Law of Sale" at Athens correct. Indeed, in this case, Epikrates (against his own interest) delineates entry into the contract, not the subsequent delivery and payment, as the source of his legal obligation: once Athenogenes "had entrapped me by contract" (*homologia*) and "I had agreed that I would assume the debts", the creditors inevitably would "later" pursue me.[29]

---

25. The transaction as originally planned—although not a sales transaction—does correspond to Pringsheim's model of simultaneous action by both parties without a prior agreement: Epikrates was to pay the money, which he had already gathered; Athenogenes was simultaneously to manumit the slaves: θεὶς ἐπὶ τὴν τράπεζαν τὰς τετταράκοντα μνᾶς... ἐπ᾽ἐλευθερίᾳ καταβάλλοιμι αὐτῶν τὸ ἀργύριον [§5, 7].

26. §§5–6: τὸ ἀργύριον ἐπ᾽ἐλευθερίᾳ καταβαλεὶς τοῦ Μίδου καὶ τῶν παίδων, ἐγὼ δὲ σοι ἀποδώσομαι αὐτοὺς ὠνῇ καὶ πράσει...Ὅσον μέντοι ὀφείλουσιν ἀργύριον... ταῦτα, ἔφη, σὺ ἀναδέξῃ. Ἔστι δὲ μικρὰ κομιδῇ, καὶ πολλῷ πλείω φορτία ἐστὶ τούτων ἐν τῷ ἐργαστηρίῳ...ὅθεν πάντα ταῦτα διαλυθήσεται ῥᾳδίως. §10: ἐγέγραπτο μὲν τὸ τοῦ Παγκάλου καὶ τοῦ Πολυκλέους ὄνομα διαρρήδην, καὶ ὅτι μύρων τιμαὶ ὠφείλοντο, ἃ ἦν βραχέα τε, καὶ ἐξῆν αὐτοῖς εἰπεῖν ὅτι τὸ μύρον ἄξιον εἴη τοῦ ἀργυρίου τὸ ἐν τῷ ἐργαστηρίῳ.

27. §13: ἐρεῖ δὲ πρὸς ὑμᾶς αὐτίκα μάλα Ἀθηνογένης ὡς ὁ νόμος λέγει, ὅσα ἂν ἕτερος ἑτέρῳ ὁμολογήσῃ κύρια εἶναι. Τά γε δίκαια, ὦ Βέλτιστε, τὰ δὲ μὴ τοὐναντίον ἀπαγορεύει μὴ κύρια εἶναι.

28. In fact, Athenian purchasers—even consumers—were the beneficiaries of virtually no legally imposed safeguards such as warranties relating to the quality or usability of the products sold. See Cohen (2005: 292–293). Epikrates accordingly is able to cite only some limited protections against the making of patently false statements and against the offering of adulterated or defective goods (cf. Dem. 20.9, Harp. s.v. κατὰ τὴν ἀγορὰν ἀψευδεῖν, [Aristot.] *Ath. Pol.* 51.1).

29. § 7: ὁμολογήσας αὐτῷ τὰ χρέα ἀναδέξασθαι...ἐπάξειν μοι ἔμελλεν ὕστερον τοὺς χρήστας καὶ τοὺς πληρωτὰς τῶν ἐράνων ἐν ὁμολογίᾳ λαβών.

As Epikrates puts it, the "great deception" giving rise to his legal travails was the reading, sealing, and guaranteeing of the *homologia*—not the later transfer of the business and its assets.[30] Throughout the speech, he refers to the homologia as the source of his liability.[31] The actual payment of the purchase price and the transfer of the assets is mentioned only in passing, and no legal significance is attributed to it.[32]

The prevalence at Athens of legally enforceable consensual contracts even generated at least one proposal of juridical reform at Athens—from Plato, who was deeply opposed to artful business practices and the profit-seeking business people who engaged in them.[33] The philosopher proposed (for the ideal state sketched in the *Laws*) the prohibition of all commercial exchange other than simultaneous "cash for goods and goods for cash" (*nomisma khrēmatōn, khrēmata nomismatos*). Plato's Magnesia, the state representing not the utopia of the earlier *Republic* but merely a "reformed" Athens (Kahn 1993: xviii–xxiii; cf. Morrow 1993: 592),[34] would deny all right of legal action to a seller seeking repayment of monies lent to a buyer to "pay" for goods acquired from the seller. A vendor financing a sale by entering into an executory contract providing for future payment would have to "grin and bear it" (*stergetō*) if the purchaser did not honor the agreement. Similarly, a buyer would be denied court access to enforce arrangements permitting delayed delivery of goods.[35] Unless consensual understandings had been legally enforceable, Plato would here have had no juridical procedure to reform. As always, "Plato's descriptions must not be taken as simply reproducing actual law" (Pringsheim 1950: 40).

---

30. §§ 7–8: Ἦν ἐνταῦθα ἡ ἐπιβουλὴ καὶ τὸ πλάσμα τὸ μέγα. Ὡς γάρ...ἐγὼ προσωμολόγησα...γραμματεῖον τὸ ἐγγεγραμμένον, ἀνεγίγνωσκεν. Ἦσαν δὲ αὗται συνθῆκαι πρὸς ἐμέ...Καὶ σημαίνεται τὰς συνθήκας εὐθὺς...προσεγγράψας μετ᾽ἐμοῦ Νίκωνα. Only after completion of the contractual arrangements did they actually go to the business premises, following which the price was paid and the assets transferred (§9).

31. Cf., e.g., §§ 10 (τὰ ἀντίγραφα τῶν συνθηκῶν ἀνεγιγνώσκομεν), 14 (συνθήκας κατ᾽ἐμοῦ ἔθου), 15 (ἕτερος νόμος κεῖται περὶ ὧν ὁμολογοῦτες ἀλλήλοις συμβάλλουσιν), 17 (πῶς Ἀθηνογένει γε, κατὰ τῶν ἐμῶν συνθεμένῳ, τοιαῦτα δεῖ κύρια εἶναι...), 18 (ἀναγκασθεὶς ὑπὸ τούτων ταῦτα συνθέσθαι· Εἶτα σὺ ταῖς συνθήκαις ἰσχυρίζῃ ἃς ἐνεδρεύσαντές με, σὺ καὶ ἡ ἑταίρα σου ἐσημήνασθε), 21 (τὰς συνθήκας ἔθεμην), 30 (τὰς κοινὰς τῆς πόλεως συνθήκας παραβὰς ταῖς ἰδίαις πρὸς ἐμὲ ἰσχυρίζεται).

32. §9: τὰς δὲ τετταράκοντα μνᾶς ἐγὼ καταβαλών, τὴν ὠνὴν ἐποιησάμην.

33. For Plato, "market people" (*agoraioi anthrōpoi*) were "defective men" (*phauloi*) who pursued monetary profit because they were incapable of more acceptable cultural and political pursuits (Plato *Republic* 371c; cf. Plato *Protagoras* 347c; *Politikos* 289e).

34. A good example of Plato's recasting of Athenian practice is his proposal for publishing laws: see Bertrand (1997: esp. 27–29).

35. 849e: ἐν τούτοις ἀλλάττεσθαι νόμισμά τε χρημάτων καὶ χρήματα νομίσματος, μὴ προϊέμενον ἄλλον ἑτέρῳ τὴν ἀλλαγήν, ὁ δὲ προέμενος ὡς πιστεύων, ἐάντε κομίσηται καὶ ἂν μή, στεργέτω ὡς οὐκέτι δίκης οὔσης τῶν τοιούτων περὶ συναλλάξεων: "Here [in Magnesia] they must exchange money for goods and goods for money, and never hand over anything without getting something in return; anyone who doesn't bother about this and trusts the other party must grin and bear it whether or not he gets what he's owed, because for such transactions there will be no legal remedy" (translation: Saunders 1951). Cf. *Laws* 915d6–e2 (no legal action for delayed sale or purchase [ἐπὶ ἀναβολῇ πρᾶσιν μηδὲ ὠνὴν]).

The Universal Appeal of Pringsheim's Legal Fiction

In contrast to the paucity of evidence supporting many generally accepted modern "re-constructions" of Athenian law,[36] consensual contracts at Athens are thus attested—as the cases cited show—by a multitude of examples occurring not in a single context, but over a broad range of situations, including taxation, personal services, testamentary transmission of wealth, the obtaining of judgments, the transfer and mortgaging of real estate, business transactions, and maritime finance. Because of the profusion and variety of evidence clearly establishing the existence of consensual contracts in ancient Athens, virtually all scholars before Pringsheim had accepted the legal efficacy of such agreements (cf. Beauchet 1969: 4.12ff; Lipsius 1966: 684ff; Vinogradoff 1922: 230; Mitteis and Wilcken 1912: 73 n. 1; Simonetos 1943: 293; Rabel 1907).[37] How then can we explain the undisputed acceptance for decades of a Greek Law of Sale in conflict with the ancient evidence?

At least part of the explanation probably lies in the appeal that Pringsheim's formulation offered to a very broad range of unrelated modern academic theses and orientations. For scholars insistent on the uniqueness of Roman legal genius, the simplicity of the commercial jurisprudence inherent in the Law of Sale seemed to confirm that at least in practical juridical matters "the Greeks did not achieve doctrines comparable with those of the Romans" (Pringsheim 1950: 4).[38] But for those scholars persuaded of the legal acuity of the Greeks, the simplicity of this formulation allowed demonstrations of the brilliance by which Greeks developed "legal fictions" to compensate for the limitations imposed by the Greek Law of Sale. Pringsheim, who devoted much of his academic career to the now largely discredited task of "discovering" interpolations in the corpus of Roman law (Honoré 2004), similarly deconstructed a broad mass of Greek evidence, purporting to demonstrate how Greek ingenuity might transform a cash sale into the legal fiction of a loan transaction through which the seller advanced to the buyer the funds required for the purchase (1950: 244–247), or how the buyer might obligate a seller through a mere downpayment on the purchase price, in effect obtaining an enforceable option (1950: 333–429). Refinements of detail have been offered by a corps of later scholars[39] who have undertaken to show further (but for jurisdictions other than Athens and at times later than the fourth century) how "the Greek genius

36. The study of ancient Greek law is notoriously bedeviled by lacunae in our evidentiary sources: scholars often consider the text of a law or the existence of a legal principle to be incontrovertibly well established if it is confirmed by two or three testimonia. The accuracy of a portion of the Law against Hybris, for example, is "assured", because it is quoted in two independent texts (Fisher 1992: 36 n. 1).

37. Maschke (1926: 165) recognized a limited number of specific consensual contracts. After the substantial acceptance of Pringsheim's thesis by Wolff (1957: 26ff; 1961: 129ff), only Biscardi continued to assert the legal significance of such agreements (1991: 232ff).

38. The Greek Law of Sale supposedly represented an earlier stage of legal development than that reached by classical Roman law, which permitted legal relationships (*obligationes*) to arise from a multitude of sources, including oral executory agreements (*stipulationes*).

39. For example, Demeyère (1952, 1953), Gernet (1953; 1951: esp. 207–211), Wolff (1957), Kränzlein (1963: 76–82). On legal fictions in Greek law, see Bertrand (2003).

used its versatility and freedom of thought for so shaping the rules of sale as to cope with the variety of daily life and the requirements of a high civilization" (Pringsheim 1950: 243). And for those modern classicists who reject the very existence of "contracts" at Athens (Mirhady 2004: 56), there is great appeal in the replacement of "contracts" by the physical reality of actual delivery and actual payment. Thus Todd claims that "Athenian law had in fact no concept of a contract whatever" and that "the great achievement of Pringsheim was to demolish the myth of the Greek consensual contract", thereby demonstrating that "the Greeks had never abandoned the principle of the cash sale" (Todd 1993: 256–257, 265).[40]

Turning to economics, we find a similar universal attraction to Pringsheim's thesis. For proponents of a "primitive" or "embedded" Athenian economy (one side of the seemingly perpetual dispute on the nature of the ancient economy),[41] "the inflexibility of such a simple system and its inability to meet the sophisticated requirements of a more developed economy" (Millett 1990: 17) have been welcomed as confirming the essentially "primitive" nature of the Athenian economy (Millett 1990: 180–182; Finley 1999: 141; cf. Finley 1985: 298 n. 28).[42] But for the proponents of a "modern" (or "market-oriented") Athenian economy, Pringsheim's rule was also welcome, as it facilitated the demonstration of a variety of sophisticated credit mechanisms.[43] Pringsheim's Law of Sale sometimes appeared to reconcile even economic historians of wildly disparate approaches: Sitta von Reden, a leading practitioner of cultural poetic analysis of the ancient economy, noting the absence in Pringsheim's work of Athenian evidence for his Law, found the missing evidence (still missing, in my opinion) in my positivistic examination of Athenian banking (von Reden 2000: 74).

Over the years, ironically, the only one truly skeptical of Pringsheim's contribution has been Pringsheim. He concluded *The Greek Law of Sale* with the announced expectation that additional research would result in the amendment and correction of many of his interpretations (1950: 502), a diffidence corresponding to his belief that "the whole Greek law of contract must be re-written, or rather must be written for the first time"—a task that he felt unable to undertake (1950: 14). He deemed his own dismissal of consensual contracts merely "a provisional hypothesis" that "may stimulate further investigation" (1950: 14). Unfortunately, the compatibility of Pringsheim's "provisional hypothesis" with so many otherwise divergent approaches has discouraged the reexamination that he called for. For a half century, Pringsheim's desire for correction and revision has remained unfulfilled.

40. In accord: Mirhady (2004: 56).

41. Polarized analysis of the ancient economy was already into its second century when Bücher published in 1893 his seminal "primitivist" exposition of the ancient economy, to which Meyer in 1895 and Beloch in 1902 issued "modernizing" responses. For the decades of dichotomized struggle that have followed, see Cohen (2002), Schaps (1998: 1), Meikle (2002).

42. Gernet considers it a "paradoxe" that the system was able to function "dans un état économique déjà avancé" (1955: 207; cf. Gernet 1955: 222 n. 1).

43. Some scholars have sought to denigrate these transactions as "exceptional" (Finley 1985: 113–114); Millett (1990: 187): "credit sales few and far between". Because of the sparse quantity and fragmentary quality of surviving evidence—limitations compounded by the absence of ancient statistics—characterization of these instances as "exceptional" (without the proffering of "standard" examples) merely confirms *a priori* assumptions.

BIBLIOGRAPHY

Beauchet, L. 1969 [1897]. *Histoire du droit privé de la république athénienne.* 4 vols. Amsterdam. Rodopi.

Beloch, J. 1902. Zur griechischen Wirtschaftsgeschichte. *Zeitschrift für Sozialwissenschaft* 5: 1–97. Reprinted in Finley (1979).

Bertrand, J.-M. 1997. De l'usage de l'épigraphie dans la cité des Magnètes platoniciens. In: G. Thür and J. Vélissaropoulos-Karakostas, eds., *Symposion 1995: Vorträge zur griechischen und hellenistischen Rechtsgeschichte (Korfu, 1.–5. September 1995)*, Akten der Gesellschaft für Griechische und Hellenistische Rechtsgeschichte, Bd. 11, pp. 27–47. Cologne: Böhlau.

———. 2003. De la fiction en droit grec. Quelques réflexions. In: G. Thür and F. Fernández Nieto, eds., *Symposion 1999: Vorträge zur griechischen und hellenistischen Rechtsgeschichte (Pazo de Mariñán, La Coruña, 6.–9. September 1999)*, Akten der Gesellschaft für Griechische und Hellenistische Rechtsgeschichte, Bd. 14, pp. 387–411. Cologne: Böhlau.

Biscardi, A. 1991. *Αρχαίο ελληνικό δίκαιο.* Trans. P. Dimakis. Athens. Originally published in 1982 as *Diritto greco antico.* Papadimas.

Bogaert, R. 1968. *Banques et banquiers dans les cités grecques.* Leyden: A. W. Sijthoff.

Bücher, K. 1893. *Die Entstehung der Volkswirtschaft.* Tübingen: H. Laupp. (Reprinted in Finley 1979).

Carawan, E. Forthcoming. *The Athenian law of agreement.*

Cohen, E. 2002. Introduction. In: P. Cartledge, E. Cohen, and L. Foxhall, eds., *Money, labour, and land: approaches to the economies of ancient Greece,* pp. 1–7. London: Routledge.

———. 2005. Commercial law. In: M. Gagarin and D. Cohen, eds., *The Cambridge companion to ancient Greek law,* pp. 290–302. Cambridge: Cambridge University Press.

Demeyère, J. 1952. La formation de la vente et le transfert de la propriété en droit grec classique. *Archives d'histoire de droit oriental—Revue internationale des droits de l'antiquité* 1: 215–266.

———. 1953. Le contrat de vente en droit grec classique: les obligations des parties. *Archives d'histoire de droit oriental—Revue internationale des droits de l'antiquité* 2: 197–228.

Dorjahn, A. 1935. Anticipation of arguments in Athenian courts. *Transactions of the American Philological Association* 55: 274–295.

Finley, M. 1951. Some problems of Greek law. *Seminar* 9: 72–91.

———. 1953a. Land, debt and the man of property in classical Athens. *Political Science Quarterly* 68: 249–268.

———. 1953b. Multiple charges on real property in Athenian law. In: *Studi in onore di Vincenzo Arangio-Ruiz nel XLV anno del suo insegnamento*, vol. 3, pp. 473–491. Naples: Jovene.

———. 1973. *The ancient economy.* London: Chatto & Windus.

———, ed. 1979. *The Bücher-Meyer controversy.* New York: Arno Press.

————. 1985. *Studies in land and credit in ancient Athens, 500–200* BC: *the horos inscriptions.* New Brunswick, N.J.: Transaction Books. (Originally published in 1951).

————. 1999. *The ancient economy.* Rev. ed. Berkeley: University of California Press.

Fisher, N. 1992. *Hybris: a study in the values of honour and shame in ancient Greece.* Westminster: Aris & Phillips.

Foxhall, L., and A. Lewis. 1996. Introduction. In: L. Foxhall and A. Lewis, eds., *Greek law in its political setting: justification not justice,* pp. 1–8. Oxford: Oxford University Press.

Fuks, A. 1951. *Kolonos misthios*: labour exchange in Classical Athens. *Eranos* 49: 171–173.

Gagarin, M. 2005. The unity of Greek law. In: M. Gagarin and D. Cohen, eds., *The Cambridge companion to ancient Greek law,* pp. 29–40. Cambridge: Cambridge University Press.

Gernet, L. 1951. Le droit de la vente et la notion du contrat en Grèce d'après M. Pringsheim. *Revue historique de droit français et étranger* 29: 560–584. (Reprinted in Gernet's *Droit et société dans la Grèce ancienne,* 1955).

————. 1953. Sur l'obligation contractuelle dans la vente hellénique. *Archives d'histoire de droit oriental—Revue internationale des droits de l'antiquité* 2: 229–247.

————. ed. 1954–60. *Démosthène, Plaidoyers civils* (Collection des Universitès de France). 4 vols. Paris.

————. 1955. *Droit et société dans la Grèce ancienne.* Paris: Recueil Sirey.

Harris, E. 1988. When is a sale not a sale? The riddle of Athenian terminology for real security revisited. *Classical Quarterly* n.s. 38: 351–381.

Harrison, A. 1968–71. *The law of Athens.* 2 vols. Oxford: Oxford University Press.

Honoré, T. 2004. Fritz Pringsheim (1882–1967). In: R. Zimmermann and J. Beatson, eds., *Jurists uprooted: German-speaking emigre lawyers in twentieth-century Britain,* pp. 205–333. Oxford: Oxford University Press.

Humphreys, S. 1978. *Anthropology and the Greeks.* London: Routledge.

Jones, J. 1956. *The law and legal theory of the Greeks.* Oxford: Clarendon Press.

Kahn, C. 1993. Foreword to G. Morrow, *Plato's Cretan city: a historical interpretation of the laws.* Princeton: Princeton University Press.

Katzouros, P. 1981. Pollux et la ῾Δίκη Συνθηκῶν Παραβάσεως᾿. In: P. Dimakis, ed., *Symposion 1979: Vorträge zur griechischen und hellenistischen Rechtsgeschichte (Ägina, 3.–7. September 1979),* Akten der Gesellschaft für Griechische und Hellenistische Rechtsgeschichte, Bd. 4, pp. 197–216. Cologne: Böhlau.

Kränzlein, A. 1963. *Eigentum und Besitz im griechischen Recht des fünften und vierten Jahrhunderts v. Chr.* Berlin: Duncker & Humblot.

Kussmaul, P. 1969. *Synthekai: Beiträge zur Geschichte des attischen Obligationemrechts.* Basel.

————. 1985. Zur Bedeutung von συμβόλαιον bei den attischen Rednern. In: C. Schäublin, ed., *Catalepton. Festschrift für Bernhard Wyss zum 80. Geburtstag,* pp. 31–44. Basel: Seminar für Klassische Philologie der Universität Basel.

Lipsius, J. H. 1966 (1905–15). *Das attische Recht und Rechtsverfahren.* 3 vols. Hildesheim.

MacDowell, D. 1978. *The law in classical Athens.* Ithaca, N.Y.: Cornell University Press.

Maffi, A. 2005. Family and property law. In: M. Gagarin and D. Cohen, eds., *The Cambridge companion to ancient Greek law,* pp. 254–266. Cambridge: Cambridge University Press.

Maschke, R. 1926. *Die Willenslehre im griechischen Recht.* Berlin: G. Stilke.

Meikle, S. 2002. Modernism, economics, and the ancient economy. In: W. Scheidel and S. von Reden, eds., *The ancient economy,* pp. 233–250. New York: Routledge.

Meyer, E. 1895. Die wirtschaftliche Entwicklung des Altertums. *Jahrbücher für Nationalökonomie und Statistik* 9, no. 64: 1–70. (Reprinted in Finley 1979).

Millett, P. 1982. The Attic horoi reconsidered in the light of recent discoveries. *Opus* 1: 219–249.

———. 1990. Sale, credit, and exchange in Athenian law and society. In: P. Cartledge, P. Millett, and S. Todd, eds., *Nomos: essays in Athenian law, politics, and society,* pp. 167–194. Cambridge: Cambridge University Press.

Mirhady, D. 2004. Contracts in Athens. In: D. Cairns and R. Knox, eds., *Law, rhetoric, and comedy in classical Athens: essays in honour of Douglas M. MacDowell,* pp. 51–63. Swansea: Classical Press of Wales.

Mitteis, L. 1891. *Reichsrecht und Volksrecht in den östlichen Provinzen des römischen Kaiserreichs.* Leipzig: B. G. Teubner.

Mitteis, L., and U. Wilcken. 1963 [1912]. *Grundzüge und Chrestomathie der Papyruskunde,* vol. 2, *Juristischer Teil.* Leipzig: B. G. Teubner.

Morrow, G. 1993 [1960]. *Plato's Cretan city: a historical interpretation of the* Laws. Princeton: Princeton University Press.

Mossé, C. 1976. Les salariés à Athènes au IVᵉ siècle. *Dialogues d'Histoire Ancienne* 2: 97–101.

Nouhaud, M. 1990. *Dinarque: Discours.* Paris: Belles Lettres.

Préaux, C. 1961. De la Grèce classique à l'Égypte hellénistique: les formes de la vente d'immeuble. *Chronique d'Égypte* 36: 187–195.

Pringsheim, F. 1950. *The Greek law of sale.* Weimar: H. Böhlaus Nachfolger.

Rougé, J. 1966. *Recherches sur l'organisation du commerce maritime en Mediterranée sous l'empire romain.* Paris: SEVPEN.

Saunders, T. 1951. *Plato: the Laws.* Harmondsworth: Penguin.

Schaps, D. 1998. Review of D. Tandy, *Warriors into traders: the power of the market in early Greece. Bryn Mawr Classical Review* 98.11.1: 1–13.

SEG: Supplementum epigraphicum graecum. 1984–. Amsterdam: J. C. Gieben.

Simonetos, G. 1939. Das Verhältnis von Kauf und Übereignung im altgriechischen Recht. In: M. Kaser, H. Kreller, and W. Kunkel, eds., *Festschrift für Paul Koschaker,* vol. 3, pp. 172–198. Weimar.

———. 1943. Τὰ ἐλαττώματα τῆς βουλήσεως εἰς τὰς δικαιοπραξίας. *Ἀρχεῖον ἰδιωτικοῦ δικαίου* 14: 290–313.

Thür, G. 1977. *Beweisführung von den Schwurgerichtshöfen: Die Proklesis zur Basanos.* Vienna.

Todd, S. 1993. *The shape of Athenian law.* Oxford: Clarendon Press.

———. 1994. Status and contract in fourth-century Athens. In: G. Thür, ed., *Symposion 1993: Vorträge zur griechischen und hellenistischen Rechtsgeschichte (Graz-Andritz, 12.–16. September 1993),* Akten der Gesellschaft für Griechische und Hellenistische Rechtsgeschichte, Bd. 10, pp. 125–140. Cologne: Böhlau.

Troianos, S., and J. Vélissaropoulos-Karakostas. 1997. *Ιστορία Δικαίου, από την αρχαία στη νεώτερη Ελλάδα.* 2nd ed. Athens.

Vélissaropoulos-Karakostas, J. 1993. *Λόγοι Εὐθήνης.* Athens.

———. 2001. Remarques sur la clause κύρια ἡ συγγραφή. In: E. Cantarella and G. Thür, eds., *Symposion 1997: Vorträge zur griechischen und hellenistischen Rechtsgeschichte (Altafiumara, 8.–14. September 1997),* Akten der Gesellschaft für griechische und hellenistische Rechtsgeschichte, Bd. 13, pp. 103–115. Cologne: Böhlau.

———. 2002. Merchants, prostitutes, and the "new poor". In: P. Cartledge, E. Cohen, and L. Foxhall, eds., *Money, labour, and land: approaches to the economies of ancient Greece,* pp. 130–139. London: Routledge.

Vinogradoff, P. 1922. *Outlines of historical jurisprudence,* vol. 2, *The jurisprudence of the Greek city.* Oxford: Oxford University Press.

von Reden, S. 2001. The politics of monetization in third century BC Egypt. In: A. Meadows and K. Shipton, eds., *Money and its uses in the ancient Greek world,* pp. 65–76. Oxford: Oxford University Press.

von Soden, H. 1973. *Untersuchungen zur Homologie in den griechischen Papyri bis Diokletian.* Cologne and Vienna.

Whitehead, D. 2000. *Hypereides: the forensic speeches.* Oxford: Oxford University Press.

Wolff, H. 1957. Die Grundlagen des griechischen Vertragsrechtes. *Zeitschrift der Savigny-Stiftung für Rechtsgeschichte. Romanistische Abteilung* 74: 26–72.

———. 1961. Zur Rechtsnatur der Misthosis. In: *Beiträge zur Rechtsgeschichte Altgriechenlands und des hellenistisch-römischen Ägyptens,* pp. 129–154. Weimar. (Published in English in *The Journal of Juristic Papyrology* 1946: 55–79).

———. 1966. Debt and assumpsit in the light of comparative legal history. *The Irish Jurist* 3: 316–327. (Reprinted in *Opuscula Dispera,* ed. J. Wolf and F. Wieacker, 123–134. Amsterdam, 1974).

Agoranomia: Studies in Money and Exchange Presented to John H. Kroll, pp. 99–108
© 2006 The American Numismatic Society

Athens and Bronze Coinage

CATHERINE GRANDJEAN*

As proof of my admiration for Jack Kroll's work, I offer him the following thoughts on the coinage of Athens, a subject that he knows better than anyone else. This chapter is built upon Jack's work, as well as the conclusions of an interdisciplinary seminar organized by the EHESS (Paris) on the subject of confidence and coinage from antiquity to the introduction of the euro.

Jack has focused several times, like other renowned specialists before him, on the difficult question of the *ponēra chalkia* ("wicked little bronzes") produced in Athens in 405 BC (Ar., *Frogs* 725–726 = Melville-Jones 1993: 86). Using the available written and numismatic sources, Jack demonstrated (Kroll 1996: 139–146; see also Kroll 1976, 1993: 7) that the silver-plated bronze tetradrachms and drachms of the Piraeus 1902 hoard (*IGCH* 46; Oikonomides 1985) belong to this issue. The drachms were struck using at least five pairs of dies—signaling a large output—and, moreover, a number of contemporary plated triobols are also known. Considering that the design of these coins is quite similar to that of the emergency gold coins struck in 407 and 406 by the Athenian mint, and considering as well that not even one bronze coin contemporary with the crisis has ever been found, it is likely that we are dealing more with an official series of plated coins than with the illicit work of counterfeiters.

Bronze coins seem to have been a cause of suspicion and even ire among the Athenians. In the mid-fifth century, Dionysios Chalkous mounted a substantial propaganda campaign in favor of minting bronze, but failed to persuade the Athenians to adopt the metal for coinage (Athenaeus 15.669d). In fact, it was not until the middle of the fourth century that Athens began to mint bronze coinage, long after many other Greek cities had already done

*Université de Tours.

so. It has been argued that Greeks in the Black Sea region and in Magna Graecia, who were in contact with bronze-using non-Greek *ethnē*, advanced this phenomenon (Psoma 2001: 121). The use of bronze for coinage also received a boost during the Peloponnesian War, when several of Sparta's allies—Syracuse, Corinth, Sicyon, and possibly Phlious—seem to have begun striking bronze. Although the chronology of these first bronze coins remains to be confirmed, it is quite clear that this innovation was implemented rather quickly in the Peloponnesus (Grandjean 1990; 2003). In general, there is little doubt that bronze coinage had spread widely in the Greek world by the end of the fifth century, and still more so by the middle of the fourth century.

Since bronze is an alloy formed from comparatively inexpensive metals (copper, tin, and lead), two of which (copper and lead) were quite easy to obtain for only a fraction of the cost of silver, bronze coins generally seem to have been valued over their bullion weight (Price 1968). Metallurgical analyses performed recently on coins of Messene, Thasos, etc., at the CNRS Centre Babelon in Orléans also indicate that some mints, after a transition period perhaps intended to gain users' confidence, reduced the tin content in the coins while increasing the lead, presumably since the latter was much less costly, which further increased the overvaluation (Picard 1998; Grandjean 2003: 245–246). The reason why bronze coinage spread so easily and quickly in the Greek world is probably to be explained by the advantages bronze had for the minting states: (1) the cities—which were fighting expensive wars almost constantly—could fix the nominal value of these coins at their will, and (2) the coins weighed approximately one to three grams, replacing minute silver coins, some of which, like the one-eighth-obol *hēmitetartēmorion*, weighed as little as 0.18 g. These tiny silver coins were difficult to handle and probably wore down quickly.

Given that it was so widely used elsewhere, the Athenians' policy of avoiding bronze coinage in the fifth and early fourth centuries is quite surprising. Why was it that the Athenians, an otherwise inventive and pragmatic people (cf. Thuc. 1.70), took such a long time to adopt bronze coinage for their city? The traditional explanation for this monetary conservatism is simplistic and consists of an apparent political paradox, that Athenian democracy impeded the adoption of bronze coinage while oligarchic regimes faced no opposition or were able to overcome any opposition to its use. More recently, however, other hypotheses concerning this phase of Athenian monetary history have been offered, which explore the link between the Athenians' wealth (*argyrion, chrēmata*) and their political power (Kallet-Marx 1993; Kallet 2001; von Reden 2002: 52–66). To understand the ramifications this work has on the question of the Athenians' adoption of bronze coinage, a brief review of fifth-century Athenian monetary history is in order.

THE ATHENIAN IMPERIAL SYSTEM AND ITS FAILURE

Soon after they became a first-rate naval power under Themistokles in the first decades of the fifth century, the Athenians had to find ways to finance their fleet. The revenue extracted from the Laurion mines was sufficient to finance the initial construction of approximately two hundred triremes (Plut., *Them.* 4.1); thereafter, the city's protection was no longer directly tied to the wealth and skills of individual horsemen and hoplites, but more to the wealth of the community as a whole. Lisa Kallet (2001; Kallet-Marx 1993) has shown that during the course of the fifth century there was a conflation in the minds of the Athenians between the financial wealth of the city and the city's military power, similar to the conflation between notions of a good government and its capacity to generate *chrēmata* (revenues, goods). In time, naval expenses were supported by the city and its wealthiest citizens, who were encouraged to perform trierarchies on a regular basis, and by the *phoros* (tribute) paid by the allies of the Delian League. Because of the additional expenses caused by the Peloponnesian War, this system proved incapable of generating enough funds for a long-term effort. Hence the levy of the *eisphora* in 428 (Thuc. 3.19.1), and then again in 413, 412, and 406, which occurred when occupied Attica could not produce the agricultural exports needed to help offset the tax; landowners and farmers subsequently suffered serious financial harm.

With the Athenians' defeat in Sicily in 413 BC, their allies grew more reluctant to pay the *phoros*, which meant that their income from tribute was drastically reduced to approximately five hundred talents, compared to the five thousand that the city received in 431. After this highpoint, Thucydides (6.12.1, 6.26.2) indicates that the city's financial situation continued to deteriorate during the period of peace, 421–415. In order to regain lost income, especially after the Sicilian disaster, the Athenians created the *eikostē*, a five-percent tax levied on all sea-borne commerce (Thuc. 7.28.4; Kallet 2001: 196–226), and then in 410 they introduced a customs tax in the Bosporus for ships coming from the Black Sea (Xenophon, *Hell.* 1.1.22), despite the fact that the *phoros* was probably once again being paid (cf. Kallet 2001: 223). The permanent occupation of Attica by the Spartans also had financial consequences, as Thucydides notes (7.28.1): "the transport of goods originating from Euboia, which, originally, was routed easily by land from Oropos, through the Decelia region, but which had to be rerouted by sea, around the Sounion Cape, transport that was very expensive: but, all imports were treated the same by the city. This was not a city economy anymore, but one of a fortress." At the same time as well, the escape of slaves from the Laurion silver mines stopped the flow of silver.

In 412 the situation became so bad that it became necessary to dig into the reserve of one thousand talents that had been set aside in 431 (Thuc. 8.15, cf. 2.24.1), and even into the reserve that had been formed during the Persian Wars (Ar., *Lys.* 649). The Athenians fared better between 411 and 407, to the other Greeks' great surprise. However, when the Athenian fleet was completely destroyed by a storm after the victory at Arginusai, there was no hope of rebuilding it because of the lack of money. In his famous oration at the beginning of the war, as recorded by Thucydides (2.13.5), Perikles noted as reserves gold offerings on the Acropolis that could be converted to coin if necessary; this was, in fact, done in 407/6, but the effort generated only fourteen talents of gold coins (the monetary equivalent of roughly 160 talents of silver). These gold coins had the same types and were produced on the same standard as their silver equivalents, but their considerable face value, compared to the silver coinage, meant that they were likely reserved for use in large payments, with the smallest denomination, the hemiobol, probably corresponding to a silver drachm (Nicolet-Pierre 2002: 173–174). It was between 406 and 405 (before the first performance of Aristophanes' *Frogs* in 405) that the plated coins noted earlier were struck. They too have the same types as the normal silver issues and the same diameter, but they are of a slightly lighter weight compared to the regular-issue silver tetradrachms and the drachms. Some silver-plated bronze triobols may be assigned to this period as well (Kroll 1996: 146, fig. 1). Although we have no way of knowing for certain, it is possible that these coins were traded at the full value of regular silver tetradrachms, drachms, and triobols. These plated issues—together with the increasing rarity of the obol fractions—may have contributed to inflation in Athens, but in absence of data to confirm it, this must remain only speculation.

THE DEFEAT OF ATHENS AND ITS CONSEQUENCES

With the worsening situation, the antidemocratic movement in Athens gained ascendancy. Hoping to install an oligarchic regime and restore peace, this movement was not successful on either count, in part because they could not agree among themselves. After the failed coup of 411, they took advantage of the opportunity of another Athenian defeat by the Spartans to seize power in 404, with the blessing of the Spartan general Lysander.

The regime of the Thirty was marked by political turmoil and violence; 1,500 people were executed over a period of eight months. Unable to install a stable regime, the Thirty were ousted from power by an uprising of Athenian citizens, helped by those exiled in Boiotia and by the *dēmos* of Piraeus, with the Spartans remaining neutral. In order to end the *stasis* as quickly as possible and to restore political stability to the city, the crimes of the Thirty were pardoned. After a heated debate on the nature of which type of political regime to install, the Athenians reinstated the democracy, which, though it had not proved itself too effective in the recent past, was still "the one that divided them the least" (Will et al. 1975: 400).

A "return to the past" was enacted in the monetary sphere as well. It is quite possible that the *ponēra chalkia* were taken out of circulation as soon as the new democracy was installed (Kroll 1976: 338–340). Otherwise, the demonetization must have happened in 394–393 at the latest, when the Athenian Konon defeated the Spartans at Knidos, at the head of the Persian fleet. At this point, Athens was reestablishing itself, taking advantage of the rivalries between Sparta and Persia: Persian funds paid for the reconstruction of the "Long Walls", which protected Athens from the threat of a Spartan attack. In any event, Aristophanes indicates that by 393/2 all the plated coins were taken out of circulation:

CITIZEN A. Do you remember when we voted for those bronzes?

CITIZEN B. Yes, and that striking was a bad one for me. I was selling grapes, and had
gone off with my mouth full of bronzes, and went to the market for barley meal. Then,
just as I was holding my bag out, the herald bellowed that no one was to use bronze in
the future: "Starting now we use silver" (*Ecclesiazousae* 815–822; trans. Melville-Jones
1993: 88).

This text leads us to believe that, despite what might have happened in other instances of
Notgeld (cf. [Arist.] *Oec.* 2.2.16b, 1348b23–32), the plated coins were not exchanged for
silver coins at the end of the crisis, but were simply declared *adokimon*, no longer legal
tender.

The evidence for the resumption of minting silver tetradrachms at Athens in the early
fourth century is varied and somewhat indirect. Lysias (*On the Property of Aristophanes*),
indicates that silver was hard to find in Athens in 387, due in part to the slow revival of
the Laurion silver mines. It was not until the foundation of the second Delian League in
378–377—with the implied return of allied monetary contributions (the *syntaxeis*)—that
the situation with Athenian silver income clearly improved. Hoards from Sicily from about
this time indicate that minting had resumed in Athens (Kroll forthcoming), as does Niko-
phon's law of 375 (Stroud 1974; *SEG* 26.72—a *nomos* [law], not merely a simple *psēphisma*
[decree], indicating its importance), wherein *argyrokopoi* are mentioned in lines 54–55; the
law also indicates just how serious the problem of imitative "owls" circulating in Athens had
become, which evidence from the excavations in the Athenian Agora further corroborates
(Kroll 1993: 9).

Evidence for renewed fractional silver and bronze issues, on the other hand, is generally
dated toward the middle of the fourth century. At the end of the 360s, the Athenian *stratēgos*
Timotheos, pressed by the necessity of paying his soldiers during his siege of Olynthos, issued bronze coins that circulated with an enforced value, which generated criticism and ire
among his troops ([Arist.] *Oec.* 2.2.23a, 1350a23–30); he later exchanged them for silver
coins as soon as he was in a position to do. There were also bronze coins that were issued by
the Athenian cleruchy in Salamis, the dating of which is not certain, but could possibly be
as early as the end of the fifth century (Taylor 1997). Also, around the middle of the fourth
century, Eleusinian bronze coinage was issued, with Triptolemos as a type and with the legend ΕΛΕΥΣΙ (Kroll 1993: 24–48). The Athenians did not stop issuing silver obol fractions
during the fourth century, and they did not regularize the use of bronze obol fractions (issued in their name) until after the middle of the fourth century, which, compared to most
Greek mints, was quite late. They started to do so only when the city was suffering from serious financial difficulties during the war against Philip II, a period when there again could
be no expectation of allied monetary contributions.

THE MONETARY QUESTIONS AT THE HEART OF THE DEBATE

The Athenians took considerably more time to integrate bronze coinage into their monetary system when compared to other states equally known for their numismatic conservatism. The use of this bronze coinage would have been an ideal way to conserve silver coinage (still a rarity at this period) for use in military operations and trade (since high-value imported goods were presumably paid for with high-denomination silver currency), while at the same time covering local transactional needs.

The Athenians' resistance to bronze currency is understandable, since their first experiment, the *ponēra chalkia*, was a disaster: this coinage was not issued in a range of fractions, as in the states of the Peloponnesian League, or at a devalued rate, but presumably bore the same face value as the silver tetradrachms and drachms for which they were meant to substitute. The fact that the payment of political indemnities in 405/4 took the form of a wheat distribution rather than coins to purchase wheat (Garnsey 1988: 182, 391), as was generally the case during times of supply crises, leads us to believe that not enough coin fractions were available in this highly monetized city. Inflation might also have been running at such a high rate that actual goods were preferred to money. The money-supply problem was likely made more problematic by the effects of Gresham's law: people still having silver coins or ingots hoarded them as soon as the plated coins were introduced (cf. Lysias 12.10–11). By the end of the fifth century, bronze coinage was no doubt associated in the Athenian mind with financial crises.

Moreover, bronze coins were a relatively new phenomenon, quite different in some respects from precious-metal issues. Because of their highly fiduciary nature they further complicated some of the conceptual problems and abstractions associated with money and coinage (Kurke 1999: 300; Picard 1998; cf. Seaford 2004: 136–146). Conceptually, bronze coins were much more "modern" than coins made of precious metals, in so far as they were much closer to the token-like coins of today, and so required absolute confidence in the issuing authority to offset their lack of recognized intrinsic value. The resistance of the Athenians in this context should not to be considered exceptional behavior. It reminds us, for instance, of the difficulties that the Scottish banker John Law encountered when he attempted to introduce currency notes in eighteenth-century France (cf. Williams 1997: 180–182). Documentation on the introduction of bronze coinage in the Peloponnesus is scarce, and nowhere do we find evidence that it met with users' opposition in the cities of the region, which were famous for their metalworking but lacked their own sources of silver. It is true, however, that some of these cities experienced *staseis* in the fourth century (e.g., Corinth at the beginning of the century, Phlious in 383, and Sicyon after the battle of Leuctra), and several of these *staseis* could have been caused, at least partially, by conflicts between debtors and lenders, and therefore, as in modern societies, could have been linked to monetary problems.

Following M. Aglietta and A. Orléan's institutionalist approach to money, confidence must be thought of as a key problem in monetary regulation. They draw a distinction between three forms of confidence. First, *methodic confidence*, linked with habit, derives from the repetition of successful operations concerning trade and debts. Secondly, *hierarchic confidence* comes from the legitimacy of the institution issuing the money, i.e., a state. Thirdly, the fact that monetary policy must be in accordance with some higher level is expressed in the last form of confidence, *ethical confidence*, so called because one must never allow monetary regulation to interfere with the value of private contracts (Aglietta and Orléan 2002: 104–105).

These three forms of confidence had certainly been shaken by both the late fifth-century Athenian financial crisis and the solutions chosen to resolve it, as Aristophanes indicates:

> CHORUS. We have often thought that the same thing has happened to the city, in respect of the good and fine men [*kalous kai kagathous*] among its citizens, as happened with the old coinage and the new gold. We do not make use of these coins, not counterfeit but the fairest of all, as it seems, of all, and the only ones struck well and ringing true among the Greeks and the Barbarians elsewhere, but [we use] these wicked little bronzes [*ponēra chalkia*], struck yesterday and the day before with the worst possible striking. And those of the citizens whom we know to be noble and respectable, just and good and fine, reared in [the traditions of] the wrestling ground, the dance and music, we threaten outrageously and we make use of the bronze ones for every purpose, foreigners, red-heads, villains from evil stock, recent arrivals whom the city in the past would not have used even in the most random way as scapegoats (*Frogs* 718–733 = Melville-Jones 1993: 86).

Aristophanes' testimony is not easy to interpret (cf. Said et al. 1997: 174), but the bronze is rejected here as foreign (and indeed, it is not an Athenian innovation), and there is an obvious association between bronze coinage and the Athenian leaders at the end of the Peloponnesian War. The chorus is opposed to certain political figures, but it is impossible to determine whether these "noble and respectable" citizens are democrats or oligarchs. Aristophanes associates the exceptionally pure silver coinage that Athens uses with its military power and the good regime under which the city is run, as the Athenians themselves did since the fifth century. They viewed themselves as autochthonous as Laurion silver, which, obviously, emanated from Attic soil. We find a similar expression of the concept of the superiority of the Athenian people tied to the wealth, in silver, of their soil in Aeschylus (*Persians* 238) and, albeit more down-to-earth, in Xenophon (*Poroi* 1.5; cf. Kallet-Marx 1993: 25, 98, 205; Kallet 2001: 197; von Reden 2002). In the *Archaeology* and throughout the rest of the *History*, Thucydides clearly associates Athens' wealth in silver with naval power (Kallet-Marx 1993); in addition, wealth and health clearly go together in his eyes and in the eyes of the Greeks more generally (Kallet 2001: 132–140). This leads us to wonder whether the quick restoration of silver coinage and the delayed adoption of bronze coinage in the fourth century cannot be considered as thoughtful measures taken in order to buttress the new democratic regime and avoid any risk of *stasis*, in quite the same way that the *nomothetes* were named to vote on the new laws, the death penalty was reinstated as a measure to safeguard the democracy, and so on. In fact, in 352, Demosthenes drew a parallel between genuine silver coinage and good laws (*nomisma/nomos*), equating those who challenged laws to those who debased silver coinage by adding copper or lead to it (*Against Timocrates* 212–214).

How do we define the connection between Athenian democracy and Athenian silver coinage? Certainly not as a "symbolic" one (Trevett 2001; cf. Kurke 1999), since silver and democracy were never fundamentally connected in ancient Greek thought (cf. Kroll 2000; 2002). As Athens was a highly monetized city whose silver tetradrachm was "the unrivaled international silver currency... in the Eastern and Central Mediterranean" (Kroll 2002), the city was compelled to restore confidence in its coinage for all its users—Athenian citizens and the numerous foreign users alike—in order to regain its financial footing in the wake of the late fifth-century monetary collapse. At home, the restoration of both *methodic* and *ethical* confidence in the Athenian monetary system was also one, if not the best, way to weaken creditor-debtor disputes, which were potentially a serious cause of *stasis*. In short, the revitalization of Athenian silver coinage contributed to the strength of the renewed Athenian democracy, in ways that no bronze coinage ever could.

The Greeks of the Classical period were well acquainted with monetary and currency concerns; they were also aware of how money changes societies (Zelizer 2005: 312–329). This is certainly clear from the debates on coinage that occurred at the end of the Peloponnesian War in Sparta and particularly in Athens, where nearly two centuries before Solon had reformed the weights and measures partly in order to stop *stasis* (Kroll 1998). This tale was quite popular in the fourth century and, we can imagine, resonated soundly in the minds of the Athenians.

ACKNOWLEDGMENTS

The original French text was translated into English by my husband, and much improved by Peter van Alfen. Warmest thanks to them both.

BIBLIOGRAPHY

Aglietta, M. and A. Orléan. 2002. *La monnaie entre violence et confiance*. Paris: O. Jacob.

Garnsey, P. 1988. *Famine and food supply in the Graeco-Roman world: responses to risk and crisis*. Cambridge: Cambridge University Press.

Grandjean, C. 1990. Le monnayage d'argent et de bronze d'Hermionè, Argolide. *Revue numismatique* 6th ser. 32: 28–55.

———. 2003. *Les Messéniens de 370/369 au Ier siècle de notre ère. Bulletin de correspondence hellénique* suppl. 44.

IGCH: M. Thompson, O. Mørkholm, and C. M. Kraay, eds. *An inventory of Greek coin hoards.* New York: American Numismatic Society.

Kallet, L. 2001. *Money and the corrosion of power in Thucydides: the Sicilian expedition and its aftermath.* Berkeley: University of California Press.

Kallet-Marx, L. 1993. *Money, expense, and naval power in Thucydides' History 1–5.24.* Berkeley: University of California Press.

Kraay, C. M. 1976. *Archaic and classical Greek coins.* London: Methuen.

Kroll, J. H. 1976. Aristophanes' *ponēra chalkia*: a reply. *Greek, Roman, and Byzantine Studies* 17: 329–341.

———. 1993. *The Athenian Agora XXVI, The Greek coins.* Princeton: American School of Classical Studies in Athens.

———. 1996. The Piraeus 1902 hoard of plated drachms and tetradrachms (*IGCH* 46). In: *ΧΑΡΑΚΤΗΡ: Αφιέρωμα στη Μάντω Οικονομίδου*, pp. 139–146. Athens.

———. 1998. Silver in Solon's laws. In: R. Ashton and S. Hurter, eds., *Studies in Greek numismatics in memory of Martin Jessop Price*, pp. 225–232. London: Spink.

———. 2000. Review of L. Kurke, *Coins, bodies, games, and gold: The politics of meaning in Archaic Greece. The Classical Journal* 96.1: 85–90.

———. 2002. Review of A. Meadows and K. Shipton, *Money and its uses. Bryn Mawr Classical Review* (2002.07.24).

———. forthcoming. Athenian tetradrachms recently recovered in the Athenian Agora. *Revue numismatique* 162.

Kurke, L. 1999. *Coins, bodies, games and gold: the politics of meaning in archaic Greece.* Princeton, N.J.: Princeton University Press.

Melville-Jones, J. R. 1993. *Testimonia numaria. Greek and Latin texts concerning ancient Greek coinage. I. Texts and translations.* London: Spink.

Nicolet-Pierre, H. 2002. *Numismatique grecque.* Paris: Armand Colin.

Oikonomides, M. 1985. Note on the Piraeus hoard of 1902 of Athenian plated coins. *Coin hoards* 7: 40–41.

Picard, O. 1998. Colloque sur 'La valeur des monnaies de bronze'. *Revue numismatique* 153: 5–61.

Price, M. J. 1968. Early Greek bronze coinage. In: C. M. Kraay and K. Jenkins, eds., *Essays in Greek coinage presented to Stanley Robinson*, pp. 90-104. Oxford: Clarendon Press.

Psoma, S. 2001. *Olynthe et les Chalcidiens de Thrace: études de numismatique et d'histoire.* Stuttgart: Franz Steiner.

Saïd, S., et al. 1997. *Histoire de la littérature grecque.* Paris.

Seaford, R. 2004. *Money and the early Greek mind: Homer, philosophy, tragedy.* Cambridge: Cambridge University Press.

SEG: Supplementum epigraphicum graecum. 1984–. Amsterdam: J. C. Gieben.

Stroud, R. S. 1974. An Athenian law on silver coinage. *Hesperia* 43: 157–188.

Taylor, M. C. 1997. *Salamis and the Salaminioi: the history of an unofficial Athenian demos.* Amsterdam: J. C. Gieben.

Thompson, W. E. 1966. The functions of the emergency coinages of the Peloponnesian War. *Mnemosyne* 19: 337–343.

Trevett, J. 2001. Coinage and democracy at Athens. In: A. Meadows and K. Shipton, eds., *Money and its uses in the ancient Greek world,* pp. 23–34. Oxford: Oxford University Press.

von Reden, S. 2002. *Demos' phialē* and the rhetoric of money in fourth-century Athens. In: P. Cartledge, E. Cohen, and L. Foxhall, eds., *Money, labour, and land: approaches to the economies of ancient Greece,* pp. 52–66. Routledge: London and New York.

Will, C., C. Mossé, and P. Goukowsky. 1975. *Le monde grec et l'orient.* Paris.

Williams, J., ed. 1997. *Money: a history.* London: British Museum.

Zelizer, V. A. 2005. *La signification sociale de l'argent.* Paris.

Agoranomia: Studies in Money and Exchange Presented to John H. Kroll, pp. 109–124
© 2006 The American Numismatic Society

Polis Economies and the Cost of the Cavalry in Early Hellenistic Athens

Graham J. Oliver*

Jack Kroll's important contributions to our understanding of the ancient world are not limited to his work on coins. I have already drawn heavily on the numismatic side of Kroll (Oliver 2001, building on Kroll and Nicolet-Pierre 1990 and Kroll 1993; see now Kroll 2003). This paper turns to another important aspect of his oeuvre: the contribution to our understanding of Athenian society, institutions, and military organization signalled by Kroll's work on other metal finds from the Athenian Agora excavations (Kroll 1977a; 1977b; Kroll and Mitchel 1980). Among the most important of these is the publication of a series of lead tokens that had been used in the administration of the Athenian cavalry from the mid-fourth to the third centuries BC (Kroll 1977a). The discovery of this material during excavations in 1971 supplemented the contents of a large deposit found in 1965 in the Kerameikos excavations and published five years later (Braun 1970). Kroll's publication offered not only a comprehensive publication of the 111 tokens from the Agora but also allowed him to review the lead tokens (574 in total) from the Kerameikos. Both the Agora and Kerameikos deposits came from wells but originated from the same offices of the Athenian administration, the cavalry headquarters, which was located on or just beyond the northwestern corner of the Agora. I return to this material now to draw out further the light they throw on the economies of early Hellenistic Athens.

The lead cavalry tokens carry details of the value and identity of horses owned by the men who served in the Athenian cavalry in the fourth and third centuries. Each token represents the value and abbreviated description of the particular horse, along with the name of a cavalryman, presumably the horse's owner. The thin strips of lead were inscribed with

*School of Archaeology, Classics, and Egyptology, The University of Liverpool.

FIGURE 1. IL 1593 (folded) (1:2) (Copyright American School of Classical Studies at Athens)

details of the brand (if one was used) that marked the horse, the color of the horse, and its assessed value, and were then rolled or folded over (see Figure 1). The details of the horse were found on the inside, while on the outside, and inscribed before the lead token was folded, was the name of the Athenian cavalryman (see Figures 2–5). The established view is that the lead tokens were probably arranged in collections by tribe, and each cavalryman and horse was subject to reassessment on an annual basis. The "value" of the horses, as Kroll argued, was not equivalent to the absolute value of the horse, but represented the value of the horse up to a *maximum* of 1,200 *drachmai* (200 *mnai*). The publication of this material by Karin Braun and Jack Kroll was the result of careful conservation in opening the lead to-kens and the outcome of the difficult process of reading the lightly incised lead tokens (see Figures 2–5). Braun's work and Kroll's comprehensive reassessment of the problems and interpretation of the cavalry tokens has been fundamental to subsequent studies.

The cavalry tokens are important not only because they help identify Athenians as mem-bers of the cavalry and therefore enhance our prosopography of Athenian society, but also because they advance our understanding of the organization and administration of the cav-alry and Athenian society in general (for a prosopographical study of the cavalry, see Bugh 1998: 225–262). The cavalry tokens supplement the relatively rich literary evidence from fifth- and especially fourth-century Athens. They add to the growing epigraphical evidence for equestrian forces in the Athenian *polis*, a body of material that has been extended by more recent discoveries from the ongoing excavations in the Agora (Camp 1996: 242–252; Bugh 1998). They throw light on the economies of the *polis* and raise two central problems: (1) the contribution of individual Athenians to the *polis* and (2) the degree to which the state in the early Hellenistic period supported central institutions such as the cavalry. This article deals with these two problems by looking first at the state provision of grain for the cavalrymen and then the relationship between state finances and the cost of the horses.

FIGURE 2. IL 1593, outside (unfolded) (1:1/2)

FIGURE 3. IL 1593, inside (unfolded) (1:1/2)

FIGURE 4. IL 1539, outside (unfolded) (1:1/2)

FIGURE 5. IL 1539, inside (unfolded) (1:1/2)
(All figures copyright American School of Classical Studies at Athens)

Some articles and books that have appeared since the publications of Braun (1970) and Kroll (1977a) have touched on these problems. They too owe a great deal to the original publication of the material and especially to the formidable analysis that Jack Kroll offered in 1977. Principal among these studies are Glenn Bugh's *The Horsemen of Athens* (1988) and Ian Spence's *The Cavalry of Classical Greece* (1993). Bugh's earlier study extends from the Archaic into the Hellenistic and Roman periods, offers a diachronic study of the organization of the Athenian cavalry, and includes a detailed prosopography of the cavalrymen (Bugh 1988: 225–262; cf. Spence 1993: 287–305 for the fifth and fourth centuries only). Spence concentrates on the military operation of the cavalry and explores the cavalry's strategic role in the *polis* (see also Spence 1990). His military and social history of the cavalry focuses on the period from 450 to 320 BC.

Both Bugh and Spence, like Kroll before them, are interested in the socioeconomic aspects that the cavalry tokens and the organization of the equestrian forces revealed. Spence (1990: 272–286) in particular has also offered an important survey of the cost of cavalry service at Athens. He underlined how cavalry service was reserved for Athenians of considerable wealth: "being a cavalryman was therefore a costly exercise, even with state aid, and horse-ownership or cavalry service clearly qualifies an individual for inclusion in J. K. Davies' propertied class. It also means that Athens expected a not inconsiderable financial sacrifice from its serving cavalry" (Spence 1993: 286; see now Davies and Oliver 1996: 306). The cavalryman was required to supplement any state aid by paying for stabling, grazing, equipping, and maintaining the horse, almost certainly requiring a slave or hired groom. Cavalry armor was an additional cost, as was the depreciation in the value of the horse. In the Classical period, the Athenian state supported the cavalryman in two ways: it paid for feeding the horse and supported the cavalrymen through an institution called *katastasis*. The operation of the state support of the cavalry in the early Hellenistic period needs to be reassessed in terms of the financial capacity of the Athenian state and its individual members.

Feeding the Cavalry

Bugh (1988: 58–62) has shown clearly that the Athenians supported the cavalry by providing a grain allowance. The evidence for this provision in the early Hellenistic period is rich. An inscription from 300/299 reveals clearly that the Athenian cavalrymen were normally given grain for their horses by the state (*IG* II² 1264; Tracy 1990: 146 for line 1). In this year, some problems arose that prevented or delayed this process. We are not told what those difficulties were. The Treasurers of Athena Polias intervened on behalf of the *hipparchoi* and ensured that the cavalry were given the grain owed to the cavalry by the state. To recognize the assistance of the Treasurers, the cavalry set up an inscription honoring them:

> (1) [Ant]iphon son of Antisthenes of Teithras made the proposal: since the Treasurers of the Goddess who in the archonship of Hegemachos [300/299] cared (5) [on behalf of] the *hipparchoi*, so that the cavalry might be supplied with the grain owed to them by the People; and they continue to perform all other kinds of services (10) that are of benefit in pursuit of honor on behalf of the cavalrymen. With good fortune the cavalrymen has passed a decision: to praise the Treasurers of the Goddess who were in office in the archonship of Hegemachos [300/299] and (15) to crown them with a gold crown on account of their excellence and pursuit of honor [*philotimia*] which they continue to have both for the cavalrymen and for the Athenian People; (20) to write up this decree and the crown and the names of the Treasurers on a stone *stele* and to set it up on the Acropolis; and the expenditure for the *stele* (25) and the writing up, whatever it happens to be, the *hipparchoi* are to pay. [*a space of ten lines is followed by several words the sense of which is difficult to make out because of the missing text*]

The people had for some reason not been forthcoming with the grain for the cavalry. The Treasurers of Athena had either facilitated the procedure or perhaps even used public monies to pay for the grain, or perhaps they had handed over the necessary funds to the *hipparchoi*.

In the fifth century, the grain for the horses had indeed been under the control of Treasurers of Athena Polias, as the record of 410/09 reveals (*IG* I³ 375 = *IG* I² 304A, for the first, third, fourth, and seventh prytanies; Bugh 1988: 60 n. 86). Financial organization in the fourth century was somewhat different from the fifth century and from the period of the Peloponnesian war in particular (Ferguson 1932: 128–140). This is not the place to enter into the complexities of Athenian financial administration (see Rhodes 1972: 88–113), but in the closing years of the fourth century, it is generally believed that financial organization in the city was creaking and unstable (Henry 1984). It is worth reviewing the context of such tensions.

The cost of erecting decrees that had been passed by the Athenian People and subsequently inscribed on stone *stēlai* in 303/02 and 302/01 was assigned at various moments to different financial officials. For much of the fourth century (since 363; see Henry 1984: 50) until 303/2, the Treasurer of the People had paid for setting up the inscriptions. In 303/2, three different bodies (The Treasurer of the People, the Single officer for the Administration, and the Treasurer of the Stratiotic Fund) exercised that function. In 302/1, two different sets of officials carried out these duties (The Treasurer of the People and the Single officer for the Administration). Three years later, in 299/98, a completely new set of officials paid the costs of setting up inscribed *stēlai* carrying state decrees: the *trittyarchoi* and *exetastes* (*IG* II² 641). Although the evidence for precise dating is difficult, this last pairing of officials is thought to have undertaken its duties from 301/00 (Henry 1984: 63–68, 91). The *exetastēs* was elected by a vote of the Athenian People, and his concerns probably extended over military institutions composed of citizens and mercenaries, as the honors awarded to this officer serving in 298/97 reveal (*IG* II² 1270.2–8). These frequent changes in the years from 303/02 suggest financial disruptions. The experience of the cavalry and the *hipparchoi* in 300/299 is likely to be a reflection of such irregularities or disruptions in the state financial administration. Some indication of the health of civic finances and the operation of state institutions is suggested in the following year (299/98), when King Lysimachus, the ruler of Thrace (*IG* II² 657), performed several services for the Athenians. Not only did he give as a gift 10,000 *medimnoi* of grain to be distributed to all the Athenians, he also ensured that the Panathenaic festival of the same year could proceed and that the *peplos* (the robe or cloth produced for that festival) be brought up to the Goddess Athena (*IG* II² 657.10–16). The problems in being provided with grain that the cavalrymen experienced in 300/299 can justifiably be located within this wider context of difficult Athenian state finances. However, such problems are not without parallels.

Financial tensions feature in decrees involving the cavalry or other equestrian bodies (and indeed other military institutions) in the early Hellenistic period. In 282/1, the Athenians were struggling to maintain their recent recovery in Athens and Attica against the Macedonian forces of Demetrius Poliorcetes, who still controlled the harbors of Piraeus and the fortress on the Mounychia hill. Two different equestrian groups, the Athenian cavalry and the *Tarantinoi* (a term describing a form of light-armed cavalry and not necessarily

men from Taras; see Launey 1987: 601–603; Martin 1887: 422) honored the *hipparchoi*
and *phylarchoi* of that year because the equestrian officers ensured that the cavalry forces
received grain. The Athenian cavalry recalled that the officials had "cared also for the grant
of grain so that the cavalrymen exist in good order in each prytany" (*SEG* 21.525.18–22 =
Moretti *ISE* I no. 36). The *Tarantinoi* praised the officials because they "cared for the grain so
that both the cavalrymen and the *Tarantinoi*, with full rations, should receive their supply"
(Camp 1996: 252 = Ag. I 7587.7–9; *SEG* 46.167, with Gauthier, *BE* 1997, no. 208 and Parker
1997 for line 9; Habicht 1997b for further prosopography; Tracy 2003, 50–52 for the letter
cutter). The Secretaries of the *hipparchoi* wrote up both honorific decrees (*SEG* 21.525.40–
44; *SEG* 46.167.40–43). The *Tarantinoi* had their stele set up at the Stoa of the Herms (*SEG*
46.167.43). The Athenian cavalry set up two copies, one near the Sanctuary of Poseidon, at
the hill of Hippios Kolonos northwest of urban Athens (Spence 1993: 188–189; Bugh 1988:
27–28)—not a location used for known state decrees (Liddel 2003)—and the other in the
same location as the stele carrying the decree of the *Tarantinoi*, in the Stoa of the Herms in
the Agora (*SEG* 21.525.40–44). These two inscriptions show clearly that the equestrian officials (the *hipparchoi* and the *phylarchoi*) had taken steps to maintain the supply of grain for
the cavalry, including the *Tarantinoi*. However, there is no emphasis in either of these texts
that the grain was owed or overdue, as the decision of the cavalry in 300/299 had suggested.

   The decree passed by the Athenian cavalry in 281/0 (*SEG* 21.525 = Moretti, *ISE* I no. 36)
refers to the "grant of grain", proving that the Classical practice, indicated still in 300/299,
continued in the early third century (Bugh 1988: 60–61). The decree passed by the Tarantinoi, on the other hand, was a decision proposed by a foreigner, Kallistratos son of Termonios of Achaea. The precise wording of the *Tarantinoi* decree adheres closely to that passed
by the Athenian cavalry but differs significantly in the specific reference to the grain:

> (1) Gods. Kallistratos son of Termonios of Achaea spoke. Since the *hipparchoi* and the
> *phylarchoi* of the archonship of Nikias [282/1] (5) have continued to serve as officials
> in the magistracy in accordance with the laws and have cared for the grain so that
> both the cavalry and the *Tarantinoi* might be supplied with full rations [*enteleis*]. And
> they have (10) continued to in all other respects both in private and in public to show
> *philotimia* to the cavalry and the *Tarantinoi*. (*SEG* 46.167.1–13)

The passing of the two decrees of the Athenian cavalry and the *Tarantinoi* in the same year
and the fact that the same Secretaries wrote them up suggest that the discrepancy with respect to the grain marks a significant difference. The decree of the Athenian cavalry (*SEG*
21.525) refers directly to the allowance of grain (Bugh 1988: 61), but the phraseology in the
Tarantinoi inscription is much more periphrastic and awkward (Parker 1997). The term
enteleis has indeed attracted attention, and both Gauthier and Parker elucidated its meaning
by underlining that it does not, *pace* Camp, here refer to *Tarantinoi* "with full rights" (L & S-
J *enteles* II) but to the fact that the two groups of cavalry received their full ration of grain.

Parker suggests that the text does not quite say that the cavalry and *Tarantinoi* received full rations, but that is the sense. Gauthier's translation of the crucial lines shows that the magistrates "ont veillé à ce que les *hippeis* et les *Tarantinoi* perçoivent leurs rations de grain complètes" (*BE* 1997 no. 208; *SEG* 46.167.7–9). The use of the adjective is important and proves that the *Tarantinoi* were included as recipients of the distribution of grain. Whether the *Tarantinoi normally* received the state distribution of grain as was the established practice for Athenian cavalry is not clear. The adjective (*entelēs*) normally refers not to people but objects (pay, food, etc.), and the word order prevents an association of *enteleis* with, for example, *isoteleis*, *ateleis*, etc. (Parker 1997).

A third decree that, like the *Tarantinoi* inscription, has been found in the recent excavations of the Athenian Agora (Bugh 1998) preserves a decision passed by an equestrian body known as the *prodromoi*, the only decree from Athens passed by this cavalry force (Bugh 1998 = *SEG* 48.122; on the *prodromoi*, see Bugh 1988: 223–224). Unfortunately, no precise date for the decree has been offered apart from that based on the lettering style, c. 330–285 BC. The hand of the mason has not yet been identified. The decree honors neither the *hipparchoi* nor the *phylarchoi* but, apparently, those who served as secretaries: Philodemos and a man whose name is lost. The restoration of the honorands as secretaries is not secure, but a better alternative has eluded the editor. The decree refers to the honorands who cared "for both all the cavalrymen and the *prodromoi* in respect of the distribution of grain allowance for the horses" (*SEG* 48.122.8–12; the initial *delta* of *d[osin]* looks secure on the photograph: Bugh 1998: pl. 14 no. 2), and it is likely that the secretaries are the same officials who assist the *hipparchoi* and who are responsible for writing up and setting up the inscribed decrees for the other equestrian bodies. It is likely that these secretaries had recorded the decision passed by the *prodromoi*, which were a military unit of the Athenian state and composed of Athenians. Their scrutiny was integrated into the regular activities of the Council ([Arist.] *Ath. Pol.* 49.1 with Rhodes 1981: 565). It is clear from their decision that they, like the Athenian cavalry in 282/1 and in 300/299, were entitled to a grain ration for their horses. Confirmation that the *prodromoi* were Athenians or were at least supported financially by the Athenian state is found in the published tokens of the cavalrymen in the third century. Two separate tokens identify horses (and their values) belonging to *prodromoi*. These tokens refer either to horses of the *prodromoi* of the Athenians named on the tokens (Charias: Braun 1970: 234 no. 565; Antimachos: Kroll 1977: 124–127 no. 62; see Figures 1–3) or to the horses of two *prodromoi* named Charias and Antimachos (Bugh 1998: 88). The second interpretation seems more likely, but for now the important conclusion is that the cavalry tokens of the third century prove that the state supported *prodromoi*. If the Athenian state underwrote the replacement value of horses used by the *prodromoi*, then the *prodromoi* decree can be seen as evidence for the distribution of the grain allowance provided by the Athenian state, and that reinforces the *normative* aspect of the wording used in 282/1 to describe the allowance of grain for the Athenian cavalry.

The epigraphical evidence therefore suggests that the Athenian state provided a grain allowance for the cavalry, Athenians serving as *hippeis* or as *prodromoi*. The *Tarantinoi* serving at Athens in 282/1 also enjoyed the full distribution of grain, but this provision that they and the Athenians received is not described in *SEG* 46.167 in terms of the normal allowance granted by the state on other occasions. The absence of the wording found in both the decrees for the Athenian cavalry of 282/1 (*SEG* 21.525) and the *prodromoi* (*SEG* 48.122) suggests that the *Tarantinoi* did not benefit from an established "distribution of the grain allowance." Perhaps the *Tarantinoi* extraordinarily benefited from a grain allowance. Perhaps the *Tarantinoi* were a recent element in the Athenian military, and so their inclusion in the grain distribution was new or, simply, their receipt of grain from the equestrian officials was unexpected. The last of these reasons at least would explain why the *Tarantinoi* deemed it right to add their own honors for the cavalry officers of 282/1 to those that were granted by the Athenian cavalrymen. Although it is not possible to establish how frequently the *Tarantinoi* were serving at Athens or precisely when they were introduced, their presence added to the burdens of supplying grain to military units that weighed on the Athenian state in 282/1. The presence of the *Tarantinoi* as a serving force in early Hellenistic Athens is confirmed by the survival of the dedication of a significant monument of uncertain but early Hellenistic date set up from the spoils of a victory (*IG* II² 2975). *Tarantinoi* at Athens had also been involved in the struggle to remove Lachares from power in the 290s (Polyainos 3.7.1). The combination of evidence for 282/1 underlines the need to quantify how much the mounted forces were costing the Athenian state.

It is not possible to quantify precisely the cost of supplying grain for the cavalry in 282/1, but some base figures can be obtained by returning to Spence's (1993: 272–274, 281–286) calculations of the cost of feeding the Athenian cavalryman for the period 450 to 320. To provide grain for the cavalry could be expensive. In the middle of the fourth century, the Athenians could spend forty talents per year on the cavalry, a sum that may have consisted largely of the grain allowance (Xen. *Hipparch*. 1.19; Bugh 1988: 60; Loomis 1998: 51). In 282/1, the Athenian cavalry praised the *hipparchoi* and *phylarchoi* for their work in maintaining the cavalrymen in good order (*eutaktōs*) prytany by prytany (*SEG* 21.525.18–21 = *ISE* I no. 36). How much did the operation cost? A calculation can be based on a daily allowance of 4 *choinikes* of barley per day for the horse (Spence 1993: 283–284). If barley cost 4 to 6 *drachmai* per *medimnos*, then the daily allowance of 4 *choinikes* would have cost 1.5 to 3 obols per horse. Spence concluded that an individual cavalryman might normally expect to need 3 to 6 obols per day for his two (?) horses, and an additional 2 obols for himself and his attendant (Spence 1993: 284–285). The fifth- and fourth-century sources suggest a rate of 1 drachma per day, or possibly 4 obols for a cavalryman (Bugh 1988: 61–62; Loomis 1998: 45–46).

The *prodromoi* inscription (Bugh 1998 = *SEG* 48.122.12) refers to the distribution of the grain allowance *for the horses*. However, the two honorific decrees of the Athenian cavalry (*IG* II² 1264 and *SEG* 21.525) and that of the *Tarantinoi* of 282/1 (Camp 1996 = *SEG* 46.167) refer in general to grain distribution but not in particular to grain for the horses. Among the given reasons for the honors awarded to the *hipparchoi* of 282/1 was their success in increasing the numbers of the Athenian cavalry by one hundred, making the force three hundred strong. The burden on the state to provide grain for this larger force would have been much greater. Somehow the *hipparchoi* (and the *phylarchoi*) procured the necessary grain rations, a service among those mentioned by the Athenian cavalrymen (*SEG* 21.525.18–21), and the principal specific service for the *Tarantinoi* (*SEG* 46.167.6–9). The monthly provision of three hundred Athenian cavalrymen, at a rate of 3 to 6 obols per cavalryman per day, would have cost the state in 282/1 around 150 to 300 *drachmai* per day and therefore 4,500 to 9,000 *drachmai* (or 1.25 to 1.5 talents) *per prytany* (of 30 days). Grain prices at the end of the 280s and in particular in that year may not have been as low as they had been in c. 330, so this estimate must be regarded as a minimum. In addition to the cost of providing grain to the Athenian cavalry, the *Tarantinoi* decree reveals that the light cavalry also benefited from a state-supported distribution of grain, and it is likely that *prodromoi* served, although these may have been included among the Athenian cavalry.

It remains unclear how many *Tarantinoi* there were. Camp's suggestion (1996: 257; cf. Bugh 1998: 188) that they provided the additional two hundred men that made up the five-hundred-man-strong cavalry force that fought the Celts in 279 lacks supporting evidence. Nor is it clear whether all *Tarantinoi* were foreigners or mercenaries (Gauthier, *BE* 1997 no. 208; Martin 1887: 422 n. 2). The sum of 1.5 talents is therefore the minimal cost to the *polis* for maintaining the Athenian cavalry force in 282/1, and would have been higher still if the *Tarantinoi* were *not* included among the three-hundred-strong cavalry force of 282/1. It is unlikely that the extra one hundred cavalrymen provided in 282/1 included the *Tarantinoi*. The Athenian cavalry praised the *hipparchoi* and *phylarchoi* who had "cared for the drafting list [*katalogē*] of the cavalrymen and added an extra 100 so that the cavalry having been made up to strength as much as possible for the time being and having become 300 in number might be able to provide what was needed [*tas chreias*] for the countryside" (*SEG* 21.525.6–11). How likely is it that the *dokimasia* and drafting of the *katalogē* were extended to the assessment of non-Athenians serving in the *Tarantinoi*, such as Kallistratos son of Termonios of Achaea, the proposer of that body's decree? Nevertheless, a non-Athenian commander could command Athenian mounted forces (see Bugh 1982: 31, with Dem. 4.27). But still the *Tarantinoi* benefited from the full ration of grain because of the qualities of the Athenian officials. Given that it is impossible to quantify the size of the *Tarantinoi* force, it is probably safe to estimate that it cost the Athenian state at least 1.5 talents *per prytany* to supply grain to their mounted forces.

THE COST OF HORSES

The other increased cost to Athens at the end of the 280s was related to the one hundred extra cavalrymen enrolled by the military officials praised in *SEG* 21.525. Any calculation of the cost to Athens of the provision of horses is difficult to compute. The literary sources (especially Lysias 16.6–7 [*In defence of Mantitheus*] and Harpocration, s.v. *katastasis*; Bugh 1988: 56) and the fourth- and third-century Athenian cavalry tokens provide the essential evidence. The current thinking is that the state was financially committed to supporting the cavalry in two forms. The *katastasis* was a financial operation whereby the state loaned money to the individual cavalryman to buy a horse. When the cavalryman retired, he would repay the state a sum of money equivalent to that which he had originally been loaned (Bugh 1988: 56–57; Spence 1993: 279–280). The other consideration is identified by the lead cavalry tokens. The state underwrote the *assessed value* (*timēsis*) of the horse being used by an Athenian cavalryman. The value of the horse may have changed year by year. If the horse was killed or maimed in action, then the state would have repaid the cavalryman a sum equivalent to the assessed value of the horse. The lead cavalry tokens are the records of the regular assessments, which provided an up-to-date archive of the values of the horses (Kroll 1977: 97–100; Bugh 1988; Spence 1993: 275).

Although there is a connection between the *katastasis* and the *timēsis*, the valuation of any specific horse recorded on the lead tablets may well be less than the original loan. However, the valuations never exceed 1,200 *drachmai* (12 *mnai*), and this sum has been identified as the limit of the sum loaned by the state as the original *katastasis*. For the state to loan the relatively large sums to individual cavalrymen to purchase their horse was a considerable expense, particularly if during any particular year a substantially increased number of cavalrymen were recruited. Kroll (1977: 89) has shown that the average assessment of a horse's value increased from the fourth to the third century. In 282/1, the average value of the horses must be closer to those values indicated by the tokens of the mid-third century. The average value for a horse in the third century, based on the evidence of the lead cavalry tablets, is 700 *drachmai* (Kroll 1977: 89). If an average of 700 *drachmai* was loaned by the state, the extra cost of providing horses for one hundred mounted recruits in 282/1 could have reached the large sum of 70,000 *drachmai*, or 11 2/3 talents. Of course, it is un-likely that every single newly inscribed cavalryman at Athens had to purchase a horse. The officials in 282/1 "have been responsible for the evaluations [*timēsis*] and scrutinies [*doki-masiai*]; and they also performed the scrutiny of the persons [*sōmata*] in accordance with the law and in partnership with the Council well and to the benefit of both the People and the cavalry" (*SEG* 21.525.14–18). No doubt part of that process involved their assessment of the horses of each of the cavalrymen, but there is no word in the text of the decree that seems to refer to their involvement in any process resembling the *katastasis*.

If the Athenian state maintained both forms of cavalry finance, namely, the *katastasis* and the assured repayments to replace horses, then how easy would the increase in cavalry numbers have been? Or, to put the question another way, what does the enlargement of the cavalry in this year say about the wealth of both the Athenian state and the Athenians themselves? If in 282/1 the Athenians found an additional one hundred cavalrymen, one wonders how that expansion was financed if the cost was anything approaching 11 2/3 talents. The fourth-century evidence suggests that *katastasis* was a loan by the state of a sum of money to cavalrymen to purchase or help toward the purchase of a horse. However, there is no direct evidence to suggest that this facility continued, nor is there anything to suggest it was disbanded (Rhodes 1981: 565 underlines that the evidence relates to the *katastasis* only to the time before and during the period of the oligarchic regime). Spence (1993: 279) has emphasized how unlikely it was that the state in the fifth and fourth centuries had financed fully the purchase of all horses by loaning the full amount to buy a horse: "It seems much more likely that each cavalryman was loaned either a fixed amount (lower than 1,200 drachmas) or, alternatively, all or part of what his horse actually cost—perhaps up to a maximum of 1,200 drachmas." The administration of the cavalry in the third century has been reconstructed based largely on the assumption that *katastasis* continued. Given the uncertainty offered by the evidence, it is difficult to draw a definitive conclusion. The administration of the cavalry was without doubt a long-standing feature of Athenian life. The scrutiny (*dokimasia*) of the cavalrymen at some stage of their service is represented on ceramic vessels in the first half of the fifth century (Bugh 1988: 14–20; Cahn 1973; see also Riccioni 1979 for another example, a red figure *kylix* from Ferrara, inv. 205008). The operation continued to involve the Boule with whom the cavalry officials (*hipparchoi* and *phylarchoi*) performed the examination (*dokimasia*) of the cavalrymen in 282/1 (*SEG* 21.525.15–18; Rhodes 1972: 174–175). The examination echoes the same sort of process described in the third quarter of the fourth century ([Arist.] *Ath. Pol.* 49.2 with Rhodes 1981: 567–568) and procedures described in Lysias 16, itself a speech written for the *dokimasia* of the defendant, Mantitheus (Rhodes 1981, 178 n. 6). But in the early Hellenistic period, the overall financial management of civic monies had perhaps moved away from the Council toward a smaller number of financial officials, such as the board for the distribution, *hoi epi tēi dioikēsei* (Rhodes 1972: 110). Of course, the Council continued to serve as a body of central importance, as is witnessed by the flurry of honorific decrees in the late 280s and early 270s (*Agora* 15.69–77). There is no surprise then that the decree honoring the *hipparchoi* and *phylarchoi* of 282/1 should give little away about financial organization, but that still leaves considerable uncertainty over the operation of *katastasis*.

The discussion of the financial organization of the cavalry leaves little doubt that the increase in cavalry numbers by one hundred in 282/1 was made possible primarily because sufficient individuals wealthy enough to be judged fit for mounted military service could be found. But to claim that the state was wealthy enough to be able to fund the *katastasis* loans in 282/1 up to the sum of 70,000 *drachmai* does seem, *a priori*, difficult to believe.

During this period, the Athenian state repeatedly praises individuals for their services to the state and on occasion highlights how some individual Athenians often in their capacity as magistrates used their own personal funds to finance all kinds of operations. So the *taxiarchoi* (with the generals) of 275/4 are praised for having personally funded the sacrifices it was necessary for them to undertake (*Agora* XVI.185.8–11). Among Athenians in this period, it is frequently individuals serving as officials who have used personal funds to finance sacrifices that receive honors (Smikros son of Philinos, Priest of Zeus Soter, *IG* II² 690.3–5, c. 262 BC; the *epimelētai* of the Mysteries in 267/6 BC, *IG* II² 661.22–24; Nikokrates son of Dion of Ankyle, treasurer of the Council in 274/3, is praised for actions including the funding of sacrifices from his own funds, *Agora* XV.85.15 = *IG* II² 678.16). Individuals were, more than ever, vital to the funding of major festivals. The *agonothetēs* was almost certainly a wealthy man capable of financially supporting major events. Philippides son of Philokles of Kephale volunteered to serve as *agonothetēs* in 284/3, and to do so using his own financial resources; he had spent vast amounts of his money in his career by providing for sacrifices and festivals (*IG* II² 657.38–40; 657.45–48). Individuals were indeed making significant personal contributions to the running of the state. However, the fact that the cavalry officials—the *hipparchoi* and *phylarchoi*—resolved problems concerning the distribution of grain does suggest that the civic structures were creaking. If this is the context against which to view the Athenian state funding *katastasis* loans to increase the numbers of cavalry from 200 to 300, then one might conclude that it is unlikely that Athens would have been able to find quickly up to 70,000 *drachmai* for the purchase of horses. It is much more likely that individual Athenians were expected to and able to fund much of their cavalry service themselves. In the early 280s, during the period of the revolution and expulsion of Demetrius Poliorcetes' forces from urban Athens, the Athenians sought and acquired several large sums of cash. Demochares of Leukonoe's role in securing various windfalls is singled out for praise later in 271/0 ([Plut.] *Vit. X Orat.* 851e): from Lysimachus, 30 talents and another 100 talents; from Ptolemy, 50 talents; from Antipatros, 20 talents (the identification is difficult: Marasco 1984: 72–74 argues against the Etesian Antipatros, proposed by Shear 1978: 82 with n. 225). How likely is it that by the end of the 280s the state had sufficient reserves to finance the purchase of horses for the cavalry? Is it not more likely that individuals exploited their own wealth to fulfil such civic obligations as military service?

The richest Athenians of the early Hellenistic period suffered fewer demands on their wealth than their counterparts earlier in the fourth century. Demetrius of Phalerum had transformed the system of *chorēgiai* (317–307) so that the Athenian *dēmos* was officially the *chorēgos*. This change also saw the introduction of one wealthy Athenian who served as *agonothetēs*, an office with responsibility for the agonistic festivals in the city (for the first known official, see Lambert 2000–2003). The reforms of the late fourth century meant that the wealthier Athenians were relieved of the burdens of serving as *chorēgoi* and that thenceforth only one individual bore the financial responsibilities for the major festivals. Another major liturgy of the fourth century was the trierarchy. The Athenian fleet had fallen in strength over the course of the late fourth and early third centuries, and what naval strength there was in the 280s was almost certainly much reduced. The Piraeus was no longer available in the period when Macedonians occupied the Mounychia fortress overlooking the principal naval harbors and installations. As a result, the cost to Athenians of paying for the trierarchies was almost certainly much less than it had been in c. 330–323. Any view of the wealth of the Athenian elite in the early third century must therefore take account of the fact that they had far fewer civic financial obligations than earlier in the fourth century.

Among the crises of the early Hellenistic period at Athens, the loss of personal property that arose from changes in government and especially the departure of individuals into exile was of some significance. Kallias of Sphettos had left Athens and not contested the apparent confiscation of his own property (Shear 1978: 4.78–83 = *SEG* 28.60). Following the expulsion of the Macedonian forces from the heart of Athens in 288/7, it is likely that similar issues of property ownership and recovery of property arose. Demochares of Leukonoe (like Kallias of Sphettos and Philippides of Kephale) had left when the government became apparently oligarchic, probably toward the end of the 300s, when Stratokles was dominating Athenian affairs (in 303, see Habicht 1997a: 126; in the mid-290s, see Shear 1978: 55). However, Demochares is praised for his own attitude toward property, which he seems to have displayed when he returned to the city after 286 ([Plut.] *Vit. X Or* 851f; for the date, see Habicht 1997a: 126; viewed in limited terms with respect to Demochares' stoicism, see Marasco 1984: 78–79). It is possible that in the 280s, as the Athenians gradually recovered control of parts of Attica, individual Athenians were not only able to recover their own property but perhaps were also able to begin to profit from it in ways that were difficult when open conflict raged in 288. The Piraeus remained under foreign control, but the Athenians had sufficient control of Attica to be able to exploit other harbors (*IG* II² 654.29–30: 286/5). It is possible then that over the course of the 280s, the revival of democracy and the reduced interference in the exploitation of Attica by Macedonian-led forces after the troubles of 288/7 allowed a measured revival in the finances of some Athenian families (Shear 1978: 2–3.14–27 = *SEG* 28.60.14–27; Habicht 1997a: 95–97). If the financial background to the later 280s in fact resembled the sort of conditions suggested here, then it would not have been surprising if individuals had been able to start enjoying some prosperity following the upheavals of 288 and the revolt against Demetrius Poliorcetes. Taxation on wealth in the form of liturgies was much lighter than it had been in the later Classical period.

CONCLUSION

The Athenian cavalry tokens provide ample evidence for the continuity of a state-supported cavalry system in the middle of the third century BC. The expansion of the cavalry force to 300 men in 282/1, a figure that may not have been reached in the middle of the third century, confirms the central importance of cavalry to the Athenian state. The individuals who were of sufficient wealth to sustain membership of the cavalry forces had been comprehensively reassessed by the cavalry officials of 282/1. Cavalry service is direct evidence of the commitment of the elite to the wider benefits of Athenian society.

It is less clear how far the state was able to maintain its mounted military contingents. Whether the *polis* was always able to continue the *katastasis* loan system is not clear. For the expansion of the Athenian cavalry from 200 to 300 men in 282/1 *may* have proved to be too big a financial burden for the state. The Athenians may have needed to find a sum of around 11 2/3 talents to support the potential costs of the *katastasis* system. It is more than likely that when the cavalry expanded, the individual Athenians, assessed and scrutinized by the *hipparchoi*, *phylarchoi*, and the Council, were expected to pay much of the costs themselves, as indeed has been suggested for the earlier operation of the *katastasis* system. Nevertheless, the state remained committed to supporting the cavalry. Once on active service, the *polis* was meant to provide the grain for the various branches of the mounted forces: the Athenian cavalrymen, including the named forces such as the *prodromoi*, and also the contingent known as the *Tarantinoi*. The cost of maintaining these forces in the field and on active service reached a minimum of 1.5 talents per prytany. It is clear that the provision of grain to the cavalry did not always operate smoothly. The numerous decrees referring to such problems from the end of the fourth and beginning of the third centuries probably indicate several kinds of difficulty. Financial provision by the *polis* may have been problematic and the logistics of securing grain for the cavalry may also have been problematic. The praise for officials in supplying grain to the mounted forces may reflect successes in overcoming problems of logistics rather than finance.

This investigation into the costs of the cavalry in the early Hellenistic period has highlighted some of the burdens that the Athenian economy absorbed. It also has made clear the degree to which key members of society were integrated into the fighting forces of the *polis*. The expansion of the cavalry and the continuing operation of a state-supported cavalry force in the mid-third century proves that the citizen continued to be a fundamental part of the fighting force of the Hellenistic *polis*, as Couvenhes (forthcoming) also shows. The extent of that commitment is highlighted by the costs that individuals were able and ready to sustain in the late 280s. This confirms evidence from other areas of Athenian society that reveal individual Athenians prepared to use their own personal funds to support communal activities, especially those related to religious rituals and festivals. However, in the early Hellenistic period, the richest Athenians no longer performed the same number of liturgies that they would have in the later Classical period. Their wealth was no longer under the same pressures as before. Cavalry service therefore was one of the few areas in which the wealthiest Athenians continued to perform civic obligations. The increase in numbers of serving cavalrymen reflects the levels of wealth and commitment of the elite families to the Athenian *polis* at a time when state finances were particularly stretched.

BIBLIOGRAPHY

Agora XV: B. D. Meritt and J. S. Traill. 1974. *The Athenian Agora* XV: *Inscriptions: the Athenian councillors*. Princeton: American School of Classical Studies at Athens.

Agora XVI: A. G. Woodhead. 1997. *The Athenian Agora* XVI: *Inscriptions: the decrees*. Princeton: American School of Classical Studies at Athens.

Braun, K. 1970. Der Dipylon-Brunnen, B: Die Funde. *Mitteilungen des Deutschen Archäologischen Instituts, Athenische Abteilung* 85: 198–269.

BÉ: *Bulletin Épigraphique*, published in: *Revue des Études Grecques*.

Bugh, G. R. 1988. *The horsemen of Athens*. Princeton: Princeton University Press.

———. 1982. Introduction of the *katalogeis* of the Athenian cavalry. *Transactions of the American Philological Association* 112: 23–32.

———. 1998. Cavalry inscriptions from the Athenian Agora. *Hesperia* 67: 81–90.

Cahn, H. A. 1973. Dokimasia. *Rossiiskaia Arkheologiia* 1973: 3–22.

Camp, J. McK. 1996. Excavations in the Athenian Agora: 1994 and 1995. *Hesperia* 65: 231–261.

Couvenhes, J.-Chr. Forthcoming. La fourniture d'armes aux citoyens athéniens du IVe au IIIe siècle avant J.-C. In: *Actes du colloque de Montpellier sur les armes dans l'antiquité (20–22 mars 2003)*. Montpellier: Université Paul Valéry.

Davies, J. K., and G. J. Oliver. 1996. A new edition of Athenian propertied families. *Zeitschrift für Papyrologie und Epigraphik* 110: 306–308.

Ferguson, W. S. 1932. *The treasurers of Athena*. Cambridge: Harvard University Press.

Habicht, C. 1997a. *Athens from Alexander to Antony*. Cambridge: Harvard University Press.

———. 1997b. Ein neues Zeugnis der athenischen Kavallerie. *Zeitschrift für Papyrologie und Epigraphik* 115: 121–124.

Henry, A. S. 1984. Athenian financial officials after 303 BC. *Chiron* 14: 49–92

ISE: L. Moretti. 1967-1976. *Iscrizioni storiche ellenistiche. Testo traduzion e commento*. 3 vols. Firenze: La nuova Italia.

Jones, C. P. 1987. Stigma: tattooing and branding in Graeco-Roman antiquity. *Journal of Roman Studies* 77: 139–155.

Kroll, J. H. 1977a. An archive of the Athenian cavalry. *Hesperia* 46: 83–140.

———. 1977b. Some Athenian armor tokens. *Hesperia* 46: 141–146.

———. 1993. *The Athenian Agora* XXVI. *The Greek coins*. Princeton: American School of Classical Studies at Athens.

———. 2003. The evidence of Athenian coins. In: O. Palagia and S. V. Tracy, eds., *The Macedonians in Athens, 322–229 BC*, pp. 206–212. Oxford: Oxbow Books.

———, and F. W. Mitchel. 1980. Clay tokens stamped with the names of Athenian military commanders. *Hesperia* 49: 86–96.

———, and H. Nicolet-Pierre. 1990. Athenian tetradrachm coinage of the third century BC. *American Journal of Numismatics* 2: 1–35.

Lambert, S. D. 2000–2003. The first Athenian *agonothetai*. Ηόρος 14–16: 99–105.

Launey, M. 1987. *Recherches sur les armées hellénistiques. (BEFAR 169). Réimpression avec addenda et mise à jour, en postface par Yvon Garlan, Philippe Gauthier, Claude Orrieux.* 2 vols. Paris: De Boccard.

Liddel, P. 2003. The places of publication of Athenian state decrees from the fifth century BC to the third century AD. *Zeitschrift für Papyrologie und Epigraphik* 143: 79–93.

Loomis, W. T. 1998. *Wages, welfare costs, and inflation in Classical Athens.* Ann Arbor: University of Michigan Press.

LSJ: H. G. Liddell, R. Scott, and H. S. Jones. 1968. *A Greek-English lexicon.* 9th edition, with Supplement. Oxford: Clarendon Press.

Marasco, G. 1984. *Democare di Leuconoe. Politica e cultura in Atene fra IV e III sec. A.C.* Firenze: Università degli Studi di Firenze.

Martin, A. 1887. *Les cavaliers athéniens (BEFAR 47).* Paris: Les écoles françaises d'Athènes et Rome.

Oliver, G, J. 2001. The politics of coinage: Athens and Antigonus Gonatas. In: A. Meadows and K. Shipton, eds., *Money and its uses in the ancient Greek world*, pp. 35–52. Oxford: Oxford University Press.

Parker, R. C. T. 1997. Full rations for the *Tarantinoi* in Athens: a note on the new decree. *Zeitschrift für Papyrologie und Epigraphik* 115: 136.

Rhodes, P. J. 1972. *The Athenian boule.* Oxford: Clarendon Press. Re-issued with addition and corrections, 1985.

———. 1981. *A Commentary on the Aristotelian Athenaion Politeia.* Oxford: Clarendon Press.

Riccioni, G. 1979. Kylix inedita de Spina del pittore di Antiphon con dokimasia. In: A. Cambitoglou, ed., *Studies in honour of Arthur Dale Trendall*, pp. 125–128. Sydney: Sydney University Press.

SEG: *Supplementum epigraphicum graecum.* 1984–. Amsterdam: J.C. Gieben.

Shear, L. T. Jr. 1978. Kallias of Sphettos and the revolt of Athens in 286 BC. *Hesperia Supplement* XVII. Princeton: American School of Classical Studies at Athens.

Spence, I. G. 1990. Perikles and the defence of Attika during the Peloponnesian War. *Journal of Hellenic Studies* 110: 91–109.

———. 1993. *The cavalry of Classical Greece.* Oxford: Clarendon Press.

Agoranomia: Studies in Money and Exchange Presented to John H. Kroll, pp. 125–150
© 2006 The American Numismatic Society

The Pseudo-Rhodian Drachms of
Mylasa Revisited

PLATES 5–6   RICHARD ASHTON* AND GARY REGER**

In 1992 Ashton observed that the pseudo-Rhodian drachms of Mylasa, distinguished by an eagle on the cheek of Helios on the obverse, were all or largely struck in a series of annual issues, most of them divided into monthly sub-issues; he suggested that the series ran for some thirty years, perhaps from the 170s or early 160s BC (Ashton 1992). At the time he wrote, the well-known Mylasean inscriptions recording land transactions, many of them effected with drachms of "light Rhodian money", were generally dated to the mid to late second century or later, in which case the pseudo-Rhodian drachms would probably not have been inaugurated specifically to cater for those transactions, although whatever the original reason for their introduction, they might well have been used later for that purpose. In Part 1 of the present article, Reger argues that the "lease" inscriptions should be redated to begin before c. 185 BC; he and Ashton agree that the evidence for dating the beginning of the eagle-on-cheek drachms to the 170s or early 160s is far from conclusive, and that there is much to be said in favor of backdating them by a decade or two to coincide with the inscriptions. In Part 2, Ashton publishes and comments on further numismatic material recorded since 1992.

PART 1

The Date of the "Lease" Inscriptions of Mylasa and the Coinage of Rhodos

The "leases" of Mylasa constitute one of the most important bodies of documentation about land tenure practices from the Hellenistic world. They record the sale of properties

*London, England
**History Department, Trinity College, Hartford, Connecticut.

to sanctuaries and their rental, usually back to the original owners for an indefinite term. Their full evaluation has been frustrated by incompleteness of publication and by imprecision of date. I plan to deal with the first problem in a book on Mylasa in which I will publish the material discovered by Louis and Jeanne Robert and reserved for their book on Mylasa, which, unfortunately, never appeared. The publication by Richard Ashton in the second part of this article of a new hoard of Mylasean pseudo-Rhodian drachms, which reinforce his interpretation of these coins published in 1992, offers a suitable opportunity to reconsider the second matter of date.[1] In the inscriptions, references to payments for the purchase price and rents paid in respect of the properties specify payments in either simply drachms of "money", ἀργύριον, or of "light Rhodian money", ἀργύριον ʽΡόδιον λεπτόν.[2] I will argue that this distinction between plain "money" and "light Rhodian money" can help set a date for these texts.

In principle, it is certainly possible that no real distinction lies behind "money" and "light Rhodian money". The phrases could have been used interchangeably to mean the same thing. But several considerations, I think, militate against this view. First, these texts

1. I originally presented my ideas about the dates of the lease texts in a paper delivered at the Annual Meeting of the American Philological Association in 1995 (see *AJA* 100 [1996]: 363). Richard Ashton got wind of this paper through Andrew Meadows; his comments helped me enormously in the reconceptualization of it and with the numismatic issues, and he encouraged me several years ago to revise it for publication in *Numismatic Chronicle*. Other work (and personal health problems) intervened, and I set it aside—always promising myself to return to it "soon". In the meantime, through Alain Bresson, I became aware of the work of Fabrice Delrieux on the Mylasean inscriptions. He shared generously with me his work, for which I am very grateful indeed. Then, late in 2002, Richard Ashton informed me that Delrieux was working on trying to date the inscriptions by the reference to "light Rhodian coinage". It seemed to me suddenly quite important to present in print my views, which had been languishing for so many years on my desk. I asked Delrieux whether he would share with me his views, and with his usual extraordinary generosity, he did (Delrieux 1998: chap. II.2.3.1.1; Delrieux 1999 deals with another question in Mylasean numismatics). I meanwhile wrote up my views, with modifications, on the basis of the arguments that had seemed to me to be right. We have taken very different approaches to dating these documents and come out with different results; it will be up to the scholarly world to debate the pros and cons once he has published his views. I am very grateful to Richard Ashton for advice and criticism and for the invitation to publish this essay with him, and to Peter van Alfen for accepting it as part of the Festschrift. Andrew Meadows has been a crucial help in many ways. I owe enormous, unpayable debts to Alain Bresson and Riet Van Bremen. To Joshua Sosin I owe observations on an earlier draft that helped sharpen my arguments. Wolfgang Blümel has shared generously unpublished material over the years. As always with Mylasa, I am grateful to Glen Bowersock, Christian Habicht, Christopher Jones, and Léopold Migeotte. I cannot express the debt I owe to the late Jeanne Robert, who entrusted me with the material from Mylasa collected by her and Louis Robert for their never-published book. Some work on this paper was undertaken during a very pleasant semester at Cologne in 1995; I am grateful to my hosts there, especially R. Merkelbach and W. Blümel. This paper is the second in a series of prolegomena to my book on Mylasa; Reger (2004) was the first.

2. "Money": *IK Mylasa* 206.12, 216.8, 221.7, 226.7, 801.6, 802.5, 807.5, 810.9, 10, 819.9, 823.4, 829.4, 850.4, Blümel (1995: 46) no. 7.5–6; "light Rhodian money": *IK Mylasa* 202.1, 203.9, 207.12, 18, 816B6, 822.10–11, 828.4; Blümel (2004: 6–8) no. 7.21–22. The phrase cannot be restored at *IK Mylasa* 205.18, as unpublished material makes clear. Texts so far published can be found at *IK Mylasa* 202–232, 207B, 801–854, Blümel (1992: 5–6) no. 217B, (1995: 46–55) nos. 7–25, (2004: 6–9) nos. 7–8 (9–10 no. 9 is probably from Hydai). There is a series of similar inscriptions from the sanctuary of Sinuri which I leave aside here; there are a few mentions of "money" only: Robert (1945: 70–77) no. 46 A–C and B speak of "drachmas" and "money" (*argyrion*) alone; in

are meticulously drafted contracts.[3] They give in great detail the capital equipment of each estate, locate it precisely with respect to its neighbors and natural features, and provide exact dates at which the acts were passed. Such precision does not sit well with sloppiness about the currency in which the prices and rents are to be paid. Second, the texts do not use the different designations for the currency in the same dossier.[4] In the first instance, in each separate inscription where a payment is mentioned, either plain "money" or "light Rhodian money" is consistently used.[5] Different dossiers dating to the same year use the same designation. Finally, the rentals were often expected to last indefinitely, so that if there could be confusion about the currency acceptable for payments, the need to specify would have been apparent.[6] It therefore seems reasonable to suppose that "money" alone was used at a time when no confusion about currencies was likely, and that "light Rhodian money" came to be used when more than one currency began to circulate at Mylasa and it became necessary to specify (by "light Rhodian money") the exact currency in which payments would be made.

Precisely this situation arose in Karia in the 180s BC. Since the 340s BC the Rhodians had been issuing silver coinage struck to a weight standard of c. 3.4 g per drachm, which Ashton calls the Rhodian standard (Ashton 2001: 79). From about 225 BC, the Rhodians began to issue the drachms of this coinage—and only the drachms—on a reduced standard of about 2.8–2.5 g per drachm.[7] These abundant coins with a head of Helios on the obverse and a Rhodian rose on the reverse were widely accepted and evidently served as the currency for towns like Mylasa,[8] which does not seem to have struck coins of its own in this period. Throughout this period, the Rhodians continued to strike *didrachma* and *tetradrachma* on the full original weight standard of c. 3.4 g per drachm. Then, certainly by the 180s, and perhaps even better c. 190, the Rhodians abandoned this coinage in favor

---

(1945: 84–85) nos. 50.9–10 we have *argyriou drachmas* precisely; and at (1945: 85) no. 50a5, *arg[yrion - - -]* (for the whole series see Robert [1945: 69–93] nos. 46–72). But there do not seem to be many close ties between these texts and the Mylasean ones, and my general impression is that the examples from Sinuri are earlier. I will reexamine all these inscriptions in my book on Mylasa.

3. The best treatment of the legal aspects of these documents remains Behrhend (1973).

4. By "dossier" I mean the set of documents (originally four) that governed a single transaction. See W. Blümel, *IK Mylasa* I: 74–76. The dossiers presented in current publications do not always consist of documents that in fact belong together; for example, *IK Mylasa* 807, 809, and 810 are part of a single dossier, but *IK Mylasa* 808 seems to belong to a different dossier. Likewise Blümel (1995: 46–8) nos. 8–9 seem to be part of another dossier, as does (1995: 51–2) no. 16.

5. The references to cash payments as simply "drachmas" in *IK Mylasa* 818.7 and 831.5 should be understood either in the context of an earlier specification, whether in the same document (as in *IK Mylasa* 216.8, where *drach[mon]* refers back to *arguriou drach[mon]* in line 9) or in a single dossier of documents referring to the same sale (as in *IK Mylasa* 206.12) or because some imprecision of terminology was acceptable before the introduction of the light Rhodian money, as discussed below.

6. See for example *IK Mylasa* 864 (Migeotte [1984: 326–9] no. 105): drachmas only are specified, but the term of the loan was a single year.

7. See for the date Ashton (2004: 97–8).

8. See Bresson (1993) on the circulation of the pre-plinthophoric Rhodian coins, with Ashton (2001: 94–6).

of a new type.[9] The so-called *plinthophoroi*, distinguished by the use of a shallow incuse square as the reverse type, were struck to a new standard of just over 3.0 g per drachm. Thus a slightly complicated change occurred. On the one hand, the *plinthophoroi* represented a *reduction* in the weight standard, because the Rhodians had continued to use the "Rhodian standard" of c. 3.4 g per drachm for their larger coins, but the new plinthophoric drachms were *heavier* than the reduced drachms the Rhodians had been issuing, at c. 2.8–2.5 g per drachm, as part of their previous coinage. The Rhodians' motivations for this major currency reform remain obscure. It has been associated with the gains of the Rhodians after the war with Antiochos the Great, which brought them control of Lykia and large parts of Karia.[10] More recently, Ashton has noted the similarity of the Rhodian reform with the Attalid cistophoric coins introduced perhaps as early as c. 190, and has suggested that the allies against Antiochos undertook a related reform at the same time in the context of the war. Be that as it may, there seems now less and less room to doubt that the new *plinthophoroi* were in circulation in Karia by the mid-180s at the latest, and that the introduction of these new coins created potential for serious confusion about the currency in which payments were to be made.[11] The Rhodian reform created a new monetary situation in Karia. Before c. 190, need for coins was satisfied (at Mylasa, in any case) by a single Rhodian monetary system, struck on the "old" Rhodian standard with reduced drachms (after c. 225). After c. 190, an entirely new system intruded, with different types— the *plinthophoroi*—struck to a different standard. As hoard and other evidence shows,

9. For a date of c. 190 for the introduction of the *plinthophoroi*, see Ashton (2001: 94; 2005), with whom I agree; Bresson (1993: 164; 1996: 68), "avant 185/184 au plus tard". Now, however, Bresson has indicated a preference for a lower date: see Ashton (2005: 85 n. 1). Melville-Jones (1979: 53–54) believed that he could date the start of the *plinthophoroi* to 177/6–173/2 on the basis of a restoration at *I. Didyma* 464.12 of Ῥοδίας μὲν [ἑκατόν] (the restoration appears also in the translation of this passage in Melville-Jones [1993: 275 no. 373]; see also Bresson [1996: 70–71]). But this restoration omits the word ὁλκή present in every other entry in this inscription. In fact, a *lambda* is faint but clear on the photograph of the stone published by Rehm in *I. Didyma*. Restore therefore: τοῦ δήμου τοῦ Ἰασ[έων φιάλη, ἐ]πιγραφὴν ἔχουσα, Ῥοδίας μὲν [ὁ]λ[κὴν . . . , Ἀλεξαν]δρε[ί]ας δὲ ἑξήκοντα δύο *vac* (lines 11–13). On the Alexandreian currencies of this period, see now Marcellesi (2000: 326–358) and Knoepfler (1997). I am very grateful to Thomas Corsten for confirming my reading of the photograph and for discussion on this matter.

10. Robert (1951: 172–173) for the suspicion. On the war, see now Grainger (2002: *passim*) (but new evidence continues to appear with dizzying rapidity; see, for example, Wiemer [2001] on the new inscription from Bargylia). For the outcome in Karia and Lykia, see now Wiemer (2002: 251–271), although Wiemer's description of the role of Rhodian coinage is unsatisfactory (258–259).

11. For example, *Milet* I 3 150, the treaty ending a war between Miletos and Herakleia by Latmos, stipulated that owners from one state could recover slaves who had run away to the other by paying a conveyance fee (ἀναγώγιον) of "twelve old Rhodian drachmas per slave", τοῦ σώματος δραχμὰς Ῥοδίας παλαιας δεκαδύο (l. 97). These "old Rhodian drachmas" are clearly precisely the pre-plinthophoric coinage, as Robert (1951: 173–174) pointed out. This inscription was long believed to belong in the 170s (some had proposed even later; for a review of the dates see Herrmann [1997: 185–186]) but has now been redated to 185/4 BC by Errington (1989: 288) (see Bresson [1996: 68]; Wörrle [2004: 49], writing "180s"), and so would imply that *plinthophoroi* were already circulating at Miletos and Herakleia by this date and created a potential for confusion, which the drafters of this text sought to avoid (see Ashton [2005: 86 and n. 7]).

the pre-plinthophoric coins continued to circulate in the region (and more widely) even after the *plinthophoroi* had begun to be issued.[12] It would therefore seem to make sense to set the new terminology in the Mylasean inscriptions in this context of the introduction of the *plinthophoroi*. If this is right, to what currency exactly did the phrase "light Rhodian coinage" refer? It is certainly possible that the coinage was that of Rhodos itself—the "old" Rhodian coinage in which Miletos and Herakleia stipulated payments were to be made. But there is another, very attractive possibility: that the "light Rhodian coinage" referred instead to the coins struck by the Mylaseans themselves using Rhodian types (head of Helios on the obverse, though with an eagle on his right cheek, and a rose on the reverse) and a weight standard at first of 2.4 g per drachm for the earliest anepigraphic issues, and later of 2.2 g per drachm—still lighter even than the standard to which the Rhodians had been striking till around 188.[13]

Richard Ashton's exhaustive studies of this Mylasean coinage have determined the order in which the various issues were struck. The earliest issue is anepigraphic and was struck in great abundance over a short period to a standard of c. 2.4 g per drachm; thereafter, production settled down to a smaller regular series of annual issues struck to a standard of c. 2.2 g per drachm. Ashton has argued that these coins "belong among the imitations of pre-plinthophoric Rhodian drachms struck in the earlier part of the second century by various states in south-west Asia Minor"; these states included Kaunos, Kos, and Miletos. On the basis of some inconclusive hoard evidence, and the thought that imitations of old-style Rhodian drachms would be unlikely to date very long after the introduction of the new-style Rhodian *plinthophoroi*, he sought a starting date for the Mylasean series "in the 180s, 170s or, at latest, 160s".[14] Some major new need for money would seem to lie behind the decision to start these new coins. In 1992, Ashton tentatively suggested the 167 BC war prosecuted by Mylasa with Alabanda against Euromos as the impetus for the start of the coinage or for some heavy issues struck a few years after the start (Ashton 1992: 32, 34). The association I have argued here of the appearance of the phrase "light Rhodian coinage" in the leases with this coinage suggests a more tempting idea: that the coins were produced as part of the financing of the purchase of private properties by the Mylasean sanctuaries.

---

12. See the hoard evidence cited at n. 22. Kos, Miletos, and Kaunos struck old-style Rhodian imitations probably as late as the late 170s or early 160s: Ashton (1999: 150–151 n. 11; 2002: 72 n. 20). The apparent imitations signed by Mousaios and attributed sometimes to Mylasa or Alabanda were probably struck at a more eastern mint and could date to as late as c. 170; see Ashton (1995: 10 n. 8).

13. See Ashton (1992: 21) on the standard.

14. See Ashton (1992: 26–29, 31–32) for relative chronology and absolute chronology and quotations, respectively. For the states issuing old-style pseudo-Rhodian drachms, see n. 12 above. As the Rhodian *plinthophoroi* became the standard coinage of southwestern Asia Minor, mints in the region began to imitate them; these imitators, including Kaunos, Kos, and the Lykian League, began striking plinthophoric coinages, i.e., coinages with a shallow square incuse on the reverse, within two decades or so of the introduction of the new Rhodian coinage (i.e., by c. 160 at the latest); see Ashton (1992: 32).

If the Mylaseans began buying up private property for sanctuaries in the 190s or early 180s, at first there would have been no question about the currency and simply designating payments in "silver money", *argyrion*, would have created no problems. This money would have been the "old" Rhodian coins, which had presumably been serving the Mylaseans for their currency needs for several decades. The introduction of the *plinthophoroi* would have created confusion, and since the Rhodians were no longer minting the "light" drachms, an obvious solution would have been to issue new Mylasean coins on the older, lighter Rhodian standard, with types imitating the old Rhodian ones, and to require payment of prices and rents in this "light Rhodian money". Not all the inscriptions preserve prices for the estates being bought by the sanctuaries, but those that do total about 50,000 dr. Obviously, a great deal of coined money would be required to carry out these transactions. Rents were also required to be paid in the same currency, creating an indefinitely continuing (but considerably smaller) demand for coinage. Ashton has suggested that the eagle on the cheek of Helios on the Mylasean drachm may represent one of the Zeuses of Mylasa (Ashton 1992: 3 n. 4). In several cases, it was indeed a Zeus on whose behalf land was purchased: Zeus Osogollos bought properties in the plain called Ombrianon (*IK Mylasa* 203.6, 204.7), and another property was bought for the Zeus of the tribe of Otorkondeis (*IK Mylasa* 216.3). Thus it would have been appropriate to mark Zeus' interest with his emblem on the coins.

Why did the Mylaseans not simply accept the new Rhodian plinthophoric coinage? There are several possible reasons. First, if the purchases had been made from the start with Rhodian coins on the old standard, continuity of practice and fairness to later sellers would favor using coins of the same standard. Moreover, because the standard for the *plinthophoroi* was heavier, accepting the new *plinthophoroi* would have raised costs for the sanctuaries. An inscription from Sinuri makes clear the interest of landowners in getting the best prices they could even when selling their properties to a god.[15] There may also have been some resistance to accepting the new types and unfamiliar appearance of the new *plinthophoroi*. But there may also have been political reasons, related to a certain ambivalence of towns like Mylasa to the Rhodians. As a reward for siding with the Romans in the war against Antiochos III, the Rhodians had been granted suzerainty over Karia and Lykia. In Lykia the Rhodians met resistance early on, and struggled for twenty years to assert authority over the recalcitrant Lykian *poleis*. The situation in Karia was different because the Romans did not simply give all of Karia to the Rhodians. A number of cities that had resisted Antiochos received grants of freedom. These cities included Alabanda, Herakleia by Latmos, Miletos, and Mylasa; other cities whose allegiances in 187–167 suggest that they too received freedom included Knidos, Myndos, Halikarnassos, and Iasos. There is plenty of evidence to show these towns acting in ways that displayed their freedom throughout the decades when Rhodos controlled much of the rest of Karia; for Mylasa, perhaps the clearest state-

---

15. See Robert (1945: 84–85 no. 50), in which the 4,500 drachmas allocated for the purchase of land did not attract any seller of a suitable property.

ment of its freedom came in 167, when it joined Alabanda to prosecute a local war against its neighbor Euromos (Reger 1999: 89–90, 96–97 n. 47). The *plinthophoroi*, issued immediately after the grant to Rhodos or at least in the context of Rhodian support for Rome and in expectation of reward, may well have been perceived as symbolic of Rhodian suzerainty. If so, the attraction of keeping to the old Rhodian-style coins and minting one's own issues would be obvious.

This suggestion brings us back to a serious problem created by redating the lease inscriptions to the early second century. The most recent attempt to date these texts depends on the connection between some of them and another inscription of Mylasa, all dated by the same *stephanēphoros* (the eponymous magistrate) and therefore of the same year. The second inscription, an honorary decree for one Menekrates passed by the Mylasean tribe of the Otorkondeis, contains the expression ʿΡωμαίοις τοῖς κοινοῖς εὐεργ[έταις]. Because this expression also appears in an inscription from Antiocheia on the Maiandros dating to about 165 BC, and because Christian Habicht argued that the Karians would have begun calling the Romans "common benefactors" after they removed Rhodian overlordship from Karia in 167, Wolfgang Blümel has put the lease texts roughly around 150 BC.[16] This date seems generally accepted.[17] But the lease texts dated by this *stephanēphoros* belong to the group using the designation "money", which by my analysis must date to before roughly 185. Can the Mylaseans have been calling the Romans "common benefactors" so early?

Although the inscription from Antiocheia in which this phrase appears dates to around 165, it is not the earliest attested use of the phrase. An inscription from Delphi dated to 182/1 issued by the Amphiktyonic Council for Eumenes II explicitly calls the Romans "common benefactors". This makes it absolutely clear that the formula was current by the late 180s (*SIG*³ 630.17–18, republished as Rigsby 1996: 375–377 no. 179).[18] I do not find it at all improbable that the phrase should have appeared at about the same time in Karia. Like many important Karian cities, the Mylaseans had taken the Roman side in the struggle against Antiochos and were rewarded in 187 by a grant of freedom that kept them outside Rhodian control. The appearance of the phrase, whatever its ultimate origins,[19] in a My-

---

16. The lease texts are *IK Mylasa* 808 and 810, which should now be read in Blümel (1995: 46–8 nos. 8–9). The honorary decree is *IK Mylasa* 111, whose first line should be restored as [Ἐπὶ στεφανηφόρου Κρατίνου τοῦ Κρατίνου κατα δὲ ὑποθεσ]ίαν Λαμπρίου τοῦ Μενίππου, etc. The inscription from Antiocheia is now *IG* XII 6.6, with the phrase at *ll.* 21–22; for the argument, see the *editio princeps* by Habicht (1957: 248). Ferrary (1988: 127 with n. 281) dates this text to after 129, taking the *stratēgoi* Louis Robert restored in line 11 (1937: 448 n. 3) as provincial governors; but it is quite clear that this word can be used to refer to Roman consuls or proconsuls or other high officials, as in the Miletos-Pidasa *sympoliteia* inscription, now dated to just after 188, perhaps precisely 187/6: see now Gauthier (2001: 117–127) and Wörrle (2003).

17. Dignas offers a new interpretation of the purpose of the sales (2000: 117–126; 2002: 95–106).

18. The restoration of *euergetas* seems certain. See Ferrary (1997: 200), giving c. 182 BC as the date of the introduction of the formula and Dmitriev (2005: 333 n. 16); "after Roman victories over Philip V and Antiochos III".

19. See the discussion by Erskine (1993: 70–87), with reference to earlier scholarship. See also the suggestion of Dmitriev (2005: 49 n. 70), that representations of Hellenistic kings as benefactors of "all Greeks" might go back to Alexander.

lasean inscription that would have to be redated to c. 185 is therefore no impediment to accepting the dating scheme here proposed.

I would therefore propose that those Mylasean inscriptions which speak of payments simply in "drachms of money", *argyriou drachmai*, should date to before the plinthophoric coinage penetrated Karia and before the Mylaseans began to strike their pseudo-Rhodians. Since the new *plinthophoroi* were already a problem for Miletos and Herakleia by c. 185, they would surely also have posed the same issues for the Mylaseans at the same time. I would therefore suggest that these inscriptions belong to the late 190s or first few years of the 180s. Presumably the Mylaseans began striking their pseudo-Rhodian drachms at this time and began requiring payments in the new "light Rhodian money". Inscriptions with this phrase will then date to the later 180s into perhaps the 170s.

Here I must digress to consider a possible objection to the dating scheme just outlined.[20] In principle, it is possible that the texts with plain ἀργύριον might be later than those with ἀργύριον Ῥόδιον λεπτόν, if we suppose enough time had passed for the difference no longer to be meaningful, i.e., long enough for the distinction between light Rhodian money and other money to have disappeared. On this view (for example) the latter set of inscriptions might belong to the second century and the former to the first.[21] In fact, however, this is impossible, for a number of reasons. First, the Rhodian drachms struck between c. 225 and 190 at c. 2.8–2.5 g per drachm continued to circulate in western Asia Minor long after the Rhodians ceased to produce them; they are found in hoards as late as c. 100–90 BC.[22] Thus the problem of distinguishing them from other coinages on other standards did not go away even so late as the latest dates that have been proposed for the leases.[23] Second, several states began to "imitate" the light Rhodian drachms after the Rhodians gave up producing them. Third, the long timespan between the two groups of inscriptions that this solution requires is contradicted by the inscriptions themselves, which give every sign of having been produced over a short period of time.[24] Indeed, two inscriptions provide a striking physical confirmation of the order. *IK Mylasa* 822 and 823 were inscribed on the same stone. The lat-

20. I had struck this argument from an earlier draft; I am grateful to Joshua Sosin for making me see that it should go back.

21. This would seem to be the view of Laumonier (1940: 212–213 n. 2), following up on the remarks of Robert (1937: 571 n. 2).

22. They appear in hoards intermixed with other coins: *IGCH* 232, the Histiaia hoard, buried c. 171–169; *CH* 1 (1975): 26 no. 85, of the mid-second century; in *CH* 1 (1975): 28 no. 91, of the late second century (one light Rhodian drachm and many *plinthophoroi*); and above all *IGCH* 1355, found at Marmaris, ancient Physkos in the Rhodian Peraia, of 100–90. See Robert (1951: 175); Hackens (1965: 716, 722); Leschhorn (1985: 11 n. 16); Jenkins (1989: 116–119).

23. This is not the place to rehearse the long bibliography on the date of these inscriptions, which I will review in my book on Mylasa. For a date in the 70s BC, see Persson (1922: 419, 423–425), whose arguments, however, cannot be sustained.

24. These indications include prosopographical links among the inscriptions, already noted by Cousin (1898: 432–439), following Waddington in Le Bas-Waddington (1870/1972: 2.125, and Buckler (1916/18: 190 with n. 1), and the similarity of the lettering.

ter was inscribed first, the former later and below it (see *IK Mylasa* 2: 58). *IK Mylasa* 823.4 speaks only of ἀργύριον, whereas 822.10–11 has ἀργύριον Ῥόδιον λεπτόν (restored but certain thanks to the preservation of the λεπτόν).

Another bit of corroborative evidence for this dating scheme comes from the texts of over 100 lines whose discovery Louis and Jeanne Robert reported on a number of occasions and parts of which, subsequently rediscovered, have been published (Robert 1946: 582, 1955: 225 n. 3, 1969: 4.98; Robert and Robert 1983: 167).[25] One text mentions a certain Melas son of Eirenaios, priest of the kings. Such an office at Mylasa is likely to have been devoted to the Seleukid royal cult and indeed may, as in other cases in western Asia Minor, have been created in the aftermath of the reconquest of the region by Antiochos III in 202.[26] But it seems improbable that the Mylaseans would have continued this cult long after the defeat of Antiochos III in 188 and their liberation by the Romans. The texts in which Melas appears use the simple designation "money" for payments, and so by the dating scheme proposed here belong before about 185.

Indeed, this whole argument can be pushed slightly farther, for this cluster of texts—the lease texts mentioning the priest of the kings and designating payments simply as "money" and the inscription calling the Romans "common benefactors"—all date to exactly the same year, under the *stephanēphoros* Kratinos son of Kratinos but by adoption of Lamprias son of Menippos. They were passed, moreover, within a month of each other: the lease texts in the Mylasean month of Dystros, the decree mentioning the Romans as common benefactors a month later, in Xandikos. This combination of circumstances—continued use of "money" only, the presence of a priest of the kings, and the Romans as "common benefactors"—points to an unusual, if not unique, set of circumstances in Mylasa. I would suggest that Kratinos son of Kratinos was *stephanēphoros* at Mylasa in precisely the period when Antiochos had just been defeated and the Romans were dealing with the aftermath of the war: thus precisely in 187 or 186. The "*stratēgoi* dispatched by the Roman people", [τοῖς ἀπε]σταλμένοις στρ[ατηγο]ῖς ὑπὸ τοῦ δή[μ]ο[υ τοῦ] Ῥωμαίων] (*IK Mylasa* 111.11) will then have been Roman officials dealing with the situation in Mylasa and Karia generally.

Further Implications of the Proposed Dating Scheme

The new scheme outlined here for the dates of the Mylasean lease inscriptions has a bearing on many aspects of the history of Mylasa and west-central Karia in the third and second centuries BC. Discussion of these issues would take us far from the purposes of this article, and I propose to deal with these matters in the book on Mylasa that I am preparing. But

---

25. Parts of the text have been published as *IK Mylasa* 816C, E, and D; *IK Mylasa* 843; and Blümel (1995: 51 no. 16). I will publish the full text with commentary in my book on Mylasa.

26. See the discussion in Ma (2002: 225); for other instances of a priest of "the kings", see Robert and Robert (1983: 151–154 no. 15.4–5) (= Ma 2002: 298–300 no. 10) of November-December 201 and Robert and Robert (1983: 154–163 no. 15B4) (= Ma 2002: 324–325 no. 23), from Xanthos in Lykia, of September-October 196.

three potential problems with this new dating must be considered here, since they may be regarded as challenging the new scheme.

Hybreas son of Polykritos. Several of the lease texts mention Ὑβρέας Πολυκρίτου κατὰ δὲ υἱοθεσίαν Ὑβρέου τοῦ Κρατέρου ἱερεὺς Σινυρι (*IK Mylasa* 217.6–7; Blümel 1992: 5–6 no. 217B lines 1–2), who is also *stephanephoros* in *IK Mylasa* 103.1–2 and probably *IK Mylasa* 864.19 (Migeotte 1984: 326–9 no. 105).[27] If W. Blümel has rightly assigned these leases to one dossier that includes *IK Mylasa* 216 (Blümel 1992: 5–6 no. 217B lines 1–2; *IK Mylasa* 217.6 [cf. 215.1]), then, under the dating scheme proposed here, Hybreas was priest of Sinuri before c. 185. However, the list of names of priests of Sinuri published by L. Robert includes neither Hybreas' name nor his father's, but does include a priest named Hiereus, who also appears in a document from Labraunda dated to the late 240s or early 230s (Robert 1945: 19–20 no. 5).[28] In the list from Sinuri Hiereus' name precedes seven others, distributed by Robert's reckoning (1945: 22) over three generations. But we must admit that we have no idea whatsoever how long any of the priests served. Another inscription from Sinuri[29] shows that at the latest the first priest on the list cannot be dated later than the joint reign of Idrieus and Ada (351–344 BC). The eight names before Hiereus must therefore cover about a century or slightly more. But, as Robert remarks himself (1945: 25), "la durée des sacerdotes pourrait être très inégale", and he cites an inscription of Halikarnassos (*SIG*³ 1020) in which length of service varies from four to thirty years. There is therefore no difficulty in inserting the seven priests who follow Hiereus into the roughly fifty years between c. 240 and c. 190. Likely confirmation comes from *IK Mylasa* 864.19, in which the Hybreas named as *stephanēphoros* is likely to be the same person. This inscription deals with Ouliades son of Hekatomnos son of Korris, who cannot be anyone but the grandson of the priest of Labraunda of the 240s and 230s.[30] He appears also in *IK Mylasa* 841.8 and possibly *IK Mylasa* 853.3, an inscription mentioning king Perseus (and so, very probably, to be dated to 179/8–168 BC). Thus if this identification is correct, Hybreas will date to the same period: the 180s would seem ideal.

IK Mylasa 631 and Dionysios son of Melas. In *IK Mylasa* 631, a decree of Tralleis honoring a *dikastēs* dispatched by Mylasa, Blümel has restored at line 24 the name of Dionysios son of Melas son of Phanias after *IK Mylasa* 806.1, where he is *stephanēphoros*. Under the new

27. A photograph of a squeeze of this inscription was published by Persson (1922: 420–426 no. 24). Louis Robert refound and photographed the stone on 3 October 1932.

28. Robert cites two other priests of Sinuri who are not on the list (1945: 13). Pixodaros is a phantom, due to a misrestoration of *IK Mylasa* 103. The other, Θαργήλιος Ἀριστομένους ὁ γενομένος ἱερεὺς Σινυρι, is known from a statue base which I will publish in my book (see *IK Mylasa* 763 for a reference to Robert's mention of this base [Robert 1945: 13]); Robert had dated the base to the second half of the first century. Debord (1969: 387), on *Labraunda* III 1 8.30, followed by Piejko (1990: 137), cf. Isager (1990).

29. Robert (1945: 94–97 no. 73), to be read in Robert (1949: 63–67), following up suggestions of Adolf Wilhelm. For the date, see Hornblower (1982: 45).

30. The idea that he belonged to this family already in Migeotte (1984: 328 n. 243); see now also *IK Mylasa* 2, p.80.

redating, *IK Mylasa* 806 belongs to the earlier group of texts (with *argyrion* only). A careful study by L. Robert revealed such close association in language and phrasing between *IK Mylasa* 631 and a decree for a judge sent from Tenos to Tralleis (*IG* XII 5.869 with *IG* XII Suppl. 136) that Robert proposed that both judges were summoned for the same court. He dated both texts to the end of the second or beginning of the first century BC. Since then, the date and association seem to have been universally accepted.[31] This dating might appear to pose an insuperable barrier to the proposed redating. Three observations are worth making. First, the restoration is far from certain. Robert reckoned about ten letters for the missing name of the grandfather (Robert 1927: 103 line 7 [= Robert 1969: 1058]). Φ[ανίου] would be short; the inscriptions of Mylasa offer many other names beginning with *phi* that would fit.[32] Second, Dionysios, Melas, and Phanias are three of the commonest names at Mylasa; it is possible that, even if the restoration is accepted, the men are not the same persons. Finally, it is not inconceivable that this Dionysios could have served as *stephanēphoros* before c. 185 and, in his old age, as a dikast at Tralleis toward the middle of the second century, given that Robert ultimately allowed for a range of dates running over a century, from 150 to 50 BC (Robert 1934: 282 [= Robert 1969: 1181]). It is perfectly possible for someone to have lived long enough to have served the Mylaseans in c. 185 and the Tralleans forty years later.[33] Thus even if the restoration of Dionysios' papponymic and the identification of the two persons be accepted, the career can be accommodated within the proposed scheme.

IK Mylasa 109. Perhaps the most serious problem is the last. One of the few well-dated Mylasean inscriptions is *IK Mylasa* 109, a decree of the tribe Otorkondeis in honor of Iatrokles. This text reports that Iatrokles was sent as ambassador to meet M. Iunius Silanus as he was crossing into Asia ([πρὸς] Μᾶρκον Ἰούνιον Δεκόμου υἱὸν Σιλανόν, στρατηγόν, πάτρωνα τῆς πόλεως, διαβαίνοντα ε[ἰς τὴν] Ἀσίαν, lines 15–16). Silanus was proconsul of Asia in 76/5 BC (Broughton 1952: 2.94). The *stephanēphoros* under whom this decree was passed was Ouliades son of Sibilos but by adoption of Euthydemos. The name Sibilos is only found in Mylasa and its vicinity, and this Sibilos has been identified with the Sibilos of *IK Mylasa* 401, a summary of honorary decrees passed for him by various Karian cities, and with the Sibilos found in several lease texts. Since a Euthydemos son of Theoxenos is known also from some of the

31. L. Robert (1927: 102–112) (= Robert 1969: 1057–1067), with the date at p. 109 (= Robert 1969: 1064). H. Englemann and R. Merkelbach, *IK Erythrai und Klazomenai* 113 (p. 205: "Wohl 1. Jahrh. V. Chr."); W. Blümel, *IK Mylasa* 1: 235; Fjodor B. Poljakov, *IK Tralleis und Nysa* 1: 29; Etienne (1990: 132). Robert's dating does not, however, rest on the basis of the lettering (so Blümel)—for, as Robert notes, the original editor gave no indication of letter forms—but on peculiarities of the orthography and style (108–109 = Robert 1969: 1063–1064).

32. For example, Phainippos, Phanodikos, Phanomenes, Philodemos, etc.

33. Robert's expanded dating range in this slightly later article was noticed by Grandjean (1979: 406). Perhaps it is worth noticing here a trend toward updating inscriptions that had been supposed to be later in earlier publications. For example, an inscription mentioning the priest Poleites son of Androsthenes (known also from *SIG*[3] 1020 B 2) from Theangela was dated to the late second or early first century BC on the basis of the lettering (see Migeotte 1992: 251–253 no. 79 with references). But we know now that he belongs in fact a century earlier, c. 201–197 BC (Descat 1997).

same lease texts, Blümel has proposed to restore Theoxenos as the father of the Euthydemos in *IK Mylasa* 109.[34] This chain seems to draw a tight bond between this late inscription and a set of lease inscriptions that on the new dating scheme belong to before about 185 BC.

It is important to recognize, first, that there is more than one Sibilos in these texts: a Sibilos (I) son of Diodoros son of Thraseas, priest of Dikaiosyne, Parembordeus, who appears in the lease inscriptions,[35] and a Sibilos (III) son of Ouliades, known from a single inscription of indeterminate date.[36] We have no patronymic either for the Sibilos (II) honored by several Karian cities, who may therefore have been either of these two or a third, or for the Sibilos whose son Ouliades was *stephanēphoros* in *IK Mylasa* 109—who may therefore have been either of the two with known patronymics, or the third, or yet a fourth. However, one might suggest a reconstruction. The Sibilos (II) honored by several Karian cities was married to Nonne daughter of Ouliades (I) (*IK Mylasa* 401.22–23). Perhaps her father's name was given to her son by Sibilos, who then could be the *stephanēphoros* of *IK Mylasa* 109, and his son could then be the Sibilos (III) son of Ouliades (II) of *IK Mylasa* 728. This reconstruction would leave the Sibilos (I) of the lease inscriptions floating free, and his father's and grandfather's names do not obviously connect him with the family just hypothetically reconstructed. He might however be an ancestor of Sibilos (II), up a couple of generations or so. Of course, one could in theory identify Sibilos (II) with Sibilos (I)—but nothing compels such an identification, and the arguments separating these two by about two generations seem to me far stronger. Since Sibilos was a name clearly passed down in alternate generations (see Sibilos [II] and [III]), I see no reason not to place Sibilos (I) farther up the chain and thus maintain the dating worked out on other, to me compelling, grounds for the lease inscriptions.

In sum, none of these difficulties poses an insurmountable problem for redating the texts, and in some cases—such as that of Ouliades son of Hekatomnos son of Korris—it considerably simplifies the dating by placing him in a time and context that fit his name. Clearly, however, this redating bears many implications about the dates of many Mylasean inscriptions, and, if it stands the test of time and the scrutiny of scholarship, will require considerable rethinking of Mylasean history. I would argue that the consequences of such rethinking will ultimately make more sense of the evidence we have and set it in better historical context.[37]

---

34. The connection was first made by Habicht (1984: 69–72); see also Habicht (1995: 87). Sibilos in the lease texts: *IK Mylasa* 801.4, 802.5, 804, 871, and see 728.1. For Euthydemos in the lease texts: *IK Mylasa* 801–804, 207.5.

35. *IK Mylasa* 801.4, 6 (but only by his name), and 22 (full designation), 803.5, 804.5–6; honorary decree, *IK Mylasa* 871.5–7.

36. *IK Mylasa* 728, a brief inscription of two lines carved on the same block as *IK Mylasa* 611 but much older (Robert 1938: 186–187).

37. As, for example, I hope to have done with the *sympoliteia* of Mylasa and Olymos in Reger (2004: 164–168). In this connection I will mention just one last example. The text of *IK Mylasa* 101 was markedly improved in Blümel's edition, most notably in the first three lines: ἀλ[λὰ] καὶ κινδύνους τοὺς μεγίστους διὰ τὸ [--------------] τοῖς Πισίδαις, τῶν δὲ περὶ Γάιον προεκπεπλευ[κότων]. I hope to be able to say something about the identity of this Gaios in another context.

PART 2

In late 1999, a group of 53 pseudo-Rhodian drachms of Mylasa, clearly a hoard or part of one, was sold to a London dealer, who kindly allowed me to examine them. It contained a fairly representative range of material from the earliest to the latest issues recorded in 1992, and was presumably buried around the middle of the second century BC: it is now recorded as *CH* 9.525. All 53 coins are illustrated on Plate 5. A further 146 drachms that have come to light piecemeal since 1992 are described in the second section of the following catalogue.

For the sake of completeness, I also reproduce on Plate 6, catalogue no. 83 in the 1992 article (SKA Bern FPL 52 [1988]: 327), whose photograph in error was not incorporated into the plate.

In addition to the drachms catalogued above, a new tetradrachm of the series came to light in 1998. It has no die in common with the two other known tetradrachms, catalogued in Ashton 1992 (nos. 21–22).

> *Obv.:* Rose with bud on either side; rose-stalk flanked by Δ–?Δ.
> *Rev.:* Eagle standing r. on groundline with open wings; to r., MY downward.
> 12 h; 9.14 g. *SNG Kayhan* 842; CNG 49 (1999), 596; Spink New York 26/6/1998, 1695.
> Here Plate 6 no. 200.

CATALOGUE

	Wt. (g)	Issue	Obv. Die	Rev. Die	Die-comb[38]
CH 9.525[39]					
1.	2.10	Anepigraphic	4	8	13
2.	2.31	Anepigraphic	9	15	27
3.	2.01	Anepigraphic	11	17	29
4.	2.28	Anepigraphic	14?	New	New
5.	2.14	Anepigraphic	19	26	43
6.	2.10	Anepigraphic	20	35	58
7.	2.19	Anepigraphic	23	42	70
8.	2.19	Anepigraphic	24	41	76

38. For the individual issues (distinguished by the presence or otherwise of various letters and monograms around the rose on the reverse), die numbers, and die-combination numbers, see Ashton (1992: 3–20).

39. The group offered in 1999 in fact contained 62 coins. The other nine were one fraction each from the Thracian Chersonese, Soloi, and Kelenderis, and a mid-third-century diobol of Rhodes with helmet symbol (Ashton 2001: 105 no. 202), none of which are likely have formed part of the hoard; a Rhodian drachm and hemidrachm of the late third century with Ameinias + trident and Ameinias + term, respectively (Ashton 2001: 106 no. 224, 107 no. 227); a Rhodian drachm and hemidrachm of c. 200 BC with Gorgos + bow in case and Peisikrates + spearhead, respectively (Ashton 2001: 109 nos. 288 and 305); and a pseudo-Rhodian drachm with uncertain moneyer + grapes struck on mainland Greece during the Third Macedonian War (*Numismatic Chronicle* 1988: 19–32). The last five could have formed part of the hoard (the pseudo-Rhodian drachm could have been carried from mainland Greece to south-west Asia Minor in 171 BC (*Numismatic Chronicle* 1995: 18–19), although I know of no other coin of that series with a provenance east of the Aegean, but on balance it seems more likely that they too are intrusive.

	Wt. (g)	Issue	Obv. Die	Rev. Die	Die-comb
9.	2.09	Anepigraphic	24	42	77
10.	1.92	Anepigraphic	24	42	77
11.	2.15	Anepigraphic	24	43	78
12.	2.22	B	28	50	86
13.	2.20	Γ	New[40]	New	New
14.	2.19	Ⱉ–Θ	31	New	New
15.	2.07	Ř	36	75	114
16.	2.06	˘ΓΡ	37	77	116
17.	2.06	Ⱥ	New	87	New
18.	2.05	M–A	54	108	New
19.	1.27[41]	M–A	54	113	156
20.	2.05	M–A	54	114	157
21.	2.32	Δ–Y/M–A	58	125	176
22.	2.31	A–Π/I–I	64	139	190
23.	2.13	Ξ–A/Ě–O	66	144	195
24.	2.23	Γ–O/ⱶ–Δ	70	New	New
25.	2.34	Y–Π/ⱶ–Δ	72	152	New
26.	2.03	Y–Π/ⱶ–Δ	72	New	New
27.	2.11	Ξ–A/ⱶ–Δ	76	160	212
28.	2.14	Ξ–A/ⱶ–Δ	76	164	New
29.	2.07	Ξ–A/ⱶ–Δ	76	New	New
30.	2.05	Ξ–A/ⱶ–Δ	77	158	New
31.	1.68	Ξ–A/ⱶ–Δ	77	158	New
32.	2.28	Ξ–A/Π–M	83	179	233
33.	2.08	Π–A/M–I	84	180	234
34.	2.16	Π–A/M–I	84	181	235
35.	1.87	Π–A/M–I	84	New	New
36.	2.04	Π–A/M–I	85	182	237
37.	2.13	Λ–Ω/M–I	New	New	New
38.	2.20	Λ–ω/M–I	85	New	New
39.	2.22	A–Y/M–I	85	187	New
40.	2.12	A–Y/M–I	86	190	245

40. This obverse die is the same as that used for coin A among the drachms of uncertain issue listed at Ashton (1992: 21). Although the reverse die is different, coin A is thus likely to belong to the Γ issue, its Γ being off flan to the right, rather than, as I had suggested in 1992, to the anepigraphic issue.
41. I have no explanation for this unusually low weight, which was double-checked.

41.	2.22	A–Υ/M–I	86	New	New
42.	2.19	ΠЄ/ ⚚ –A	91	New	New
43.	2.05	O–Π/Ξ–A	93	201	258
44.	1.92	O–Π/Ξ–A	93	201	258
45.	2.10	Ξ–A/Θ–A	95	205	262
46	2.19	Ξ–A/M–M	New	New	New
47.	1.93	Ξ–A/M–M	As last	As last	As last
48.	2.07	Π–Є/Λ–M	96	210	267
49.	2.20	Υ–Π/Δ–Δ	99	215	273
50.	2.03	Ξ–A/Δ–Δ	101	223	New
51.	2.02	Ξ–A/Δ–Δ	102	231	292
52.	2.13	Π–A/ ⚚ –Є	102	233	294
53.	2.11	Λ–ω/ ⚚ –Є	103	241	305

Miscellaneous new material[42]

54. Henzen FPL Sept. 2002 294		Anepigraphic	3	3	9
55. eBay 804262192 (7/12/2002)	2.45	Anepigraphic	3	6?	11?
56. Milas Museum, inv.	538	Anepigraphic	5	7	17
*57. SNG Tübingen 3627 (Lot)[43]	1.89	Anepigraphic	5	New	New
58. SNG Kayhan (2000), 501; CNG 53 (2000) 501	2.15[44]	Anepigraphic	6	12	22
59. SNG Tübingen 3626 (Lot)	2.15	Anepigraphic	6	12?	22?
60. Milas Museum, inv. 495		Anepigraphic	9	15	27
*61. Milas Museum, inv. 484		Anepigraphic	New	New[45]	New
62. Milas Museum, inv. 537		Anepigraphic	11	19	31
*63. SNG Tübingen 3624 (Lot)	2.25	Anepigraphic	12	17	New
64. SNG Tübingen 3628 (Lot)	2.11	Anepigraphic	15	22?	37?
*65. SNG Tübingen 3625 (Lot)	2.02	Anepigraphic	17	New	New

42. Recent pedigrees for coins already known in 1992 are not recorded here. Asterisked coins are illustrated on Plate 6. I am grateful to Koray Konuk for providing photographs of the eagle-on-cheek drachms in Milas (Mylasa) Museum, of which only one, no. 61, can be illustrated here. To judge from their respective degrees of wear and their nonconsecutive inventory numbers, they are unlikely to represent a single hoard, and seem to have come to the museum in several separate batches. Their presence at Milas is further proof, not that any was needed, that the series was struck at Mylasa: see *Numismatic Chronicle* 1997: 29, n. 32. Note also Fellows (1840: 285 and pl. 35, 6): a drachm of the anepigraphic issue [seen] at Mylasa. Not included above is Malloy 65 (2002), 139, an anepigraphic drachm whose condition and unclear photograph preclude die identification.

43. *SNG Tübingen* 3616–47, designated "(Lot)" here and in *SNG Tübingen*, entered the collection (at a date not recorded in the *SNG*) as a single group, together with the four Rhodian coins 3555, 3578, 3595–96. It is probable that the Mylasean drachms formed all or part of a single hoard; of the Rhodian coins, 3555 seems too early and 3595–96 too late to be regarded as likely members of this putative hoard, but 3578 (a drachm with Gorgos + bow in case) could have belonged to it.

44. This is the weight recorded in CNG 53; the 2.54 g given in *SNG Kayhan* may be an error, since the the great bulk of anepigraphic drachms fall in the range 2.10–2.49 g (see weight table at Ashton 1992: 21).

45. The new reverse die has, uniquely, an ivy leaf and a thyrsos in the field on either side of the rose. See below.

	Wt. (g)	Issue	Obv. Die	Rev. Die	Die-comb
*66. Ashton coll.; eBay late 1999	2.12	Anepigraphic	18	As last	New
67. Berk 122 (2001), 226; Berk 119 (2001), 237	2.20	Anepigraphic	19	26	43
68. *SNG Tübingen* 3621 (Lot)	1.99	Anepigraphic	19	27	44
69. *SNG Keckman I* 804	2.24	Anepigraphic	19	28	45
70. Milas Museum, inv. 497		Anepigraphic	19	28	45
71. Milas Museum, inv. 491		Anepigraphic	19	29	46
72. eBay 505198965 (27.11.2000)		Anepigraphic	19	30	47
73. *SNG Tübingen* 3619 (Lot)	2.10	Anepigraphic	19	31	48
74. Fitzwilliam CM 1995–82 (Konuk)	2.43	Anepigraphic	19	31	48
75. Milas Museum, inv. 540		Anepigraphic	19	32	49
76. Milas Museum, inv. 539		Anepigraphic	19	33	50
77. *SNG Tübingen* 3620 (Lot)	2.06	Anepigraphic	19	35	52
78. Milas Museum, inv. 576		Anepigraphic	19	New	New
79. Spink America 7/12/1995, 2125	2.4	Anepigraphic	20	28	53
80. *SNG Tübingen* 3615 (Hommel)	2.24	Anepigraphic	20	29	54
*81. *SNG Tübingen* 3616 (Lot)	2.11	Anepigraphic	20	31	New
82. Milas Museum, inv. 536		Anepigraphic	20	32	55
83. Milas Museum, inv. 488		Anepigraphic	20	32	55
84. Malloy 37 (1994), 144		Anepigraphic	20	32	55
85. eBay 358681994 (24.6.2000)		Anepigraphic	20	32	55
86. Zwicker 1996 Z1531[46]	2.09	Anepigraphic	20	32	55
87. Grunow FPL 48 (1998/9), 486	2.14	Anepigraphic	20	33	56
88. Tkalec 29/2/2000, 154	2.37	Anepigraphic	20	37	57
89. *SNG Kayhan* 843; CNG 25 (1993), 330	2.50	Anepigraphic	20	37	57
90. Milas Museum, inv. 494		Anepigraphic	20	35	58
91. Malloy 48 (1998), 178, ex W. Turner coll.		Anepigraphic	20	?	?
*92. Elsen 8 (1987), 81	2.43	Anepigraphic	20	31[47]	New
*93. eBay 515016400 (7.12.2000)	2.05	Anepigraphic	20	New	New
94. Milas Museum, inv. 578		Anepigraphic	21	31	61
95. *SNG Tübingen* 3623 (Lot)	1.89	Anepigraphic	21?	?	?
*96. *SNG Tübingen* 3622 (Lot)	1.99	Anepigraphic	22	29	New
97. eBay 1390981657 (28.10.2002)		Anepigraphic	23	39	67
98. Milas Museum, inv. 493		Anepigraphic	23	41	69

46. Note also the metal analysis at Zwicker (1996: 161).

47. The relatively clear and full depiction of the reverse die on this coin indicates that I erred in the 1992 catalogue in identifying the reverse die of that catalogue's no. 48 with that used for nos. 61 and 63. The reverse die on the Elsen coin is almost certainly that used for nos. 61 and 63, but is not the one used for no. 48.

99. *SNG Tübingen* 3618 (Lot)	1.97	Anepigraphic	23	41	69
100. *SNG Tübingen* 3617 (Lot)	2.22	Anepigraphic	23	41	69
101. Ashton coll.; Künker 54 (2000), 1992 part	2.26	Anepigraphic	23	41	69
102. Milas Museum, inv. 490		Anepigraphic	23	44	72
103. Berk 59 (1989), 300		Anepigraphic	24	41	76
104. Milas Museum, inv. 501		Anepigraphic	24	42	77
105. Sadberk Hanım Museum 275	2.15	Anepigraphic	24	43	78
106. eBay 1290010149 (5.11.2001)		Anepigraphic	24	44	79
107. *SNG Keckman I* 805		Anepigraphic	24	45	80
108. eBay 1214369808 (19.2.2001)		Anepigraphic	24	45	80
109. Malloy 56 (2000), 100		Anepigraphic	24	45?	80?
*110. Berk 119 (2001), 238	2.38	Anepigraphic	24	New	New
111. Malloy LXVIII (2003), 101		Anepigraphic	?	?	?
112. Antioch Associates 45 (2003), 49		A–Z	31	65	102
*113. *SNG Tübingen* 3637 (Lot)	1.92	A–Z	31	New	New
*114. Antioch Associates 47 (2003), 39		A–Z	31	New	New
*115. Ashton coll.; eBay 1214368663 (19.2.2001)	2.12	K	?	New	New
*116. *SNG Kayhan* 845, acq. 1992	1.82	ΓP	37	New	New
117. Milas Museum, inv. 503		ΓP	38	79	120
118. Milas Museum, inv. 580		?	New	New	New[48]
119. Ashton coll.; eBay 410331066 (Aug. 2000)	2.31	X	40	81	122
120. *SNG Keckman I* 806		X	42	84?	?
121. eBay 1218666321 (8.3.2001)		Δ–H	45	89	131
122. Milas Museum, inv. 492		M–A	50	98	140
123. G. Hirsch 236 (2004), 1922		M–A	51	102	145
124. Milas Museum, inv. 485		M–A	52	10	150
125. Hirsch 217 (2001), 1514		M–A	54	111	154
126. Milas Museum, inv. 498		M–A	54?	113	156?
127. Malloy 62 (2001), 153; Malloy 56 (2000), 101		M–A	55	111?	158?
128. Malloy LXVIII (2003), 102		M–A	?	?	?
129. *SNG Tübingen* 3646 (Lot)		Δ–Y/M–A	58	125	176
130. G. Hirsch 233 (2004), 1484		Δ–Y/M–A	58	125	176

48. The issue to which this coin belongs is uncertain, but the upright eagle clinging to Helios' cheek like a woodpecker to a tree-trunk is very similar to that found on one obverse die (A40) of the X issue; hence this coin is assumed to belong to or close to that issue.

	Wt. (g)	Issue	Obv. Die	Rev. Die	Die-comb
131. Milas Museum, inv. 416		Π–Є/A–M	59	New	New
132. Milas Museum, inv.?		Π–Є/A–M	59	New	New
*133. *SNG Tübingen* 3638 (Lot)	2.00	Π–Є/A–M	59	New	New
134. Ashton coll., acq. 1993[49]	2.24	Ξ–A/M–A	58	129	180
135. Milas Museum, inv. 486		Δ–Υ/I–I?	?	New	New
136. Milas Museum, inv. 499		Ξ–A/[I]–I	64?	New	New
*137. *SNG Tübingen* 3639 (Lot)	1.96	Π–A/⋈–Δ	67?	New	New
138. *SNG Tübingen* 3640 (Lot)	1.67	Π–A/⋈–Δ	68?	147?	198?
*139. Peus 369 (2001), 203	2.06	Π–A/⋈–Δ	69?	146	New?
140. Berk 114 (2000), 214		Λ–Ω/⋈–Δ	70?	149?	200?
141. *SNG Tübingen* 3641 (Lot)	2.12	Λ–Ω/⋈–Δ	70	150	201
*142. Henzen FPL June 2002, 290; id., FPL July 2001, 268		Λ–Ω/⋈–Δ	70	New	New
143. Milas Museum, inv. 483		Υ–Π/⋈–Δ	70	New	New
*144. *SNG Tübingen* 3645 (Lot.)	1.99	Δ–I/ ⋈–Δ	75?	New	New
*145. Malloy 63 (2001), 133		A–Π/⋈–Δ	75?	New	New
146. Milas Museum, inv. 417		[Ξ]–A/⋈–Δ	76	New	New
*147. eBay 1217437877 (3.3.2001)	2.12	Ξ–A/⋈–Δ	76	New	New
*148. *SNG Tübingen* 3633 (Lot)	2.19	Ξ–A/⋈–Δ	77	As last?	New
*149. *SNG Tübingen* 3647 (Lot)	2.19	Δ–Υ/Π–M	79	New	New
*150. Ashton coll.; eBay 3005474282 (12.2.2003)	2.14	Δ–Υ/Π–M	79?	As last?	New
151. Milas Museum, inv. 579		Ξ–A/Π–M	79	New	New
152. *SNG Tübingen* 3630 (Lot)	2.14	Ξ–A/Π–M	79	173	225
153. Milas Museum, inv. ?		Ξ–A/Π–M	?	174	?
154. Milas Museum, inv. 577		Ξ–A/Π–M	New?	New	New
155. Milas Museum, inv. 489		Ξ–A/Π–M	New?	New	New
*156. *SNG* Tübingen 3631 (Lot)	2.00	Ξ–A/Π–M	?	New	New
157. Milas Museum, inv. 418		Π–M/Ξ–A	80	175	227
158. Malloy 67 (2002), 130		Ξ–A/Π–M	81	174	228
159. *SNG Tübingen* 3642 (Lot)	1.87	Π–A/M–I	85	182	237
160. UBS 59 (Basel, 2004), 5763	2.31	Π–A/M–I	85	182	237
*161. *SNG Tübingen* 3644 (Lot)	2.59	Π–A/[M–I]	85?	New	New
162. Ashton coll., acq. 1992	1.99	Λ–Ω/M–I	86	184	239
163. eBay 489808320 (11.11.2000)	2.04	Λ–Ω/M–I	86	184?	239?

49. I acquired coins 134, 162, 186, 189, 195, and 197 from two London dealers in 1992 and 1993. They almost certainly came from a common source, for they appear to have been subjected to the same cleaning methods, which made their surfaces very bright, and a common hoard provenance is likely. Their wear would be consistent with this.

164. Ashton coll.; eBay 250770104 (Jan./Feb. 2000)	2.19	Υ–Π/Μ–Ι	806	186	241
165. Milas Museum, inv. 496		Α–Υ/Μ–Ι	85	187	New
166. eBay 1212393559 (10.2.2001)		Α–Υ/Μ–Ι	86	190	245
167. eBay 1208523794 (26.1.2001)		Δ or Α–Υ/ Μ–Ι	86	192[50]	247
168. Milas Museum, inv. 502	2.15	⋀–Ι/Μ	87	193	248
*169. eBay 3009452444 (2.3.2003)		Ι/Μ–Π	87	New	New
*170. UBS 59 (Basel, 2004), 5762	2.18	Α–Υ/⚕–⚕	91	New	New
171. *SNG Kayhan* 846; *CNG* 47 (1998), 491; id. 24 (1992), 294	2.17	ΠΕ/⚕–Α	91	198	255
*172. *SNG Tübingen* 3634 (Lot)	1.95	Ξ–Α/⚕–Α	91	New	New
173. *SNG Tübingen* 3635 (Lot)	1.94	Ξ–Α/⚕–Α	91	As last	As last
174. *CNG* 53 (2000), 502		Ο–Π/Ξ–Α	93	201	258
175. *SNG Tübingen* 3636 (Lot)	2.04	Ο–Π/Ξ–Α	93?	201?	258?
176. Malloy 55 (1999), 120		Λ–Μ/Α–Υ	96	209	266
177. G. Hirsch 178 (1993), 399		Λ–Μ/Α–Υ	96	209	266
*178. G. Hirsch 173 (1992), 421	1.66	Π–Ε/Λ–Μ	96	New	New
179. G. Hirsch 178 (1993), 398	2.5	Ξ–Α/Λ–Μ	96	211	268
180. Ashton coll.; eBay late 1999	1.71	Ξ–Α/Λ–Μ	96	212	269
181. *SNG Tübingen* 3629 (Lot)	2.51	Ξ–Α/Λ–Μ	96	212	269
*182. KMK 69 (1998), 147; KMK 66 (1997), 117	1.93	Π–Α/Δ–Δ	98	New	New
183. G. Hirsch 178 (1993), 400	1.87	Λ–ω/Δ–Δ	97	213	270
184. Malloy 52 (1999), 179; id. 48 (1998), 177; ex Wm Turner coll.		Λ–ω/Δ–Δ	98	213	271
*185. Antioch Associates 25 (1999), 23		Υ–Π/Δ–Δ	99	New	New
*186. Ashton coll., acq. 1993	2.26	Π–Ε/Δ–Δ	New	216	New
187. *CNG* 37 (1996), 543	2.15	Δ–Υ/Δ–Δ	100	220	278
*188. G. Hirsch 175 (1992), 404	2.15	Δ–Υ/Δ–Δ	100	New	New
189. Ashton coll., acq. 1993	2.12	Ξ–Α/Δ–Δ	101	223	284
*190. *SNG Tübingen* 3632 (Lot)	1.85	Ξ–Α/Δ–Δ	101	New	New
191. G. Hirsch 202 (1998), 219; id. 191 (1996), 536; id. 187 (1995), 544	2.25	Π–Α/⚕–Ε	102	232	293
192. KMK 72 (2000), 57	2.05	Π–Α/⚕–Ε	102	233?	294?
193. *SNG Tübingen* 3643 (Lot)	2.00	Π–Α/⚕–Ε	105	240	303
194. eBay 375773544 (13.7.2000)	1.69	Γ–Ο/⚕–Ε	103	243	309
195. Ashton coll., acq. 1992	1.97	Γ–Ο/⚕–Ε	103	244	310

50. The poor illustration available to me of this new coin does not resolve the question as to whether reverse P192 belongs to Dystros or Audnaios (Ashton 1992: 16 n. 12).

196. KMK 60 (1994), 207	2.08	Γ–O/ ⚹ –Є	103	244	310
197. Ashton coll., acq. 1993	1.96	Γ–O/ ⚹ –Є	107	245	313
198. Milas Museum, inv. 500		Γ–O/ ⚹ –Є	107	245	313
199. Milas Museum, inv. 487		Uncertain	?	New	New

COMMENTARY

1. The new material does not require any radical change in the relative dating proposed in 1992. The wear of the coins on the 1999 hoard is consistent with the ordering of issues proposed in 1992, for the anepigraphic coins are significantly more worn than those with one or two letters or single monogram, while the latter in turn are more worn than those with four letters/monograms.

2. The new material produces a hitherto unrecorded annual issue signed by the initials M and M in the month Xandikos (nos. 46 and 47 in the 1999 hoard). The obverse die used for these two die-duplicate coins is new, but its style suggests that the issue should be placed near the Θ–A issue.

3. New months are recorded for several annual issues already known: A–M are now known to have struck in Peritios (cat. nos. 131–133); I–I (probably) in Dystros and Xandikos (cat. nos. 135–136); ⊠–Δ in Apellaios (cat. no. 145);[51] M–I in Peritios (probably: cat. no. 169);[52] ⚹–A in Audnaios and Xandikos (cat. nos 170, 172, 173); and Δ–Δ in Panemos (cat. no. 182).

4. The new drachms produce seven certain and two probable new obverse dies, and include 192 coins with identifiable obverse dies. Adding these figures to the 107 obverse dies from 620 coins with identifiable obverse dies recorded in the 1992 article,[53] we reach new totals of 116 obverse dies from 812 coins, and an increase in the ratio of coins to obverse dies from 5.79 to 7.00.

5. The new coins produce 50 new reverse dies to be added to the 246 recorded in 1992[54] to give a total of 296.

6. All the recorded die-axes from the above coins (those in the 1999 hoard and in my own collection) are upright. I did however notice that, among the coins of the

51. This new and indisputable issue for Apellaios in the ⊠–Δ year makes one wonder whether coin 207 in the 1992 catalogue, there read as A – ?Υ/⊠–Δ and classed as the only known coin for Audnaios in that magistrate year, should not be regarded an issue of Apellaios.

52. This coin shows yet again the experimentation practised by the die-cutter in the position of the letters on the reverse dies of the M–I magistrates (Ashton 1992: 16, 24 n. 19). This time the I is placed above the M to the left of the rose, and to the right, the month is apparently represented by a single letter Π rather than by the usual two letters. Given that its obverse die, A87, is otherwise recorded only for Audnaios and Xandikos, the single letter presumably stands for the immediately preceding Peritios rather than the much earlier Panemos. (The magisterial year seems to have ended in Xandikos; hence, although no coins of any issue have been recorded for the months Artemisios and Daisios, which immediately follow Xandikos, the letter Π is most unlikely to stand for the following month, Panemos, in the next magisterial year; see Ashton 1992: 25.)

53. 619 + coin A, whose obverse die can now be identified: see footnote 40 above.

54. Including one each for coins 48 and A in the 1992 catalogue: see footnotes 40 and 47 above.

new hoard, the earlier coins tended to have axes at precisely 12 o'clock, while the later coins, with consistently cursive lettering and cruder style, tended to have axes which veered towards 1 o'clock, although there were many exceptions.

7. Cat. no. 61, an anepigraphic coin in Milas Museum, is unique in having an ivy leaf and a *thyrsos* on either side of the rose. In 1992, I suggested that the *thyrsoi* found on either side of the rose on the ⋈/Δ issue may suggest that the monogram Δ should be resolved as a name beginning Dionys . . . .[55] The occurrence of Dionysiac symbols on the anepigraphic issue suggests that they have a wider reference than a single individual. As Reger reminds me, Dionysos was worshipped at Mylasa from at least the Hellenistic period (*IK Mylasa* 101. 61–62; 330; 501.7–8), but his connection, if any, with the coins remains obscure.

8. The second monogram on the new reverse die of cat. 170 shows that the name of the second magistrate of the ⚹–A year began Ar… This remarkable coin also supplies a new month for its year, as we have seen, and, unlike any other recorded coin of the series, it is lozenge-like in shape, as if broken off the end of a thin bar of silver.

9. The new tetradrachm seems to belong to the year of the magistrate pair Δ–Δ (nos. 271–292 of the 1992 catalogue); it has no month initial. The squat globular shape of its rose suggests a date early within the series as a whole, and contrasts with the rather elongated roses of the Δ–Δ drachms, which must come near the end (Ashton 1992: 25, 27–29). Likewise, the elegance of the eagle on the tetradrachms contrasts with the crude eagle-on-cheek heads of the Δ–Δ drachms. It would be farfetched to suggest that the Δ–?Δ of the tetradrachm are mere simplifications of the monograms ⋈ and Δ found on an earlier series of drachms. In the absence of other evidence, we should accept that the new tetradrachm belongs with the Δ–Δ drachms, and might speculate that for this rare emission of tetradrachms the mint decided to employ a more competent engraver than the one used for the contemporary drachms.

10. The new high dating proposed for the "leases" and for the start of the Mylasean eagle-on-cheek coinage, before the mid-180s, casts doubt on the integrity of *IGCH* 1335, which is reported to have contained some 200 Mylasean drachms ranging from the earliest to the latest issues, and a quantity of Rhodian plinthophoric hemidrachms, both sets of coins in roughly the same state of wear. Fifteen of the Rhodian hemidrachms have been identified, nine from Jenkins (1989), Group B, six from Group D. Group D belongs to roughly the last quarter of the second century (with some issues perhaps a little earlier and some a little later) (Ashton 1992: 1 n. 2, and 31). Although the Mylasean and Rhodian coins could have been buried together in ancient times, it is perhaps more likely that the assemblage is a modern conflation of two ancient hoards or parts of hoards.

---

55. The *thyrsoi* are usually, perhaps always, filleted.

Bibliography

Ashton, R. H. J. 1987. Pseudo-Rhodian drachms and the beginning of the Lycian league coinage. *Numismatic Chronicle* 147: 8–25.

———. 1992. The pseudo-Rhodian drachms of Mylasa. *Numismatic Chronicle* 152: 1–39.

———. 1995. Pseudo-Rhodian drachms from central Greece. *Numismatic Chronicle* 155: 1–20.

———. 1998. The coins of the Macedonian kings, Lysimachos and Eupolemos in the museums of Fethiye and Afyon. In: A. Burnett, U. Wartenberg, R. Witschonke, eds., *Coins of Macedonia and Rome. Essays in honour of Charles Hersh*, pp. 19–48. London: Spink.

———. 1999. The Hellenistic hemidrachms of Kaunos. *Revue belge de numismatique et de sigillographie* 145: 141–54.

———. 2001. The coinage of Rhodes 408–c. 190 BC. In: A. Meadows and K. Shipton, eds., *Money and its uses in the ancient Greek world*, pp. 79–115. Oxford: Oxford University Press.

———. 2002. Clubs, thunderbolts, torches, stars and caducei: more pseudo-Rhodian drachms from mainland Greece and the islands. *Numismatic Chronicle* 162: 59–78.

———. 2004. Redating the earliest Alexanders of Rhodes. *Numismatic Chronicle* 164: 93–102.

———. 2005. Recent epigraphic evidence for the start of the Rhodian and Lykian league plinthophoroi. *Numismatic Chronicle* 165: 85–89.

Behrend, D. 1973. Rechtshistorische Betrachtungen zu den Pachtdokumenten aus Mylasa und Olymos. In: *Akten des VI. internationalen Kongresses für griechische und lateinische Epigraphik*, pp. 145–68. Munich: C. H. Beck'sche.

Blümel, W. 1992. Neue Inschriften aus Mylasa (1989–1991) mit Nachträgen zu I.K. 34. *Epigraphica Anatolica* 19: 5–18.

———. 1995. Inschriften aus Karien I. *Epigraphica Anatolica* 25: 35–76.

———. 2004. Inschriften aus Karien II. *Epigraphica Anatolica* 37: 1–35.

Bresson, A. 1993. La circulation monétaire rhodienne jusqu'en 166. *Dialogues d'histoire ancienne* 19: 119–69.

———. 1996. Drachmes rhodiennes et imitations: une politique économique de Rhodes? *Revue des Études Anciennes* 98: 65–77.

———. 1998. Rhodes, Cnide et les Lyciens au début du IIᵉ siècle av. J.-C. *Revue des Études Anciennes* 100: 65–88.

Broughton, T. R. S. 1952. *Magistrates of the Roman republic,* vol. 2. New York: American Philological Association.

Buckler, W. H. 1916/1918. Documents from Mylasa. *Annual of the British School at Athens* 22: 190–215.

CH: Coin Hoards. 1975–. London: Royal Numismatic Society.

Cousin, G. 1898. Voyage en Carie. *Bulletin de correspondance hellénique* 22: 361–402.

CRAI: Comptes rendus de l'Académie des inscriptions et belles-lettres.

Agoranomia: Studies in Money and Exchange Presented to John H. Kroll, pp. 151–176
© 2006 The American Numismatic Society

Amyntas, Side, and the Pamphylian Plain

PLATES 7–12   ANDREW R. MEADOWS*

It is a pleasure to be able to honor one who has done so much over the years to remind us that numismatics is but one aspect of the broader pursuit of historical research.[1] It has its own methods, of which he is an undisputed master, but its goals should be those of any historian of the ancient world. The present I offer will, I hope, be fitting for a number of reasons. At one level, it deals with a problem with which Jack has had to wrestle in the field of Athenian coinage: that of imitation, the borrowing of the types of one mint by a different issuing authority (in the case of Athenian imitations at some geographical remove). On the other hand, my subject is one of the rare but wonderful cases where the understanding of a decade or more of the history of an entire region may depend upon the correct understanding of a single die link. It is also a case where, for us to be able to appreciate its historical importance, we must move beyond basic numismatic method and begin to question what coinage meant to the individuals who made and used it.

I. AMYNTAS

We begin in the area of southern Asia Minor, during the period of Mark Antony's imperium in the East.[2] In 40 BC, a Parthian army penetrated deep into Asia Minor under the command of Quintus Labienus, a former lieutenant of the tyrannicides Brutus and Cassius. In

*Department of Coins and Medals, The British Museum, London.

1. I am very grateful to Wolfgang Leschhorn for his comments on a draft of this paper, and for sharing the results of his own work on the mint of Side. I am also indebted to Oliver Hoover for comments and for the use of unpublished work on Seleucid countermarks.

2. Another numismatic consequence of this, at Aigion in Achaia, has been suggested by Jack himself: Kroll (1993: 233, *ad* no. 733). Note also the comments on Athenian coinage of Antonian date (1993: 104–105, *ad* nos. 144–145).

the following year, the Antonian forces went on the counterattack under the leadership of
Publius Ventidius Bassus and recovered Asia Minor. Antony appears to have taken the opportunity in 39 BC to rearrange certain aspects of the administration of the area. Deiotarus,
the king of Galatia, had recently died, and Antony now made some strategic alterations to
the former Galatian dominions. A kingdom of Pontus was created to the north, including
some of Galatia's northern territories, and bestowed upon Darius son of Pharnaces. The
central part of the Galatian kingdom, along with parts of Paphlagonia, was given to Deiotarus' grandson Castor. To Polemo son of Zeno of Laodikeia was given the governorship of
an area described by Appian as "parts of Cilicia" (*BC* 5.75), which seems to have included
Iconium in Lycaonia (Strabo 12. 6. 1 C 568). Control of an area described by Appian (*BC*
5.75) as Pisidia was handed to Amyntas son of Dyitalos, a former commander in the army
of Deiotarus.[3] However, this state of affairs did not survive for long. Most probably during
the winter of 37/6 BC further change was precipitated by the end of Castor's rule in Galatia.[4]
The northeastern part of his kingdom passed to his son Deiotarus, but the bulk of Galatia
now passed to Amyntas together, it appears, with some of the areas that had previously belonged to Polemo. This last was more than compensated for by the award of the Kingdom
of Pontus in the place of the territory ceded to Amyntas.

The literary sources for this latter settlement of 37/6 BC are fragmentary, and the precise territory covered by Amyntas' new kingdom has been the matter for some debate in
the past. Of particular interest is the fate of the large and fertile plain of Pamphylia and the
wealthy cities that occupied it. In such circumstances, the evidence of coinage has often
although not always been invoked.

In an article now largely forgotten, Ronald Syme (1934) gathered together the evidence
for the areas of Galatia and Pamphylia under Augustus.[5] His starting point was Strabo's account of the kingdom granted to Amyntas by Mark Antony in 37/6. Strabo informs us that
Amyntas' kingdom consisted of Galatia proper (the territory of the three tribes), as well as
regions to the southwest: Lycaonia (including Isauria), Cilicia Tracheia, Pisidia, and Phry-
gian Pisidia. As Syme noted, the southernmost and westernmost cities described by Strabo
as belonging to this kingdom are, respectively, Selge and Sagalassos. He added:

> This is unimpeachable testimony. It is further to be noted that Strabo nowhere says
> anything about the status of the cities of the Pamphylian coast either before or after the
> death of Amyntas; indeed, he implies a contrast between Selge (which was Pisidian,
> and therefore had belonged to Amyntas), and both Side and Aspendos, which he calls

---

3. For Amyntas' earlier career and his recently discovered patronymic, see Mitchell (1994: 101). On the extent
of this early award and the evidence of Strabo 12.6.4 C 569, see Mitchell (1993: 2.152 n. 17).

4. On the chronology, see Mitchell (1993: 1.39).

5. Although Syme would later single out the piece as the beginning of his interest in Asia Minor and the province of Galatia (in the preface to the Italian edition of *Colonial Elites* [= 1978–91: VI.xi]), it was not included in
the *Roman Papers*.

Παμφυλικαὶ πόλεις [Pamphylian cities]. The argument from silence is dangerous, but is here perhaps to be admitted. If the Pamphylian cities were not in the kingdom of Amyntas, Strabo was not bound to state the fact; if they were, such a remarkable fact was worth recording in view of the abundant detail he provides about the extent of Amyntas' kingdom. Seleuceia, on the coast of Cilicia Tracheia, so we are informed by Strabo, did not belong to Amyntas. It would be strange if Pamphylian cities like Attaleia, Side and Aspendos did. (Syme 1934: 123)

Syme goes on to add that Dio (49.32.3), in his account of Antony's settlement, states that the Roman gave Galatia to Amyntas and added to this Lykaonia and *parts* of Pamphylia (Παμφυλίας τέ τινα αὐτῷ προσθεὶς). As Syme says, "There must therefore have been other parts which did not belong to him. We know from Strabo that he held Pisidia and Cilicia Tracheia [which could fall under the heading of Pamphylia at this period]. Therefore the only 'part of Pamphylia' left, the only part which did not belong to him was the Pamphylian coast" (1934: 124).

   Syme's application of logic was as usual impeccable, and the solution he proposed made sense of all the evidence, or so it momentarily seemed. But Syme had committed an uncharacteristic gaffe. He had overlooked one crucial piece of evidence that appeared to prove incontrovertibly that his reconstruction was wrong, and that the Pamphylian plain must have belonged to Amyntas. And this piece of evidence is numismatic.

   Syme was soon made to realize his mistake. A. H. M. Jones would point out in his *Cities of the Eastern Roman Provinces* (1937: 412 n. 20) that there existed a silver coinage of Amyntas, minted with the designs of the city of Side, and firmly attributed by such authorities as Barclay Head and the *British Museum Catalogue* to a mint in the city operating for Amyntas. The similarity is indeed undeniable. On the obverse appears a head of Athena in crested Corinthian helmet facing to the right, her hair falling from underneath the back of the helmet. On the reverse stands a figure of Nike facing to the left. On the issues of Side she holds a wreath, on the issues of Amyntas a scepter or sheathed sword. To the left on the Sidetan issues is a pomegranate, the symbol of the city, and a magistrate's name or monogram, the latter sometimes extending into the right field. On the issues of Amyntas there is no symbol or magistrate's identifier, just the clear statement ΒΑΣΙΛΕΩΣ ΑΜΥΝΤΟΥ (See Plate 8 no. 9 [Side] and no. 10 [Amyntas]). Ever since the coins of Amyntas first appeared in 1845, the attribution of Amyntas' coinage to Side had been obvious, and an obvious conclusion had been drawn: Side, and with it the rest of Pamphylia, must have belonged to the Galatian kingdom.[6]

   Syme was clearly aghast at his omission: he returned to the matter and pointed out his mistake on at least three occasions in print.[7] Subsequent writers have tended to regard the

---

6. The first coins of Amyntas to be published were two acquired in London and three that appeared in Paris. On the publication of these coins and the circumstances of their discovery, see below.

7. Syme notes that "In a matter irrelevant to the main purpose of that paper, but arising from Dio's account of the dominions of King Amyntas (49.32.3) and of their disposal after his death in 25 BC (53.26.3) the writer, in

argument from coinage as decisive and have accepted that the Pamphylian plain, or at least the city of Side, must have been within Amyntas' kingdom.[8]

But I now wonder whether Syme was correct to give in so easily. Amyntas' coinage is extraordinary, indeed I think unique in the world of the Hellenistic rulers. For while it was a relatively common phenomenon for cities to copy the designs of kings to produce acceptable specie, such as in the cases of the many posthumous Alexander coinages (Price 1991), the first-century silver of Antioch in the name of the Seleucid king Philip I (*RPC* I 4124–4149), and the silver of Aradus in the name of the Ptolemaic king, in the silver of Amyntas we find the reverse of this phenomenon occurring. A king copies the designs of a city and adds his name. This singularity requires closer examination than it has received, not least because the evidence has undergone such a transformation since Syme wrote. There have been major advances, both in the evidence available for the coinage of Side and in our understanding of its relationship to the coinage of Amyntas. To understand fully the impact of these advances, a detailed look at these coinages will be necessary.

II. Side and Its Coinage

The Hellenistic silver coinage of Side began in the very late third century. Unlike their neighbors at Aspendos, Perge, Sillyum, and Phaselis, who all began at around this time to produce coinage with types of Alexander the Great,[9] the Sidetans introduced a coinage with its own distinctive types: a helmeted head of Athena on the obverse and a figure of Nike on the reverse. In place of an ethnic, the city's badge, a pomegranate, also featured prominently on the reverse. Unlike the other Pamphylian cities, which marked their coinage with a sequence of letters that are generally taken to be dates according to one or more civic eras, the citizens of Side controlled their coinage with abbreviated forms of the names of the men responsible for them. In recent years, the hoard evidence for the beginning of this coinage has become remarkably clear (see Table 1). A first group of hoards (H1–3), buried within the decade c. 205–195, allows us to pin down the earliest three issues. Thereafter, another horizon is provided by a group of nine hoards (H4–12), all apparently buried around the time of the war between Rome and Antiochus III in the late 190s, providing another clear chronological point before which almost all of the remainder of the magistrates' issues must be placed. Just one magistrate seems to postdate this horizon, whose name is abbreviated as ΚΛΕ, ΚΛΕΥ, or ΚΛΕΥΧ (*Kle, Kleu,* or *Kleuch*) and usually taken to have been "Kleuchares"

order to give meaning to Dio's words, felt compelled to assume that the Pamphylian Coast had not been a part of the Galatian kingdom of Amyntas. This appears to be false—Amyntas coined at Side in Pamphylia" (1937: 227 = 1978–91: I.42); cf. Syme (1939: 330 = 1978–91: I.145): "a mistake"; and Syme (1995: 179): "this argument was adduced . . . wrongly".

8. A. H. M. Jones had suggested that Amyntas ruled all of Pamphylia. Others have been more cautious, confining the assumption to Side. See, e.g., Magie (1950: 434, 1284 n. 21); Bowersock (1965: 51–52); Levick (1967: 26 n. 6).

9. On the Pamphylian Alexanders and their date(s), see most recently Price (1991: 346–348) and Boehringer (1999). They seem to have begun slightly earlier than the issues of Side.

TABLE 1.

H	Date	Hoard[a]	Side	Magistrates	Cmk[b]
1	c. 205	Diyarbakir (1735)	1	AΘ	
2	c. 201	Pergamum, Asklepieion (1303)	2	AP, ΔI	
3	c. 200–195	Oylum Höyüğü	1	ΔI	
4	c. 190	Mektepini (1410)	4	AP (2); A; ΔI	
5	c. 190	Kosseir (1537)	9	AK (2); AP + helmet; Δ E; ΔH; ΔIOΔ; ΣH (3)	
6	c. 190	Latakia (1536)	6	AP + helmet (2); AP + wreath (2); XPY	
7	c. 190	Sardes pot (1318)	13	ΔEI; ΔEIN; ΔEINO; ΔI (2); ΔIN; ΔIO (2); Δ ; Σ (2); Σ H; CT.	
8	c. 190	Pisidia? (1411)	3+2	(A) ΔI; Δ E; Σ (B) ΔI; ΔIOΔ	
9	c. 190	Ayaz In (1413)	34	AP; AP + wreath (2); ΔEI; Δ E (3) ; ΔEIN; ΔEINO (2); Δ I; Δ I + fulmen; ΔIO (6); ΔIOΔ (5); Σ (4); Σ H (5); CT (2).	
10	c. 190?	Karacalar (9.505)	2	Δ E; Σ; H	–
11	c. 190	Aleppo (1539)	?	Unknown	
12	c. 190	Syria (2.81)	22	Unknown	?
13	c. 180	Alicante (8.411)	1	CT	–
14	c. 180	Çeltek[c]	33	ΔIO (2); ΔIOΔ (4); Σ H (2); ΔE; ΔEI (4); ΔEINO (4); ΔH (5); ΔHM (5); AK; XPY (4); uncert.	C
15	c. 170–150	Unknown[d]	198	Unknown (no KΛEYX I)	Yes
16	c. 175–160	Konya (7.105)	1	KΛEY	A, R
17	c. 175–160	Beqa'[e]	1	KΛEY	A
18	c. 175–160	Unknown[f]	1	KΛEY	A
19	c. 170–160	Khan Cheikhoun (1547)	22	Δ E; ΔH; ΣT (3); CT; Σ H (2); KΛE (3); KΛEY (5); KΛEYX I (6)	A, R
20	c. 169	Latakia (1544)	1+1	AP + wreath	A
21	c. 165	Aleppo (1546)	12	ΔE; ΔIOΔ; CT (2); ΣT; KΛEY (7)	A
22	c. 170–55	Tell Kotchek	3	ΣT; KΛEY; KΛEYX I	A, R
23	c. 162	Ma'Aret en-Nu'man (8.433)	38	AP; fulmen (2); helmet; ΔEI (4); ΔEIN (2); CT (2); ΣT (3); ΔH; ΔHM; XPY; KΛE (2); KΛEY (14); KΛEYX I (4?)	A, R
24	c. 155–150	Babylon (1774)	6	℞; Σ; ΔHM; KΛEY; KΛEYX I (2)	A
25	c. 150	S. Anatolia (1432)	2	ΔEINO; CT.	A
26	c. 150–140	E. Anatolia (9.517)	13	AP; ΔIO; ΔHM (2); KΛEY (3); KΛEYX I; KΛE[--]; CT; uncert. (2).	A, R, T
27	c. 144/3	Gaziantep (9.527)[g]	20+3	ΔI; ΔH (2); ΔEINO; CT; ΣT; Σ H (2); KΛE (3+1); KΛEY (6+2); KΛEYX I (3)	A
28	c. 200–150	Asia Minor (1457)	25	Unknown (no KΛEYX II)	Yes
29	c. 150–140	Asia Minor (1453)	5	XPY; KΛEYX II	–
30	c. 138	Susiana (1806)	1	ΔH	A, R
31	c. 150–100	Unknown (9.521)[h]	560 + 127	All magistrates up to and including KΛEYX II	A, R, C, O
32	c. 150–100	Çığlık[i]	53	AΘ, ΓP (2); helmet; wreath (2); ΔI (2); ΔIOΔ; Σ H (2); ΣH (?3); ΔEI (2); ΔEINO; ΔHM; AK; XPY; KΛE (13); KΛEY (6); KΛEYX I (3); KΛEYX II (8)	A, C

33	c. 150–100	Karakuyu (9.518)	269	KΛEYX II	–
34	c. 125–100	Unknown Findspot[j]	111	ΔIO; ΔIOΔ (5); AP; ΣT (4); CT (5); E; Δ E; ΔH ; AK ; XPY (2); KΛEY (4); KΛEYX (82); uncert. (3)	–
35	1st cent.?	Egypt (1721)	43	ΔH; ΔIO (2); ΔEI; ΔEINO (2); ΣT (2); KΛEY and KΛEYX (26) uncert. (9)	A, C.
36	1st cent.	Unknown (9.551)	15	KΛEYX II and III	–
37	1st cent.	Side environs (3.80; 8.532; 9.569)	85	KΛEYX III	–
38	1st cent.	Asia Minor (1463)	11+	KΛEYX II, III, and IV?	–

a. Numbers in brackets are references (where available) to *IGCH* or volumes of *CH*.

b. C = cistophoric; A = anchor; R = radiate head; T = tyche head; O = other.

c. Arslan (1998, 2001).

d. Leschhorn (1988: 24).

e. Elayi (1999).

f. Davesne and Lemaire (1996: 65–67). It is here assumed that the group of ten coins published by Davesne and Lemaire form, as they suggest, two distinct groups. The contents of the earlier of these (including the coin of Side) suggest a burial date of c. 180–160.

g. This remarkably interesting hoard remains to be fully published. Part was listed as *CH* 9.527, part was published by Augé et al. (1997), and a further portion was dispersed in commerce. The relatively precise date for its burial emerges from both the dated Seleucid issues and the Athenian New Style tetradrachms that it contained. A full publication is being prepared by the author and A. Houghton.

h. Professor Leschhorn informs me that the 560 coins of the Saarbrücken hoard were most probably from the same hoard as those recorded in Frankfurt by H. Schubert. For the latter group see, Leschhorn (1998: 23); Schubert (1998) "Münzschatz A". The number of coins given for this hoard by both authors is 127; the table provided by Schubert (592) lists only 126 coins, however.

i. Büyükyörük (2001).

j. Schubert (1998) "Münzschatz D". This hoard contained far fewer of the early issues of Side than Schubert's "Münzschatz A" and a greater proportion of Kleuchares II issues. It seems reasonable to suppose that D was buried later than A.

(Seyrig 1962: 59 with n. 1). However, the issues in the name of this man are far from easy to interpret, and some detailed analysis of these is necessary if we are to begin to understand the relationship between the coinage of Side and that of Amyntas. There appear to be four distinct groups in the name of this magistrate.

Kleuchares I

The first group of issues in the name of Kleuchares has generally been the best understood. The hoard evidence makes it clear that it was not among the earliest issues of the mint, since it is absent both from the group of hoards (H1–3) that closed around 205–195 BC and also from the larger group (H4–12) that seem to have closed by c. 190 BC. The issues of Kleuchares I do not begin to appear in the hoard record until the 170s and 160s (H16–23). When the group begins, the coins are signed simply KΛE (Subgroup 1: plate 7 no. 1). These issues were followed by coins with the fuller abbreviation KΛEY (Subgroup 2: plate 7 no. 2), and although no obverse die link between these subgroups has yet been published, hoard evi-

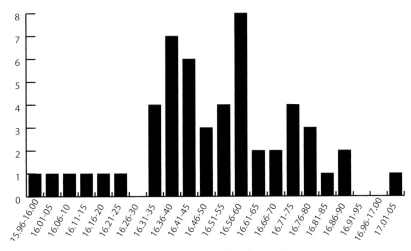

FIGURE 1. Kleuchares I

dence and style suggest that they belong together. The third subgroup was signed with the letters ΚΛΕΥΧ in the form that would remain in use until the late first century BC (Subgroup 3: plate 7 no. 3). An obverse die link between issues of Subgroup 2 (ΚΛΕΥ) and 3 (ΚΛΕΥΧ) is known, confirming that these issues belong together.[10] Issues of all three subgroups regularly bear the anchor countermarks that seem to have been applied to coins by the Seleucid authorities c. 175–170 BC.[11] By contrast, they never bear the cistophoric countermarks applied by the Attalid authorities, probably in the period c. 188–183 BC (Bauslaugh 1990). These facts suggest a relatively precise period of production between c. 183 and 175 BC for the Kleuchares I group as a whole. This range is confirmed by the evidence of the Gaziantep hoard (H27), which can be dated with some precision to the year 144/3 BC and contained issues of Kleuchares I exhibiting a noticeable degree of wear. This was apparently not a large coinage. Professor Leschhorn informs me that up until 1990 he had recorded 26 obverse dies. This suggests a strike rate of around two to three obverse dies per annum.

The weight table for Kleuchares I (Figure 1), based on 80 specimens recorded in the British Museum photofile, allowing for the fact that many surviving specimens of this group exhibit some wear and consequent weight loss, suggests that the target weight standard was in the range 16.8–17.0 g, comparable to the Attic standard that was in the use by neighbouring Pamphylian cities for their Alexander coinages and that of the Seleucid kingdom in the late third to early second centuries BC (Mørkholm 1982a; Colin 1996: 28–29).

10. Compare Lanz 62 (1992) no. 98 (ΚΛΕΥ) and Berlin (Babylon Hoard), *Zeitschrift für Numismatik* 38 (1928): 125 no. 83 (ΚΛΕΥΧ).
11. On the date of these countermarks, see, e.g., Mørkholm (1982b: 303–304), Price (1990: 7–9), and Metcalf (1994: 45–47). A full survey of the Seleucid countermarks by O. Hoover will appear in vol. II of A. Houghton et al. (eds.), *Seleucid Coins* (forthcoming).

Kleuchares II

While the Kleuchares I issues clearly belong both stylistically and chronologically with the earlier issues of Side in the names of other magistrates, it has long been recognized that there are later phases of Kleuchares coinage that are stylistically distinct from the earlier Sidetan issues.

The stylistic distinction between Kleuchares I and II is unmistakeable, particularly in the latter part of group II. This is clearest in the treatment of the hair of Athena. In group II this changes from a relatively naturalistic layering effect of curls in alternate directions to become more stylized and regular later in the group (compare plate 7 nos. 4 and 5). The facial features of the goddess likewise move from a more naturalistic delicacy to a bulbous-eyed, large-nosed ugliness (plate 7 no. 6). On the reverse, the detail of the wing of Nike is reduced to a series of dots, while the folds of her dress at the rear lose any semblance of natural flow.

Two hoards, Gaziantep (H27) and Asia Minor (H29), provide us with a fairly narrow chronological bracket for the beginning of group II. They are absent from the Gaziantep hoard, which contained a significant quantity of group I coins and can be dated fairly accurately to c. 144/3 BC. Group II coins are present, however, in the Asia Minor hoard, the deposit of which came most probably in the decade c. 150–140. A date in the latter half of the 140s seems most likely for the beginning of Kleuchares group II.

Otherwise, the best published evidence for the group II coinage comes from the Kara-kuyu hoard (H33), which contained 268 coins of the Kleuchares II group but no other types of coinage (Table 2). These coins were struck from 53 obverse dies, which are tabulated below according to an order based on stylistic criteria.[12] The opportunity has been taken to add to the table details of dies of the few specimens of this group recorded in the British Museum photofile, which add a further five obverse dies, bringing the total recorded for the group to 58.

Even so, we do not yet have clear picture of the totality of this coinage. For this we must await the publication of the substantial hoard *CH* 9.521 (H31) by Wolfgang Leschhorn. Professor Leschhorn informs me that in 1990 (excluding the specimens from the Karakuyu hoard) he had recorded 75 obverse dies from 836 specimens. The Carter estimate from these figures for the total number of obverse dies is 89–96. This was a large issue, and probably not complete by the time of deposit of the Karakuyu hoard.

As we have already noted, the evidence of the Asia Minor 1962 (H29) and Gaziantep hoards (H27) suggests that these issues were in circulation shortly after 145 BC. At first sight, the stylistic development of the Kleuchares II group that is evinced by the Karakuyu

---

12. The die numbers used are those assigned by Arslan and Lightfoot (1999) in their publication of the hoard. Their ordering of the coins was based on the treatment of the pomegranate symbol on the reverse and has here been revised. Moreover, a number of die identities seem to have been missed by the original editors, who recorded 84 obverse dies. Numbers given in quotation marks are die numbers wrongly assigned in the original publication (the dies listed as OD 74, 76, 77, and 78, on plates 28–29 are not the same as those similarly designated on plates 36–37).

TABLE 2.

Obverse Die	Other Specimens	Karakuyu Total	Overall Total
OD28; OD84	Hirsch 191, 617	2	3
OD16		1	1
OD13		1	1
OD"78"	Hirsch 34, 1303 (*IGCH* 1453); Schlessinger 4.ii.35, 1380	1	3
OD45		7	7
OD12		1	1
OD25		1	1
OD7		1	1
OD5	Hirsch 34, 1302 (*IGCH* 1453); Hirsch 35, 443 (*IGCH* 1453)	1	3
OD6	Hirsch 35, 444 (*IGCH* 1453)	4	5
OD1		2	2
OD11	Knobloch FPL 34, 1240?; *SNG* Newcastle 520	1	3
OD79		1	1
OD2		2	2
OD54; OD57		2	2
OD20; OD52		4	4
OD10		1	1
OD21; OD22; OD53		4	4
OD60		1	1
OD62	BM 1955-11-10-24; Freeman & Sear MB 11, 135; Paris 697?	10	13
OD19	GM 115, 1198	2	3
OD8		1	1
OD4; OD59		2	2
OD14; OD58		2	2
OD15		1	1
OD55		1	1
OD51		3	3
OD56		1	1
OD9		1	1
OD61	Leschhorn Pl. I. 3 (*CH* 9.521)	3	4
OD75		4	4
OD74		2	2
OD68		7	7
OD38	Lanz 102, 280; Freeman & Sear MB 11, 138	14	16
OD71		2	2
OD65	Oxford (Milne 1924)	6	7
OD33; OD35; OD42; OD"77"	GM 52, 339; Peus 366, 214	9	11
OD37		4	4
OD29		2	2
OD17; OD23		15	15
OD66		3	3
OD36; OD44; OD70	"1994 Hoard" (*CH* 9.551) no. 335	18	19
OD64	Rauch 37, 167	5	6
OD24; OD39; OD40; OD"76"	Leschhorn Pl. I. 4 (*CH* 9.521)	15	16

Table 2 continued

Obverse Die	Other Specimens	Karakuyu Total	Overall Total
OD26; OD30; OD32; OD80; OD83		6	6
OD41; OD43	"1994 Hoard" (*CH* 9.551) no. 334	4	5
OD46; OD72; OD73; OD"74"	Oxford, Ashmolean (1971)	25	26
OD18; OD31		3	3
OD34		1	1
OD76		6	6
OD67	GM 133, 248; Cederlind 135, 76	9	11
OD27; OD63; OD69; OD77; OD78; OD81	Glendining 31.i.51 (Cunningham), 241; GM 113, 5266; D. Markov 11, 78; Künker 104, 289	38	42
OD3	Freeman & Sear MB 11, 136	5	6
New (early style)	Ars Antiqua 4, 279		1
New (early style)	Ars Antiqua 4, 280		1
New (early style)	GM 15, 1979		1
New (early style)	Hirsch 97, 167		1
New (early style)	Hirsch 152 (1986) 215; *SNG Turkey* I 1056.	2	
	Totals	268	304

hoard, together with the substantial number of dies, might seem to suggest that the period of production for this group was fairly long. However, the relatively uniform freshness of the Karakuyu hoard coins speaks against such a conclusion.[13] Closer inspection of the dies within this group suggests that the disparate styles are the result not of a gradual change but of the employment of die cutters of substantially different abilities. This looks more like a large group of coins struck over a relatively short space of time. Moreover, the relatively heavy use of some of the dies in this group also suggests haste in their production.[14]

Another characteristic of the Kleuchares II group deserves comment, and may not be unrelated to the circumstances of the production of this coinage. Whereas the Kleuchares I issues turn up in relatively large numbers, and relatively consistently in mixed hoards from Asia Minor and the Levant, the coins of Kleuchares II do not. Our only hoard provenances are the Asia Minor 1962, Çığlık, Karakuyu, unknown findspot 1994, and Asia Minor 1845 hoards (H29, 32, 33, 36, and 38). In the first case, only what appear to be the earliest coins of the group are represented; in the last three, the coins do not appear with coins of other mints. Interestingly, three of the hoard provenances are local to the point of production: Çığlık and Karakuyu are both on the Pamphylian and Pisidian borders (the former about ten kilometers northeast of Termessos, the latter a little less to the northwest of Ariassos), while the 1994 hoard seems to have been acquired from within the Antalya administrative region.

The weight table for the issues of Kleuchares II (Figure 2) suggests that these issues were aiming at a "reduced Attic" standard of 16.4–16.5 g, akin to that in use in the Seleucid

13. On this point see Arslan and Lightfoot (1999: 36).
14. Compare e.g., Arslan and Lightfoot (1999) nos. 389 and 612 (same obv. die) and 458–464 (same obv. die).

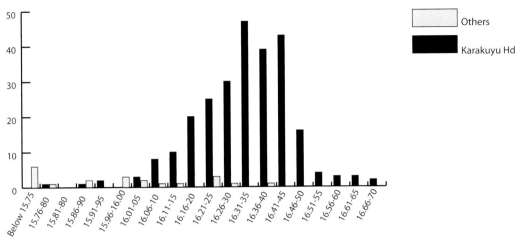

FIGURE 2. Kleuchares II

kingdom in the latter half of the second century (Mørkholm 1982a: 143–147). The generally higher weight of the Karakuyu hoard coins also confirms the impression gained from their appearance that this hoard consists of fresh coin.

Kleuchares III

A third, radically different style of coinage with the Sidetan types and in the name of KΛEYX has long been identified as a later issue of the mint of Side, although the chronology and precise identification has remained unclear. In his publication of the Babylon hoard in 1928, Regling noted the existence of what he took to be two different styles of Kleuchares issues, which he described as I and II. The first of these was exemplified by the coins found in the Babylon hoard, as well as other coins in the Berlin collection that exhibited countermarks. This style equates here to Kleuchares I (see above). In the identification of his second style, however, Regling conflated the two groups that are here identified as Kleuchares III and IV. As an example of his group II, he illustrated a coin in Berlin of Kleuchares group III. The style is markedly different to either of the two previous styles (I and II). The hair of Athena on the obverse falls in long, lank strands, often with a dominant central lock curling downward as if hanging from a globular feature apparently representing the ear (see plate 7 no. 7). The crest of the helmet is generally represented with a series of transverse lines. The rim of the helmet above the face curves inward from front and back to meet in a point just above and in front of the ear. Nike on the reverse is crudely realized, with a "hairy" edge to her wing. The upper portion of the wing is decorated with large dots, in contrast to the more delicate dots or lines of groups II and I (see plate 7 nos. 1–6).

The best evidence for group III is now provided by the publication of the Near Side 1963 hoard (H37) and the unknown findspot 1994 hoard (H36). Between them, these two hoards provide evidence for 17 obverse dies. The two hoards overlap closely in their content

TABLE 3.

Obverse die	Other specimens	1963+1994 Hd total	Overall total
O1	Hirsch 179, 553	5	6
O2; OD12	Grabow 14, 504; CNG 51, 485	1+1	4
O3; O29	Künker 71, 397; Aufhäuser 16, 174; Hirsch 223, 1825 = 227, 220 = 237, 389; S. Gibbons FPL 9, 61	2	6
O4; O27	Münz Zentrum 56, 303; ANA Conv. Auction 1952, 1210	5	7
O5; O6	Oxford (Milne 1924)	11	12
OD6	Ars Antiqua 4 (2003), 281	1	2
O7; O22; O23; O24; O25; O26; OD9; OD10; OD11	Hirsch 182, 344; Egger 46 (Prowe), 1978 = NFA MB 12.x.88, 349; Cambridge, *SNG* 5101; Hirsch 197, 330 = 218, 391; SKB FPL21, 68 = 25, 88; Vecchi FPL 7, 26; *SNG* Blackburn 1018 (double struck, die uncertain)	222+5	33
O8; O28	CNG online no. 197807837; Hirsch 159, 381 = Rauch 42, 3079	3	5
O15; OD2	Hirsch 177, 391; Paris, *SNG* 700; Münz Zentrum 50, 139	2+1	6
O10; O13; O21; OD8	SBV 23, 123; Freeman & Sear MB 11, 137; Kress 138, 419; NFA/Leu 1/18.x.84, 277; Kurpfälzische MH 49, 228 = 54, 59; Numifrance 2.vi.82, 81; Hirsch 180, 341	9+1	17
O11; O18	SBV 45 (1998) 274; Naville 4.vi.21 (Pozzi), 2802 = *SNG* Lockett 3026; ANS 1905–57–447; Ciani FPL x.1929, 142; BM 1979–1–1–927 = *SNG* vA 4797; Bourgey 7/8/xi/83, 85 = 26/8.vi.89, 47; Florange & Ciani 17/21.ii.25 (Allotte de la Füye 597 = Ciani 14.vi.34, 72 = NAC "O", 1663; KMK 73, 67	4	12
O12; O14; OD1	*SNG* Manchester 1297; Kurpfälzische MH 35, 85; *BMC* 43;	7+1	11
O9	Naville 7 (Bement), 1602; Platt 27.iii.22, 696; Hirsch 178, 435; Kricheldorf FPL 61, 384 = 11, 194;	7	
OD7	GM 79, 257; Athena 2, 203; Auctiones 12, 125; R. Ball 6, 360; SBV 27.x.77, 359 = Hirsch 162, 301; UBS 59, 5836	1	7
O16; O17	Naville 4.vi.21 (Pozzi), 2801; NFA MB 14.xii.89, 615; ANS 1944–100–50925; Auctiones 13, 323; Paris, *SNG* 695; Rauch 13, 44 = Kurpfälzische MH 10, 23	5	11
O19		1	1
O20; OD3	SBV 33, 344; Glendining 1.ix.76, 181	1+2	5
–	Burgan MB 18.vi.91, 405	–	1
–	Oxford (Evan beq.)	–	1

A1	Lanz 52, 248; ACNAC Davis 241 = NFA 9, 202 = Berk 115, 295; NAC 'D', 1515; KMK 22, 79 = 24, 124; Monnaies de Collection, 13/5.x.80, 419; Myers 1, 239.	–	6
A2	Sotheby (Zurich) 27/8.x.93, 754 = GM 67, 315 = Leu 83, 358; Asta Ceresio 26.ix.87; Tradart 12.xii.91, 175; Sternberg 16, 159; Lanz, 40, 353; BMC 44.	–	6
A3	SBV 43, 176; Hirsch 148, 103; Rauch 20/2.x.86, 166	–	3
A4	SBV 6, 74; Hirsch 148, 104	–	2
A5	Ciani 20/2.ii.35 (Grandprey), 182; Lanz 70, 21; Hirsch 151, 146; BMC 46.	–	4
A6	Lanz 38, 296; Sternberg 16, 158; BMC 41.	–	3

of Kleuchares III dies. In Table 3, as with group II, I list all of the dies known to me from the hoards and from the photofile of the British Museum.[15]

As can be seen, the two hoards do not contain all of the coinage to be attributed to this phase of production. The dies represented in these hoards are relatively close stylistically. The British Museum photofile adds a further two dies[16] that seem to belong with this core of dies, bringing the total to 19 observed dies from 158 specimens. The Carter estimate for the total number of obverse dies for this group is 19 or 20. However, a distinct subgroup of Kleuchares III is formed by a further six obverse dies (above A1–A6) recorded from 24 specimens, including three in the British Museum collection (see plate 7 no. 8 and plates 11–12, BMC 44, 41, and 46).[17] Although certain features such as the rendering of the crest and rim of Athena's helmet and to a degree the treatment of the hair link these dies to the main group, the rendition of the facial features of the goddess are sufficiently different to make them an identifiably separate phase of production. None of these dies appear to have been present in the 1963 and 1994 finds, and these may perhaps be regarded as the final issues of Kleuchares group III. The evidence of the Asia Minor 1845 hoard (H38) may confirm this (see below).

The weight distribution of Kleuchares group III (Figure 3) suggests that the standard aimed at by these issues is around 16.10–16.20 g. This is lower than group II, and close to the "reduced" Attic standard in use in the Seleucid kingdom in the first half of the first

15. The die numbers used are those assigned by Arslan and Lightfoot (1999) in their publication of the 1963 and 1994 hoards. The die numbers assigned to coins in the 1963 hoard I have abbreviated to "Oxx"; for those in the 1994 hoard I have retained the format "ODxx". Their ordering of the coins has been revised here. Again, a number of die identities seem to have been missed by the original editors, who recorded 38 obverse dies in the two hoards (excluding the two coins of Kleuchares group II in the 1994 hoard).

16. Burgan MB 18.vi.91, 405, and Oxford, Evans beq.

17. The estimated number of obverse dies is 6–7.

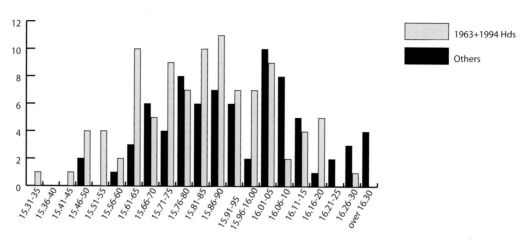

Figure 3. Kleuchares III

century BC (Mørkholm 1982a: 148, Table IV).[18] However, it remains to be seen whether the Kleuchares III coins belong to this period. There is clear evidence, as we shall see, in the case of Kleuchares IV, for a substantial gap opening up between the "Attic standard" of Sidetan issues and that used at Antioch.

Kleuchares IV

The issues of group IV are the least well attested of all the Kleuchares groups. Stylistically, group IV is markedly different from the two preceding groups. The obverse style bears in the depiction of Athena's head a superficial resemblance to Kleuchares group I. The treatment of the helmet and hair all mark a step away from the stylization of group III back toward the more naturalistic treatment of group I. The facial features are less flattering, however. The reverse style is markedly different from group I, showing a similar clumsiness to that achieved by the cutters of the dies of group III (see plate 8 no. 9).

The following die study of group IV is based predominantly on published specimens and the photofile of the British Museum. It thus makes no pretensions to completeness, but offers an overview to set alongside the contemporary coinage of Amyntas. All die combinations are illustrated on plates 8–11.[19]

As can be seen, with a ratio of ten observed obverse dies from 42 specimens, it is likely that we now have most of the obverse dies (Table 4). The nature and chronology of this group, together with its significance for the broader history of Side and the Pamphylian plain, depend upon the group's relationship to the coinage of Amyntas.

18. The Seleucid tetradrachms of c. 105–92 BC seem to be aiming at a slightly higher weight of c. 16.20–16.30 g, while those of 89–69 BC probably aim closer to 15.90–16.00 g.

19. I am grateful to Peter van Alfen for providing information on the unpublished specimens in the ANS, and to Richard Ashton for his help with the Oxford collection.

A1/P1
a.	15.60	o	Cambridge, McClean pl. 317, 2

A1/P2
a.			Frankfurt. Atlan "I"

A1/P3
a.	15.54		Künker 77 (2002) 209

A1/P4
a.	16.00		Rauch 43 (1989) 417; 46 (1991) 257. Hirsch 160 (1988) 241

A1/P5
a.	16.00	o	*BMC* 38

A1/P6
a.	15.87		CNG 46 (1998) 459

A1/P7
a.*	15.94	o	Cambridge, Leake, *SNG* 5100
b.	15.90		Rosenberg 72 (1932, Lejeune) 683

A1/P8
a.	15.87	o	*BMC* 39; Atlan "M"

A1/P9
a.	16.20		Coin Galleries 14.xii.04, 174

A1/P10
a.	15.98		Sotheby 15.v.74, 53

A1/P11
a.*	15.95	o	*BMC* 40A
b.	15.71		Auctiones 20 (1990) 450

A2/P12
a.	15.62		Kölner MK 46 (1988) 2111
b.*	15.84	o	Lanz 97 (2000) 332

A2/P13
a.	15.67	o	*BMC* 42

A2/P14
a.	16.05	o	*BMC* 45

A2/P15
a.	15.70	o	*SNG Lewis* 1034

A2/P16
a.	15.88		Paris, *SNG* 699

A2/P17
a.	15.72	o	Oxford (Keble), Spink 7.i.1889

A3/P18
a.	15.27		Paris, *SNG* 696. Atlan "N"

A4/P19
a.	15.97		Rauch 41 (1988) 287

A4/P20
a.	15.79	o	Lanz 120 (2004) 170

A4/P21
a.	15.70	o	Brussels, de Hirsch 1589

A4/P22
a.	15.87	o	ANS 1944.100.50928. Newell

A5/P22
a.	15.87	o	Brussels, du Chastel 271. Atlan "K"
b.*	15.40		Künker 94 (2004) 1300

A6/P23
a.	15.67	o	ACNAC Dewing 2473

A6/P24
a.	15.27		Hess 1.xii.31 (Otto), 609; Münzhandlung Basel 10 (1938) 354; Kricheldorf 15.x.55, 488; Kurpfälzische MH 31 (1986) 101; Peus 369 (2001) 222.

A7/P25
a.			Berlin. Atlan "L"

A8/P26
    a.   15.80 o *BMC* 40
A9/P27
    a.   Kölner MK 54 (1991) 97
A9/P28
    a.   15.55   Maison Platt FPL iii.98, 261
    b.*   15.66   Künker 89 (2004) 1434
A9/P29
    a.   15.39   Naville 4.iv.21 (Pozzi) 2800
A9/P30
    a.   St. Petersburg. Atlan "H"
A9/P31
    a.   Knobloch FPL 34 (1968) 1239
    b.*   Cederlind 98 (1993) 128
A9/P32
    a.   16.07 o *SNG* Lewis 1035
A10/P33
    a.   15.65   GM 46 (1989) 325
A10/P34
    a.   15.84   Hirsch 175 (1992) 448
A10/P35
    a.   15.64 o Berlin (Fox); Atlan "O"

Table 4.

Specimens	Obverse dies	Reverse dies	Combinations	Carter est.
42	10	35	36	11.52 ± 0.95

Amyntas

The coinage of Amyntas was the subject of a die study by S. Atlan (1965), who identified six obverse and 33 reverse dies for the issue. Regling had already noted a stylistic similarity between some of the coins he classified amongst his later group of Kleuchares issues (1928: 127).[20] Atlan was able to discover the obverse die link between Amyntas' coinage and a coin of Kleuchares IV (her O1 and above A10). To the corpus assembled by Atlan, fifteen more specimens may be added, providing evidence for a further two reverse dies not recorded in her work.[21] The dies of the Amyntas coinage and their use are summarized in Tables 5 and 6.

20. It was undoubtedly the confusion in Regling's discussion between Kleuchares III and IV, and his illustra-tion of a Kleuchares III coin that led Seyrig to question this similarity (1962: 61).

21. Credit Suisse 3.xii.85, 147 = 42 (1987) 301: O2/Rnew; Ciani 27.vi.34, 14: O2/Rnew. The other 13 coins to be added are: Sotheby 16.xi.1880, 163 = *SNG Lewis* 1050: O1/R1; Münz Zentrum 56 (1985) 385 = Künker 94 (2004), 1377: O1/R4; *SNG Newcastle* 546: O1/R5; Künker 83 (2003) 396: O1/R7; Schulman 30/1.iii.36, 175: O2/R8; Hess/Leu 25.iv.72, 271 = Kurpfälzische MH 29 (1985) 46: O2/R9; SBV 57 (2003) 286 = CNG 69 (2005) 503 286: O2/R10; Sternberg 34 (1998) 49: O4a/R18; Auctiones 22 (1992) 342 = Triton 6 (2003) 442: O5/R25; MMAG 54 (1978) 350: O6/R22; *SNG Delepierre* 2927 = *SNG Paris* 2351: O6/R22; Kress 102 (1956) 62: O6/R27; *SNG Paris* 2350: O6/R33. For specimens recorded by Atlan, the following references may also be added: Atlan 8.5 = Ars Antiqua 4 (2003) 289; Atlan 9.6 = Vedrines MB 30.xii.94, 43; Atlan 12.7 = Peus 371 (2002) 210 and 374 (2003) 115; Atlan 17.1 = NAC "L" (2001) 1393; Atlan 26.1 = Kress 109 (1958) 762; Atlan 30.2 = NFA 16 (1985) 236; Atlan 30.4 = Burgan MB 22.xii.90, 52; Atlan 39.1 = Bourgey 21/2.ii.72, 64.

TABLE 5. The Dies of Amyntas' Coinage

Issue	Specimens	Obverse dies	Reverse dies	Combinations	Carter est.
Amyntas	112	6	35	45	5.8 ± 0.13

TABLE 6. The Die Structure of Amyntas' Coinage

O1	r2												
	r3												
	r4			O3	r4								
	r5												
	r6												
	r7												
	r8	O2	r8		r8			O4a	r8a[a]				
	r1		r1										
			r–										
			r–										
			r9										
			r10										
			r11		r11								
			r12										
			r13										
					r14								
					r15								
						O4	r16						
							r17		r17a				
									r18				
									r20				
									r19	O5	r19		
											r21		
											r23		
											r24		
											r25		
											r26		
											r22	O6	r22
													r27
													r28
													r29
													r30
													r31
													r32
													r33

a. This die is designated no. 8 by Atlan, but is in fact a recut state of 8, with the numerals IB added, just as reverse die 17a is a recut version of reverse 17 (see the note ad *BMC* 2). It is the die on which Nike is portrayed with an elephant scalp headdress.

A weight table (Figure 4) for the issues of Amyntas, combined with those of the die-linked Kleuchares IV coins, suggests that the standard aimed at for these coins was around 16.00–16.10 g, although in fact fairly fresh-looking specimens regularly fall short of this mark. This standard looks to be fractionally lighter than that adopted for Kleuchares group III. It is, nonetheless, significantly higher than the "reduced" Attic weight standard in use at the end of the Seleucid kingdom and for the Roman production of posthumous Philips

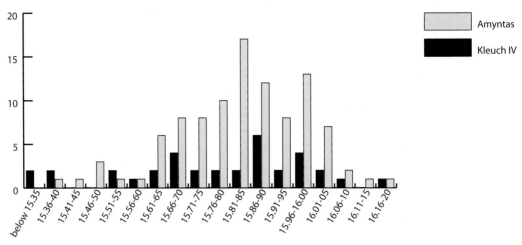

FIGURE 4.

at Antioch, which must be broadly contemporary with Amyntas' tetradrachms: the Attic standard at the mint of Antioch dropped from c. 15.61–65 g under Philip and 15.66–70 g under Tigranes to c. 14.80 g in the 30s BC.[22]

The chronology of Kleuchares III and IV

The date of Kleuchares group IV is relatively clear, thanks to the discovery of the die link with the issues of Amyntas. The precise dates for Amyntas' coinage remain to be resolved, but must belong within the period of his rule (c. 39–25 BC). Kleuchares IV will belong at around the same time. The chronology of Kleuchares III is less clear, however, and appears to hinge on the testimony of two poorly recorded hoards of the first century BC.

The first of these hoards has a somewhat murky history. During the year 1845, Henry Borrell sent to the English collector and curator Thomas Burgon two of the hitherto un-known tetradrachms in the name of King Amyntas. Burgon immediately announced this new find in a lengthy communication to the editor of the *Numismatic Chronicle* (Burgon 1845–6).[23] At the same time, apparently, two similar coins were received in Paris, and simultaneously announced as new by the Duc de Luynes to the readership of the *Revue numismatique* (Luynes 1845).[24]

Neither of these collectors and authors seem to have been informed by their source or sources either of the other's coins or—initially at least—of the context of the find. During

22. For the figures for Philip and Tigranes, a refinement over those presented by Mørkholm (1982a: 148, table IV), I am grateful to Oliver Hoover; for the later period see *RPC* I 609.

23. The coin engraved at the head of the first page is *BMC* 3.

24. The two coins described are de Luynes 2789 and 2790 (*SNG Paris* 2353 and 2345). Interestingly, by the time that Burgon's article went to press a third piece had been received in Paris (Luynes 1845: 69 [editor's note]), and it is clear that a third piece did enter the de Luynes collection (de Luynes 2791; *SNG Paris* 2348), presumably after the latter's article had gone to press.

the course of the work on the publication of the coins in London, Burgon became aware that the coins of Amyntas had been found with coins of Side (Burgon 1845–6: 82 n. 39). Two such coins of Sidetan type came into his possession and can now perhaps be identified in the collection of the British Museum (*BMC* 44 and 39).[25] But this was still not the whole story. As E. H. Bunbury was later to put it: "A much larger number of specimens of both coins [sc. Amyntas and ΚΛΕΥΧ issues of Side] subsequently emerged from the 'find' in question than were known to that distinguished numismatist at the time he wrote his paper. See the Sale Catalogue of Borrell's Coins (1852), pp. 30, 41" (Bunbury 1883: 199 n. 21).[26] In the 1860s, the find from which these coins derived was said to have numbered close to 500 coins, and it is clear from the sale of Henry Borrell's own collection after his death that numerous pieces from the hoard were still in his possession (Hoffmann 1862–64: no. 2534 with note).[27] In the meantime, between Burgon's publication in 1845/6 and Borrell's death in 1852, the British Museum had acquired four specimens of Amyntas' coinage (three from Henry Borrell's brother Maximilian) and eight specimens of Kleuchares III and IV, all from the same source. In addition, a coin of Amyntas was acquired from the dealer Whelan in October 1852, which may have been among those sold at the Borrell sale in July that year.

	Side					Amyntas	
1	1845-12-17-205	(*BMC* 44)	Kleuch III	1	1846-3-13-1	(*BMC* 7)
2	1845-12-17-206	(*BMC* 39)	Kleuch IV	2	1846-3-13-2	(*BMC* 6)
3	1846-4-15-1	(*BMC* 45)	Kleuch IV	3	1846-4-15-7	(*BMC* 3)
4	1846-4-15-2	(*BMC* 41)	Kleuch III	4	1847-2-2-1	(*BMC* 1)
5	1846-4-15-3	(*BMC* 46)	Kleuch III	5	1852-10-25-1	(*BMC* 2)
6	1846-4-15-4	(*BMC* 42)	Kleuch IV	6	1855-3-20-3	(*BMC* 5)
7	1846-4-15-5	(*BMC* 40)	Kleuch IV	7	1866-12-1-3811	(*BMC* 4)
8	1846-4-15-6	(*BMC* 38)	Kleuch IV			

Two other coins of Amyntas in the British Museum collection were acquired from a Mr. Langdon in 1855 (*BMC* 5) and from the Woodhouse collection in 1866 (*BMC* 4), and are highly likely to have come from the same find as the others. The coins acquired by the British Museum in this period, and likely to derive from the Borrell "find", may be listed thus (all coins are illustrated on plate 11–12).

25. These two coins were acquired by the British Museum together and have weights that seem to correspond to the two pieces described by Burgon.

26. The note appended to the coins of Side in the Borrell catalogue reads: "All these tetradrachms of Side are in fine condition, being a selection from an extensive 'trouvaille', which fell into the hands of the late proprietor in 1845" (30).

27. Sotheby 12.vii.1852 (H.P. Borrell), 30, lots 257–261 (Side), 41, lots 359–366 (Amyntas).

If, as seems likely, the attribution of all of these coins to the Asia Minor 1845 hoard is correct, then this find provides us with important evidence for the dating of Kleuchares groups III and IV. That issues of Kleuchares IV were present alongside the coins of Amyntas causes no surprise, since the die link discovered by Atlan between the two issues indicates approximate contemporaneity. Interestingly, the issues of Kleuchares III in the hoard look similarly fresh, and this may suggest that they are not far removed in time from the Kleuchares IV coins, despite the considerable stylistic difference. It should be noted, however, that the three coins of group III listed above (*BMC* 41, 44, and 46) were struck from dies not included in the Side 1963 and 1994 hoards (H37 and 36). As has been noted above, the likelihood is that these dies, which show some stylistic difference to the dies included in those hoards, may represent the last issues of group III and have been used after the closure of the two hoards in question. It also possible, however, that we have in these "late Kleuchares III" dies a distinct later group (IIIb), which was struck after the main body of group III present in the two Side hoards. This later subgroup would be closer in date to the Kleuchares IV group. Nonetheless, if the late Kleuchares III issues (IIIb) do belong with the main group, then the conclusion to be drawn is probably that the whole of group III and group IV are either consecutive or at least partially contemporary.

The considerable stylistic difference between the two groups, if not the result of radically different dates of production, as seems to be the case whichever of the above two hypotheses is accepted, is surely more likely to be indicative of two separate mints. This conclusion, as we shall see, must have profound implications for our interpretation of these late "Sidetan" coinages.

The other hoard apparently of first-century date is that recorded by E. Dutihl (1898), as having appeared on the market in Alexandria in 1897 (H35). Dutihl recorded 43 tetradrachms of Side and eight examples of what he took to be tetradrachms of Ptolemy Auletes. The Sidetan element is familiar from numerous earlier hoards. It contained eight coins of magistrates preceding the Kleuchares I coinage, at least one coin of Kleuchares group I, subgroup 2 (ΚΛΕΥ), and perhaps as many as 25 coins with the signature ΚΛΕΥΧ. Amongst these, Dutihl noted "deux types différents de tête de Pallas". Without illustration of these pieces, we can only speculate what these two different types of Pallas head might have been. Within Kleuchares group I there is arguably sufficient difference in style to give rise to such a notice. On the other hand, and perhaps more likely, is the suggestion that the hoard contained some coins of Kleuchares I and a later Kleuchares group. It is impossible to say which on the basis of Dutihl's account, but it seems unlikely that a hoard would contain issues of group I and, say group III or IV, without also including a specimen of the substantial group II. Moreover, if it did include issues of the early second century (group I) alongside issues of the late first century (groups III or IV), then it would be unique in the hoard record for Sidetan coinage. Similarly unique would be the appearance of late issues (group III and IV) away from their immediate area of issue. The mention of the Ptolemaic coins is more tantalizing still. Dutihl recorded coins with the regnal years 4, 16, and 22. He assumed these to be coins of Ptolemy Auletes, and thus arrived at a date around or after 59 BC for the deposit of the hoard. But the attribution of these coins to Auletes must be open to question.[28] The issues of Auletes and Cleopatra VII have in the past been extremely difficult to tell apart, and it was not until 1975 that Mørkholm established definitively the means to distinguish certain issues of the two rulers from each other (Mørkholm 1975). Since the three years in question are all recorded on coins for Cleopatra, the hoard could have been buried as late as 30 BC. But the date could move the other way too. Coins of the Alexandrian mint with regnal years 4, 16, and 22 would have been circulating together also during the reign of Ptolemy X Alexander, whose twenty-second year ran from 93/92 BC.[29] A date of c. 90 BC would certainly suit the Sidetan material if only issues down to Kleuchares II were included. But certainty is impossible, and Dutihl's hoard is perhaps best set aside as too poorly recorded to be used.

III. Amyntas, Side, and the Pamphylian Plain

On the basis of the above discussion of the four groups of Kleuchares coinage and that of Amyntas, the following broad summary of production may be offered:

Kleuchares I	c. 183–175 BC	c. 26 obverse dies
Kleuchares II	c. 145–125 BC	c. 89–96 obverse dies
Kleuchares III	c. mid-first century BC?	c. 25–27 obverse dies
Kleuchares IV	c. mid-first century BC?	c. 10–12 obverse dies
Amyntas	c. 39–25 BC	c. 6 obverse dies

Plainly, the same Kleuchares cannot have been responsible for all phases of Sidetan coinage. It is possible that groups I and II were the product of the same man over a span of forty-odd years, or even that these two groups were the product of a father and son of similar civic position. But it surely stretches credulity to breaking point to suggest that a homonym over a century later should again have been responsible for two distinct phases of coinage (groups III and IV) and, moreover, should have been the only citizen of Side to sign coins in this way. Yet, if we cannot accept the unlikely scenario that the city of Side confined itself to homonymous monetary magistrates over a period of a century and a half, what is the alternative?

The answer is at once obvious and surprising. The last two groups of Sidetan issues produced in the middle part of the first century must be imitations of the plentiful issues of Kleuchares that were produced around the middle of the second century. The phenomenon of imitation is familiar, as we have already noted, from the world of Athenian coinage of the fourth century BC. It continued, of course, throughout the Hellenistic period, most obvi-

---

28. So already for Regling (1928: 127).

29. Year 4 coinage is known from the earlier reign of Ptolemy IX (114/3 BC), year 16 from the reign of Ptolemy X (99/8 BC). See Mørkholm (1975).

ously in the form of posthumous coinage in the name of Alexander the Great. Pamphylia saw a huge burst of such imitation at the end of the third century BC. At the period that interests us, the mid-first century BC, the Roman administration in Syria was busy turning out imitation issues of the Seleucid king Philip, while in Asia, the cistophorus of the Attalid kingdom was produced for the Roman proconsular governors. The second-century coins of Side, we must presume, still dominated in a local circulation area and thus were still desirable and practical coins for the issuing authority of the first century. But who might this issuing authority have been?

An obvious answer might be that it was the city of Side itself. But a simple point tells against such a solution: the repetition of the magistrate's name. This feature must be a deliberate element of the imitation of the earlier types by the later. When the engravers came to produce the dies for the first-century issues, they slavishly copied the most common of the issues of the earlier period, down to the detail of reproducing the magistrate's name. This small detail of design is of profound significance, for the magistrate's name on a Hellenistic city's coinage is one of those signs, like the erection of statues, the choosing of ambassadors, and the voting of honorific decrees, that stands as an expression of the role of the individual in civic activity. It is one of the signs of a healthy citizen body.

The fact that the "posthumous" issues of Side groups III and IV could not muster a new magistrate's name but rather imitated an earlier one strongly suggests that the first-century Kleuchares issues are not issues of Side at all. Paradoxical though this suggestion might appear, if it is correct to view these issues as "imitations", then there is no good reason to insist that they must have been produced at Side. Just as anybody could issue posthumous Alexanders, so, potentially, anyone could issue "posthumous" coinage of Side. We might add the proviso here that, whoever they were, they probably existed within the circulation area of this coinage, that is, in Asia Minor or Syria.

If not the city of Side, then who might have been responsible? Again there is an obvious answer. Kleuchares group IV is die-linked to the coinage of Amyntas. The most natural conclusions to draw from this are that both the Kleuchares IV and Amyntas' coinages were produced by the same mint, and that this was the royal mint of Amyntas. But we have no independent basis for saying where this mint was. Whether it was at the city of Side or not is debatable, and will depend in part on whether we believe Side to have been within Amyntas' kingdom, not vice versa.

Upon receiving his new kingdom from Antony in 39 BC, Amyntas presumably needed a silver coinage with which to pay his troops. It is highly plausible that he adopted as his model a coinage that would have been recognizable and desirable to them, such as that of Side. As we have already noted, the Roman governors of Asia, Cilicia, and Syria had found themselves similarly bound by conservative monetary convention. But by itself this imitation does not prove that Side was the mint any more than the posthumous Philips of Antioch prove that the Romans had reinstalled a dead king to the throne of Syria.

Logically, we must also question the location of the production of the Kleuchares group III and the agency behind it. Might these also have been issues of Amyntas, and if so, does their stylistic variation from group IV indicate a separate mint? And what relation might these silver coinages have to the bronze coinage in the name of Amyntas (*RPC* I: 536–7), which certainly does appear to be the product of two mints? Detailed consideration of these questions I must reserve for elsewhere.

To conclude, we should return to the sources for the history of first-century Pamphylia as they appeared to Syme in 1934. The literary evidence, as Syme saw, strongly suggested that the Pamphylian plain was not ceded to Amyntas by Antony. The coinage, which was once taken as evidence for Amyntas' occupation of Side, cannot now with certainty be attributed to that city. The new evidence for Amyntas' activities that has emerged since then, in the form of the honorific decree for Trokondas son of Obrimoas, has served merely to reinforce the impression of a kingdom anchored firmly in the uplands. All the evidence suggests that Amyntas was preoccupied for much of his reign with the subjection of the querulous natives of the mountainous spaces of Lykaonia and Pisidia.[30] That he was required in doing so to pay his troops in coin masquerading as that of the peaceful, wealthy city of Side was an irony perhaps not lost on this remarkable king. If imitate coins he must, he would at least, in the end, have his name on them.

Key to plates 7–8.

1. *NFA* 14, 174
2. Lanz 62, 398
3. *NFA* MB 1980, 822
4. Karakuyu Hoard 613
5. Freeman and Sear MB 11, 135
6. Freeman and Sear MB 11, 136
7. Freeman and Sear MB 11, 137
8. Lanz 40, 353
9. Hirsch 175, 448
10. *BMC* Amyntas 7

Bibliography

Arslan, M. 1998. Yeşilova-Çeltek Side tetradrahmi definesi 1995. *Adalya* 2: 51–69.

———. 2001. Burdur müzesi'ndeki Side tetradrahmi definesi. *Belleten* 65 no. 242: 37–61.

Arslan, M., and C. Lightfoot. 1999. *Greek coin hoards in Turkey: the Antalya archaeological museum and the C.S. Okray collection.* Ankara: UDAS.

Atlan, S. 1965. Side'de basılan Amyntas sikkeleri. *Belleten* 39: 575–611.

---

30. On the new inscription and its place in the record for Amyntas' activities, see Mitchell (1994: 104–105).

Augé, C., A. Davesne, and R. Ergeç. 1997. Le début des tétradrachmes d'Athènes du 'nouveau style': un trésor trouvé près de Gaziantep en 1994. *Anatolia Antiqua* 5: 44–82.

Bauslaugh, R. 1990. Cistophoric countermarks and the monetary system of Eumenes II. *Numismatic Chronicle* 150: 39–65.

BMC: G. F. Hill. 1897. *Catalogue of the Greek coins of Lycia, Pamphylia, and Pisidia*. London: British Museum Press.

Boehringer, Chr. 1999. Beobachtungen und Überlegungen zu den Ären der Pamphylischen Alexandreier. In: M. Amandry and S. Hurter, eds., *Travaux de numismatique grecque offerts à Georges Le Rider*, pp. 65–75. London: Spink.

Bowersock, G. W. 1965. *Augustus and the Greek world*. Oxford: Clarendon Press.

Bunbury, E. H. 1883. Additional tetradrachms of Alexander the Great. *Numismatic Chronicle* 3: 1–17.

Burgon, T. 1845–6. On two newly discovered silver tetradrachms of Amyntas, King of Galatia: with some remarks on the diminution in weight of the Attic drachma. *Numismatic Chronicle* 8: 69–96.

Büyükyörük, F. 2001. Side tetradrahmi definesi 1997. *Türk Tarih Arkeologya ve Etnoğrafya Dergisi* 2: 95–110.

CH: *Coin hoards*. 1975–2002. London: Royal Numismatic Society.

Colin, H. J. 1996. *Die Münzen von Perge in Pamphylien aus hellenistischer Zeit*. Köln: Kölner Münzkabinett.

Davesne, A., and A. Lemaire. 1996. Trésors hellénistiques du Proche-Orient. *Revue numismatique* 151: 51–76.

De Luynes: J. Babelon. 1924–36. *Catalogue de la collection de Luynes: monnaies grecques*. 4 vols. Paris: Bibliothèque Nationale de la France.

Dutihl, E. D. J. 1898. Monnaies de Side et d'Égypte. *Journal international d'archeologie numismatique* 1: 148–156.

Elayi, J. 1999. Un trésor de tétradrachmes aux types d'Alexandre trouvé dans le Beqa'. In: M. Amandry and S. Hurter, eds., *Travaux de numismatique grecque offerts à Georges Le Rider*, pp. 135–138. London: Spink.

IGCH: M. Thompson, O. Mørkholm, and C. M. Kraay, eds. 1973. *An inventory of Greek coin hoards*. New York: American Numismatic Society.

Jones, A. H. M. 1937. *Cities of the eastern Roman provinces*. Oxford: Clarendon Press.

Kroll, J. 1993. *The Athenian Agora XXVI. The Greek coins*. Princeton: American School of Classical Studies at Athens.

Leschhorn, W. 1988. Ein Schatzfund sidetischer Münzen. In: P. R. Franke et al., eds., *Side. Münzprägung, Inschriften und Geschichte einer Antiken Stadt in der Türkei*, pp. 23–42. Saarbrücken: Landesbank Saar Girozentrale.

Levick, B. M. 1967. *Roman colonies in southern Asia Minor*. Oxford: Clarendon Press.

Luynes, Duc de. 1845. Médailles inédites d'Amyntas. *Revue numismatique* 10: 253–265.

Magie, D. 1950. *Roman rule in Asia Minor: to the end of the third century after Christ.* Princeton: Princeton University Press.

Metcalf, W. E. 1994. A late second-century hoard of posthumous Alexanders. *Schweizerische Numismatische Rundschau (Revue suisse de numismatique)* 73: 19–53.

Mitchell, S. 1993. *Anatolia: land, men, and gods in Asia Minor.* Oxford: Clarendon Press.

———. 1994. Termessos, King Amyntas, and the war with the Sandaliôtai. A new inscription from Pisidia. In: D. French, ed., *Studies in the history and topography of Lycia and Pisidia in memoriam A. S. Hall,* pp. 95–105. Ankara: British Institute of Archaeology at Ankara.

Mørkholm, O. 1975. Ptolemaic coins and chronology: the dated silver coinage of Alexandria. *American Numismatic Society Museum Notes* 20: 7–24.

———. 1982a. The Attic coin standard in the Levant during the Hellenistic period. In: S. Scheers, eds., *Studia Paulo Naster oblata I. Numismatica antiqua,* pp. 139–149. Leuven: Departement Oriëntalistiek (Katholieke Universiteit).

———. 1982b. Some reflexions on the production and the use of coinage in ancient Greece. *Historia* 31: 303–304.

Price, M. J. 1990. A silver crisis in the 170s BC. *NNF-NYTT* 2: 7–9.

———. 1991. *The coinage in the name of Alexander the Great and Philip Arrhidaeus.* 2 vols. London: British Museum; Zurich: Swiss Numismatic Society.

Regling, K. 1928. Hellenistischer Münzschatz aus Babylon. *Zeitschrift für Numismatik* 38: 92–132.

RPC: A. Burnett, M. Amandry, P. P. Ripollès, eds. 1998. *Roman provincial coinage. Vol. 1, From the death of Caesar to the death of Vitellius (44 BC–AD 69).* London: British Museum Press.

Schubert, H. 1998. Ein unbekannter Gegenstempel auf einer Tetradrachme von Side. In: U. Peter, ed., *Stephanos Nomismatikos. Edith Schönert-Geiss zum 65. Geburtstag,* pp. 591–600. Berlin: Akademie Verlag.

Seyrig, H. 1962. Monnaies hellénistiques. X. Sidé. *Revue numismatique* 4: 57–63. (= Seyrig, Scripta Numismatica [Paris, 1986], 61–67).

SNG Paris: E. Levante, ed. 1994. *Sylloge nummorum graecorum. France 3. Cabinet des Médailles: Pamphylie, Pisidie, Lycaonie, Galatie.* Paris: Bibliothèque Nationale de la France.

Syme, R. 1934. Galatia and Pamphylia under Augustus: the governorships of Piso, Quirinius, and Silvanus. *Klio* 27: 122–148.

———. 1937. Pamphylia from Augustus to Vespasian. *Klio* 30: 227–231 (= *Roman papers* I, no. 4).

———. 1939. Observations on the province of Cilicia. In: W. M. Calder and Josef Keil, eds., *Anatolian studies presented to William Hepburn Buckler,* pp. 299–332. Manchester: Manchester University Press (= *Roman Papers* I, no. 10).

———. 1978–91. *Roman papers.* 7 vols. Oxford: Clarendon Press.

———. 1995. *Anatolica: studies in Strabo,* Anthony Birley, ed. Oxford: Clarendon Press.

Agoranomia: Studies in Money and Exchange Presented to John H. Kroll, pp. 177–200
© 2006 The American Numismatic Society

Greek Coins from Archaeological Excavations:
A Conspectus of Conspectuses and a Call for Chronological Tables

François de Callataÿ*

In his monumental and acclaimed publication of the Greek coins of the Athenian Agora, Jack Kroll starts with a conspectus of coins, which summarizes the catalogue. This is placed after the preface and the bibliography, but before the introduction, still within the Roman-numbered pages (Kroll 1993: xvii–xxvi). This conspectus itself is summarized on page xxvi, in what appears as a chronological table running from the sixth century BC to the fourth century AD. Devoted to such a paramount archaeological site, dealing with such a huge amount of material (16,557 identifiable coins), and compiled by no one other than Jack, this conspectus deserves particular attention.

With this conspectus, organized century by century, Jack Kroll offers a unique tool, one that we should welcome with gratitude, for three reasons. (1) It deals with more material than the currently published archaeological coin finds. To focus on the centuries BC, the 12,676 Greek coins from the Athenian Agora come well ahead of the 5,682 coins from Priene, the 3,817 coins from Olynthus, or the 2,176 from Susa (see Table 1A). Huge numbers of coins indeed have been found in regular archaeological excavations but, as a rule, they are still waiting to be truly published.[1] In practice, archaeological publications with at least five hundred Greek coins remain few (no more than twelve; see Table 1A). (2) It deals with

*Bibliothèque royale de Belgique (Brussels) and École pratique des Hautes Études (Paris/Sorbonne). I wish to thank Peter van Alfen, who took the time to improve my English, and Jean-Baptiste Forestier, who supplied me with bibliographical information not available at the Brussels coin cabinet.

1. Around 54,000 for the Athenian agora (Rotroff 1997: 9), more than 30,000 ancient coins found at Seleucia on the Tigris (McDowell 1935: preface), 26,521 at Corinth for the campaigns 1936–1939 (Harris 1941: 143), 13,500 for the campaigns 1925–1930 (Theater area) (MacIsaac 1987: 98), 25,862 for Karanis (Haatvedt and Peterson 1964: 4–7), more than 20,000 at Thasos (Picard 1997: 29), 14,486 ancient coins for Antioch and Seleucia Pieria (Waage 1952), etc.

a longer span of time, starting from the very beginning of widespread coin use, i.e., the sixth century BC. To the best of my knowledge, this is unique. (3) There was no interruption as there is with many other sites (e.g., Olynthus [nearly nothing after c. 348 BC] or Seuthopolis [nearly nothing after c. 275 BC]).

It is the aim of this article to emphasize the value of that conspectus as well as to put it into perspective with other publications of its type. This seems appropriate, since it affords the possibility first to pay a vivid tribute to the opus of Jack Kroll, to whom this Festschrift is dedicated, then and more generally to honor the American School of Classical Studies at Athens, which has played a prominent role in the publication of Greek coins recovered from archaeological sites, as made clear in the bibliography at the end of this chapter, and finally—although not accidentally—to quote the names of Tony Hackens and Georges Le Rider, my masters in numismatics, who have both contributed to these matters.

THE ABSOLUTE PREPONDERANCE OF BRONZE SINCE THE FOURTH CENTURY BC

A basic and unmistakable fact with the Greek coins from the Athenian Agora is the absolute preponderance of bronzes. As with all the other data in this article, I eliminate the evidence for the present era, and stop, arbitrarily, at 31 BC. This involves some extra calculations since, in most publications, Greek imperial or Roman provincials are mixed with the coins struck before 31 BC. Consequently, out of 12,676 Greek coins, 12,515 are in bronze (98.7%), 161 in silver (1.3%), 3 in gold, and 1 in electrum. It may be added that the three gold pieces and the unique electrum piece were discovered in unexpected—apparently disturbed—contexts (Rotroff 1997: 9). Is that particularly unbalanced distribution typical for the Greek world, or does the Athenian Agora give an exaggerated image of bronze issues? Table 1A below summarizes a large part of the useful and available evidence for Greek coins found in official excavations in the eastern part of the Greek world (from continental Greece to Afghanistan).[2] For each site, it is advisable to refer to Appendix 1, which provides more information.[3] Sites are classified in decreasing order of quantities.

The documentary gap between Athens and other published sites is very large indeed. In the list, the number of archaeological reports with more than 1,000 Greek coins is not higher than seven (twelve with a minimum of 500 and eighteen with at least 250). This is a poor situation in comparison with the Roman world. It may suffice to remember that Richard Reece (1991) was able to produce a much more abundant list for Roman Britain only, both

---

2. The Western evidence, Italy and Spain, has been deliberately left aside. Less deliberately, some valuable evidence is clearly missing (e.g., I did not try to sort out many excavation reports from Crimea). However, it is unlikely that this additional material would modify substantially the nature of the comments presented here.

3. As with the other tables of this article, much data had to be calculated or recalculated. In many instances, factual errors, although minor most of the time, were discovered and rectified. It would be surprising in turn if these calculations stand beyond the reach of any criticism.

TABLE 1A. Distribution by metals (in numbers of coins)

Sites	AE	AR	AU	EL	Total
Athens (Kroll 1993)	12,515	161	2	1	12,676
Priene (Regling 1927)	5,682	10	–	–	5,692
Olynthus (Robinson and Clement 1938)	3,480	337	–	–	3,817
Susa (Le Rider 1965)	2,074	102	–	–	2,176
Antioch (Waage 1952)	1,298	16	–	–	1,314
Seuthopolis (Dimitrov and Pentchev 1984)	1,270	35	–	–	1,305
Olynthus (Robinson 1931)	1,093	82	–	–	1,175
(1000)					
Megara (Waage 1935)	682	–	–	–	682
Pergamum (Regling 1914)	631	3	–	–	634
Cyrene (Buttrey 1997)	629	111	4	–	744
Paphos (Nicolaou 1990)	595	1	–	–	596
Delos (Hackens 1970)	503	4			507
(500)					
Corinth, forum area (Fisher 1972–80)	465	23	–	–	488
Olympia (Moustaka 1999)	450	15	–	–	465
Sardis (Buttrey et al. 1981)	442	9	1	–	452
Pergamum (Voegtli 1993)	443	3	–	–	446
Karanis (Haatvedt and Peterson 1964)	278	4	–	–	282
Al-Mina (Robinson 1937)	252	21	–	–	273
(250)					
Tanis (Amandry 1997)	239	3	–	–	242
Mecyberna (Robinson and Clement 1938)	214	2	–	–	216
Dura Europos (Bellinger 1949)	189	8	–	–	197
Corinth, East of the Theater (Zervos 1982–88)	191	–	–	–	191
Aï Khanoum (Bernard 1985)	181	3	–	–	184
Tarsus (Cox 1950)	179	3	–	–	182
Kenchreai (Hohlfelder 1978)	152	–	–	–	152
Aphrodisias (MacDonald 1976)	142	9	–	–	151
Sardis (Bell 1916)	121	13	–	–	134
Corinth, Demeter and Kore (Fisher 1972–74)	115	3	–	–	118
Masada (Meshorer 1989)	115	1	–	–	116
Cyzicus (Köker 2003)	107	4	–	–	111
Corinth, Frankish Corinth (Zervos 1989–98)	99	4	–	–	103
Corycean cave (Picard 1984)	99	1	–	–	100
Corinth 1925 (Bellinger 1930)	48	6	–	–	54
Abou Danne (Doyen 1987)	51	1	–	–	52
Phanagoreia 1996 (Ashton 2003)	32	–	–	–	32
Sagalassos (Scheers 1993–2000)	21	1	–	–	23
Failaka (Callot 1984)	15	–	–	–	15
Jerash (Bellinger 1938)	10	–	–	–	10
Total	35,102	997	7	1	36,107
	97.2%	2.8%	0.0%	0.0%	100.0%

in terms of the number of sites (140, instead of the thirty-seven here) and in the number of coins (an astonishing 168,828, if calculations are correct, compared to 35,966).[4]

Converted into percentages, this gives the distribution in Table 1B (sites are classified in a decreasing order of percentages for bronze coins).

TABLE 1B. Distribution by metals (in percentages)

Sites	AE	AR	AU	EL
Megara (Waage 1935)	100.0	–	–	–
Corinth, East of the Theater (Zervos 1982–88)	100.0	–	–	–
Kenchreai (Hohlfelder 1978)	100.0	–	–	–
Phanagoreia 1996 (Ashton 2003)	100.0	–	–	–
Failaka (Callot 1984)	100.0	–	–	–
Paphos (Nicolaou 1990)	99.8	0.2	–	–
Priene (Regling 1927)	99.8	0.2	–	–
Pergamum (Regling 1914)	99.5	0.5	–	–
Pergamum (Voegtli 1993)	99.3	0.7	–	–
Delos (Hackens 1970)	99.2	0.8	–	–
Masada (Meshorer 1989)	99.1	0.9	–	–
Mecyberna (Robinson and Clement 1938)	99.1	0.9	–	–
Corycean Cave (Picard 1984)	99.0	1.0	–	–
Antioch (Waage 1952)	98.8	1.2	–	–
Tanis (Amandry 1997)	98.8	1.2	–	–
Athens (Kroll 1993)	98.7	1.3	0.0	0.0
Karanis (Haatvedt and Peterson 1964)	98.6	1.4	–	–
Troy (Bellinger 1961)	98.6	1.4	–	–
Aï Khanoum (Bernard 1985)	98.4	1.6	–	–
Tarsus (Cox 1950)	98.4	1.6	–	–
Abou Danne (Doyen 1987)	98.1	1.9	–	–
Sardis (Buttrey et al. 1981)	97.8	2.0	0.2	–
Corinth, Demeter and Kore (Fisher 1972–74)	97.5	2.5	–	–
Seuthopolis (Dimitrov and Pentchev 1984)	97.3	2.7	–	–
Olympia (Moustaka 1999)	96.9	3.2	–	–
Cyzicus (Köker 2003)	96.4	3.6	–	–
Corinth, Frankish Corinth (Zervos 1989–98)	96.1	3.9	–	–
Dura Europos (Bellinger 1949)	95.9	4.1	–	–
Sagalassos (Scheers 1993–2000)	95.5	4.5	–	–
Corinth, Forum area (Fisher 1972–74)	95.3	4.7	–	–
Susa (Le Rider 1965)	95.3	4.7	–	–
(95%)				
Aphrodisias (MacDonald 1976)	94.0	6.0	–	–
Olynthus (Robinson 1931)	93.0	7.0	–	–
Al-Mina (Robinson 1937)	92.3	7.7	–	–
Olynthus (Robinson and Clement 1938)	91.2	8.8	–	–
Sardis (Bell 1916)	90.3	9.7	–	–
Corinth 1925 (Bellinger 1930)	88.9	1.1	–	–
Cyrene (Buttrey 1997)	84.5	14.9	0.5	–

4. The average number of coins per site is thus close (1,206 for Roman and 999 for Greek).

It turns out that the Athenian Agora is located in the upper part of the list (with fifteen sites producing even higher percentages of bronzes, and twenty-two lower percentages). But, with 98.7% for bronze coins, Athens stands very close indeed to the median value (98.4%). This is likely to represent a more realistic percentage than those that Table 1A calculated from absolute numbers (97.2% for bronzes, 2.8% for silver [for which, although for different reasons, sites like Cyrene or Olynthus are clearly atypical]).

Of course, we have to remember that people's behavior differed, depending on whether they lost silver or bronze coins. In the case of silver, it was worthwhile to actively look for the missing coin, as best exemplified by Luke (15: 8–9, the Parable of the Lost Sheep and Coin): "Or what woman, if she has ten silver drachms and loses one of them, does not light a lamp, sweep the house, and search thoroughly until she finds it? Then when she has found it, she calls together her friends and neighbours, saying, 'Rejoice with me, for I have found the coin that I had lost.'" The recovery of a bronze coin was not so exciting or desired. The tenth character of Theophrastus is devoted to "pennypinching", an immoderate sparing of expense: "And if his wife drops a three-penny piece [trichalkon], he is capable of moving the dishes, couches, and chests, and searching in the floorboards" (Theophrastus Characters 10.1). What was true in ancient times also holds true now. Excavation workmen may be quicker to conceal a silver coin than a bronze one. It is thus likely that silver coins published in official reports may be fewer than the real number discovered by modern excavations, and surely underestimated in terms of real ancient circulation compared to bronzes (for these questions, see Reece 1987; 1991).

Kroll's conspectus allows a chronological study of the repartition by metals as shown in Table 2. The intermediary columns are for coins whose current date falls across two centuries. Visualized on a graph, these numbers indicate almost exclusively bronzes (intermediary columns have been excluded from the count) as shown in Figure 1. However, if we look at the data in terms of percentages, we see the pattern in Figure 2. Unsurprisingly, and as

TABLE 2. Athenian Agora—repartition by metals (Kroll 1993)

	6th c.		5th c.		4th c.		3rd c.		2nd c.		1st c.
Gold (2)	–		–	1	1		–		–		–
Electrum (1)	–		1		–		–		–		–
Silver (161)	11	3	61		56	5	16		7		2
Bronze(12,515)	–		5	2	2,642	620	2,131	136	2,915	104	3,959
		–										
Total (12,676)	11	3	67	3	2,699	625	2,147	136	2,922	104	3,961

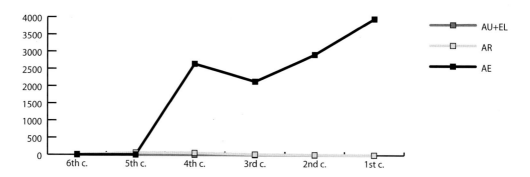

FIGURE 1. Athenian Agora—repartition by metals in numbers of coins (Kroll 1993)

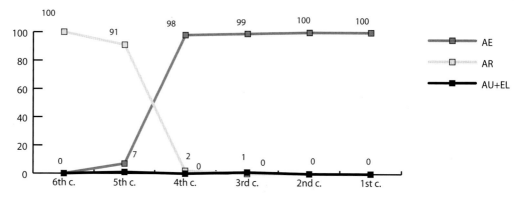

FIGURE 2. Athenian Agora—repartition by metals in percentages (Kroll 1993)

observed by Kroll (1993: 4): "Once a bronze coinage was introduced in the fourth century, bronze began to replace the smaller silver denominations in petty transactions and lessened dependency on silver in general".

This profound change between the fifth and the fourth centuries BC is also illustrated by other sites, such as the external sanctuary of Demeter and Persephone at Cyrene (Table 3), for which T. V. Buttrey provides some chronological statistics as well (Buttrey 1997).

Table 3. Extramural sanctuary of Demeter and Persephone at Cyrene—repartition by metals (Buttrey 1997: 2)

	6th–5th c.	4th c.	3rd/early 1st c.	Total
Gold	–	4	–	4
Silver	103	4	4	111
Bronze	–	76	553	629
Total	103	84	557	744

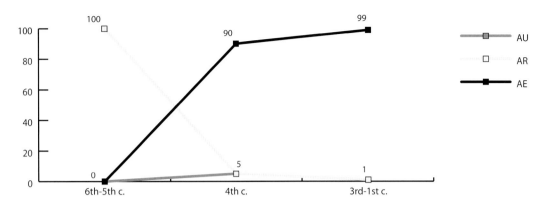

FIGURE 3. Extramural sanctuary of Demeter and Persephone at Cyrene—repartition by
metals in percentages (Buttrey 1997: 2)

TABLE 4. Susa—repartition by metals (Le Rider 1965)

	4th c.	3rd c.	2nd c.	1st c.	Total
Silver	33	26	8	35	102
Bronze	11	316	1,045	702	2,074
Total	44	342	1,053	737	2,176

Again, these data are more explicit when converted into a graph (Figure 3). The
same pattern—a massive preponderance of bronze coins very soon after they started to
be struck—may be observed everywhere. It may have been slower, as in the case of Susa
(Table 4, Figure 4), where coinage was unknown before the arrival of Alexander the Great,
and where bronze coins were not much in use before the third century BC (Le Rider 1965:
234–239).

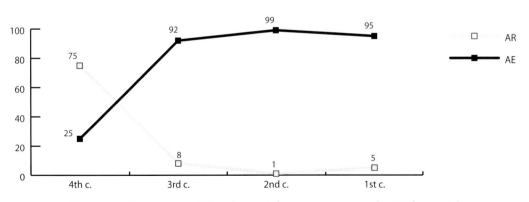

FIGURE 4. Susa—repartition by metals in percentages (Le Rider 1965)

LOCAL VERSUS FOREIGN COINAGES

Out of the 12,676 Greek coins published from the Athenian Agora, 10,809 are Athenian (85.3%). Again, is this a normal value for the Greek world? Tables 5A and 5B put these data into perspective.

TABLE 5A. Local versus foreign coins (count by decreasing number of foreign coins)

Sites	Local	Coinage	Foreign
Athens (Kroll 1993)	10,809	(Athens)	1,867
Zone (Gallani-Krikou 1996)	729	(Zone)	1,406
Olynthus (Robinson and Clement 1938)	2,443	(Chalcidic coins)	1,374
Olynthus (Robinson 1931)	647	(Chalcidic coins)	528
Seuthopolis (Dimitrov and Pentchev 1984)	849	(Seuthes)	456
Corinth 1936–1939 (Harris 1941)	657	(Corinth)	444
Olympia (Moustaka 1999)	136	(Elis)	329
Antioch (Waage 1952)	1,048	(Antioch and Seleucids at Antioch)	266
Priene (Regling 1927)	5,433	(Priene)	259
Sardis (Buttrey et al. 1981)	200	(Sardis)	252
Pergamum (Regling 1914)	443	(326 Pergamum and 117 Pergamene kingdom)	191
Pergamum (Voegtli 1993)	285	(192 Pergamum and 93 Pergamene kingdom)	161
Corinth, Forum area (Fisher 1972–74)	325	(Corinth)	163
Troy (Bellinger 1961)	85	(Ilium)	124
Sardis (Bell 1916)	25	(Sardis)	109
Delos (Hackens 1970)	406	(378 Athens and 28 Delos)	101
Aphrodisias (MacDonald 1976)	58	(Aphrodisias)	93
Kenchreai (Hohlfelder 1978)	64	(Corinth)	88
Corinth, East of the Theater (Zervos 1982–88)	108	(Corinth)	83
Corinth, Frankish Corinth (Zervos 1989–98)	46	(Corinth)	57
Corinth, Demeter and Kore (Fisher 1972–74)	76	(Corinth)	42
Cyzicus (Köker 2003)	81	(Cyzicus)	30
Corinth 1925 (Bellinger 1930)	29	(Corinth)	25
Masada (Meshorer 1989)	92	(Jewish)	24
Cyrene (Buttrey 1997)	725	(Cyrene)	19
Tanis (Amandry 1997)	232	(Ptolemaic coins)	10
Phanagoreia 1996 (Ashton 2003)	29	(Pantikapaion 27 and Phanagoreia 2)	3
Karanis (Haatvedt and Peterson 1964)	282	(Ptolemaic coins)	0

TABLE 5B. Local versus foreign coins (percentages by increasing proportion of foreign coins)

Sites	Local	Foreign
Karanis (Haatvedt and Peterson 1964)	100.0%	0.0%
Cyrene (Buttrey 1997)	97.4%	2.6%
Tanis (Amandry 1997)	95.9%	4.1%
Priene (Regling 1927)	95.8%	4.2%
Phanagoreia 1996 (Ashton 2003)	90.6%	9.4%
(95%)		
Thasos (Picard 1997, 31)	more than 90%	less than 10%
Athens (Kroll 1993)	85.3%	14.7%
Delos (Hackens 1970)	80.1%	19.9%
Antioch (Waage 1952)	79.8%	20.2%
Masada (Meshorer 1989)	79.3%	20.7%
(75%)		
Cyzicus (Köker 2003)	73.0%	27.0%
Pergamum (Regling 1914)	69.9%	30.1%
Corinth, Forum area (Fisher 1972–80)	66.5%	33.5%
Seuthopolis (Dimitrov and Pentchev 1984)	65.1%	34.9%
Corinth, Demeter and Kore (Fisher 1972–74)	64.4%	35.6%
Olynthus (Robinson and Clement 1938)	64.0%	36.0%
Pergamum (Voegtli 1993)	63.9%	36.1%
Corinth 1936–1939 (Harris 1941)	59.7%	40.3%
Corinth, east of the Theater (Zervos 1982–98)	56.5%	43.5%
Olynthus (Robinson 1931)	55.1%	44.9%
Corinth 1925 (Bellinger 1930)	53.7%	46.3%
Corinth, Frankish Corinth (Zervos 1989–98)	44.7%	55.3%
Sardis (Buttrey et al. 1981)	44.2%	55.8%
Kenchreai (Hohlfelder 1978)	42.1%	57.9%
Troy (Bellinger 1961)	40.7%	59.3%
Aphrodisias (MacDonald 1976)	38.4%	61.6%
Zone (Gallani-Krikou 1996)	34.1%	65.9%
Olympia (Moustaka 1999)	29.2%	70.8%
Sardis (Bell 1916)	8.7%	91.3%

It comes as no surprise to learn that, here, the Athenian evidence is not close to the average. With six cases higher and twenty-two lower, the proportion of local coins at Athens (85.3%) was high. Here we may distinguish between at least three categories: sites embedded in a closed monetary economy (e.g., Karanis and Tanis in Egypt), sites that were also major ancient mints (e.g., Athens and Thasos—but see Corinth), and others where foreign coins were naturally more abundant.

There is no reason to think that foreign coins entered into local circulation in the same proportion at every point in history. For the Athenian Agora, we do indeed observe strong variations (Table 6). Leaving aside the intermediary columns, which are for coins dated "à cheval" (between two centuries, e.g., fifth–fourth century), we are able to construct the following graphs expressed first in numbers, then in percentages (Figures 5 and 6).

TABLE 6. Local and foreign coins of the Athenian Agora (Kroll 1993)

	6th c.	5th c.	4th c.	3rd c.	2nd c.	1st c.
Athenian (10,809)	10	59	2,230	1,512	2,752	3,890
			356			
Non-Athenian (1,867)	1	8	469+	635+	170+	69
		3	3	269+	136+	104+
Total (12,676)	11	67	2,699+	2,147+	2,922+	3,959
		3	3	625+	136+	104+

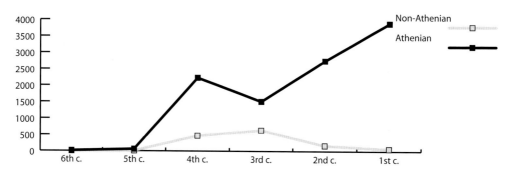

FIGURE 5. Local and foreign coins of the Athenian Agora—in numbers (Kroll 1993)

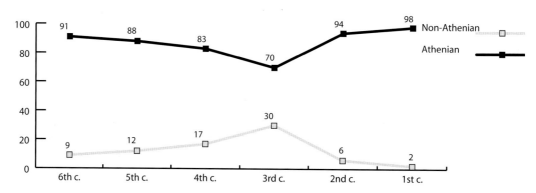

FIGURE 6. Local and foreign coins of the Athenian Agora—in percentages (Kroll 1993)

It appears that the percentages of foreign coins in Athens fluctuated between 2% and 30%. Here again we may well wonder if there are biases in our data. As everywhere else, the chances of discard were higher for foreign coins, which were not legal tender in Athens, than for Athenian coinages. Kroll sees an analogy with Canadian coins now circulating in the United States, mainly along the frontier. It is likely that foreign bronzes were not legal tender but were still used, especially the very small denominations. Still, variations remain and I have no difficulty in sharing Kroll's point of view: "After the Athenian restriking of this Macedonian bronze in the 220s, therefore, the inflow of supplementary outside bronze currencies was sharply reduced, either because the supply of Athenian bronze had become more abundant or, more probably, because a new attitude or policy discouraged the use of non-Athenian bronze now that bronze coins were more commonly issued in larger denominations and were playing a larger role vis-à-vis silver in the monetary economy" (Kroll 1993: 169).

CHRONOLOGICAL TABLES AND GREEK NUMISMATICS

To produce a recapitulative and chronological table of all the coins found in a single archaeological site is by no means a novelty, even if it occurs only sporadically today and is less common for the Greek world than for the Roman world. For the Greek world, with its endless number of cities and dynasts, and their bronze issues being often so loosely dated in the literature, it may look discouraging to adopt a chronological division of the material. Many catalogues of archaeological finds even avoid giving a date for some coinages they deal with. Certainly, it is less trouble to list all the coins, city after city, and to include a map displaying all the provenances. Table 7 summarizes the evidence drawn from the references in this paper's bibliography. For each site, it gives the number of Greek coins, as well as information (with references to pages) on the existence of a map of provenances (six cases out of forty-three), a conspectus (twenty-six cases), or a chronological table of the finds (nine cases).

How much simpler the imperial Roman world looks, especially the High Empire, with its one international currency, struck by emperors the length of whose reigns is known. It is thus easy to calculate how many coins per year have been found for Trajan, for Hadrian, and so on. Consequently, what is known as the "Ravetz index" is of common use to Roman field archaeologists, but practically ignored by Greek numismatists (Ravetz 1964).[5]

However, a chronological table is not a new practice in Greek numismatics (Robinson and Clement 1938: 364–368 [very schematic: before and after 348 BC] and Harris 1941: 156). The graph published by J. M. Harris (1941) for the coins found at Corinth resembles, and thus anticipates, the ones Roman numismatists are familiar with (Figure 7).

It has to be noticed that the practice of providing a chronological table for Greek coins was a common rule in Russian publications for many decades. Reproduced in Table 8 are the combined results of two articles for the Crimean sites of Tiritake and Myrmekion (Zograf 1952: 383 [Tiritake] and 384 [Myrmekia]; Belova 1955: 347–348 [Tiritake] and 348–349 [Mirmekion]). These data are the basis for the graph in Figure 8.

---

5. The Ravetz index, adapted by Casey (1988: 41–45), is calculated for each period by the formula: (number of coins per period $\times$ 1,000) / (length of each period $\times$ total number of coins found on the site). On the uses and abuses of the so-called Ravetz index (since the idea and the formula is not very elaborated), see Reece (*passim*) and, very explicitly with nice fictional examples, van Heesch (1998: 23–26, "De Ravetz-methode").

TABLE 7. Publications of Greek coins found in archaeological excavations—some criteria of their quality

Sites	Greek Coins	Map	Conspectus	Chronological Table
Athens (Kroll 1993)	12,676	–	xviii–xxvi	xviii–xxvi
Priene (Regling 1927)	5,692	–	179–87	–
Olynthus (Robinson and Clement 1938)	3,817	–	364–8	364–8
Susa (Le Rider 1965)	2,176	–	234–41	–
Zone (Gallani-Krikou 1996)	2,135	–	68–9	–
Antioch (Waage 1952)	1,314	–	173–5	–
Seuthopolis (Dimitrov and Pentchev 1984)	1,305	–	126–7	–
Olynthus (Robinson 1931)	1,175	2/3	6–7	–
Corinth 1936–1939 (Harris 1941)	1,101	–	147–52	156
Cyrene (Buttrey 1997)	744	–	2–3	2
Sardis (Buttrey et al. 1981)	710	–	4–5	4–5
Megara (Waage 1935)	682	–	–	–
Pergamum (Regling 1914)	634	–	–	–
Paphos (Nicolaou 1990)	596	–	123–30	–
Delos (Hackens 1970)	507	413	409–12	417
Corinth, forum area (Fisher 1972–80)	488	–	–	–
Olympia (Moustaka 1999)	465	154	–	–
Pergamum (Voegtli 1993)	446	–	5–6	–
Mirmekia (Zograf 1952 and Belova 1955)	409	–	347–51, 382–6	347–50, 382–4
Tiritake (Zograf 1952 and Belova 1955)	333	–	347–51, 382–6	347–50, 382–4
Karanis (Haatvedt and Peterson 1964)	282		4–7	–
Al-Mina (Robinson 1937)	273	–	–	–
Tanis (Amandry 1997)	242	–	364–5	–
Mecyberna (Robinson and Clement 1938)	216	–	373	–
Troy (Bellinger 1961)	209	–	–	–
Dura Europos (Bellinger 1949)	197	11	–	–
Corinth, East of the Theater (Zervos 1982–88)	191	–	*passim*	–
Aï Khanoum (Bernard 1985)	184	–	154–8	–
Tarsus (Cox 1950)	182	–	–	–
Kenchreai (Hohlfelder 1978)	152	–	92	92
Aphrodisias (MacDonald 1976)	151	43	41–2	–
Curium (Cox 1959)	149	–	–	–
Sardis (Bell 1916)	134	–	iv	–
Corinth, Demeter and Kore (Fisher 1972–74)	118	–	–	–
Masada (Meshorer 1989)	116	–	–	–
Cyzicus (Köker 2003)	111	–	–	–
Corinth, Frankish Corinth (Zervos 1989–98)	103	–	*passim*	–
Corycean cave (Picard 1984)	100	282	–	–
Corinth 1925 (Bellinger 1930)	54	–	–	–
Abou Danne (Doyen 1987)	52	–	–	–
Phanagoreia 1996 (Ashton 2003)	32	–	–	–
Sagalassos (Scheers 1993–2000)	22	–	–	–
Failaka (Callot 1984)	15	–	–	–
Jerash (Bellinger 1938)	10	–	8–9	–

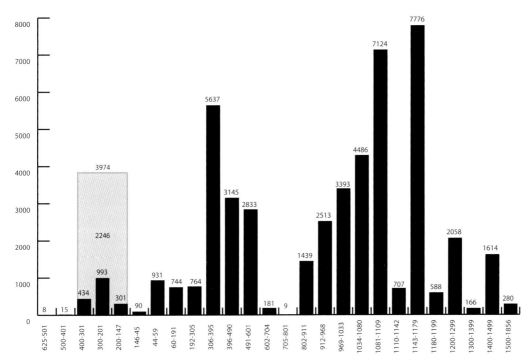

FIGURE 7. Chronological distribution of coins found at Corinth (after Harris 1941: 156)

TABLE 8. Greek coins found in Tiritake and Myrmekion (Zograf 1952; Belova 1955)

	5th c.	4th c.	3rd c.	2nd c.	1st c.	Total
Tiritake (Zograf)	–	44	106	58	81	289
Tiritake (Belova)	–	2	10	7	14	44
			1	10		
Total	–	46	116	65	95	333
Mirmekia (Zograf)	–	61	103	42	35	241
Mirmekia (Belova)	–	3	72	28	26	168
		2	8	29		
Total	–	64	175	70	61	409

It is all too clear how dangerous it would be to draw general conclusions about the mon-etization of these two sites, not that distant from each other, from these graphs alone. Let us repeat that secure chronologies are of paramount importance, and that this simple re-quirement is rarely met with Greek bronze coinages. There is a wider range of data available for the northern Pontic shores. For Chersonesus, still in Crimea, A. M. Gilevich provides us with a detailed list of all the coins that were not struck in Chersonesus (Gilevich 1968).

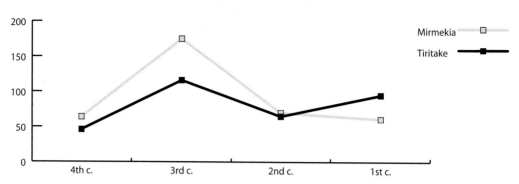

FIGURE 8. Greek coins found in Tiritake and Myrmekion (Zograf 1952; Belova 1955)

She puts this decent number of coins (682) into chronological perspective, with a different result (Table 9).

TABLE 9. Foreign Greek coins found in Chersonesus (Gilevich 1968)

	5th	4th c.	3rd c.	2nd c.	1st c.	Total
Chersonesus (Gil.)	1	44	73	100	212	682
		8	9	236[a]		

a. The massive import of Mithridatic bronzes is mainly dated here to the second and first centuries BC (129 for Amisus and 37 for Sinope, thus 166 out of 236 coins).

It would be tempting to amalgamate all the available data in order to produce what would resemble for archaeological coins the "Master Hoard" ventured by M. Crawford (Crawford 1974: 642–671; Buttrey 1993: 335). Let us add, for this purpose, two other sets of information coming from two very different sites: the foreign coins[6] found by French archaeologists in the House of the Comedians on Delos and the royal (both Seleucid and Parthian) coins found at Seleucia on the Tigris (Table 10; Figure 9).

TABLE 10. Coins found in Delos and Seleucia on the Tigris

Delos: îlot de la Maison des Comédiens (Hackens 1970: 387–419)					
	4th c.	3rd c.	2nd c.	1st c.	Total
Foreign coins	6	10	28	42	86
Seleuceia on the Tigris (Le Rider 1998: 72)					
	4th c.	3rd c.	2nd c.	1st c.	Total
Italian excavations		36	162	263	461
McDowell		147	410	430	987
Total		183	572	693	1448

6. This excludes the Athenian and Delian coins, which are highly abundant on Delos.

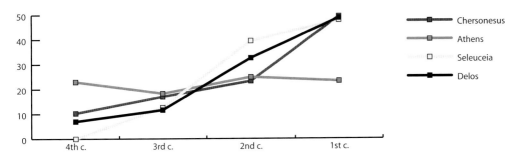

FIGURE 9. Athens, Chersonesus, Delos, and Seleucia on the Tigris—percentages of coins recovered per century, calculated out of the total for the last four centuries BC

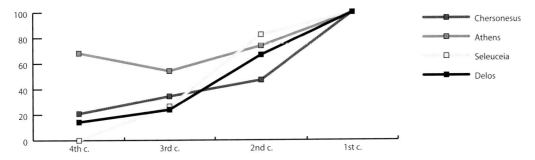

FIGURE 10. Athens, Chersonesus, Delos, and Seleucia on the Tigris—percentages of coins recovered per century, with a base 100 for the first century BC

It has often been noted that the so-called Ravetz index could be easily misused, if comparing percentages derived from sequences of different chronological lengths (which is not here the case). A way to manage this kind of distortion is to attribute the same value to a certain set of data (here the final one) and to calculate the percentages from what we had before. In this case, it does not affect very much the shape of the graph (Figure 10).

What do these chronological tables say about the monetization of ancient societies? There is no shortage of warnings for those who would be tempted to find in these rough numbers the much desired model of the growing monetization of ancient economies. Referring to coinage production, Olivier Picard once argued that the Ravetz index would be of very limited use if applied to the Greek world. "On the other hand, how exhaustive and precise it could be, this productivity table does not allow any estimate of how the economical activities vary… monetary production is not the result of the richness or the importance of the activities of a city" (Picard 1997: 33). He rightly dissociates production and circulation. The production of coins is just one face of the problem, as Reece has continuously insisted (Reece 1987, 1991–93, 1996). And, as numismatists seem more ready to accept than historians, coins (even in bronze) were rarely struck for commercial reasons. But coins found in excavations and hoards form another side of the information available to us; they are the forgotten remnants of actual circulation.

TABLE 11. The number of Greek coins found per square meter in Delos and Paphos

Sites	Number of Greek coins	Surface excavated	Surface per coin
Delos, Îlot des Comédiens	507	1,920 m²	1 coin for c. 3.8 m²
Paphos, House of Dionysos	596	5,000 m²	1 coin for c. 8.4 m²

In regard to these questions, Roman numismatists are far ahead of their colleagues who deal with Greek coinages; there is much to learn from them. This article is a call for more audacious studies about the levels of monetization in the Greek world, studies that should take advantage of chronological tables such as the illuminating one produced by Jack Kroll for Athens.

ADDITIONAL REMARK: A SURFACE INDEX

It is a pity that, as a rule, archaeological publications of coins fail to mention excavated surfaces. It would be of prime interest to get some quantitative ideas about the number of coins recovered per unit of surface, and some cases favor such a treatment: the Hellenistic block of houses in Delos known as "L'îlot de la Maison des Comédiens" (about 50×100 m), fully excavated by the French School (Hackens 1970); and the Hellenistic "House of Dionysos" in Paphos (roughly 48×40 m), fully excavated as well (Nicolaou 1990). Table 11 summarizes the data.

To take these numbers at face value, and with everything else being equal, it appears that Delos was more monetized than Paphos, hardly a surprising conclusion. It is difficult to estimate the entire surface excavated by the American School in the Athenian Agora up to 1990, but 6 hectares (60,000 m²) must not be too far off the mark. If so, it would mean the recovery of one Greek coin for every 4.8 m² (12,515 coins). At first sight, these results, which seem plausible, appear meager: one coin for every 5 square meters is paucity indeed, especially since this covers all the strays from the sixth to the first century BC. But what then to think of the excavations of Aï Khanoum, which in many digs (1965–1978) mounted in many areas (no fewer than twenty-one; see Bernard 1985: 115–116) brought to light 184 Greek coins (out of a total of 224)? More detailed information such as "5 coins for the Theater area" illustrates even more dramatically the paucity of coins recovered there. Despite the many dangers of extrapolation, it is much to be hoped that, in the future, such kind of calculations may be extended.

BIBLIOGRAPHY

Amandry, M. 1997. Monnaies isolées découvertes en fouille à Tanis (1976–1994). In: Ph. Brissaud and Ch. Zivie-Coche, eds., *Tanis. Travaux récents sur le Tell Sân el-Hagar. Mission française des fouilles de Tanis* 1987–97, pp. 353–377. Paris: Noêsis.

Ashton, R. H. J. 2003. Excavation coins from Phanagoreia. *Numismatic Chronicle* 163: 379–385.

Bell, H. W. 1916. *Sardis XI: coins. Part I: 1910–1914.* Leyde.

Bellinger, A. R. 1930. *Catalogue of the coins found at Corinth, 1925.* New Haven: Yale University Press.

———. 1938. *Coins from Jerash, 1928–1934.* Numismatic Notes and Monographs 81. New York: American Numismatic Society.

———. 1949. *The excavations at Dura Europos. Final report VI: the coins.* New Haven: Yale University Press.

———. 1961. *Troy: the coins.* Princeton: Princeton University Press.

Belova, L. N. 1955. Moneti iz raskopok Tiritaki, Mirmekia i Ilurata, b 1946–1953 gg. *Materiali i Issledobania po Archeologii SSSR* 85: 330–351.

Bernard, P. 1985. *Fouilles d'Aï Khanoum IV. Les monnaies hors trésors; questions d'histoire gréco-bactrienne.* Mémoires de la Délégation archéologique française en Afghanistan 28. Paris: Diffusion de Boccard.

Buttrey, T. V. 1993. Calculating ancient coin production: facts and fantasies. *Numismatic Chronicle* 153: 335–351.

———. 1997. Part I: the coins. In: D. White, ed., *The extramural sanctuary of Demeter and Persephone at Cyrene, Libya: final reports.* Philadelphia.

———. 1999. The content and meaning of coin hoards. *Journal of Roman Archaeology* 12: 526–532.

———., A. Johnston, K. M. MacKenzie, and M. L. Bates. 1981. *Greek, Roman, and Islamic coins from Sardis.* Archaeological exploration of Sardis 7. Cambridge: Harvard University Press.

———., K. T. Erim, and R. R. Holloway. 1989. *The coins.* Morgantina studies II. Princeton: Princeton University Press.

Callot, O. 1984. Les monnaies. In: J.-F. Salles et al., *Failaka. Fouilles françaises 1983*, pp. 157–167. Lyon: GDR-Maison de l'Orient; Paris: Diffusion de Boccard.

Cox, D. H. 1950. The coins. In: H. Goldman, ed., *Excavations at Gözlu Kule, Tarsus*, pp. 38–84. Princeton: Princeton University Press.

———. 1959. *Coins from the excavations at Curium, 1932–1953.* Numismatic Notes and Monographs 145. New York: American Numismatic Society.

Crawford, M. H. 1974. *Roman republican coinage.* Cambridge: Cambridge University Press.

Dimitrov, K., and V. Pentchev. 1984. *Sevtopolis II: Antichni I srednovekovin moneti.* Sofia.

Doyen, J.-M. 1987. *Les monnaies antiques du Tell Abou Danne et d'Oumm el-Marra (campagnes 1976–1985).* Bruxelles.

Edwards, K. M. 1933. *Corinth VI.* Cambridge: Cambridge University Press.

Fisher, J. E. 1972–74. The sanctuary of Demeter and Kore on Acrocorinth. *Hesperia* 41.3 (1972): 318–331; *Hesperia* 43.3 (1974): 292–307.

———. 1972–80. "The forum area." *Hesperia* 41.2 (1972): 174–184; *Hesperia* 42.1 (1973): 34–44, pl. 12; *Hesperia* 43.1 (1974): 46–76 = data not usable; *Hesperia* 44.1 (1975): 30–50, pl. 11; *Hesperia* 45.2 (1976): 138–162, pl. 25; and *Hesperia* 49.1 (1980): 1–29.

Gallani-Krikou, M. 1996. The mint at Zone: the evidence of the excavations at Aegean Mesembria-Zone. In: *ΧΑΡΑΚΤΗΡ. Αφιέρωμα στη Μάντω Οικονομίδου*, pp. 63–80. Athens.

Gilevich, A. M. 1968. Ancient coins of other cities from excavations at Chersonesus. *Numizmatika i Sfragistika* 3: 3–61.

Haatvedt, R., and E. E. Peterson. 1964. *Coins from Karanis: the University of Michigan excavations 1924–1935.* Ann Arbor: University of Michigan Press.

Hackens, T. 1970. XVI. Les monnaies. In: Ph. Bruneau et al., eds., *L'Îlot de la Maison des Comédiens*, pp. 387–419. Exploration archéologique de Délos 27. Paris.

Harris, J. M. 1941. Coins found at Corinth. *Hesperia* 10.2: 143–162.

Hohlfelder, R. L. 1978. *Kenchreai, eastern port of Corinth. III. The coins.* Leiden: Brill.

Köker, H. 2003. The Greek coins from the 1952–3 excavations at Cyzicus. *Numismatic Chronicle* 163: 385–392, pl. 49.

Kroll, J. 1993. *The Athenian Agora XXVI. The Greek coins.* Princeton: American School of Classical Studies at Athens.

Le Rider, G. 1965. *Suse sous les Séleucides et les Parthes. Les trouvailles monétaires et l'histoire de la ville*, 234–241. Mémoires de la mission archéologique en Iran XXXVIII. Paris : Paul Geuthner.

———. 1998. *Séleucie du Tigre. Les monnaies séleucides et parthes.* Firenze: Casa Editrice Le Lettere.

MacDonald, D. J. 1976. *Greek and Roman coins from Aphrodisias.* BAR Suppl. Ser. 9. Oxford: British Archaeological Reports.

Meshorer, Y. 1989. The coins of Masada. In: *Masada I. The Yigael Yadin excavations 1963–1965. Final Reports*, pp. 71–132, pl. 61–81. Jerusalem.

Moustaka, A. 1999. *Die Fundmünzen der Südostgrabung.* In: *Bericht über die Ausgrabungen in Olympia*, IX, 152–180, pl. 42–45. Berlin and New York.

Nicolaou, I. 1990. *Paphos II: the coins from the house of Dionysos.* Nicosia.

Picard, O. 1984. Monnaies. In: *L'Antre corycien*, II, *Bulletin de correspondance hellénique* Suppl. 9, 281–306. Athens and Paris.

———. 1997. Monnaies de fouilles et histoire grecque: l'exemple de Thasos. In: K. A. Sheedy and Ch. Papageorgiadou-Banis, eds., *Numismatic archaeology. Archaeological numismatics. Proceedings of an International Conference held to honour Dr. Mando Oeconomides in Athens 1995*, pp. 29–39. Oxford: Oxbow Books.

Ravetz, A. 1964. The fourth-century inflation and Romano-British coin finds. *Numismatic Chronicle* 7, no. 4: 201–231.

Reece, R. 1987. Coin finds and coin production. In: G. Depeyrot et al., *Rythmes de la produc-*

tion monétaire, de l'antiquité à nos jours, pp. 335–341. Louvain-la-Neuve : Séminaire de Numismatique Marcel Hoc, Collége Erasme.

———. 1991. *Roman coins from 140 sites in Britain.* Cirencester: Coswold Studies.

———. 1991–93. Coins as minted and coins as found. *Acta Numismàtica* 21–23: 57–62.

———. 1996. The interpretation of site finds: a review. In: C. E. King and D. G. Wigg, eds., *Coin finds and coin use in the Roman world: Oxford symposium on coinage and monetary history 13*, pp. 341–355. Berlin: Gebr. Mann Verlag.

Regling, K. 1914. Münzfunde aus Pergamon. *Blätter für Münzfreunde* 49.10–11: 5671–5685, 5703–5718.

———. 1927. *Die Münzen von Priene.* Berlin.

Robinson, D. M. 1931. *Excavations at Olynthus. Part III: The coins found at Olynthus in 1928.* Baltimore: Johns Hopkins University.

———., and P. A. Clement. 1938. *Excavations at Olynthus. Part IX: The Chalcidic mint and the excavation coins found in 1928–1934.* Baltimore: Johns Hopkins University.

Robinson, E. S. G. 1937. Coins from the excavations at Al-Mina (1936). *Numismatic Chronicle* 5th series 65: 182–196.

Rotroff, S. I. 1997. Coins and stratigraphy. In: K. A. Sheedy and Ch. Papageorgiadou-Banis, eds., *Numismatic archaeology. Archaeological numismatics. Proceedings of an international conference held to honour Dr. Mando Oeconomides in Athens 1995*, pp. 8–16. Oxford: Oxbow Books.

Rusten, J., and I. C. Cunningham. 2002. *Theophrastus, Characters, Herodas, Mimes, Sophron and other mime fragments.* Loeb 225, Cambridge-London, pp. 82–85.

Scheers, S. 1993–2000. Catalogue of the coins. In: M. Waelkens and J. Poblomme, eds., *Sagalassos*, II (1993): 249–260; III (1995): 307–323; IV (1997): 315–350; V (2000): 509–549. Leuven: Leuven University Press.

van Heesch, J. 1998. *De muntcirculatie tijdens de romeinse tijd in het Noordwesten van Gallia Belgica. De civitates van de Nerviërs en de Menapiërs (ca. 50 v.C.–450 n.C.).* Brussels.

Voegtli, H. 1993. *Die Fundmünzen aus der Stadtgrabung von Pergamon.* Berlin and New York: Walter de Gruyter.

Waage, D. B. 1952. *Antioch-on-the-Orontes, IV.2: Greek, Roman, Byzantine and Crusaders' coins.* Princeton.

Waage, F. O. 1935. *Greek bronze coins from a well at Megara.* Numismatic Notes and Monographs 70. New York: American Numismatic Society.

Walker, A. 1997. Excavations coins: the use and misuse of numismatic evidence in archaeology. In: K. A. Sheedy and Ch. Papageorgiadou-Banis, eds., *Numismatic archaeology. Archaeological numismatics. Proceedings of an international conference held to honour Dr. Mando Oeconomides in Athens 1995*, pp. 17–26. Oxford: Oxbow Books.

Zervos, O. H. 1982–88. East of the theater: the coins. *Hesperia* 51.2 (1982): 145–163, pl. 47; *Hesperia* 52.1 (1983): 33–47, pl. 12; *Hesperia* 54.1 (1985): 81–96, pl. 18; *Hesperia* 55.2 (1986):

163–175, pl. 37; *Hesperia* 56.1 (1987): 33–46, pl. 8; and *Hesperia* 57.2 (1988): 132–146, pl. 44.

———. 1989–98. Frankish Corinth: the coins. *Hesperia* 58.1 (1989): 37–50, pl. 13; *Hesperia* 60.1 (1991): 41–58, pl. 8; *Hesperia* 61.2 (1992): 179–191, pl. 45; *Hesperia* 62.1 (1993): 36–52, pl. 12; *Hesperia* 63.1 (1994): 41–56, pl. 13; *Hesperia* 64.1 (1995): 40–60, pl. 15; *Hesperia* 65.1 (1996): 40–55, pl. 9; *Hesperia* 66.2 (1997): 173–192, pl. 53; and *Hesperia* 67.3 (1998): 265–281, pl. 49.

Zograf, A. N. 1952. Opisanie monet, naidennykh pri raskopkakh Tiritaki i Mimrmekiya v 1935–1940 gg. *Materialy i issledovaniia po archeologii SSSR* 25: 363–386.

Appendix 1: Alphabetical List of Archaeological Sites with Published Greek Coins

Abou Danne (Doyen 1987)
52 Greek coins (1 in silver [1.9%] and 51 in bronze [98.1%]) out of 83
48 for the Seleucids (92.3%) (47 struck in Antioch), 2 for Antioch,…

Aï Khanoum (Bernard 1985)
184 Greek coins (3 in silver [1.6%] and 181 in bronze [98.4%]) out of 224
68 for the Seleucids, 49 for Euthydemus I,… (149? [81.0%] for the mint of Aï Khanoum)
Comment: This is a small amount for many campaigns (1965–1978) covering no less than 21 areas on the site (for example: 5 coins for the Theater, etc.—see p. 115–16).

Al-Mina (Robinson 1937)—mainly fourth century BC
273 Greek coins (21 in silver [7.7%] and 252 in bronze [92.3%])
194 for Alexander III, 20 for Aradus, 8 for Ptolemies, 6 for Athens,…

Antioch (Waage 1952)
1,314 Greek coins (1,298 in bronze [98.8%] and 16 in silver [1.2%]) out of 14,486
1,009 for the Seleucids (out of which 898 for the mint of Antioch), 150 for Antioch, 55 for Seleucia Pieria, 33 for the Ptolemies (10 in silver), 18 for Demetrius Poliorcetes,…

Aphrodisias (MacDonald 1976)
151 Greek coins (9 in silver [6.0%] and 142 in bronze [94.0%]) out of 615
58 for Aphrodisias (38.4%), 6 for Ephesus, 4 for Tabai,…

Athens (Kroll 1993)
12,676 Greek coins (2 in gold, 1 in electrum, 161 in silver [1.3%], and 12,515 in bronze [98.7%])
10,809 for Athens + 1,867.

Corinth, 1925 (Bellinger 1930)
54 Greek coins (48 in bronze [88.9%] and 6 in silver [10.1%]) out of 1,305
29 for Corinth (53.7%), 6 for Sicyon,…

Corinth, 1936–1939 (Harris 1941)
1,101 Greek coins (no details by metal available) out of 26,521
657 for Corinth (59.7%), Sicyon,...

Corinth, Forum area (Fisher 1972–80)
488 Greek coins (23 in silver [4.7%] and 465 in bronze [95.3%]) out of 1,144
325 for Corinth (66.6%), Sicyon,...

Corinth, Sanctuary of Demeter and Kore (Fisher 1972–74)
118 Greek coins (3 in silver [2.5%] and 115 in bronze [97.5%]) out of 208
76 for Corinth (64.4%), Sicyon,...

Corinth, East of the Theater (Zervos 1982–88)
191 Greek coins (all in bronze) out of 1,117
108 for Corinth (56.5%), Sicyon,...

Corinth, Frankish Corinth (Zervos 1989–98)
103 Greek coins (4 in silver [3.9%] and 99 in bronze [96.1%]) out of 2,028
46 for Corinth (44.7%), Sicyon,...

Corycean Cave (Picard 1984)
100 Greek coins (1 in silver and 99 in bronze) out of 110
16 for the Locrians, 14 for the Phocidians, 10 for the Etolians, 8 for the Boeotians,...

Curium (Cox 1959)
149 Greek coins (all in bronze)
30 for Ptolemy II, 21 for Ptolemy I, 10 for Ptolemy VIII, 8 for Alexander III, 5 for Curium,
    5 for the Seleucids,...

Cyrene, Sanctuary of Demeter and Persephone (Buttrey 1997)
744 Greek coins (4 in gold [0.5%], 111 in silver [14.9%], and 629 in bronze [84.5%]) out of
    834
725 for Cyrene (97.4%), 9 for Euesperides, 3 for Rhodes, 3 for Corcyra, 2 for Barce,...

Cyzicus, 1952–53 (Köker 2003)
111 Greek coins (4 in silver [3.6%] and 107 in bronze [96.4%]) out of 193
81 for Cyzicus (73.0%), 7 for Alexander the Great, 3 for Lampsacus and Pergamum,...

Delos, L'Îlot des Comédiens (Hackens 1970)—second century / beginning of first century BC.
507 Greek coins (4 in silver [0.8%] and 503 in bronze [99.2%]) out of 509
378 for Athens (74.6%), 28 for Delos, 8 for Ptolemies, 8 for Tinos, 7 for Myconos, 7 for
    Bargylia (found together),...
Comment: The surface of L'Îlot de la Maison des Comédiens is roughly 1,920 m² (48 × 40 m).
    It means, as an average, 1 Greek coin for 3.8 m².

<u>Dura Europos</u> (Bellinger 1949)

197 Greek coins (189 in bronze [95.9%] and 8 in silver [4.1%]) out of 2,179

132 for the Seleucids, 21 for the Parthians, 4 for Alexander the Great, 5 for Aradus, 4 for
      Seleuceia on the Tigris, 3 for Laodicea,...

<u>Failaka</u> (Callot 1984)

16 (identifiable) Greek coins (all in bronzes) out of 32

9 for the Seleucids (6 Antiochus III),...

<u>Jerash</u> (Bellinger 1938)

10 Greek coins (all in bronze)

4 for John Hyrcanus, 2 for Ptolemais-Ace,...

<u>Karanis</u> (Haatvedt and Peterson 1964)

282 Greek coins (4 in silver [1.4%] and 278 in bronze [98.6%]) out of 25,862

282 for Ptolemaic coinages

<u>Kenchreai</u>, Eastern Port of Corinth (Hohlfelder 1978)

152 Greek coins (all in bronzes [100.0%]) out of 1,315

64 for Corinth (42.1%), 12 for Sicyon, 10 for Athens, 7 for Demetrius Poliorcetes,...

<u>Masada</u> (Meshorer 1989)

116 Greek coins (115 in bronze [99.1%] and 1 in silver [0.9%]) out of 4,642

92 Jewish (nos. 19–110), 12 for the Ptolemies, 5 for the Seleucids, 3 for Ascalon,...

Comment: no. 111 and after (several hundred specimens) were struck in 37–34 BC.

<u>Mecyberna</u> (Robinson and Clement 1938, 251–260)

216 Greek coins (2 in silver [0.9%] and 214 in bronze [99.1%])

73 for Philip II, 29 for Alexander III, 24 for Chalcidic coinage,...

<u>Megara</u>, a well (Waage 1935)—only Hellenistic

682 Greek coins (only bronze)

357 for Sicyon (52.3%), 261 for Megara (38.2%), 6 for Athens, 3 for Argos,...

<u>Olympia</u> (Moustaka 1999)

465 Greek coins (15 in silver [3.2%], 450 in bronze [96.8%]) out of 528

136 for Elis (29.2%), 91 for Sikyon,...

<u>Olynthus</u> (Robinson 1931)

1,175 Greek coins (82 in silver [7.0%], 1093 in bronze [93.0%])

647 for Chalcidic coins (55.1%), 67 for Bottiaea, 48 for Potidaea, 35 for Acanthus, 34 for
      Amphipolis

Comment: 7% in silver (fourth century BC).

Olynthus (Robinson and Clement 1938)

3,817 Greek coins (337 in silver [8.8%] and 3,480 in bronze [91.2%])

2,443 for Chalcidic coins (64.0%), 172 for Potidaea (4.5%), 142 for Bottiaea (3.7%), 107 for Amphipolis (2.8%), 96 for Amyntas III (2.5%), 95 for Acanthus (2.5%)

Paphos, House of Dionysos (Nicolaou 1990)

596 Greek coins (1 in silver [0.2% = drachm of Alexander III] and 595 in bronze [99.8%])

554 for the Ptolemies (93.0% [517 struck in Cyprus]), 6 for Alexander III, 6 for Demetrius Poliorcetes, 5 for Timarchus, 4 for the Seleucids,…

Comment: The surface of the House of Dionysos is roughly 5,000 m² (50 × 100 m = 0.5 hectare). It means, as an average, 1 Greek coin for c. 5 m².

Pergamum (Regling 1914)

634 Greek coins (3 in silver [0.5%] and 631 in bronze [99.5%])

326 for Pergamum (51.4%), 117 for the Pergamene kingdom (18.5%), 42 for Elaia, 25 for Gambreion, 15 for Kyme

Pergamum (Voegtli 1993)

446 Greek coins (3 in silver [0.7%] and 443 in bronze [99.3%]) out of 1,093

192 for Pergamum (43.0%), 93 for the Pergamene kingdom (20.9%) + 161

Phanagoreia, 1996 (Ashton 2003)

32 Greek coins (all in bronze) out of 53 identified coins

27 for Pantikapaion (84.4%), 2 for Phanagoreia (6.3%), 1 for Sinope, 1 for Rhodes

Priene (Regling 1927)

5,692 Greek coins (5,682 in bronze [99.8%] and 10 in silver [0.2%]) out of 6,100

5,433 for Priene (95.8%), 70 for Miletus, 55 for Magnesia, 28 for Ephesus,…

Sagalassos (Scheers 1993–2000)

22 Greek coins (1 in silver [4.5%] and 21 in bronze [95.5%])

11 for Sagalassos, 6 for Selge,…

Sardis (Bell 1916)

134 Greek coins (13 in silver [9.7%] and 121 in bronze [90.3%])

26 for the Seleucids, 25 for Sardis (18.7%), 17 for Pergamum, 15 for Ephesus,…

Sardis (Buttrey et al. 1981)

452 Greek coins (1 in gold, 9 in silver [2.0%], and 442 in bronze [97.8%]) out of 1,575

200 for Sardis (57.3%), 92 for Pergamum, 73 for the Seleucids, 24 for Ephesus,…

Comment: A lot of Seleucid bronzes were actually struck at Sardis.

Seuthopolis (Dimitrov and Pentchev 1984), mainly c. 360–275 BC

1,305 Greek coins (35 in silver [2.7%] and 1,270 in bronze [97.3%])

849 for Seuthes (65.1%), 134 for Philip II (10.3%), 73 for Alexander III (5.6%), 55 for Cassander, 41 for Lysimachus, 19 for Lysimacheia, 14 for Adaios,...

Susa (Le Rider 1965)
2,176 Greek coins (102 in silver [4.7%] and 2,074 in bronze [95.3%])
384 for Mithridates II, 352 for Antiochus III,...

Tanis (Amandry 1997)
242 Greek coins (3 in silver [1.2%] and 239 in bronze [98.8%]) out of 304
232 for Ptolemaic kings (95.9%), 8 for Alexander III (3.3%),...
Comment: This holds for 14 campaigns of excavations (c. 17 Greek coins per campaign).

Tarsus, Gözlu Kule (Cox 1950)
182 Greek coins (179 in bronze [98.4%] and 3 in silver [1.6%]) out of 345
73 for Tarsus (40.1%), 64 for the Seleucids (21 Antiochus III, 12 Antiochus I,...),...

Troy (Bellinger 1961)
209 Greek coins (3 in silver [1.4%] and 206 in bronze [98.6%]) out of 575
85 for Ilium (40.7%), 14 for Alexandreia Troas, 11 for Sigeum,...

Zonè (Gallani-Krikou 1996)
2,135 Greek coins (not details given)
729 for Zonè (34.1%), 466 for Maroneia, 217 for Alexander III, 86 for Philip II, 23 for Abdera, 21 for Cassander, 19 for Ainus, 17 for Orthagoreia, 13 for Samothrace, 10 for Lysimachus

Agoranomia: Studies in Money and Exchange Presented to John H. Kroll, pp. 201–246
© 2006 The American Numismatic Society

Cooperative Coinage

EMILY MACKIL[*] AND PETER G. VAN ALFEN[**]

INTRODUCTION[1]

One of the striking features of late Archaic and Classical Aegean and Mediterranean economies is the frequency with which cities cooperated with one another to form monetary unions, as can be seen in the following overview. Although a number of these unions are posited rather than confirmed, the uncontested extent of the catalogue nevertheless underscores what a significant and widespread phenomenon monetary cooperation was in the Greek world from the sixth century onward. If we accept Georges Le Rider's arguments, shortly after the first coins appeared in Lydia and Ionia several of the cities of the region had already formed a monetary union and were producing coins to the same standard with identical designs on the reverse.[2] Numismatists believe they have identified other coin-producing unions established before the end of the sixth century that were formed between the

[*] Department of History, University of California, Berkeley.
[**] American Numismatic Society, New York.

1. Over the years, through graduate school and beyond, Jack has been our numismatic mentor and good friend. As a steady and cheerful guide, he has devoted many long hours to steering us through the intricacies of ancient money; we still turn to him constantly for criticism and advice. (We both realize too how much better this paper would have been had we let him see it in draft!) In his own work and in conversation Jack has often stressed a functional approach to coinage and money, placing economic function above any social or political considerations. We have learned much from this approach, as can be seen here, and it is with some trepidation, real pleasure, and great respect that we offer him this study. We are most grateful to François de Callataÿ, Lisa Kallet, Andrew Meadows, Josiah Ober, and Ute Wartenberg Kagan for reading this paper in draft and providing suggestions and critical comments.

2. Le Rider's (2001: 45) suggestion that there was a formal monetary union between the Lydian kingdom and several of the Ionian *poleis* has been challenged by Kroll (2001: 200), who instead argues that the shared types were merely due to the imitation of an established prototype. For more on the problem of imitation see below.

major *poleis* of Lesbos, Mytilene and Phokaia, Lampsakos and Khios, Lampsakos and an unknown city, Khalkis and Boiotia, various Macedonian *ethnē*, numerous cities in southern Italy, and a handful of cities in and around Ionia.[3] The practice continued in the fifth century with unions recognized or posited between various Lykian cities or dynasts, Gortyn and Phaistos, Gortyn and Sybrita, Phokaia and Teos, Aspendos and Selge, Karystos and Eretria, Kumai and Akragas, and several Campanian communities in Italy.[4] In the fourth century new unions were formed between eight cities in and around Ionia, Byzantion and Khalkedon, Apollonia and Dyrrhakhion, cities in southern Italy, and in Sicily.[5] In addition there are the monetary ties and coinages related to the *koina* of Boiotia, Phokis, Thessaly, Arkadia, Khalkidike, Euboia, Akhaia, Akarnania, Keos, and the synoikisms in Elis, Rhodes, and Kos.[6] Nor should we overlook the monetary connections found between *metropoleis* and their *apoikiai*, such as Phokaia and Massalia, Abdera and Teos, Dikaia and Eretria, Kydonia and Aigina, and Korinth and her many colonies.[7]

It is quite clear that not all of these monetary unions and coinages were created to serve similar purposes, and numismatists and historians have long attempted to categorize them in a more manageable way. Classification has proceeded on the assumption that the coins reflect political, religious, or social relationships between cities and, rather more rarely, economic ones. Historically, political relationships in particular have been at the forefront. J. L. Warren in his study of "Greek federal coinage" was willing to presuppose political motivations for any monetary union between two or more cities, and accordingly called

3. *Lesbos*: billon (silver-base metal alloy) coinage: Wroth (1894: lxiv); *Mytilene/Phokaia*: see below; *Lampsakos/ Khios*: Babelon (1907: 193 no. 336); *Lampsakos/unknown*: SNG ANS 7: no. 989; Price and Waggoner (1975: no. 57); Triton VIII no. 229; *Khalkis/Boiotia*: Kraay (1976: 90–91, 109); but see MacDonald (1987/88: 23–29) who questions the actuality of the union; *Macedonian ethnē*: Raymond (1953: 46–48) proposed a "monetary convention" and coin types shared between various Thraco-Macedonian *ethnē*, a notion that Kraay (1976: 139) called into question; *southern Italy*: see below; *Ionia*: the so-called "Ionian Revolt staters" (Kraay 1976: 30).

4. *Lykian dynasts*: Kraay (1976: 270), Troxell (1982: 9), Spier (1987: 31–36); *Gortyn/Phaistos*: Kraay (1976: 50, 53), Le Rider (1966: 162–172); *Gortyn/Sybrita*: Le Rider (1966: 160–162); *Phokaia/Teos*: Kraay (1976: 243), Balcer (1970); *Aspendos/Selge*: Kraay (1976: 277–278); *Karystos/Eretria*: Kraay (1976: 92); *Kumai/Akragas*: Kraay (1976: 178); *Campania*: Rutter (2001: 67–72).

5. *Ionia*: the contested "ΣΥΝ" coinage for which see Kraay (1976: 113, 248; 1984), Karwiese (1980), Ashton (2001: 80), Ashton et al. (2002); *Byzantion/Khalkedon*: Le Rider (1971); *Apollonia/Dyrrhakhion*: Kraay (1976: 129), Picard and Gjongecaj (1998); *southern Italy*: Rutter (1997: 95); cf. Rutter et al. (2001: 96); *Sicily*: Kraay (1976: 229), Rutter (1997: 168).

6. *Boiotia*: Kraay (1976: 108–114), Psoma and Tsangari (2003: 113–118), and see below; *Phokis*: Williams (1972), Kraay (1976: 120–121), Psoma and Tsangari (2003: 115); *Thessaly*: Kraay (1976: 115–116), Liampi (1996), Psoma and Tsangari (2003: 114), cf. Martin (1985: 36–37); *Arkadia*: Williams (1965), Kraay (1976: 97–101), Gerin (1986), Psoma and Tsangari (2003: 116); *Khalkidike*: Kraay (1976: 138), Psoma and Tsangari (2003: 112, 115); *Euboia*: Wallace (1956), Kraay (1976: 92), Psoma and Tsangari (2003: 117); *Akhaia*: Kraay (1976: 101), Psoma and Tsangari (2003: 116–117); *Akarnania*: Kraay (1976: 129), Psoma and Tsangari (2003: 119); *Keos*: Papageorgiadou-Banis 1993; *Elis*: Kraay (1976: 103–107), Walker (2004); *Rhodes*: Kraay (1976: 257), Ashton (2001); *Kos*: Kraay (1976: 256).

7. *Phokaia/Massalia*: Balcer (1970: 29); *Abdera/Teos*: May (1966, esp. p. 54), Kraay (1976: 35, 152–153), Matzke (2000), and Kagan (2006); *Dikaia/Eretria*: Kraay (1976: 91, 134); *Kydonia/Aigina*: Kraay (1976: 50); *Korinth*: see below.

them all "leagues" (1863: 10). Barclay Head's (1911: lxxxiii–lxxxiv) quadripartite analysis of the phenomenon has been the most influential. Head saw the coinages minted by multiple communities on the same standard, with the same type and frequently common legends, as the products of one of the following: (a) a political or federal alliance, (b) a commercial alliance, (c) a military alliance, or (d) a religious alliance. It is immediately striking that only one of the four motives for the production of these joint coinages was, strictly speaking, commercial. Head's schema presupposes a radical disjunction between economic behavior on the one hand, and political, religious, and military behavior on the other. So the "political alliance" coinages, the most notorious example of which is that of the Boiotian "league", are seen simply as expressions of a collective political will (or, less optimistically, of the subordination of less powerful communities by a mightier hegemon). Reinach, for example, saw the "monnaie commune" of the Arkadians, Boiotians, Akarnanians, Khalkidians, Lykians, and so on as "ne . . . qu'une des conditions de l'union politique" and concluded that their study "dépasse l'histoire économique et rentre dans l'histoire consitutionnelle" (Reinach 1911: 352–353; cf. Warren 1863: 8). The interpretation of coinage broadly speaking (not just "alliance coinages") as a narrowly political phenomenon retains current support.[8] Likewise, the interpretation of "religious alliance" coinages, like that of the Delphic amphiktiony, tends to put more emphasis on their presumed expression of religious sentiment or festival commemoration than on any actual monetary function (Head 1911: lxxxiii).[9] While it would be foolish to deny the religious and political messages conveyed by many coin types (wherein lies a great deal of scholarly interest), in our view it is essential to reassert in this context the fact that coins served as monetary instruments above all else.[10]

In order to do so, we shall explore here the economic motives of individual *poleis*, and groups of *poleis*, for arranging what we call cooperative coinage. We use this term in a functional sense to denote coinages in which multiple communities operate together in minting (and using) money. In some cases (like Mytilene and Phokaia) the cooperation was entirely voluntary; in other cases (like Boiotia in the second half of the fifth century), it was almost certainly affected by hegemonic behavior and attempts by one *polis* to subordinate one or more other *poleis*, though even here we should consider the possibility that such hegemonic

8. Austin and Vidal-Naquet (1977: 57), for example, state "in the history of the Greek cities coinage was always first and foremost a civic emblem. To strike coins with the badge of the city was to proclaim one's political independence." More recently Trevett (2001: 23) argued that "coinage is after all nothing if not a political phenomenon", echoing Finley's assertion (1985: 166) that "the Greek passion for coins…was essentially a political phenomenon". In his review of the volume in which Trevett's paper appears, Kroll (2002) forcefully reasserts the economic function of coinage over the political.

9. For the coinage of the Delphic amphiktiony, see Kraay (1976: 121–122), Raven (1950), Kinns (1983).

10. The development of the semiotic value of coin types is a topic that has not been explored in depth. While it is clear that by the Classical period most coin types had political associations in so far as they referred to the political body responsible for the coinage, and thus could serve a range of political and social functions as expressions of a corporate identity, the political expressions on Archaic coinage are less than clear (Kroll 1981; Papadopoulos 2002). For coinage and identity generally see the papers in Howgego et al. (2005).

behavior was driven by economic motives. In still other cases (like fourth-century Akhaia), it is impossible to detect any signs of hegemonic behavior, but it would be rash to conclude categorically that such "silence" necessarily implies entirely voluntary cooperation. We shall discuss each of these cases in detail below. If, however, in each case it is possible to provide an economic explanation for the (functional) cooperation of multiple cities in minting coinage, then we need to ask whether any hegemonic factor is really significant. We shall argue that categorical schemata like Head's, which seek to break down the larger phenomenon of cooperative coinage into separate groups distinguished by primarily noneconomic motives, fail to grasp the significance of the larger phenomenon. Placing all such cooperative monetary arrangements on a single spectrum of economic behavior and monetary practices highlights the rather neglected fact that the political fragmentation of the Archaic and Classical Greek world does not translate easily to economic fragmentation. This has interesting implications. With coinage we see one of the most tangible intersections of political authority and economic behavior. If states became less fragmented over time in this period (which is one way of seeing the rise in importance of both the *koinon* and monarchy), then we should at least consider the possibility that the need for institutions to protect and further patterns of economic cooperation between *poleis* may have been a significant motivating factor in the development of political authorities capable of doing that.

Analysis of the pressures, opportunities, and institutions behind these cooperative arrangements suggests that beneath the variety of motives and means there lies a single, underappreciated fact: namely, that the local and regional economies of the ancient Mediterranean were deeply interconnected, so that state practices such as the minting of coinage, the issuing of civic decrees regulating interstate commerce, and functional cooperation in monetary production should be seen as responses to that fact. These state practices served at least three functions: first, to protect economic cooperation between *poleis*; second, to facilitate exchange and increase revenues; and third, to serve economic exigencies.[11]

It is also important to emphasize that minting coins cooperatively was one of the more radical strategies a *polis* might adopt in its attempt to align, whether multilaterally or unilaterally, its finances and financial instruments with those of other *poleis*. The most obvious, for example, was simply to adopt a widely accepted currency (like the Athenian owls) as a *nomisma koinon* (cf. Pl. *Leg.* 5.741e–742d).[12] The decision to mint coins, even within

11. In this direction, Bresson (2000: 109–130) has underscored the fact that *autarkeia*, vaunted by Aristotle as the purpose for which *poleis* come into being (e.g. *Pol.* 1252b28–3a2, 1261b10–15, 1275b17–22, 1326b2–9, 1328b15–19), was in practice only an ideal, with the state controlling and regulating the economy in order to come asymptotically closer to it.

12. Cities might also abandon local weight standards used for their coinage and embrace one that was more widely accepted, like the Aiginetan or Athenian. Samian weight standards saw a great deal of fluctuation in the Archaic period particularly, which Barron (1966) attributes to attempts to align the standards on Samos with popular standards elsewhere for commercial purposes. Likewise, in Macedonia, Thrace, and Ionia there were frequent changes of standards, which again were likely due to commercial or other alignments (May 1966; Matzke 2000).

a single *polis*, implies a whole litany of impediments and resolutions; when multiple communities were involved, the complications themselves multiplied. The bargaining processes implicit in the making of decisions and arrangements are necessary preliminaries to the actual production of coinage, particularly when it involved multiple autonomous or semi-autonomous communities, could be drawn out, engender bitterness, and collapse at any moment. So, we might ask, why bother? Even in the case of pressing joint military operations, we can imagine that it would simply have been easier to pool economic resources in the form of an already existing *nomisma koinon* than in the form of a cooperative coinage. Obviously, whatever advantages there were to minting cooperatively greatly outweighed the inconvenience of the multilateral undertaking; the political will to forge the agreement was driven by economic advantages. These advantages included, among others, facilitation of exchange, taxation, and accounting between the cities; closer control over the coinage in circulation within designated areas; and profit. To illustrate our point, we discuss in what follows two quite different cases, one the cooperative coinage of Mytilene and Phokaia, and the other the cooperative coinages of the Boiotian and Akhaian *koina*. Before turning to Mytilene and Phokaia, however, we need to address several general problems associated with the interpretation of the numismatic evidence.

IMITATION, DOMINATION, OR COOPERATION?

Despite the lengthy overview of cooperative coinages found above, there are concerns that some of them may not, in fact, be the products of a cooperative accord.[13] The ability to identify cooperative coinages, or, more accurately, the cooperative practices behind them, is complicated by our reading (or misreading) of the numismatic evidence. The coins produced by cooperative arrangements were, of course, made to an agreed weight standard, alloy, and denomination determined by their economic function; these basics of economic function pose comparatively fewer problems. Because of their inherent political associations, however, the types and inscriptions on the coins are more problematic; to many commentators, shared types reveal not just a cooperative monetary arrangement, but are emblematic of more nuanced political and social practices/behaviors as well. For example, the presence of the bull of Sybaris on the obverse of a coin with a Poseidonian type/legend on the reverse is frequently taken to indicate the political subordination of Poseidonia by Sybaris in the late sixth century (see below). Numismatists reading these signs, and often lacking textual evidence for additional support, have therefore deduced a broad range of relationships between the cities, from benign equality-based partnerships to oppressive hegemonies, focusing again more on the political than the economic aspects of the arrangements. All such interpretations, however, are questionable, as is the basic premise that shared types and fabrics are always indicative of cooperative arrangements.

13. E.g., MacDonald (1987–88: 29): "In this context of experimentation and copying, variations in coin types cannot be vested automatically with the sorts of political implications that have been read into the shield/wheel issue".

By the end of the sixth century, as the example of the Boiotian *poleis* demonstrates (see below), a general format for cooperative coinage had developed: the coins had on the obverse some symbol or badge representing the group of cooperating communities as a whole, while the reverse was left primarily for the discrete civic symbols and inscriptions of the individual participating cities. This format was also adopted on occasion by less enduring cooperatives, such as those established for the sake of military or other specific endeavors.[14] There is, therefore, the understandable assumption that shared types in general are markers of monetary cooperation between cities. But there were other possible formats for cooperative coinages, some of which eschewed shared types and minimized the promulgation of a group identity for the communities involved. In the case of the cooperation between Mytilene and Phokaia (see below), for example, it was enough that the weight and alloy of the coins be shared, whereas all the imagery on the coins and individual identifiers, if any, were left to the discretion of each city. Confidence in our ability to identify cooperative coinages by type-sharing alone is further shaken by the phenomenon of imitative coinage.

With a high degree of regularity, many Archaic- and Classical-period cities imitated the coins of other cities with no formal arrangements in place. The scale and degree of the imitation varied: only the obverse or reverse type might be copied with different degrees of adherence to the original, and, in some cases, the types might be applied to coins of different denominations or metals than the prototypes. In more extreme cases, the entire coin— obverse, reverse, denomination, etc.—was copied. At times the imitators made it clear who was responsible for the issue by marking the coins with their own ethnic or other symbols, but at other times they did not. Although some scholars have suggested that monetary imitation was politically motivated, it is more likely that artistic, or, likelier still, economic motives were the impetus.[15] A tour-de-force design, like the late fifth-century facing head of Arethusa, which the artist Kimon produced for Syracuse, might inspire dozens of copies among far-flung cities, some of which undoubtedly aspired to the prestige of producing an artistically arresting coinage.[16] Other imitators, however, sought to ride freely on the coat-tails of an economically successful coinage. Imitations of this sort were not counterfeits per se—their weight and metal content were often good—but rather a means of disbursing payments by mimicking a widely accepted foreign coin without entering into formal arrangements with the producers of the prototype. Often, as in the case of the imitators of Athenian coins operating in Egypt and the Near East, the distance between the imitators and original producers could be great, not only geographically, but politically and culturally as well. Where there was less distance, and perhaps even a tradition of close contact, the line

14. As seems to have been the case with the early fourth-century "ΣΥΝ" coinage. For a bibliography see above n. 5.

15. For an overview of the imitation phenomenon and problems of interpretation see van Alfen (2005).

16. For Kimon's masterpiece see Kraay (1976: pl. 47 no. 810). The type appears to have inspired copies at nearly a dozen mints scattered about the Mediterranean, including those at Larissa (Kraay 1976: pl. 21 nos. 392–396), Amphipolis (Kraay 1976: pl. 32 nos. 568–570), and Tarsus (Kraay 1976: pl. 60 no. 1037).

between imitation and cooperation might be blurred. Some neighbors, and *metropoleis* and *apoikiai*, for example, shared coin types and weight standards, but we cannot be certain that this reflects formalized monetary arrangements between the cities.[17]

In some cases, like that of Korinth and her colonies, there is evidence for the production of coinage jointly organized by *metropolis* and *apoikia*. As early as the late sixth century, for example, a mint at Leukas was producing pegasi, and by around 480 one at Ambrakia had joined in as well, perhaps to provide funds in the war against the Persians. Again in the 430s, Korinth, Leukas, Ambrakia, Anaktorion, and at least two other mints produced pegasi simultaneously, presumably in order to assist the Korinthians economically in their intervention in Epidamnos in 435 and Corcyra in 433 (Kraay 1976: 82–85; Figueira 1998: 489–493; Kagan 1998).[18] Nearly a century later, fifteen different mints scattered across western Greece, southern Italy, and Sicily began to issue pegasi, initially, it would seem, in order to assist the Korinthians in yet another military endeavor, Timoleon's western adventure.[19] Other potential examples of *metropolis-apoikia* cooperative coinages can be found, but the sharing of common types could often indicate no more than an assertion of a shared cultural legacy.[20]

Aside from the basic problem of securely identifying monetary alliances using coins as primary evidence, there are inherent risks in deciphering from coinage alone the nature of the political relationships between two (or more) partners. The imagery and legends on

17. For example, in Crete in the mid-fifth century Gortyn and Phaistos both employed identical types on their coins (Europa on bull/facing lion) with the distinction that generally at Gortyn the obverse type faced left, at Phaistos to the right. While it has been assumed that the cities formed a "monetary alliance" (Kraay 1976: 50; Le Rider 1966: 153–172), their long history of conflict might suggest otherwise, that Phaistos simply imitated the coinage of its problematic neighbor in order to take advantage of its regional acceptance. Also, we cannot be entirely certain that the widespread and constant use of the *triskeles* symbol on the reverse of Lykian coinage hints at the existence of *koinon*-like institutions predating the Hellenistic *koinon* (Kraay 1976: 270; Troxell 1982: 9), or that the shared types and fabrics of coinages produced in the late sixth century by various Macedonian *ethnē* indicate anything more than imitation.

18. Note, however, that Figueira, following Kagan, suggests that a number of the pegasi bearing the initial letters of the *apoikiai* may, in fact, have been minted in Korinth for the sake of the other communities.

19. There is no consensus on the circumstances or reason(s) for the fifteen mints to produce these coins. It would seem that Timoleon's campaign was very likely the impetus for the initial surge in production, mostly among Korinth's colonies, and that this was organized by Korinth. Later issues, such as those by the Italian mints, may have been imitative with the producers attempting to cash in on the flood of pegasi in the west (Head 1911: 407; Talbert 1971; Kraay 1976: 82–87, 235–237, 126–134; 1984; Foraste 1993; Salmon 1993; Kagan 1998; Rutter et al. 2001: 179–180).

20. For example, Corcyra and her two Illyrian colonies, Apollonia and Dyrrhakhion, produced parallel series on at least two occasions, suggesting that the three cities had coordinated monetary arrangements; see above n. 5 for bibliography. Teos and Abdera also produced similar coinages in what Kraay (1976: 35) termed a "planned conjunction" (see also Kagan 2006). On the other hand, the Aiginetans who founded Kydonia in Crete produced obol and triobol "turtles" rather similar to those produced in Aigina (Kraay 1976: 50), the Samians who settled briefly in Zankle in Sicily in the 490s produced coins with Samian types (Kraay 1976: 213), and the Athenian-led founders of Thurii in the mid-440s produced coins in their new city that had an obverse type—Athena—which called to mind the similar type on Athenian coins (Kraay 1976: 173). In all three of these cases, Kydonia, Zankle, and Thurii, the use of familiar types likely had more to do with cultural attachments than economic ties with the motherland.

coins could be vehicles for the construction and expression of political identity, and could also reflect political agendas and interests; this holds true for collective as well as individual producers.[21] One way to read the widespread format for cooperative coinages (shared obverse, discrete reverses), for example, would be to see it as a reflection of the political sensibilities of a collection of cities that were united for the sake of common economic, religious, or military purposes, and that sought to express this allegiance through the use of a common symbol but were at the same time keen to maintain their individual (political) identity within the collective. We should note that even a lack of shared symbols could have political implications. With their bilateral cooperative coinage, for example, the citizens of Mytilene and Phokaia avoided collective political expression of any sort on their coins (see below). Theirs was a conscious decision to make their cooperative coinage outwardly apolitical, in so far as their cooperation was concerned, suggesting that the nature of their cooperative effort was divested of nearly all political content and that economic concerns were of greater importance. Recognition of the fact that the political content of coinage generally played a secondary role to its monetary function requires that the political interpretations of coinage be well balanced with economic explications; this is especially true when reading evidence from coins for hegemonic and other uneven partnerships between cities.

Because the obverse of a coin, which often bears the head of state or a patron deity, traditionally is given greater symbolic importance than the reverse, which by contrast bears lesser symbols, the nature of the relationship between two cities has been inferred from the obverse or reverse positioning of their symbols on a single coin. The dominant partner, presumably, claimed the obverse for its type as a symbol of its greater prestige or power.[22] This method has been repeatedly employed in discussions of the Archaic coinage of Magna Graecia, which therefore offers an example for further explication. Sometime around 530, the four Akhaian *apoikiai* of southern Italy, Sybaris, Kroton, Kaulonia, and Metaponton, began to produce a highly distinctive type of incuse coinage (plate 13 nos. 1–4), which in its initial phase featured a relief design on the obverse that was repeated intaglio on the reverse; because the flans were unusually thin, the effect gave the appearance of *repoussé* work. Although each city maintained its own civic types, the weight standard, which was used nowhere else in the Greek world, and the peculiar fabric of the coins suggest that the cities had entered into some type of cooperative arrangement, the precise nature of which, if it did in fact exist, has exercised scholars for generations.[23] Not long after these four mints

21. On the "minting" of political identity by means of coinage see especially Papadopoulos (2002) and the papers in Howgego et al. (2005).

22. We should note, however, a case where the opposite was true. Following Theron of Akragas' capture of the city c. 483, the citizens of Himera (under Theron's orders?) adopted the Akragantine weight standard for their coinage and employed the Akragantine crab as a device, but on the reverse, not the obverse (Kraay 1976: 208–209).

23. See Kraay (1976: 163–164) for more on the weight standard (based on a unit of c. 8 g for the stater) and the technical and political implications of the fabric.

began production, Poseidonia and Taras (plate 13 nos. 5–6) also joined in with their own coins on the same model.[24] Because Sybaris achieved considerable power in the region, that city is generally thought to have initiated this type of coinage, which then spread to the others by imitation, cooperation, or hegemonic design.[25] This last possibility seems to receive support from three series of coins that have the bull of Sybaris on the obverse coupled with the reverse type and/or inscription of another city.[26] Since the Sybaritan bull appears on the dominant side of the coins (the obverse), Sybaris, it is assumed, must have been the dominant partner in the joint efforts; the interpretation of Sybaris' role, in fact, often shades into imperialism.[27]

With the fall of Sybaris to Kroton in 510, the Sybaritan "empire" was replaced by what has been called the Krotoniate "alliance", the evidence for which is primarily numismatic.[28] Seven series of coins, not all of the same date, have on the obverse Kroton's tripod, while their reverses bear the types and inscriptions of seven other cities: Pandosia, Sybaris, Laus, Temesa, Terina, Himera, and Kaulonia. Again, Kroton's dominant political role in these "alliances" is inferred by the position of the Krotoniate tripod on the obverse (plate 13 no. 7, cp. nos. 1 and 2).

Although cooperative economic motives have been suggested for the initial production of coinage by Sybaris, Kroton, Kaulonia, and Metaponton, this has not been the case for the coinage of the Sybaritan "empire" or Krotoniate "alliance".[29] The usual interpretive ap-

---

24. While the earliest coins of Taras (c. 510?) were minted on the same standard (c. 8 g) as that of the four Akhaian *apoikiai*, Poseidonia's standard seems to have been slightly reduced to around 7.5 g, suggesting that this city copied the technique of the coinage, but was not necessarily part of whatever union may have existed (Kraay 1976: 163, 169; Rutter 1997: 31–32).

25. For a general overview of the south Italian coinages see Kraay (1976: ch. 9), Rutter (1997), and Rutter et al. (2001: s.v. the various mints). A somewhat analogous situation existed in Sicily in the fifth and fourth centuries, where the quadriga obverse type, which was first used by Syracuse, was later found on the coinage of Leontini, Himera, Gela, Selinos, Akragas, Katana, Kamarina, and Segesta, and was likewise imitated by Punic mints. Syracusan hegemony and the close (economic?) ties between local tyrants likely account for the adoption in some cases. In Leontini, for example, a change in the local weight standard to that used in Syracuse and an obverse die (a quadriga) shared between Syracuse and the newly conquered city indicate Syracusan involvement in local coin production (Kraay 1976: 211). In other cases, the adoption of the quadriga type might not have been due to direct Syracusan involvement, but simply reflected the imitation of a locally successful coinage (see in general Kraay 1976: ch. 10).

26. These are the Sybaris/Sirinos-Pyxoes series, the Sybaris/Serd series, and the Sybaris/Poseidonia series (Kraay 1976: 166–169; Rutter et al. 2001: 143–145).

27. Strabo (6.1.13 C 263) writes that the Sybaritans ruled over four neighboring *ethnē*, had twenty-five subject cities (πόλεις ὑπηκόους), and campaigned against Kroton with 300,000 men. Greco's (1990; 1998) studies of an inscription on bronze found at Olympia recording a treaty between Sybaris and the Serdaioi has reinforced the image of the Sybaritan "empire", supported in part by numismatic studies such as Stazio (1983) and Rutter (1997: 24).

28. For an overview of the series and the term "alliance" used to describe the nature of the arrangements see Kraay (1976: 168), Stazio (1983: 130–133), Rutter (1997: 36–37), Rutter et al. (2001: 167). The choice of the term "alliance" might in part be influenced by Polybios' mention (2.39.6) of a fifth-century arrangement with *koinon*-like institutions established by a number of the Akhaian cities in Italy.

29. Le Rider (1989), for example, suggests that the four Akhaian *apoikiai* established a closed economic zone

proaches to these series have focused more on political relationships than economic ones, which does not take us far in answering, or even posing, questions related to the economic need or function of the coins.[30] For example, if Sybaris and perhaps Kroton were in fact hegemonic powers, what would be the point, economically and even politically, of the "alliance" coinages? Approaches to economic hegemony, as perhaps witnessed by Athens' fifth-century Coinage (or Standards) Decree (*IG* I[3] 1453), might easily become an attempt to eradicate competing systems and coinages in favor of the hegemon's, rather than expending the effort to negotiate a joint project, even if only for appearance's sake.[31] The prospect of two cities negotiating the joint production of coinage diminishes the political concept of domination; allowing another city's symbols on the coin implies that the "dominant" partner approached the negotiating table in a spirit of bilateralism, rather than dictating its will. Economic needs can trump unilateral politics.

In sum, the numismatic evidence, which is often the only evidence, for cooperative economic arrangements between cities can be highly problematic and so must be handled with caution. Imitative coins, for example, or shared designs between *metropolis* and *apoikia*, might imply a cooperative effort where one never existed. Danger also looms where coins are most politically suggestive, as in the case of the Sybaritan "empire" or Krotoniate "alliance". If indeed political or economic hegemony was a factor in the relationship between two or more cities, we cannot take it for granted that this would find expression on any jointly produced coinage.

MYTILENE AND PHOKAIA

An inscription (*IG* XII 2, 1) found at Mytilene in 1852 is the only extant text from antiquity that details an agreement between two *poleis*, in this case Mytilene and Phokaia, to mint

within which traders would be compelled to exchange their popular Korinthian pegasi for the local incuse-type staters at a one-to-one rate, despite the fact that the local issues weighed 0.6 g less than the pegasi. The weight difference resulted in an immediate 7% profit for the cooperating cities. This reduction also meant that there would be no incentive for the incuse coinage to leave the zone, thus preserving local silver supplies. The hoard evidence, in fact, indicates that the incuse coinage circulated almost exclusively in southern Italy. Other commentators (e.g., Kraay 1976: 163; Rutter 1997: 20) have been more circumspect about organized economic cooperation between the four cities.

30. Although Kraay (1976: 166–168) is hesitant to commit to any clearly defined schemata for the production of the various coinages, it is clear that his thinking tends more toward the political than the economic to explain their existence. He speaks (1976: 166), for example, of "Sybarite interest" and "Sybarite influence, and perhaps political power" in regard to the production of some issues. In the case of Kroton, he suggests (1976: 168): "These issues are better regarded as the products of subsidiary mints in territories controlled by Croton, which sign their local types on the reverse." Rutter (1997: 24, 30) follows Kraay's lead.

31. A new volume of studies on the Coinage Decree, edited by Charles Crowther and Andrew Meadows, is forthcoming. In the meantime see Kallet (2001: 205–226), who presents an economic rationale for the decree, and Figueira (1998). Figueira (1998: 493) also touches upon the political economy of appearances and coinage, summing up his section on "Corinth and Monetary Hegemony" thus: "Corinth provides an alternative model for a fifth-century hegemonistic [*sic*] state that chose to exploit the symbolic possibilities of coins as a means for an expression of its ideological leadership".

coins cooperatively.[32] The document, rich in certain details, is frustratingly elusive on other issues. Only the final twenty-one lines of the agreement survive (though the inscription was likely not much longer), and these focus not on the issues we might expect to see in a coin-age agreement, like designs, denominations, mintage, and metal sources, but rather on the individual responsible for mixing the alloy used for the coins.[33] We learn from the inscription the following details: (1) the metal used for the coinage was a gold alloy (ln. 5); (2) the official responsible for mixing the alloy answered to both *poleis* (ln. 5); (3) an audit of his performance was to be completed within six months of the end of his tenure (lns. 11–12); (4) the audit board was to be composed of local officials (ln. 9); (5) the punishment for will-ingly debasing the alloy mixture was death, while unintentional mis-mixing was punished by noncapital means (lns. 14–16); (6) each of the two cities was to mint every other year on a rotating basis (lns. 18–19); (7) the lot decided that Mytilene was to mint first (ln. 20). The coins in question are almost certainly the electrum *hektai*, one-sixth staters weighing about 2.5 g, which were produced in Mytilene and Phokaia from c. 521 until c. 326 BC (plate 13 nos. 8–13).[34] The issues of each city have in common only the *hektē* denomination, the "Phokaic" weight standard, and their gold-silver alloy. The cities never shared designs,

32. The most recent commentary on the inscription, listing earlier bibliography, can be found in Figueira (1998: 487–489). See also Burelli (1978), Giacchero (1980), Bodenstedt (1981: 29–31), and Heisserer (1984).

33. The full text of the inscription is as follows: - 7 - ε [- 18 - ὅττι | δέ κε αἰ] πόλις [ἀ]μφότ[εραι - 10 - | - 5 -] γράφωισι εἰς τὰν [στάλλαν ἢ ἐκκ|ολάπ]τωισι, κύ[ρ]ιον ἔστω. τ[ὸν δὲ κέρναν||τα τὸ] χρύσιον ὑπόδικον ἔ[μμεναι ἀμφο|τέρ]αισι ταῖς πολίεσσι· δικ[άσταις δὲ | ἔμ]μεναι τῶι μὲν ἐμ Μυτιλήναι [κέρναν|τι] ταὶς ἄρχαις παίσαις ταὶς ἐμ Μ[υτιλή|η]ναι πλέας τῶν αἰμίσεων, ἐμ Φώκαι δὲ [τ]||αὶς ἄρχαις παίσαις ταὶς ἐμ Φώκαι πλ[έ]||ας τῶν αἰμίσεω[ν]· τὰν δὲ δίκαν ἔμμεναι | ἐπεί κε ὠνίαυτος ἐξέλθηι ἐν ἒξ μήννε|σ<σ>ι· αἰ δέ κε καταγ[ρ]έθηι τὸ χρύσιον κέρ|ναν ὑδαρέστε[ρ]ο[ν] θέλων, θανάτωι ζαμι||ώσθω· αἰ δέ κε ἀμυφύγηι μ[ὴ] θέλω<ν> ἀμβρ[ό]||την, τιμάτω τ[ὸ] δικαστήριον ὄττι χρὴ α|ὐτ<ο>ν πάθην ἢ κατθέ[μ]εναι, ἀ δὲ πόλις ἀναί|τιος καὶ ἀζάμιος [ἔσ]τω. Ἔλαχον Μυτιλή|ναοι πρόσθε κόπτην. ἄρχει πρότανις ὁ || πεδὰ Κόλωνον, ἐ[μ Φ]ώκαι δὲ ὁ πεδὰ Ἀρίσ[τ]||αρχον. ("...let what both cities agree to inscribe on the stele or erase, be valid. The one who mixes the gold is to be legally responsible in both cities. As judges there are to be for the one who mixes at Mytilene, more than half of the officials at Mytilene, and at Phokaia more than half of the officials at Phokaia, and an audit is to take place when a year has ended, within six months; and if anyone is convicted of mixing the gold too weakly willingly, he is to be punished with death, and if he is found not guilty of willingly erring, let the court decide what is a fitting penalty for him to suffer or pay, and the city is to be guiltless and free from penalty. The Mytilenaeans drew by lot the right to strike first, beginning in the prytany following that of Kolonos, and at Phokaia, following that of Aristarchos" [trans. Melville Jones].) It appears that only the initial clause, providing for amendment on the agreement of both cities, is missing (Tod 1948: 35). For more on the alloy, see below.

34. The only other coins that the agreement could refer to are the elusive electrum "Phokaic staters" mentioned by Thukydides (4.52.2), [Demosthenes] (40.36), Kallisthenes (*FGrH* 124 F 4), and in the inventories of various Athenian cults from the fifth and fourth centuries (*Hekatompedon*: IG II² 1382.8–9, 18; 1384.5–6; 1386.14–15, 17; 1388.42, 44; 1389.4, 5; 1390.3, 5; 1393.23–25; 1400.19–21, 44. *Treasurers of the Other Gods*: IG I³ 383.19–20. *Eleusinian inventories*: IG I³ 384.5; 386.1.50; 387.1.57; 388.7; 389.8. *Asklepios*: IG II² 1533.46). There is not, however, a single example of this coin in any numismatic collection, which calls into question its existence. This problem is resolved if we accept "stater" as a unit of account, and "Phokaic" as the common term for the nearly indistinguishable Phokaian and Mytilenean *hektai* issues; see Kraay (1976: 266) and Figueira (1998: 98). Bodenstedt's dates for the cooperative *hektai*, 521 to 326 BC, are presented here for lack of a well-argued alterna-tive. The traditional start date for the series is c. 480 BC (Head 1911: 558; Kraay 1976: 266).

which changed with great regularity and had no obvious civic connection, and only on rare occasions is an inscription found on the coins.[35] Commentators generally believe that the inscribed agreement, which has been dated variously in the last quarter of the fifth century BC and the opening years of the fourth, was a renewal of a pact that had been in operation for decades and that continued to function for decades longer, making this also the longest-lasting cooperative monetary arrangement known from antiquity, producing 189 emissions in 206 years.[36]

Beyond the inscription and coins, the available evidence does not allow for any speculation about political, military, or religious motivations for the joint project, if they existed, but it does allow us at least to explore and reconstruct economic motives. However, explaining why these two cities in particular would maintain a bilateral agreement for generations on end in order to mint small electrum coins poses difficulties. The two harbor cities were not exactly neighbors; in favorable weather, it would take a full day to sail from one to the other. Both cities had played active and important roles as trade centers and colonizers in the sixth century BC, and both were among the first cities to coin, but each pursued its ambitions separately. This is especially clear in the later fifth century: the Phokaians quietly stayed out of the way when their partners in Mytilene revolted from Athens in 428 and subsequently paid a heavy price for their intransigence.[37] It is because there seems no other clear reason for the two cities to have formed a monetary agreement that this pact has remained the classic example of Head's "Commercial Alliance", an alliance struck "for the practical advantages to be gained by increased facilities of exchange" (1911: lxxxiii). Based on the diminished political nature of the coinage and focus of the inscription, the Mytilene-Phokaia coinage arrangement appears to be entirely devoid of obvious political, religious, and military motivations.[38] It is therefore reasonable to reconstruct the basic motivation as

35. Inscriptions are found only on the *hektai* from Mytilene: Bodenstedt (1981) Emission (Em.) 1 ("M", 521 BC); Em. 13 ("ΛΕ", c. 485); Em. 14 ("ΛΕ", c. 485); Em. 23 ("ΛΕ", 477); Em. 28 ("ΛΕ", 467); Em. 35 ("ΛΕ", 454); Em. 40 ("M", 448); and Em. 45 ("A", 443 BC). It is unclear what the inscriptions mean; while "M" is generally taken to stand for Mytilene, and "ΛΕ" Lesbos, "A" by analogy should refer to Antissa (?), a problematic solution since it implies a third party involved in the Mytliene-Phokaia agreement. Nearly all of the *hektai* from Phokaia bear a tiny seal (*phokē*) on the obverse, a punning reference to the name of the city.

36. The limited scope of the inscription as well as the fact that the *hektai* had been in production long before 400 BC give ample reason to believe that this was not the first pact concluded by the cooperating cities. Bodenstedt (1981: 38–45), in fact, has identified die-cutters who worked in both cities as early as c. 500, strengthening the supposition for an earlier accord. Most likely this inscription was merely an update of a long-standing agreement dealing with a particular issue that had in the meantime arisen, namely the culpability and responsibility of the "mixer". Heisserer (1984: 119–122) has argued for a high date of c. 426 BC, while Bodenstedt (1981: 30), at the low end, prefers a date of 394 (see also Figueira 1998: 488; Tod 1948: 35). For our arguments, the precise date does not matter.

37. Heisserer (1984: 125) reviews in detail the individual relationships that Mytilene and Phokaia had with Athens (and Persia) through the fifth and fourth centuries.

38. Here it should also be noted that while expenditures associated with military operations were often one of the prime motivating factors in the minting of coins in antiquity (de Callataÿ 2000), there is no case to be made that Phokaia and Mytilene were in annual need of the *hektai* to cover their (joint?) military expenses over the

purely commercial but not centered on economic facilitation, which, as we discuss below, seems to have been a primary motivating factor in many other economic arrangements, particularly in the *koina*. We argue instead that this arrangement was intended to generate revenue from coins that were produced primarily as a commodity to be bought and sold. The unusual characteristics of these coins—the longevity of the series, the use of electrum, the lack of stable types,[39] their single denomination—are best explained by this profit-oriented, specialized use and make it doubtful that they were intended to cover the usual types of state expenditures, like military activity (see n. 38) or internal debts.

We begin with the denomination. Despite its small size, the electrum *hektē* had about the same value as the much larger silver Athenian tetradrachm, meaning that the coins were not well suited for low-value, daily transactions.[40] Better suited to everyday internal exchange was the small denomination silver coinage minted in Mytilene (and for a briefer period in Phokaia) (plate 13 nos. 14–17), which was produced concurrently with the *hektai*; this indicates that the electrum coinage was meant for other purposes.[41] Some of the *hektai* saw circulation in Mytilene and Phokaia, as we might expect, but the hoard evidence shows that their circulation was generally oriented externally, toward the Propontis and the hinterland of Phokaia; from textual evidence it appears that the coins traveled to Athens as well (see n. 34).[42]

Scholars have sometimes explained the large value and circulation patterns of the *hektai* through an analogy with "trade coinages", meaning that these coins, like special high-value trade coins in later centuries, were manufactured not for home consumption but for use in

course of two centuries. In fact, around the time of their revolt from Athens in 428, the Mytileneans independently produced a series of low-quality electrum staters, marked with the ethnic MYTI, which were likely special issues associated with the city's military operations (Figueira 1998: 103). While it is clear that the electrum coins of Kyzikos, Mytilene, and Phokaia were used as mercenary pay (Kyzikos: Xen. *Anab.* 5.6.23, 6.2.4–5, 7.2.36, 7.3.10; Mytilene/Phokaia: [Dem.] 40.36), particularly in the Pontic region, it was secondary users of the coins, not the producers, who employed the soldiers. This secondary, military use of the coins no doubt contributed to their general demand (see below), but cannot be tied specifically to their production.

39. Head's (1911: 558) suggestion that the many types represent magistrate's symbols is problematic because, in Mytilene, both obverse and reverse types change; double-sided magistrate symbols are unheard of elsewhere. Kroll (1981: 4) is correct to point out that the changing types of the joint coinage of Mytilene and Phokaia, and of the sixth- to fourth-century electrum issues of Kyzikos (more on this below), relate to the earlier Ionian use of changing types as "pictorial signatures" of individual moneyers. While a similar function is possible for these issues, it is curious that this function would be limited to just the electrum issues of these cities and not used on the contemporary silver clearly meant for internal use.

40. Kroll (1981: 14–15, following Kraay 1956) argues that the Athenian tetradrachm denomination, and the Athena head/owl type particularly, was instituted for the sake of exporting Athens' surplus silver as a commodity abroad, and was only secondarily relevant for local use. See also below n. 50.

41. Kraay's (1976: 261) doubts about the internal use of electrum at Kyzikos were expanded by Figueira (1998: 102) to include electrum use at Phokaia and Mytilene. In all three places, Figueira argues, locally produced silver coinage played a secondary role to foreign, e.g., Athenian, silver coinage in internal and even external transactions.

42. The hoards with cooperative electrum are *IGCH* 1184 (Erythai), 1188 (Troas), 1221 (Khios), 1226 (Akhissar), 1227 (Lesbos), 1232 (W. Asia Minor), 1234 (Isiklıköy, Bithynia); *CH* 1.22 (Pergamum?), 2.23 (NW Turkey), 3.18 (Canakkale-Yenidce), 3.29 (Edremid), 9.458 (unknown). In all of these hoards the *hektai* of both cities are found circulating together, usually as the only component of the hoard, the exception being hoards *IGCH* 1184 and 1234, which contain a large number of silver coins in addition to the *hektai*.

long-distance trade, often for a specific overseas market that demanded specie of a defined size, weight, fineness, and, typically, design.[43] Because they were often made of alloys and weights that differed from the coinage at home, many trade coins were not legal tender in their country of origin and were not always accepted in payment for taxes by the issuing authority.[44] In the overseas arena some trade coins (like the Spanish eight reales) achieved very widespread use, a situation that was entirely dependent on the willingness of the foreign market to accept the coins, and subsequently were traded at a premium, while others (like the U.S. trade dollar) were ultimately less successful. If a state had a successful trade coin, it could then benefit handsomely from the demand by charging elevated (re-)minting fees or by pricing the coin well over its denominational value or the intrinsic value of its bullion content.[45] Even a slight overvaluation, half a percent for example, could result in substantial profits when the volume of production was in the several millions of coins.

A similar trade-coin analogy has been offered for the electrum issues of Kyzikos, the only other mint to strike electrum continuously through the fifth and fourth centuries, and whose issues share the same general characteristics with the cooperative *hektai*, including their unusual weight standard and constantly changing types (plate 13 no. 18, plate 14 no. 19) (Kraay 1976: 261).[46] It is important to note too that, like the cooperating cities, the Kyzikenes also produced (small-denomination) silver issues for internal use (plate 14 nos. 20–21), again indicating a specialized use for their electrum. Kyzikene electrum coins were also found in Athens.[47] However, they saw their heaviest circulation in locales around the Black Sea, where there is little doubt that they were the preferred coinage in regional trade (Kraay 1976: 261). To date, virtually no other major trade-type coins of the period, including Athenian and Aeginetan silver, have been found in the Black Sea region.

While the trade-coin analogy is useful for explaining some aspects of the production and circulation of the electrum coins, it does not address the question of how the coins entered circulation. Most coins in antiquity were produced and subsequently entered circulation in order to fulfill an authority's financial obligations through direct payment, but it

43. For an overview of trade coinages see Willem (1965: especially ch. 3) and Mossman (1993: 53–77).

44. A case in point is the trade dollar minted in the United States in the last quarter of the nineteenth century for use in trade in the Far East. Because of their nonstandard weight and fineness, these dollars were not legal tender in the U.S., although many found their way into circulation in California and on the East Coast regardless (Taxay 1966: 282).

45. The Dutch lion dollar (*leeuwendaalder*), issued from 1575 to 1713, was another highly successful trade coin, particularly from the standpoint of profitability. Although it had a low silver content (.750 fine), the popularity of the coin, especially in the Levant, meant that it was often considerably overvalued. The coin was so popular, in fact, that states in Germany and Italy imitated it for their overseas markets as well (Mossman 1993: 65).

46. The Kyzikene electrum coins were minted, however, in a greater range of denominations, which included the stater and several fractions, including *hektai*.

47. Many cults in Athens held Kyzikene electrum coins in their treasuries in the later fifth and early fourth centuries, as can be seen in their inscribed inventories; for a complete listing of this extensive evidence see Figueira (1998: 100).

is difficult to see how this mechanism would have continuously operated in the case of an-
nually produced electrum trade coins.[48] It is possible that at times some governmental obligations, perhaps even direct payments for grain, the primary Black Sea export, were made
by the electrum-producing states with their electrum coinage. However, the near-exclusive
use of electrum in trade in the Pontic regions, which would presumably have created a constant, intense primary and secondary demand for the coinage, suggest that there were other
mechanisms by which the electrum coinages of Mytilene-Phokaia and of Kyzikos entered
circulation. One possible mechanism is that the coins were simply offered for sale by the
producers. The commodification of coins in this manner was certainly a component of the
exchange of foreign coinage for local issues that took place in many *emporia* and *agorai* and
which was a potential source of income for both moneychangers and states alike through
changing fees and taxes. Beyond the necessity of foreign exchange, there are indications
that there were specialized currency markets as well, wherein coins of various cities were
bought and sold like other commodities.[49] Xenophon (*Poroi* 3.2), in fact, explicitly states
that traders could obtain coins as an export commodity at the source, in this case Athens,
to sell elsewhere at a profit.[50] It is therefore not unreasonable to think that electrum producers earned revenue by selling their coins to traders and others, who in turn might have
sold the coins elsewhere down the line or simply used them in monetary transactions or as
stores of wealth.[51] Even so, this mechanism does not immediately explain the odd choice

48. Howgego (1990), de Callataÿ (2000), and Bresson (2005) highlight the erratic nature of ancient coin production and its use in fulfilling governmental obligations, among other uses.

49. Martin (1985), for example, interprets a fourth-century inscription from Olbia (*Syll.*[3] 218) regulating coinage exchange as an attempt by the Olbians to establish an international "free market" for currency (1985: 213).
The decree was, he argues (1985: 211), "a measure which in effect turned Olbia into a duty-free port open to all
for the sale and purchase of gold and silver coinage. This measure would have facilitated trade in precious metals
in the form of coinage and boosted trade in general by making it easy for traders to import and export coinage
used in financial transactions of all kinds". Note also Plato *Pol.* 289e: νόμισμά τε πρὸς τὰ ἄλλα καὶ αὐτὸ πρὸς
αὐτὸ διαμείβοντες, οὕς ἀργυραμοιβούς τε καὶ ἐμπόρους καὶ ναυκλήρους καὶ καπήλους ἐπωνομάκαμεν, μῶν τῆς
πολιτικῆς ἀμφισβητήσουσί τι; ("The men exchanging coin for goods and coin for coin, whom we call bankers,
merchants, shippers, and retailers, do they lay claim to statesmanship?")

50. ἢν δὲ μὴ βούλωνται ἀντιφορτίζεσθαι, καὶ ἀργύριον ἐξάγοντες καλὴν ἐμπορίαν ἐξάγουσι. ὅπου γὰρ ἂν
πωλῶσιν αὐτό, πανταχοῦ πλεῖον τοῦ ἀρχαίου λαμβάνουσιν. ("If they [sc. the traders] do not wish ship back a
return cargo, they can still make a good profit by exporting silver [sc. coinage]; for wherever they sell it, they
always make more than the original outlay.") On the Athenian tetradrachm as an export commodity, see also
n. 40. It is not clear whether Xenophon means that the coins are to be obtained through sale of imports or
purchased directly from the mint *vel sim.* If by purchase, and if the Athenians viewed their coinage as a critical
export commodity, we might imagine that they would seek to protect it from price gouging, etc., by regulating
its sale either through government outlets or price fixing (cp. the Olbia inscription, n. 49). In this respect, Kallisthenes' notice (*FGrH* 124 F 4) of the poet Persinos obtaining a better exchange rate for his Phokaic *hektē* at
Mytilene than at Atarneos could be an indication of price-fixing by Mytilene and Phokaia to protect their export
coinage (Figueira 1998: 488).

51. Kraay (1976: 261), perhaps, had this in mind when he wrote that Kyzikos "marketed a traditional trade
currency". Melville Jones (1998: 267–268) argues that the fixed price on Kyzikene electrum in the Olbian decree
(n. 49), the only type of coinage in the decree to be so regulated, was necessary to rein in unfair profiteering in

of metal—electrum—for these coins, which in some respects could not have been cheap to produce by comparison with silver coins.[52]

When Mytilene and Phokaia began their cooperative program in the late sixth century, electrum had been all but phased out as a coining metal. Despite their earlier use of it, most mints in Asia Minor had abandoned electrum by the third quarter of the sixth century, switching instead to silver and (rarely) gold coinage, no doubt because of the problems posed by electrum as a monetary metal. In both its natural and manufactured forms, the gold content of electrum varies from as little as 30% to as much as 70%, with the remaining bulk of the alloy being made up by silver and smaller amounts of other metals, like copper (Keyser and Clark 2001). The tremendous discrepancy between the value of gold and silver (recall that the exchange ratio of the two metals varied from 1:10 to 1:14 through the Archaic and Classical periods) opened the door to conflict among those conducting transactions with electrum; without taking a touchstone to every coin or nugget, users could never be entirely certain how much their piece of electrum was worth. These same problems with monetary electrum are directly related to the beginnings of coinage in Lydia around 600 BC, when the state attempted to regulate the use of electrum in exchange by issuing small ingots of the troublesome metal with a stamp guaranteeing a set value.[53] Because electrum was so problematic, and was deemed unfit for coinage by most authorities (including Mytilene and Phokaia for their own internal coinage!), it is apparent that the choice to use this metal lies close to the heart of the reason why Mytilene and Phokaia initiated and maintained their monetary arrangement. While we might conclude that the initial *hektai* were simply a restyled continuation of each city's earlier sixth-century electrum issues, that does little to explain the remarkable fact that electrum was retained for this cooperative coinage throughout the entire fifth and almost to the end of the fourth century, long past the point when we would expect any lingering adherence to the old-fashioned electrum tradition.[54] At any point in time the partners had the option to switch to a joint silver coinage,

the trade of this coinage. The various recorded exchange rates for Kyzikene electrum have suggested to some scholars (e.g., Cohen 1992: 150) that it was possible to buy an electrum stater in Athens for 21 drachmas and sell it in the Bosphoros for 28. There are, however, considerable problems with the evidence and this interpretation (Figueira 1998: 524–527).

52. None of these three electrum-producing cities had access to native electrum, gold, or silver within their territories. The purchase of commodity electrum or gold, one of the priciest commodities in antiquity, in sufficient amounts to strike coins required a tremendous outlay, far more than what was necessary for the purchase of commodity silver. The costs of operating the mint, on the other hand, especially if state-owned slaves were used, would be negligible by comparison.

53. The critical role that electrum played in the origin of coinage in Asia Minor is well recognized, but pinpointing the underlying concepts and adaptations is currently a hotly contested issue. The major positions are presented in Wallace (1987), Le Rider (2001), Kroll (2001), the papers in Balmuth (2001), Seaford (2004), and Schaps (2004).

54. Without breaking stride, Phokaia produced electrum coinage from c. 600 BC onward. The earlier series (Bodenstedt 1981 Series E and 1) are characterized by a more limited type repertoire (griffin heads and seals), but were minted in a full range of denominations, from the tiny 1/96 to full staters. The pre-521 electrum issues

and in the process save themselves unnecessarily high production costs (see n. 52). They obviously found it advantageous not to do so. How then do we explain the enduring use of this otherwise undesirable monetary metal?

Profit is perhaps the most obvious answer. Georges Le Rider has argued that the producers of early electrum coins took advantage of the use of electrum as money by diluting the naturally occurring alloy with pure silver and then issuing the coins at full (i.e., non-diluted) value in order to make substantial profits on every coin they paid out.[55] Whether or not we accept Le Rider's arguments for profit-driven overvaluation in the earliest electrum issues, we must recognize that the situation facing Mytilene and Phokaia (as well as Kyzikos) a century later had changed. There was no electrum crisis to solve; nearly all other mints had moved on to silver. It is therefore conceivable that in their planning the authorities at Mytilene and Phokaia consciously chose to retain electrum for its profit-generating potential. Perhaps they realized that electrum was the only precious metal alloy that had the ability to be widely accepted yet, at the same time, could be manipulated well beyond what was possible with near-pure silver or gold. There was no expectation of purity in electrum coinage, since as an alloy "pure" electrum does not exist. Users therefore must have been more generous in their expectations of what constituted a good electrum coin than they were with straight silver or gold coins. Any handful of electrum coins, for example, was bound to exhibit variation in color between individual pieces, indicating variations in gold content. Since it would be impractical to check every individual coin every time with a touchstone, some amount of conventional overvaluation of the coins, which could absorb variations in intrinsic value, was acceptable; even a slight amount of difference in the gold content, it should be remembered, could alter this value significantly. If electrum producers were careful not to abuse this allowance, they had an opportunity to profit to a greater degree on the production of electrum coins than was generally possible with silver coinage.

It is clear from the inscribed agreement that Mytilene and Phokaia mixed their electrum to carefully predetermined gold:silver ratios; the liability for failing to conform to this ratio fell, quite literally, on the mixer's head.[56] It is also clear from metallurgical analysis that the coins contained far less gold than was commonly found in native electrum, and that this amount changed at times.[57] The use of a carefully controlled artificial alloy suggests that

at Mytilene (Bodenstedt 1981 Series E) were more spotty, but also exhibit a range of denominations including 1/6, 1/12, and 1/48 staters, but not on the Phokaic standard. The cooperation clearly set new guidelines for the electrum coins issued by both mints.

55. Le Rider (2001) argues that the profit margin was as great as 15% to 20%. In his review, Kroll (2001) counters the notion of profit as a motivating factor for states producing early electrum coinage, and instead follows Wallace's (1987) earlier proposal that the states were effectively performing a public service by setting values and issuing coins during a crisis in order to quell disputes. Throughout the history of coinage states often did overvalue their precious metal coins vis-à-vis bullion, but this was only enough to cover minting costs, generally no more than 3% to 5%.

56. Note especially lines 13–15. Also see Healy (1957).

57. The results of Bodenstedt's (1981: appendix 4) analysis show that Phokaian electrum from c. 600–522 BC

the partners were highly conscious of the commodity prices of gold and silver, while at the same time they had in mind a valuation for their coinage set at some fixed point in relation to these prices. Small fluctuations in the gold content of the *hektai* could also indicate that the mixers adjusted the gold content according to the market value of the metal in order to maintain a set margin of overvaluation for every batch of coins.[58] The margin of overvaluation was likely nowhere near the 15% to 20% suggested by Le Rider for the early electrum coinage, for the simple reason that such intense overvaluation would be difficult to maintain outside a closed system. There is little point in speculating on an exact figure, but we should note that with a lower margin of overvaluation profits would be greatest if there was a consistently high demand for the coins, which there seems to have been for over two centuries.[59]

Although the general economic environment favored simple silver coins, electrum coinage was able to occupy a specialized, liminal zone in purpose and use, one perhaps reflected in its ever changing, noncivic types.[60] Demand for electrum coinage came from at least two sources. The northern trade, which for reasons unknown had developed a preference for electrum, unquestionably fueled a large proportion of the coins' production, but it is also evident that in Athens and no doubt elsewhere in the Aegean electrum was hoarded as a convenient, internationally accepted, and reliable means of storing wealth.[61] Hoarders therefore had the capability to increase the demand for the coins enormously.[62] Figueira (1998: 101) has in fact already stressed the connection between hoarding as a significant factor in the demand for the coins and their commodification more generally. It was, in the end, this commodification of electrum coins that made the partnership between Mytilene and Phokaia desirable and comparatively simple to maintain. Why the two cities did not go their separate ways and produce *hektai* for themselves individually must have had to do, at least in part, with the inherent financial risks involved in the production of electrum

contained around 55% gold; during the initial period of joint minting by Phokaia and Mytliene down to c. 478 the figure falls to 46% for both mints. Thereafter it remains around 40%. Native Ionian electrum contained on average close to 70% gold. Bodenstedt explains the drop in gold content c. 478 as an attempt to align the value of the *hektai* with the Athenian tetradrachm for the purpose of facilitating military payments in *hektai* at the onset of the Delian League; Figueira's (1998: 105) far simpler solution is to attribute the fluctuation to changes in the value ratio between gold and silver.

58. The percentages for gold content noted above (n. 57) are averages for each period. The actual gold content in some batches varied by as much as +/- 5% (Figueira 1998: 94). For gold prices and fluctuation see Melville Jones (1999).

59. On the question of volume and profit see Giacchero (1980: esp. p. 9).

60. It has long been noted that the Athenian Coinage Decree (*IG* I³ 1453) makes no mention of electrum coinage, perhaps because the uses for electrum were more restricted and specialized than those for silver coinage.

61. The Athenian orator Lysias, for example, kept a cache of 400 Kyzikene electrum coins and 100 gold darics in his house (Lys. 12.11). The considerable number of electrum coins listed in Athenian temple inventories (see n. 34) were likely donations given out from such personal reserves. Figueira (1998: 101) notes concerning electrum hoarding in Athens that "electrum coins served as an emergency reserve that could be spent beyond the borders of the *arkhê* in predicaments of last resort".

62. On hoarding and its effects on the production of ancient coinage see Bresson (2005).

trade coins; the necessity of obtaining commodity gold or electrum meant that the annual financial outlay for production was likely greater than it was for the production of more standard silver issues. Furthermore, while certainly not in a backwater, Mytilene and Phokaia were not as well situated as Kyzikos vis-à-vis the flow of heavy trade, and so could not necessarily rely on a constant and healthy stream of revenue from passing traffic to offset the risks of producing the electrum coins individually. By not competing with each other and by buffering the risks through joint production, the partners would be able to maintain a constant output of coinage, and thus ensure a constant revenue stream for themselves. The profits from the paying out or sale of the coins would accrue immediately, would be accountable, and so could be easily shared between the partners however they chose to divide the proceeds.

The very fact that the Mytileneans and Phokaians cooperated on an annual basis to produce for over two centuries a single-denomination electrum coinage, and not one in silver or gold, demands explanation. We have tried to show that this unusual practice can best be explained by considerations of maximizing revenues while concurrently offsetting risks. The ability of the two *poleis* to generate significant income from the issuance of the coinage seems to have been the basic underlying motivation for the monetary cooperation; it was, in effect, a business deal pure and simple. How many other such coinage "deals" there might have been remains unknown, and, without the benefit of textual support, essentially unknowable. However, in regions where there were closer ties between neighboring cities, and shared economic concerns beyond the generation of state revenues, a profitable coinage might not have been as desirable as a simply functional coinage, one that was part of a larger schema of regional economic cooperation.

COINAGES OF THE GREEK *KOINA*

The coins issued by or under the auspices of the regional power structures, which the Greeks called a *koinon* or (more commonly in the parlance of the Classical period) an *ethnos*, represent one of the most significant and complex cases of the larger phenomenon of cooperative coinage. Since the nineteenth century, historians of "Greek federal states" have looked to the numismatic record for what they have seen as relatively unproblematic evidence for the existence of a "federal state" in coins marked by the authority of a regional power structure encompassing multiple *poleis*, such as ΒΟΙΩΤΩΝ, ΑΧΑΙΩΝ, or ΧΑΛΚΙΔΕΩΝ, to name only a few. But if we regard coins first of all as monetary instruments, providing evidence for political arrangements only insofar as they are stamped by the (state) minting authority that stands behind their quality and legality, then we need to consider the economic needs and opportunities that may have motivated the development of a centralized state power that could undertake such actions. Indeed, the tacit assumption that *autonomia* can be understood without any reference to *autarkeia* is deeply problematic: Mogens Hansen and other members of the Copenhagen Polis Centre (CPC) have persuasively (we think) undermined the scholarly orthodoxy that holds up autonomy as a strict condition for the existence of a *polis*, with the result that a whole spectrum of political dependency in Archaic and Classical Greece emerges (Hansen 1995a; 1997). Insofar as political power resides in the ability to control and distribute resources—economic among them—then we should at least be asking (and the CPC has not) how economic dependence or interdependence relates to political dependence.

In the case of the cooperative coinages issued by groups of *poleis* under the auspices of a *koinon*, few scholars have considered the possibility that there might be real relationships of economic interdependence among the minting communities. Instead, the participation of multiple *poleis* in an arrangement to mint on the same standard with a shared type tends to be seen *simpliciter* as an unproblematic indication of the membership of that community in a "federal state", and issues are correspondingly dated by major events in the history of each *koinon* known from literary and epigraphic evidence (e.g., Kraay 1976: 166 on Thessaly; on the Arkadikon coinage, Williams 1965; Kraay 1976: 97–101). So the various issues of the Boiotian *poleis* in the Classical period, which Head dubbed "more clearly federal in character" than any other "ancient money" (Head 1881: 10), are typically dated by, for example, the medism of Thebes in 480, the battle of Oinophyta in 457, the Peace of Antalkidas in 386, the destruction of Thebes in 335, the sack of Korinth in 146, and so on. Ascribing dates to particular issues is tricky and is generally accomplished by a kind of cautious circular reasoning in which the coins and the literary sources are taken to be complementary and mutually reinforcing (because we want them to be). But by considering the monetary instruments adopted and produced by the Greek *koina* as part of the much larger phenomenon of cooperative coinage in general, and as part of a regional economic strategy in particular, it should be possible to break that circularity and to situate what used to be called "Greek federal coinage" on a larger spectrum of cooperative monetary arrangements that the ancient Greek world made in various different political contexts. Recent work has begun to move in this direction. Both Peter Franke and Thomas Martin rejected Kraay's federal interpretation of the Thessalian coinage, Martin emphasizing that the common type and standard could only be taken as indications of the coinage's function in meeting broader regional economic needs (Franke 1970: 91–93; Martin 1985: 38, 41–42). Catherine Morgan has recently argued that these regional coinages are better understood as "a form of response to a range of possible needs", which "offers greater potential for understanding both the level at which decisions to coin were taken and the register of the problems which coinage was intended to solve" (Morgan 2003: 82). In fact, as we shall argue below (and as Mackil argues in greater detail in a forthcoming book on the *koinon*), one of the most significant functions of a *koinon* was to protect and manage fragile and highly interdependent regional economies; the phenomenon of cooperative coinage, whether more or less institutionalized, should be seen as an intrinsic part of that function.[63]

63. Cf. Morgan (2003: 84), who remarks that if we accept that there was no fifth-century Arkadian federation

The participation of a *polis* mint in issuing according to a shared type and weight standard, for example the silver obol issued by Mykalessos with the Boiotian shield on the obverse (plate 14 no. 22), or the silver triobol issued by Pellene with the Akhaian wreath on the reverse (plate 14 no. 23), has suggested to most commentators membership of that *polis* in the *koinon*. That hypothesis is much easier to verify in the case of Mykalessos than of Pellene, simply because we know so much more of the Boiotian *koinon* in the fourth century, when both coins were minted, than we do of the Akhaian. We cannot be certain of Pellene's formal membership in an Akhaian *koinon* at the time when that triobol was issued, but we do know that Mykalessos was a member of the Boiotian *koinon* when its triobol was probably issued.[64] That different political arrangements may lie behind very similar minting arrangements in these two examples, chosen almost at random, suggests the value of looking first at economic motives for this kind of cooperative minting arrangement. The Mykalessos triobol is of course part of an enormous Boiotian coinage, unified by the appearance of a heroic shield on the obverse of every coin minted in the region, with the exception of some early, small-denomination issues of Orkhomenos (see below). This coinage, beginning in the last quarter of the sixth century, is typically cited as the major "source" for the existence of a Boiotian *koinon* from the same date. But as Hansen (1995b: 31) has cogently pointed out, these coins "need [not] be evidence of a proper federation; they may simply reflect the continued cooperation between cities belonging to the same region". The case of Boiotia will be treated in some detail below, but for now it is worth asking of Boiotia, as of every other region that adopted a cooperative coinage, why the *poleis* that participated did not mint coins independently, as Athens, Korinth, Sikyon, and so many others did. Or why, if the aim was simply to facilitate trade within a region, they did not adopt a coinage like the Aiginetan "turtles" or (later) the Athenian "owls", which had an extraordinarily wide circulation throughout the eastern Mediterranean, on the grounds apparently of their recognizability and reliably good silver content. We need an explanation that accounts for the economic as well as the political implications of these arrangements, and in the next section we shall present an overview of the economic obligations and responsibilities of the *koinon* vis-à-vis the entire group of its member *poleis* and their territories.

and that in that period in Arkadia political power lay primarily with individual cities, then "the Arkadikon coinage becomes a crucial piece of evidence for the nature of cross-regional collaboration, in that it implies a widely shared need to make a large number of payments at standard rates over a reasonably long period of time."

64. The Mykalessos triobol is only one in a voluminous series of coins issued by thirteen *poleis* in Boiotia; it used to be pressed into the narrow window between the King's Peace of 387 and 374, when all the Boiotian *poleis* except Orkhomenos were reintegrated into the *koinon*. It was argued that these coins were replaced by the Theban magistrate issues from 371 to 338, but Hepworth's die-study of the magistrate coinage (Hepworth 1998: 63 n. 16) has shown it to go back to the first decade of the fourth century, well before the *polis* issues are usually thought to have begun. It is therefore probably not necessary to press the voluminous *polis* issues into that narrow thirteen-year period. They may go back to the late fifth century, and certainly to the very earliest years of the fourth. Both Akhaian and Boiotian coinages will be discussed in detail below.

Koinon Economies

From their very inception, almost every *koinon* in the Greek world created and protected economic rights and privileges, which the citizens of its constituent *poleis* could exercise throughout the territory of the entire *koinon*. As the *koinon* of the Khalkideis was forming in the early fourth century, rights of intermarriage (*epigamia*) and property ownership (*enktesis*) in every member *polis* were extended to all citizens; opponents to the growth of the *koinon* in the early fourth century cited such privileges as major incentives to participation (Xen. *Hell.* 5.2.18–19). The same rights became widespread in the Hellenistic period, if not before, and are securely attested in Akhaia, Aitolia, and Boiotia.[65] The right to own property throughout the region, regardless of one's own *polis* citizenship, is particularly significant for it facilitated access to a broader array of resources than was typically available in a single locality. If the Mediterranean is indeed characterized, as Horden and Purcell (2000) have recently argued, by extreme fragmentation and microregions supporting highly localized resources, then this kind of individual mobility is fundamental to economic success.[66]

The territory of any single *koinon*, by virtue of its size and the fragmentation of the landscape typical of the Mediterranean, provided more resources, in terms of both quantity and variety, than could the territory of any single *polis*. The *koinon* of the Khalkideis in the early fourth century provides an excellent example. The land under its control produced timber for shipbuilding and plentiful grain, while the harbors and ports created a significant source of income in the form of taxes on goods imported to and exported from the region (Xen. *Hell.* 5.2.16).[67] In combination, this set of resources made the members of the *koinon*, and perhaps the state itself, quite wealthy; but if political boundaries had complicated the export

65. Evidence for rights in Hellenistic Akhaia (c. 280–146): *Syll.*³ 490 lines 11–13 (decree integrating Arkadian Orkhomenos into the Akhaian *koinon*, by which all Akhaians are granted the right to own property in Orkhomenos); *Syll.*³ 675 lines 16–17; Plut. *Arat.* 41.4, 42.3; cf. *Kleom.* 19. In Hellenistic Aitolia: *IG* IX 1² 1, 1.10b lines 2–4 (273/2); *IG* IX 1² 1, 1.8 lines 4–9 (mid-third century); *IG* IX 1² 1, 1.6 (269/8–265/4 or 251/0–249/8); *IG* IX 1² 1, 1.3A lines 11–13 (late 260s or early 250s). In Boiotia, the right of *eppasis* extended throughout the territory of the *koinon* to all its members must be inferred from a proxeny decree of the *koinon* that bestows the right on a *proxenos* from Akhaian Pellene (*SEG* 25.553) and from a proxeny decree of Akraiphia for a citizen of Kopai (*IG* 7.2708) that does not explicitly bestow the right, presumably because he already had it as a citizen of a member *polis*. The inference from these decrees to all citizens is in our view much facilitated by comparison with the more straightforward evidence for other regions; cf. Roesch (1973: 276). Dittenberger (*IG* 7.2708 with commentary on 7.3059) placed the text after 171, when the Boiotian *koinon* was forcibly dissolved by the Romans (Plb. 27.2.7, 27.2.10; Liv. 42.44.6), on the assumption that no member *polis* would grant proxeny to a citizen of another member *polis* while the *koinon* was still functional. However, we can be certain that a decree of Akraiphia bestowed proxeny upon a citizen of Haliartos (Perdrizet 1899: 95), and because Haliartos was destroyed in 171 along with the dismantling of the *koinon* (Liv. 42.63), we can be certain that the bestowal occurred earlier; cf. a decree of Khorsiai for Kapon of Thisbe, c. 191 (*SEG* 22.410), and a decree of Akraiphia for a Theban (Perdrizet 1899: 93 lines 17–21, on the same stone as the decree for the Haliartian, and therefore presumably earlier).

66. Cf. Purcell (2005) for an analysis of one institutional response ("tax morphology") to the economic advantages of mobility.

67. Also Rhodes and Osborne (2003: no. 12 lines 15–18), a treaty recording an alliance between Amyntas III of Macedon and the Khalkidians (390s or 380s). The regularity of taxation on exports in the ancient Mediterranean is underscored by Purcell (2005: 206).

of timber or the shipment upland of grain from the coastal plains, the economic success of individual citizens, *poleis*, and the region as a whole would have been significantly reduced. Similarly, in Boiotia in the Hellenistic period we know that the *poleis* around Lake Kopais had a surplus of arable and pasturable land (*SEG* 3.356, 3.359, 22.432; *IG* VII 3171; Osborne 1985), while those nearer the coasts, like Anthedon (Herakleides Kretikos [*GGM* 1.97ff.] 23–24) and Tanagra (Herakleides Kretikos 8–10), had little land suitable for grain production but enjoyed direct access to marine resources, vines, and olives.[68] Resource complementarity depends upon access and mobility; without them, resources are only localized and shortage of nonlocal goods is predictable. The incorporation of so many microregions with their own specialized and often complementary resources into a single political entity created a remarkable potential for the development of economic power within a given region. This potential was partially actualized from at least the early fourth century in the *koinon* of the Khalkideis, by extending rights of intermarriage and property ownership throughout the region to citizens of all member communities. The same can be said with certainty of Hellenistic Boiotia and Akhaia, and it may be true of those regions in the fourth century as well.

However, the Boiotians, Khalkidians, and Akhaians, along with many others (like Thessaly), were issuing cooperative coinages well before the Hellenistic period, and we need to consider carefully the other economic interactions between member communities and the *koinon* itself that may have necessitated, or at least been significantly facilitated by, monetary cooperation. They are essentially two: military expeditions and taxation. In the early fourth century the member *poleis* of the Boiotian *koinon* were grouped into eleven districts (μέρη), each of which was obligated to contribute troops to the regional army on what appears to have been a fixed basis of 1,000 hoplites and 100 cavalry (Hell. Oxy. 16.4 [Bartoletti]). Nothing is known about how (or whether) they were paid, but in the early third century this arrangement persisted, and an inscribed agreement between Orkhomenos and Khaironeia (part of the same district) makes it clear that the cavalrymen who served in the *koinon* army were required to keep track of the time they served, because they were to receive pay from the district itself (that is, from the combined treasuries of the member *poleis*), at different rates for service within Boiotia than for service outside the region.[69] It is by no means certain that this precise arrangement should be retrojected to the fifth century, but the document is useful in considering the reasons underlying the decision to adopt a cooperative coinage, for it illustrates in some detail the kinds of common transactions for which they might be responsible. Other wartime expenses, like the payment of garrison

---

68. Variations on the same theme could be repeated for virtually every *koinon* of the Classical or Hellenistic world.

69. Étienne and Roesch (1978: lines 26–29): τιθέσθη δὲ τὰς στροτειίας τάς τε ἐν τῆ Βοιωτίη κὴ τὰς ἐ|χθόνδε τᾶς Βοιωτίας χωρὶς ἑκατέ||[ρ]ας ἅς κα τὰ ἐφόδια λάβωνθι. ("Let an account be recorded separately for campaigns in Boiotia and outside of Boiotia, for which they have taken their travel allowances.") For Orkhomenos and Khaironeia as part of the same district see Knoepfler (2000) (who does not, however, cite the cavalry agreement as part of his evidence).

troops and mercenaries, and the purchase of supplies while on campaign, were likewise incurred by *koina* just as by *poleis*, and the need to pay expenses incurred directly by the state, when that state was a complex entity composed of multiple *poleis*, must have been remarkably facilitated by the use of a cooperative coinage.[70]

The other context in which member *poleis*, the regional government, and the economy necessarily interact is in taxation. Less is known about regional taxation practices, but there is enough evidence to make a few fairly general claims with some confidence. The earliest indisputable evidence for taxes levied on member *poleis* by a *koinon* is provided by the Oxyrhynchus Historian, who states that in Boiotia *poleis* were obligated to pay an *eisphora* to the *koinon* in proportion to their population.[71] Just as for military contributions, the *poleis* were grouped into districts to pay these contributions. Whether the *eisphora* in this period was an emergency military levy or a regular tax is unknown. Some kind of regular and compulsory financial obligations, however, along with military contributions along the lines already mentioned, must have been involved in the earliest attempts by the Thebans, around 519 BC, to persuade or compel other Boiotian *poleis* to "take part in the Boiotians", (ἐς Βοιωτοὺς τελέειν: Hdt. 6.108).[72] This arrangement is clearly related to *synteleia*, a term frequently used in the ancient sources to describe the relationship of member communities to a regional government, and although it sometimes implies an asymmetry in power relationships, it consistently connotes participation by contribution (Bakhuizen 1988; 1994).[73] The "contributions" were certainly as often made in manpower as in money. In the Hellenistic period both member *poleis* and the *koinon* could levy a *telos* on landowners, though it looks as if these levies were also extraordinary.[74] The bestowal of *ateleia* by the Boiotian *koinon* as early as the fourth century BC probably amounted to an exemption from

70. Examples will be discussed below.

71. Hell.Oxy. 16.4 [Bartoletti]: ἁπλῶς δὲ δηλῶσαι κατὰ τὸν ἄρχοντα καὶ τῶν κοινῶν ἀπέλαυον καὶ τὰς ε[ἰ]σφορὰς ἐποιοῦντο καὶ δικασ<τὰς> ἔπεμπον καὶ μετεῖχον ἁπάντων ὁμοίως καὶ τῶν κακῶν καὶ τῶν ἀγαθῶν. τὸ μὲν οὖν ἔθνος οὕτως ἐπολιτεύετο. ("To put it simply, depending on the number of its magistrates, each community shared in the common treasury, paid its taxes, appointed jurymen, and shared equally in public burdens and benefits. This was the constitution of the whole people..." [trans. McKechnie and Kern].)

72. In 519 the Plataians were being "pressed" by the Thebans, according to Herodotos, but we do not know what sort of organization they were "pressing" them to join. We have no incontrovertible evidence for the nature of the institutions in place at this time in Boiotia, but the coins do tell us incontrovertibly that some kind of cooperative arrangement involving economic relations was in place, and that it was wrapped up with a sense of common "Boiotian" identity. This will be discussed further below. The date of Plataia's first schism with Thebes has been questioned by scholars wishing to emend Herodotos; for a full discussion of the issues see Hornblower (1991: 464–466). The problem here is closely paralleled by the situation in southern Italy in the late sixth and early fifth centuries, discussed above, pp. 208–210.

73. Cf. Isocr. 14.9: Thespiai was in a position of *synteleia* to Thebes between 373 and 371.

74. The clearest evidence comes from the land leases of Hellenistic Thespiai, e.g. Feyel (1936: 182 face B lines 26–27): Εἰ δέ τί κα δείει τέλος ἐμφερέμεν ἐν τὰν πόλιν εἴ ἐν τὸ κοινὸν | βοιωτῶν, ὔσι ὁ γ[αϝ]εργός. ("If it is necessary to pay some tax to the *polis* or to the *koinon* of the Boiotians, let the farmer pay it.") Cf. A.5–6 and B.1–2 (where the same phrase is restored on the basis of B.26–27) with Migeotte (1994: 8; 1984: 68) for other examples; cf. Roesch (1982: 298).

such extraordinary levies (cf. *IG* VII 2407, 2408). We know of a regular tithe imposed in Thespiai on agricultural produce (or on the rents received from the leasing of agricultural land) (Feyel 1937: 218 lines 13–14; *IG* VII 1729; Plassart 1935: 343 line 15), and we know of exceptional levies, again called *eisphorai* (Feyel 1937: 224, with a new reading in Roesch 1982: 299), instituted by several cities in the Hellenistic period to raise funds for debt repayment and participation in the Ptoia and Basileia, both festivals involving other Boiotian cities (Roesch 1982: 205 lines 25–27; Vollgraff 1901: no. 19 line 24; cf. Roesch 1982: 298–301). The Akhaian *koinon* in the Hellenistic period likewise imposed levies on its member *poleis*, and although we cannot be entirely certain, it appears that they were exceptional, just as in Boiotia, and were raised to fund military expeditions and/or the payment of mercenaries (Plb. 4.59–60 [esp. 4.60.2], 5.95.7–9, 38.16.4; Grandjean 2000). Other fees were also levied by the *koinon*, for example a fee to be paid by newly enrolled citizens of Dyme to the secretary "of the Akhaians" in the early third century (Bingen 1954: 86–87 no. 4; Rizakis 1990: 110 lines 4–6). As a final example, *telea* on imports and exports appear to have been imposed and collected by the *koinon* of the Khalkideis (*Syll.*³ 135; Tod 1948: 111; Rhodes and Osborne 2003: 12 lines 15–18), and likewise by the Thessalian *koinon*, in the fourth century (Dem. 1.22).

Our survey of prevailing conditions of regional resource complementarity and of the economic rights accruing to individual citizens of a *koinon* suggests the need for high levels of mobility within the region and attests to the commitment of the *koinon* to protecting mobility and the economic advantages deriving from it by granting and enforcing the rights of intermarriage and property ownership throughout the territory. The financial obligations of the *poleis* and their individual citizens to the *koinon* in the form of payment of *eisphora* and *telea*, combined with the intraregional economic mobility that was promoted and legally protected by the *koinon*, suggest a situation in which a cooperative arrangement for the minting of coinage would best suit the monetary needs of the entire region. If a regional political authority protected and promoted exchange structures among a particular group of *poleis*, which enjoyed local autonomy in all but matters of war, peace, and alliance, demanded payment of taxes from those *poleis*, and had its own monetary needs at the regional scale, for example to pay garrison or mercenary troops or to meet other expenses associated with military expeditions or building projects, then it would make excellent sense to develop a monetary system that reflected the multiscalar political authority that supported this system and at the same time authorized the quality of the coinage produced by stamping it with types and legends indicative of the multiscalar nature of that state. This argument, posited on a functional analysis of money within a particular political system, suggests that the coins served regional economic needs above all. The only way to test that hypothesis is to look at the minting patterns and hoard evidence, which we shall do in the next sections.[75]

75. We shall not be inclusive. For a full and recent survey of "common money" issued by "federal states" see Psoma and Tsangari (2003).

Boiotia

In 1881, Barclay Head (1881: 10) declared that "even if we had known nothing from other sources of the Boeotian Confederacy, its coinage would be alone sufficient to throw some light upon the subject, for no ancient money is more clearly federal in character". There is in practice nothing terribly unusual about the cooperative coinage minted by the Boiotian *poleis* and their *koinon*, but it remains one of the most voluminous and best studied, and for these reasons it provides a good case study. It may be helpful to review in broad outlines the main stages in the historical development of the Boiotians' cooperative coinage.

In the last quarter of the sixth century, three *poleis*, Thebes, Tanagra, and Hyettos (or possibly Haliartos), began issuing silver coins with a cut-out shield on the obverse and an incuse punch on the reverse.[76] In this period, the first letters of the *polis* responsible for each issue appear on the obverse in the shield cut-outs (plate 14 nos. 24–26). These three *poleis* were joined by another four—Akraiphia, Koroneia (plate 14 no. 27), Mykalessos, and Pharai (plate 14 no. 28)—shortly after the first issues, and the initials were transferred to the center of the incuse punch on the reverse. This series continued until probably the mid-fifth century. In this series, it is important to note that the minting arrangement was decentralized: three and then seven *poleis* minted coins of the same type on the same standard, but they continued to mint in their own names, and there appears to have been no arrangement for specialization by particular *poleis* in the minting of particular denominations.

Kraay argued that the Athenian occupation of Boiotia after the battle of Oinophyta in 457 marked the start of a series of civic issues bearing the shield on the obverse and various symbols on the reverse, associated with the *poleis* whose names appear in the legends. So the reverse of Akraiphian issues has a *kantharos*, that of Tanagra the forepart of a horse (plate 14 no. 29), that of Thebes an amphora (plate 14 no. 30), and so on. He seems to regard this as an indication of the temporary collapse of a Boiotian federal state, restored after Koroneia in 446, but this is probably (a) to overlook the significance of the continued employment of the shield on the obverse and (b) to overestimate the importance of a series attested by only three specimens carrying the legend BO or BOI on the reverse, inside a mill-sail incuse punch or a four-spoked wheel, respectively, and the legend T-A (for Tanagra) on the obverse (Fowler 1957; *BMC Central Greece* p. 60 nos. 8–10; Kraay 1976: 110 with n. 1).[77] The Tanagra-Boiotia coins were explained by Fowler (1957) as evidence of an attempt by Tanagra to seize hegemony of the Boiotian *koinon* after the disgraceful medism of Thebes in 480, until the Spartans restored Thebes to a position of regional leadership in 457 at the battle of Tanagra, shortly before the Athenian victory at Oinophyta. There is in fact a greater degree of similarity in these types, belonging generally to the period from c. 525 to c. 446, than

76. Several instances were found in the Asyut hoard, buried c. 475 (Price and Waggoner 1975), and that context, along with the material of the coins, requires a late sixth-century start to the coinage.

77. Note also a stater of Tanagra with four-spoked wheel reverse and legend TA but no BOI legend in the ANS collection (ANS 1944.100.19846).

there is between the coins of the period 525–446 on the one hand and the types that were introduced in the second half of the fifth century on the other. This, we would submit, is of greater significance than the appearance of civic emblems (probably) in 457. The shield was adopted as the obverse device by every *polis* minting in Boiotia except Orkhomenos, which, in the late sixth century, issued an independent series of small-denomination coins (obols and fractions) bearing an ear of grain on the obverse. And during this period, all the coins carried marks to designate the *polis* that produced them. Tanagra remarkably declared on its coins that it also belonged to Boiotia (as if the shield were not proclamation enough?), and that may or may not be evidence of Tanagran attempts to claim some sort of leadership of the region in this period (cf. Lewis 1992: 96, 116; Hornblower 1991: 171).

Historians and numismatists alike have noted the significance of this cooperative arrangement, but have generally misunderstood it. Because of the prevalent assumption that coinage was primarily a political phenomenon in the Greek world, it has frequently been argued that the coins themselves provide clear evidence for the existence of a "federal state" or "confederacy" in Boiotia from the late sixth century. In fact, the coins tell us only that a group of *poleis*, initially three and then seven, were minting coins on the same standard with a common type and a legend to demarcate the various *polis*-mints whence they derived. Behind this we might search speculatively for itinerant die-cutters; no die-study of the early Boiotian coinage has ever been made, so we cannot rule out the possibility that multiple *poleis* shared dies.[78] If such a study were ever performed, we might learn of an arrangement like that, but in the meantime historical sources can tell us more about why these three, and then seven, *poleis* minted cooperatively. According to Herodotos, the Boiotians suffered defeat in 507/6 at the hands of the Athenians, who attacked them in retaliation for their support of Kleomenes, and the Thebans, seeking approval for retribution, consulted the oracle at Delphi. The Pythia told them that they would not achieve vengeance on their own, but should ask those nearest them. When this response was reported in Thebes, the citizens replied in some confusion, "But are not those who live nearest to us the men of Tanagra, Koroneia, and Thespiai? And these are already our staunch allies in war".[79] The list does not include every city that minted coins with the heroic shield obverse in the late

78. Frustratingly little is known about the institutional and operational structure of mints in the Archaic and Classical periods. Many of the unanswered questions regarding mint operations in a single *polis*, such as the acquisition of metals, the authorization and sinking of dies, the employment of mint workers (or conversely, contracting outside workshops to produce coins), security issues, etc., are compounded greatly in the case of cooperative coinages. Although we have seen above (Mytilene and Phokaia) an example of decentralized cooperative minting, there is a great likelihood that *poleis* in a regional context of monetary cooperation acted with more coordination or centralization. It would certainly make economic sense, for example, for cooperating regional mints to share dies (as in the case of Syracuse and Leontini, see Kraay 1976: 211) in light of the highly skilled labor and time required to produce them. It might also make sense for a central mint to produce coinage in the individual names of the cooperating *poleis* based on the source of the metal supplied to the mint, as suggested by Kagan (1998) regarding Korinth and one of her colonies.

79. Hdt. 5.79.2: οὐκ ὦν ἄγχιστα ἡμέων οἰκέουσι Ταναγραῖοί τε καὶ Κορωναῖοι καὶ Θεσπιέες; καὶ οὗτοί γε ἅμα ἡμῖν αἰεὶ μαχόμενοι προθύμως συνδιαφέρουσι τὸν πόλεμον.

sixth century, but it does attest to a committed and active military alliance. It is impossible to doubt that meeting the expenditure associated with such activities was a catalyst to the development of cooperative coinage in Boiotia.

It was, however, only one factor among many. Before the second series, in which the poliadic initials were moved from the obverse to the reverse, the largest denomination minted was the drachma; obols and hemiobols were also produced. The prevalence of small denominations certainly suggests that trade was, from the earliest period, another significant factor in addition to the military one, and if the picture we have sketched above of resource complementarity and regional autarky is correct, then that should not be at all surprising.[80] The inclusion of Akraiphia among the earliest *poleis* to participate in this cooperative arrangement might be associated with the remarkable prominence of the city's sanctuary of Apollo Ptoios in this period. In addition to Akraiphian dedications, we have record of an Akraiphian sculptor being commissioned by a group of Thebans to produce works for dedication at the Ptoion in the period c. 540–520, and if anything is clear from Herodotos' narrative of Mys' visit to the sanctuary (Hdt. 8.135), it is that Thebes had close ties to it (Ducat 1971: 379–383 nos. 232–234, pls. 128–129).[81] The importance of minting activity to a community in charge of a sanctuary of wide repute is well illustrated by the coinage of Elis for Olympia (Milne 1931; Seltman 1975 [1921]; Kraay 1976: 103–107; Walker 2004). This connection is complicated when the catchment area of a sanctuary is not panhellenic but regional, and when it appears to play a role in the articulation of a regional group identity and the state power that governs in the name of that group. This is precisely what seems to have been happening at the Ptoion in the late sixth and early fifth centuries. In the same period, the Ptoion, as well as the regionally significant sanctuary of Poseidon at Onkhestos, saw significant building activity, and this must be yet another factor contributing to the early appearance and wide regional diffusion of coinage in Boiotia. In each case, multiple Boiotian *poleis* were involved in the adornment of sanctuaries, the pursuit of military activities, and exchange, and this helps us to understand why the coins should have been minted as they were, with a common type and on a common standard. The cooperative coinage of late sixth- and early fifth-century Boiotia should not be taken as the mark of a highly evolved and fully institutionalized "federal state", for which we have no clear evidence before the mid-fifth century (cf. Hansen 1995b: 31; Hansen in Hansen and Nielsen 2004: 431–432).

---

80. As Kagan (2006) notes, a prevalence of smaller denominations at the outset of coining operations has implications for the extent of internal monetization within a *polis* (or *koinon*) as well as the economic orientation of the issuing authority. Even if state expenses were predominantly military in character, i.e., paying locally based troops, they were being met with monetary instruments that were versatile enough to serve in smaller, daily transactions. Large denominations, like staters and possibly even drachmas, were far less versatile in so far as they were functionally limited to high-value transactions, or at least transactions taking place in a context where small change could be readily found to make up the difference between low price and high-value payment.

81. In the early fifth century, a group that described themselves as "the Boiotoi" dedicated a statuette to

A significant change occurs around that time in the coinage of the region, a change that has always, and probably correctly, been understood as an indication of a political change. The *polis* issues seem to stop and are replaced by Theban issues, which continue to carry the now iconic heroic shield on the obverse with Herakles on the reverse in a variety of belligerent attitudes—advancing to combat, kneeling or standing to string a bow (plate 14 no. 31), carrying off the Delphic tripod, or strangling snakes as a child (plate 14 no. 32) (*BMC Central Greece* 70–72 nos. 29–40, pl. 42 nos. 1–8; cf. Kraay 1976: 111). All carry legends (of varying lengths) referring explicitly to Thebes. Herakles, of course, figures prominently in Theban myth and cult (Schachter 1981–94: 2.14–30), and there is every reason to associate this remarkable shift with the expulsion of Athens from the region after the battle of Koroneia in 446 and Thebes' increasingly hegemonic and belligerent role in the *koinon* of Boiotian *poleis*. In the last quarter of the fifth century, Thebes retained its exclusive control of minting authority in the region and adopted reverse types with portrait heads of Herakles and Dionysos (plate 14 nos. 33–34), likewise particularly closely associated with the city. Theban types proliferate in the first quarter of the fourth century, and though it has proved remarkably difficult to establish a firm chronology for the various issues, it is clear that until the early fourth century (perhaps 387), the mints of the other Boiotian *poleis* were entirely inactive.[82] It is important to note that this kind of extreme centralization of minting activity for an entire region in a single *polis* is unparalleled elsewhere.

The economic independence of the other Boiotian *poleis*, whether partial or full, seems to be reflected in two series that must belong to the period of greater *polis* autonomy ushered in by the King's Peace and weakened by the Thebans' victory over Sparta at Leuktra in 371, which secured their hegemony over the region until 338. The first is a series of coins issued by individual *poleis*; the obverse of these coins uniformly bears the heroic shield, while the reverse carries types specific to each *polis*, clearly labeled in a legend (plate 14 nos. 22, 35) (Kraay 1976: 112-114, pls. 363-366 [type III]).[83] The second is a series that seems to build on the first by retaining the symbols appropriate to each *polis* but making them subordinate to a common, larger symbol of an amphora, with the legend BOIΩ. The *polis* symbols become, effectively, mintmarks in an otherwise uniform regional coinage.[84]

(Athena) Pronaia at the Ptoion, suggesting that the sanctuary had become regionally marked (the statuette base survives: Holleaux 1885: 523; Ducat 1971: no. 257 with photo, pl. 141).

82. Kraay (1976: 112–114) is very clear and helpful. He suggests that the King's Peace of 387 allowed the *polis* mints to return to activity, but without explicit evidence that the peace treaty had such far-reaching effects (the autonomy clause is notoriously vague), we remain wary of pinning the change to a single date.

83. For example, the coins of Haliartos have Poseidon hurling a thunderbolt, Tanagra the forepart of a horse (as it did in the mid-fifth-century *polis* issues), Orkhomenos a wreath, Mykalessos a thunderbolt, Pharai an amphora, and Thebes a more elaborate amphora. The types are most easily seen together in Head (1881: 43–60, pl. 4), though he does not include a specimen from Akraiphia (Brett 1955: 137 no. 1011, pl. 53), which brings the total number of attested participating mints to thirteen.

84. Some of the devices, including club and ivy leaf, seem to be associated with the Theban deities who feature so prominently on other indisputably Theban coinage. But others, like the thunderbolt and crescent (plate 14

Thebes appears, however, to have gradually assumed full control of all minting activity in Boiotia, a shift marked by the appearance of the Theban "magistrate coinage" in the early fourth century; it assumed an exclusive role perhaps after 371, and likely continued until Thebes was destroyed in 335.[85]

Attempting to trace patterns in minting activity from coins that survive in wildly various quantities can tell us only the barest facts about the cooperative arrangement: that it existed and that its precise configuration shifted slightly over time, perhaps in response to particular political changes, but it cannot tell us why the arrangement was adopted or maintained or how the coinage was used. From a systematic study of hoards, however, we can learn about circulation patterns, trade regions, and, by extension, the scale of the monetized economy of the participating states.

The only Boiotian coins discovered in hoards buried outside Boiotia in the period from 500 to 400 are issues of Tanagra and Thebes, and these in extremely small numbers. The massive Asyut hoard contained four Boiotian coins minted sometime before 480; two are Tanagran, and the other two appear to be anepigraphic (Price and Waggoner 1975: nos. 246–249). A single Tanagran stater was included in a hoard of 32 coins otherwise composed entirely of Aiginetan and Elian issues, buried in Agrinion in northwestern Aitolia sometime in the fifth century (*IGCH* 37). And a hoard buried in Arkadia (?) in the late fifth century included 1 drachma and 2 triobols of Thebes along with 84 Peloponnesian and 4 Aiginetan coins (*IGCH* 40).[86] By contrast, the two known hoards buried within Boiotia in the same period include issues of Orkhomenos, Haliartos, and Pharai, along with those of Thebes and Tanagra, in far greater volume.[87] The fifth-century hoards thus suggest that the coins of the Boiotian *poleis* stayed for the most part within the region, where they appear to have circulated quite freely. It is thus plausible to suggest that the coins were struck as they were, on a common standard with a common obverse type and indication of the *polis* mint from which they issued, to meet expenses associated with the variety of undertakings in which multiple Boiotian *poleis* participated in this period, ranging from templebuilding and large-scale sculpture to shipbuilding and military expeditions.[88] The small denominations, we

nos. 22, 37), can be exclusively tied to Mykalessos and Thespiai (*BMC Central Greece* pl. 16 nos. 5–9).

85. Kraay (1976: 114) noted that the beginning of this coinage was difficult to determine, and he speculated that it could have overlapped with the BOIΩ issues, but Hepworth (1998: 63 n. 16) has shown, with his die-study, that they must have, beginning in the period 400–390.

86. This hoard was formerly in the collection of T. L. Shear, and was stolen in December 1968. A note from Mrs. Shear on file at the ANS dates the three Theban issues to the period c. 550–480, based on the chronology of Head (1881). According to the chronology we have outlined above, they belonged to the period c. 525–456, and were thus in circulation for a rather long time before being buried.

87. *CH* 5.10: Agoriani 1972 (buried c. 450); *CH* 2.31: Boiotia 1955 (buried c. 410). A third hoard, *IGCH* 42: Euboia or Boiotia 1951, is of uncertain provenance but contained, out of 143 total coins, 68 to 70 Theban issues and 1 coin of Tanagra.

88. In 413 "the Boiotians" were required to supply Agis with 25 ships (Th. 8.3.2). Demosthenes' attempt to take Siphai and Delion in the winter of 424/3 suggests some relatively significant Boiotian ship-holdings at that time (Th. 4.89–101).

suppose, were used to engage in the exchange relations between communities in the region that the *koinon* sought to protect. The agreement that was reached, whether by cooperation or by coercion, between three and then seven cities to mint coins on the same standard with a common type, in practice facilitated regional trade and payments on a scale far greater than it did any extraregional transactions.

In the fourth century, a slightly different pattern emerges. Boiotian coins still appear not to have traveled far, but of those found in hoards outside the region in the period 400-335, 99.13% were staters. These hoards were found primarily in Thessaly, but also in Elis, Khalkidike, and Arkadia.[89] The general picture is also corroborated anecdotally: the enormous Myron hoard (*IGCH* 62), found near Karditsa in Thessaly and buried sometime in the second half of the fourth century, included more than 1,647 coins in total: 1,078 were coins from Boiotian mints; 99.26% of these were staters.

For Boiotia itself and its mints, the hoard evidence thus maps extraordinarily well onto the economic picture developed above, of resource complementarity and economic autarky occurring at the regional scale within a landscape fragmented at the microregional scale, and of the regional power structure, the *koinon*, taking steps to secure intraregional economic mobility. The arrangement for monetary production adopted by the *poleis* of Boiotia reflects their economic behavior and the monetary needs that arose from that behavior. Given the frustrating paucity of evidence, such a well-tailored "fit" is, to adopt a metaphor used by John Lewis Gaddis, perhaps the most compelling historical explanation we can provide.[90]

Akhaia

We began with Boiotia as a case study for cooperative coinage within the framework of an evolving *koinon* not only because it is the most familiar instance of the phenomenon, but also because there is more evidence for it than for most other cases. The coinage of Akhaia is, by contrast, most familiar in the Hellenistic period, but it begins in the fourth century and, like the Boiotian material, suggests that cooperative coinage should be understood primarily as an economic phenomenon. The silver triobol of Pellene, mentioned above (plate 14 no. 23), is one of a group of coins issued by Akhaian *poleis* in the early fourth century that must be seen as the product of some kind of cooperative arrangement. Pellene, Dyme, Helike, Aigai, and Aigeira issued triobols, obols, and bronzes that carry on the obverse the head of a local deity and on the reverse either the initial letters of the name of the *polis* or a small image related to the cult of the deity represented on the obverse, all within a wreath

---

89. *CH* 1.27: Thessaly c. 1966; *CH* 1.33: Thessaly 1969; *IGCH* 58 (*CH* 5.20, 8.128): Atrax 1968; *IGCH* 62: Myron 1914; *CH* 9.77: Thessaly 1996; *CH* 8.131: Lamia; *CH* 7.43: Domokos 1979; *IGCH* 48: Andritsaina (Elis) 1948 (The Katoche hoard); *CH* 1.37 (possibly part of *IGCH* 385): Olympias (Khalkidike) 1965?; *CH* 8.147: Kato Klitoria (Arkadia) 1980.

90. Gaddis (2002) explores the metaphors of both cartography and tailoring (inter alia) in his stimulating analysis of historical method.

(plate 14 no. 38).[91] The wreath is the symbol that points to cooperation; it appears on the reverse of every coin issued by the Akhaian *koinon* in the Hellenistic period, but its origins clearly lie in the fourth century. The participation of Helike in this cooperative arrangement allows us to give a fixed *terminus ante quem* of 373, when the *polis* was destroyed by earthquake and tsunami.[92] Although the number of known specimens of this series is very small, there is no evidence for the production of any denomination larger than the triobol by any of the *polis* mints of Akhaia in the early fourth century. There are, however, several specimens of staters, drachmas, and triobols minted with the reverse legend AXAIΩN. The drachma (plate 14 no. 39) has on the obverse an elaborate and carefully executed female head, with hair bound up in a *krobylos*, and on the reverse an armed Athena, charging right with spear and shield, the legend in the left field, and a small crested helmet (perhaps a mintmark?) in the right field. Precisely the same obverse and reverse types are found on the triobols, known from only three specimens (*SNG Cop. Phliasia-Laconia* 226; Imhoof-Blumer 1883: 156.2; *BMC Thessaly to Aetolia* 48, pl. 10 no. 17).[93] The stater, known from only one coin in the British Museum, has a very similar obverse type, but on the reverse is an enthroned Zeus, who holds in his outstretched right hand an eagle, and in his left a long scepter resting on the ground. Here the small crested helmet is in the left field with the legend in the right (plate 14 no. 40).[94] It is important to note that the fourth-century AXAIΩN coinage does not bear the wreath on the reverse, although the contemporary *polis* issues all do. It seems likely that the full, cooperative legend was thought to obviate the need for the visual symbol of cooperation—the wreath—but this is only speculation. What is of significance for our argument is that the wreath was adopted as the reverse type (with *polis*-monogram) by multiple Akhaian *poleis* in the early fourth century, and on the league coinage of the Hellenistic period.

These little-studied coins are typically dated, on the basis of stylistic similarity with other northern Peloponnesian coins, to the second quarter of the fourth century, but there are good historical reasons for thinking that they were probably issued concurrently with

---

91. Pellene triobols: Bloesch (1987: 2150); ANS 1944.100.39485; *SNG Cop. Phliasia-Laconia* 209–210; Boutin (1979: 4040); *SNG Lockett* 2350; *SNG Fitzwilliam* 3567–3569; *SNG Manchester* 1069; *SNG Delep.* 1968; Babelon (1925: 2239). Three triobols of Pellene were found in the Kato Klitoria (1980) hoard, buried c. 340–330, thus securing the fourth-century date for the issues. See Warren 1989; *CH* 8.147. Two known specimens of obols from Pellene have a kithara on the reverse in place of, or in addition to, the legend: *SNG Cop. Phliasia-Laconia* 212; *SNG Fitzwilliam* 3569a. Dyme bronzes: *SNG Cop. Phliasia-Laconia* 145–146; *SNG Fitzwilliam* 3559. Only three examples of the Helike bronzes are known: Lambros (1891: 16, pl. 1.15); Babelon (1907, no. 831, pl. 223.3); Walker (2006: 134 lot 497, illustrated in pl. 14, no. 38 here). Aigai silver triobols: *SNG Cop. Phliasia-Laconia* 125, *SNG Fitzwilliam* 3553, ANS 1944.100.37614. Aigeira: *SNG Cop. Phliasia-Laconia* 127.

92. Helike has been the subject of ongoing research; see Katsonopoulou et al. (1998) and, on the events of 373, Mackil (2004: 497–499).

93. The British Museum coin was attributed by Gardner to Phthiotic Akhaia, which, in light of its comfortable fit with the rest of this remarkable Akhaian series, and the relevance of the types to the cultic landscape of the *koinon* (see below), should be disregarded.

94. Wroth (1902: 324–326, pl. 16 no. 14); Head (1911: 416); Kraay and Hirmer (1966: 516).

the wreath coinages of the Akhaian *poleis* in the first quarter of the fourth century.[95] First, sometime before 389 the Akhaians captured Kalydon, across the Korinthian Gulf, and made the inhabitants "Akhaian citizens", but in that year they were compelled to install a garrison to combat the acquisitive designs that the Akarnanians, with Athenian and Boiotian allies, had on the place (Xen. *Hell.* 4.6.1).[96] Kalydon, and also Naupaktos, were still garrisoned by the Akhaians in 367, when they were "liberated" by Epaminondas (D.S. 15.75).[97] This episode, narrated in the barest fashion by Xenophon, tells us that "the Akhaians" had some-time before 389 developed a political organization sufficiently sophisticated as to bestow citizenship upon the whole populations of other cities (this incident is our earliest evidence for the existence of an Akhaian *koinon*), and also that they were engaged in some extraordinarily expensive military activities. The (apparent) concentration of the early fourth-century ΑΧΑΙΩΝ coinage on higher-denomination issues suggests that it was produced to meet the kinds of high costs associated above all with military activity requiring the transfer of large sums. Psoma and Tsangari (2003: 116–117) suggest that this coinage should be associated with Akhaian participation in the Third Sacred War during 352/1, and while that is possible, it is certain that the maintenance of a garrison over more than twenty years would have been a more significant expense and would have required some form of high-denomination coinage in the first quarter of the fourth century. Whether it was the annexation of Kalydon and Naupaktos, the Third Sacred War, or some other major military commitment of which no record survives is perhaps not important. These are only examples and possibilities to show that in the first half of the fourth century the Akhaians were undertaking joint actions that incurred high expenditures and that would likely have demanded coinage in larger denominations than that usually circulating in the region for trade purposes. Second, it is also likely that the ΑΧΑΙΩΝ coinage was issued contemporaneously with the *polis* issues precisely because there is little denominational overlap. The cooperative coinage of fourth-century Akhaia might reflect an arrangement in which the cities minted denominations that would be useful at the local level, while the *koinon* minted larger denominations to meet the expenses of extended, joint military action.

The significance of the wreathed *polis* issues and the ΑΧΑΙΩΝ coinage of the fourth century is highlighted when we consider its place on the broader trajectory of Akhaian coinage. It appears that minting activity in Akhaia was concentrated in the hands of the *koinon* from its refoundation in 280 until around 191, when several *poleis* again minted coins,[98] simply adding the first letters of the *polis* to the wreathed ΑΧ(ΑΙΩΝ) monogram

95. Stylistic similarities with the female head on the obverse of drachmas and triobols to types at Stymphalos, Messene, and Pheneos: *BMC Peloponnesus* pls. 37 no. 4, 22 no. 1, 36 no. 7.

96. Bommeljé (1988: 314) suggests that the Akhaian occupation of Kalydon might extend back to 426 (with Th. 3.102.5).

97. We do not know when the garrison was installed at Naupaktos.

98. These issues are best known from the Agrinion hoard (Thompson 1968: 85–104, esp. 90; cf. Grandjean 2000: 324–327).

on the reverse. This appears to reflect not simply the political might of the *koinon* in this period but its increasing control over the regional economy of Akhaia. Polybios' famous assertion that the Akhaians unified "almost the entire Peloponnese" by imposing a uniform set of laws, weights, measures, and coins, along with common magistrates, councillors, and judges, is a clear indication of the significant economic role played by the *koinon*, even if it lacks nuance.[99] We noted above that in the third century member *poleis* were obligated to pay an *eisphora* to the *koinon*, which in turn levied and dispatched military forces, but in the same period the *koinon* appears also to have had the authority to impose embargoes on the export of grain from the entire territory it governed (*SEG* 25.445 lines 15–17). These are only a few examples among many of the kinds of large, group expenditures incurred by the *poleis* of the Akhaian *koinon* in the Hellenistic period for which cooperative coinage would have been an extremely useful monetary instrument. Fourth-century Akhaia is much less well attested, but some of the same arrangements may have been in place, for which *polis* issues with wreath reverse, as well as the ΑΧΑΙΩΝ coinage, would have beeen useful. What is important is to see those early issues an early phase of the same developmental trajectory of state-produced instruments for the entire region.

Little hoard evidence exists that might shed light on the circulation of Akhaian coins before the mid-second century, but what there is suggests that Akhaian coinage in all periods did not travel far outside the region. The Kato Klitoria hoard (*CH* 8.147; Warren 1989), buried in northern Arkadia around 340–330, included three obols of Pellene in a remarkably diverse hoard of small silver denominations from the entire Korinthian Gulf region, and a hoard found near Itea (*CH* 8.254), on the northern shore of the gulf, included a single triobol from Aigai in an enormous collection of silver coins buried around 290–270.[100] The current state of the evidence makes it impossible to isolate with any confidence the primary purposes behind Akhaian monetary issues, but the gradual shift from decentralized, cooperative minting in the fourth century, as the *koinon* began to develop and expand its interests beyond its own borders, to centralization of production in the hands of the *koinon* in the third century, suggests that "political alliance coinages" rather constitute a regularization and protection of economic practices in a process that might best be thought of as institutionalization.

The *poleis* of Boiotia in the fifth century, and Akhaia in the fourth, produced and used cooperative coinages not so much to advertise their developing regional political arrangements as to facilitate the payment by multiple *poleis* of taxes into a common treasury, pat-

---

99. Plb. 2.37.10: τοιαύτην καὶ τηλικαύτην ἐν τοῖς καθ᾽ ἡμᾶς καιροῖς ἔσχε προκοπὴν καὶ συντέλειαν τοῦτο τὸ μέρος ὥστε μὴ μόνον συμμαχικὴν καὶ φιλικὴν κοινωνίαν γεγονέναι πραγμάτων περὶ αὐτούς, ἀλλὰ καὶ νόμοις χρῆσθαι τοῖς αὐτοῖς καὶ σταθμοῖς καὶ μέτροις καὶ νομίσμασι, πρὸς δὲ τούτοις ἄρχουσι, βουλευταῖς, δικασταῖς, τοῖς αὐτοῖς, καθόλου δὲ τούτῳ μόνῳ διαλλάττειν τοῦ μὴ μιᾶς πόλεως διάθεσιν ἔχειν σχεδὸν τὴν σύμπασιν Πελοπόννησον.

100. The Agrinion hoard, although aberrant in the sheer volume of Akhaian (and other) coins included, does accord quite well with these two hoards in suggesting that the coinages of the states on or near the Korinthian Gulf circulated relatively widely within that region.

terns of regional exchange, economically motivated mobility (instantiated particularly by the rights of *enktesis/eppasis* extended to all citizens of member *poleis* throughout the *koinon*), and collective activities like construction of shared sanctuaries, manning garrisons, and undertaking military campaigns. This deeper economic context for the production of cooperative coinage suggests that the *koinon* itself developed as it did, granting such rights and protecting the regional economy, in part to facilitate patterns of economic behavior that were, on a fundamental level, necessary for the survival of the participating communities.

CONCLUSIONS

The phenomenon of cooperative coinage stands in need of new interpretative approaches, since older frameworks, like Head's, are limited and limiting in their heuristic power and do not penetrate deeply enough into the motivations, practices, and institutions that brought the coins into existence. Our approach has been to consider the coins as only one part of the broader economic context, in which economic needs, practices, and strategies are considered alongside the issue of coin production. Dispensing with traditional categorizations, it becomes possible to see that, taken as a whole, the phenomenon is both vertically and horizontally expansive. It occurred across multiple scales, from formally institutionalized bilateral treaties to multilateral actions carried out by up to a dozen cities in an increasingly formalized manner. Significantly, it also occurred within a variety of political contexts. The phenomenon was, in short, a great deal more pervasive and adaptable than has ever been suggested; it is also now clear that the benefits provided by cooperative coinages were widely recognized and desirable. While we readily acknowledge that there were context-dependent complexities in each instance of cooperative coinage, we argue that the phenomenon of cooperative coinage should be seen as representing a whole spectrum of interstate economic strategies. The political import of coins has long been recognized but, we believe, it has been overemphasized at the expense of their economic import. If we shift the focus to consider coinage as an economic instrument created and made useful by political authorities, then the phenomenon of cooperative coinage points to the extremely important fact that Greek *poleis*, in the Archaic and Classical periods as well as in the Hellenistic, cooperated across their political boundaries in economic activity in ways more complex, and more intimately bound up with political power, than trade. This politically sanctioned inter-*polis* economic cooperation was motivated in the case of the Boiotian and Akhaian *koina* (to mention only the two examples explored in detail here) by an economic interdependence created by small settlement size, fragmented landscapes, and regional resource complementarity, and in the case of Mytilene and Phokaia by a strategy for increasing state revenues while buffering risk, by sharing both. Detailed studies of other instances may raise other motivations but will, we believe, still contribute to the larger point, that we should begin to think seriously about complex economic cooperation across political boundaries in the ancient Greek Mediterranean.

Key to Plates 13–14

1. Lucania, Sybaris, c. 530 BC, AR stater, 7.97 g (ANS 1957.172.321, Hoyt Miller bequest).

2. Bruttium, Kroton, c. 530 BC, AR stater, 8.19 g (ANS 1957.172.395, Hoyt Miller bequest).

3. Bruttium, Kaulonia, c. 530 BC, AR stater, 8.26 g (ANS 1980.109.13, Arthur J. Fecht bequest).

4. Lucania, Metaponton, c. 530 BC, AR stater, 8.27 g (ANS 0000.999.3445).

5. Lucania, Poseidonia, c. 520 BC, AR stater, 7.28 g (ANS 0000.999.3472).

6. Kalabria, Taras, c. 520 BC, AR stater, 7.49 g (ANS 1967.152.17, Adra M. Newell bequest).

7. Lucania, Kroton-Sybaris, c. 500, AR stater, 7.83 g (ANS 1968.19.1).

8. Lesbos, Mytilene, c. 501 BC, EL *hektē*, 2.56 g, 9:00 (ANS 1941.153.813, W. Gedney Beatty bequest).

9. Lesbos, Mytilene, c. 356 BC, EL *hektē*, 2.56 g, 12:00 (ANS 1975.218.41, gift of Burton Y. Berry).

10. Lesbos, Mytilene, c. 328 BC, EL *hektē*, 2.55 g, 6:00 (ANS 1967.152.427, Adra M. Newell bequest).

11. Ionia, Phokaia, c. 518 BC, EL *hektē*, 2.57 g (ANS 1967.152.449, Adra M. Newell bequest).

12. Ionia, Phokaia, c. 506 BC, EL *hektē*, 2.57 g (ANS 1977.158.32, Robert F. Kelley bequest).

13. Ionia, Phokaia, c. 394 BC, EL *hektē*, 2.53 g (ANS 1944.100.46741, Edward T. Newell bequest).

14. Lesbos, Mytilene, c. 410 BC, AR hemidrachm, 1.94 g, 11:00 (ANS 1967.197.4).

15. Lesbos, Mytilene, 4th century, AR diobol, 1.35 g, 6:00 (ANS 1944.100.44355, Edward T. Newell bequest).

16. Ionia, Phokaia, c. 500 BC, AR trihemiobol, 1.33 g (ANS 1977.158.325, Robert F. Kelley bequest).

17. Ionia, Phokaia, c. 500 BC, AR *tetartēmorion*, 0.19 g (ANS 1944.100.46730, Edward T. Newell bequest).

18. Mysia, Kyzikos, 5th century, EL stater, 15.96 g (ANS 1977.158.19, Robert F. Kelley bequest).

19. Mysia, Kyzikos, c. 500 BC, EL *hektē*, 2.67 g (ANS 1944.100.42713, Edward T. Newell bequest).

20. Mysia, Kyzikos, 5th century, AR obol, 1.13 g, 6:00 (ANS 1983.178.2, gift of Nancy M. Waggoner).

21. Mysia, Kyzikos, late 6th century, AR trihemiobol, 0.97 g (ANS 1987.2.3).

22. Boiotia, Mykalessos, c. 380 BC, AR obol, 0.86 g, 12:00 (ANS 1944.100.19911, Edward T. Newell bequest).

23. Akhaia, Pellene, c. 370 BC, AR triobol, 2.56 g, 11:00 (ANS 1944.100.39485, Edward T. Newell bequest).

24. Boiotia, Thebes, late 6th century, AR stater, 6.12 g (ANS 1980.109.53, Arthur J. Fecht bequest).

25. Boiotia, Tanagra, late 6th century, AR stater, 6.06 g (ANS 1944.100.19806, Edward T. Newell bequest).

26. Boiotia, Haliartos/Hyettos, late 6th century, AR obol, 0.96 g (ANS 1944.100.19804, Edward T. Newell bequest).

27. Boiotia, Koroneia, late 6th century, AR obol, 0.86 g (ANS 1944.100.19827, Edward T. Newell bequest).

28. Boiotia, Pharai, late 6th century, AR stater, 12.06 g (ANS 1941.153.447, W. Gedney Beatty bequest).

29. Boiotia, Tanagra, mid-5th century, AR stater, 12.15 g (ANS 1944.100.19849, Edward T. Newell bequest).

30. Boiotia, Thebes, mid-5th century, AR stater, 11.93 g (ANS 1944.100.19847, Edward T. Newell bequest).

31. Boiotia, Thebes, mid-5th century, AR stater, 12.17 g (ANS 1944.100.19851, Edward T. Newell bequest).

32. Boiotia, Thebes, mid-5th century, AR stater, 11.75 g (ANS 1944.100.19854, Edward T. Newell bequest).

33. Boiotia, Thebes, late 5th century, AR stater, 11.98 g (ANS 1944.100.19856, Edward T. Newell bequest).

34. Boiotia, Thebes, late 5th century, AR stater, 11.04 g (ANS 1941.153.456, W. Gedney Beatty bequest).

35. Boiotia, Haliartos, early 4th century, AR stater, 11.47 g, 1:00 (ANS 1948.25.1).

36. Boiotia, Plataia, early 4th century, AR triobol, 2.69 g (ANS 1944.100.20056, Edward T. Newell bequest).

37. Boiotia, Thespiai, early 4th century, AR stater, 12.08 g (ANS 1952.128.2).

38. Akhaia, Helike, early 4th century, AE *dichalkon*, 2.98 g, 2:00 (LHS auction 96, lot 497).

39. Akhaia, Akhaian *koinon*, early 4th century, AR drachm, 5.79 g, 12:00 (ANS 1950.53.6).

40. Akhaia, Akhaian *koinon*, early 4th century, AR stater (courtesy of the Trustees of the British Museum).

BIBLIOGRAPHY

Ashton, R. H. J. 2001. The coinage of Rhodes 408–c. 190 BC. In: A. Meadows and K. Shipton, eds., *Money and its uses in the ancient Greek world*, pp. 79–115. Oxford: Oxford University Press.

Ashton, R. H. J., P. Kinns, K. Konuk, and A. R. Meadows. 2002. The Hecatomnus hoard (*CH* 5.17, 8.96, 9.387). In: A. R. Meadows and U. Wartenberg, eds., *Coin hoards,* vol. 9: *Greek hoards,* pp. 95–158. London: Royal Numismatic Society.

Austin, M. M., and P. Vidal-Naquet. 1977. *Economic and social history of ancient Greece: an introduction.* Berkeley: University of California Press.

Babelon, E. 1907. *Traité des monnaies grecques et romaines*. Part II, vol 1. Paris: Ernest Leroux.

———. 1925. *Catalogue de la collection de Luynes. Monnaies grecques II. Grèce continentale et îles*. Paris: Académie des Inscriptions et Belles-Lettres.

Bakhuizen, S. C. 1988. A note on syntely: the case of Boeotia. Ἐπετηρὶς τῆς Ἑταιρείας Βοιωτικῶν Μελετῶν 1a: 279–289.

———. 1994. Thebes and Boeotia in the fourth century BC. *Phoenix* 48: 307–330.

Balcer, J. 1970. Phokaia and Teos: a monetary alliance. *Schweizerische numismatische Rundschau (Revue suisse de numismatique)* 49: 25–33.

Balmuth, M. S. 2001. ed. *Hacksilber to coinage: new insights into the monetary history of the Near East and Greece: a collection of eight papers presented at the 99th annual meeting of the Archaeological Institute of America*. New York: American Numismatic Society.

Barron, J. P. 1966. *The silver coins of Samos*. London: Athlone P.

Bingen, J. 1954. Inscriptions d'Achaie. *Bulletin de correspondance hellénique* 78: 74–88, 395–409.

Bloesch, H. 1987. *Griechische Münzen in Winterthur*. Winterthur: Münzkabinett Winterthur.

BMC Central Greece: B. V. Head, edited by Reginald S. Poole. 1884. *Catalogue of Greek coins in the British Museum. Central Greece (Locris, Phocis, Boeotia, and Euboea)*. London: British Museum.

BMC Peloponnesus: P. Gardner, edited by R. S. Poole. 1887. *Catalogue of Greek coins in the British Museum. Peloponnesus*. London: British Museum.

BMC Thessaly to Aetolia: P. Gardner, edited by R. S. Poole. 1883. *Catalogue of Greek coins in the British Museum. Thessaly to Aetolia*. London: British Museum.

Bodenstedt, F. 1981. *Die Elektronmünzen von Phokaia und Mytilene*. Tübingen: Verlag Ernst Wasmuth.

Bommeljé, S. 1988. Aeolis in Aetolia. Thuk. III.102.5 and the origins of the Aetolian ethnos. *Historia* 37: 297–316.

Boutin, S. 1979. *Catalogue des monnaies grecques antiques de l'ancienne collection Pozzi. Monnaies frappées en Europe*. Maastricht: A. G. van der Dussen.

Bresson, A. 2000. *La cité marchande*. Bordeaux: Ausonius.

———. 2005. Coinage and money supply in the Hellenistic age. In: Z. H. Archibald, J. K. Davies, and V. Gabrielsen, eds., *Making, moving and managing: the new world of ancient economies, 323–31 BC*, pp. 44–72. Oxford: Oxbow.

Brett, A. B. 1955. *Catalogue of Greek coins*. Museum of Fine Arts, Boston. Boston: Museum of Fine Arts.

Burelli, L. 1978. L'Accordo monetale tra Focea e Mitilene (I.G., XII, 2, 1). *Numismatica e Antichità Classiche* 7: 43–51.

Callataÿ, F. de. 2000. Guerres et monnayages à l'époque hellénistique. Essai de mise en perspective suivi d'une annexe sur le monnayage de Mithridate VI Eupator. In: J. Andreau, P. Briant, and R. Descat, eds., *Économie antique. La guerre dans les économies antiques*, *entretiens d'archéologie et d'histoire*, pp. 337–364. Saint-Bertrand-de-Comminges: Musée archéologique départmental.

CH: *Coin Hoards*. 1975–. London: Royal Numismatic Society.

Cohen, E. E. 1992. *Athenian economy and society: a banking perspective*. Princeton: Princeton University Press.

Ducat, J. 1971. *Les kouroi du Ptoion*. Paris: Boccard.

Étienne, R., and P. Roesch. 1978. Convention militaire entre les cavaliers d'Orchomène et ceux de Chéronée. *Bulletin de correspondance hellénique* 102: 359–374.

Feyel, M. 1936. Études d'épigraphie béotienne. *Bulletin de correspondance hellénique* 60: 175–183, 389–415.

———. 1937. Études d'épigraphie béotienne. *Bulletin de correspondance hellénique* 61: 217–235.

FGrH: F. Jacoby. 1923–1958. *Die Fragmente der griechischen Historiker*. Leiden.

Figueira, T. 1998. T*he power of money: coinage and politics in the Athenian empire*. Philadelphia: University of Pennsylvania Press.

Finley, M. I. 1985. *The ancient economy*. London: Hogarth Press.

Foraste, D. D. 1993. The fourth century mint of Anaktorian. In: *Convegno del Centro Internazionale di Studi Numismatici. La monetazione corinzia in Occidente: atti del IX Convegno del Centro internazionale di studi numismatici, Napoli, 27-28 ottobre 1986*, pp. 43–59. Roma: Istituto italiano di numismatica.

Fowler, B. 1957. Thucydides I.107–8 and the Tanagran federal issues. *Phoenix* 11: 164–170.

Foxhall, L. 2002. Access to resources in classical Greece: The egalitarianism of the *polis* in practice. In: P. Cartledge, E. E. Cohen, and L. Foxhall, eds., *Money, labour and land: approaches to the economies of ancient Greece*, pp. 209–220. London: Routledge.

Franke, P. 1970. ΦΕΘΑΛΟΙ-ΦΕΤΑΛΟΙ-ΠΕΤΘΑΛΟΙ-ΘΕΣΣΑΛΟΙ. Zur Geschichte Thessaliens im 5. Jahrhundert v. Chr. *Archäologischer Anzeiger*: 85-93.

Gaddis, J. L. 2002. *The landscape of history. How historians map the past*. Oxford: Oxford University Press.

Gerin, D. 1986. Les statères de la ligue arcadienne. *Schweizerische numismatische Rundschau (Revue suisse de numismatique)* 65: 13–31.

GGM: K. Müller. 1855–61. *Geographici graeci minores*.

Giacchero, M. 1980. I motivi finanziari e commerciale dell'unione monetaria fra Mitilene e Focea. *Rivista Italiana di Numismatica* 82: 1–10.

Grandjean, C. 2000. Guerre et monnaie en Grèce ancienne: le cas du *koinon* achaien. In: J. Andreau, P. Briant, and R. Descat, eds., *Économie antique: la guerre dans les économies antiques*, pp. 315–336. Saint-Bertrand-de-Comminges: Musée archéologique départmental.

Greco, E. 1990. Serdaioi. *A.I.O.N. Annali di archeologia e storia antica. Dipartimento di studi del mondo classico e del mediterraneo antico* 12: 39–57.

———. 1998. Le fondazioni degli Achei in Occidente. In: D. Katsonopoulou, S. Soter, and D. Schilardi, eds., *Helike II. Ancient Helike and Aigialeia. Proceedings of the Second*

International Conference, Aigion, 1–3 December 1995, pp. 335–347. Athens: The Helike Society.

Hansen, M. H. 1995a. The 'autonomous city-state'. Ancient fact or modern fiction? In: M. H. Hansen and K. Raaflaub, eds., *Studies in the ancient Greek polis*, pp. 21–43. Stuttgart: Franz Steiner Verlag.

———. 1995b. Boiotian *poleis*—a test case. In: M. H. Hansen, ed., *Sources for the ancient Greek city-state. Acts of the Copenhagen Polis Centre*, vol. 2, pp. 13–63. Copenhagen: Royal Danish Academy of Sciences and Letters.

———. 1997. A typology of dependent *poleis*. In: T. H. Nielsen, ed., *Yet more studies in the ancient Greek polis*, pp. 29–37. Stuttgart: Franz Steiner Verlag.

———, and T. H. Nielsen, eds. 2004. *An inventory of Archaic and Classical poleis. An investigation conducted by the Copenhagen Polis Centre for the Danish National Research Foundation*. Oxford: Oxford University Press.

Head, B. V. 1881. *On the chronological sequence of the coins of Boeotia*. London: Rollin and Feuardent.

———. 1911. *Historia numorum*. 2nd edition. Oxford: Clarendon Press.

Healy, J. F. 1957. Notes on the monetary union between Mytilene and Phokaia. *Journal of Hellenic Studies* 77.2: 267–268.

Heisserer, A. J. 1984. *IG* XII, 2, 1 (the monetary pact between Mytilene and Phokaia). *Zeitschrift für Papyrologie und Epigraphik* 55: 115–132.

Hepworth, R. G. 1998. The 4th century BC magistrate coinage of the Boiotian confederacy. *Νομισμάτικα Χρόνικα* 17: 61–90.

Holleaux, M. 1885. Fouilles au temple d'Apollon Ptoos. *Bulletin de correspondance hellénique* 9: 520–524.

Horden, P., and N. Purcell. 2000. *The corrupting sea: a study of Mediterranean history*. Oxford: Blackwell.

Hornblower, S. 1991. *A commentary on Thucydides*. Volume I: Books I–III. Oxford: Clarendon Press.

Howgego, C. 1990. Why did ancient states strike coins? *Numismatic Chronicle* 150: 1–25.

———, V. Heuchert, and A. Burnett, eds. 2005. *Coinage and identity in the Roman provinces*. Oxford: Oxford University Press.

IG: Inscriptiones Graecae. 1873–.

IGCH: M. Thompson, O. Mørkholm, and C. M. Kraay, eds. 1973. *An Inventory of Greek Coin Hoards*. New York: American Numismatic Society.

Imhoof-Blumer, F. 1883. *Monnaies grecques*. Amsterdam: J. Müller.

Kagan, J. H. 1998. Epidamnus or Ephyre (Elea): a note on the coinage of Corinth and her colonies at the outbreak of the Peloponnesian War. In: R. Ashton and S. Hurter, eds., *Studies in Greek numismatics in memory of Martin Jessop Price*, pp. 163–173. London: Spink.

———. 2006. Small change and the beginning of coinage at Abdera. In: P. G. van Alfen, ed., *Agoranomia: studies in money and exchange presented to John H. Kroll*, pp. 49–60. New York: American Numismatic Society.

Kallet, L. 2001. *Money and the corrosion of power in Thucydides. The Sicilian expedition and its aftermath.* Berkeley: University of California Press.

Karwiese, S. 1980. Lysander as Herakliskos Drakonopnigon. *Numismatic Chronicle* 20: 1–27.

Katsonopoulou, D. 1998. Η λατρεία του Ελικωνίκου Ποσειδώνος. Μια νέα θεώρηση. In: D. Katsonopoulou, S. Soter, and D. Schilardi, eds. *Helike II: Ancient Helike and Aigialeia*, pp. 251–265. Athens: P. Hatziyiannis.

———, S. Soter, and D. Schilardi, eds. 1998. *Helike II. Ancient Helike and Aigialeia. Proceedings of the Second International Conference, Aigion, 1–3 December 1995.* Athens: P. Hatziyiannis.

Keyser, P., and D. Clark. 2001. Analyzing and interpreting the metallurgy of early electrum coins. In: M. S. Balmuth, ed. *Hacksilber to coinage: new insights into the monetary history of the Near East and Greece: a collection of eight papers presented at the 99th annual meeting of the Archaeological Institute of America*, pp. 105–126. New York: American Numismatic Society.

Kinns, P. 1983. The Amphictionic coinage reconsidered. *Numismatic Chronicle* 143: 1–22.

Knoepfler, D. 2000. La loi de Daitôndas, les femmes de Thèbes et le collège des béotarques au IVe et au IIIe siècle avant J.-C. In: P. A. Bernardini, ed., *Presenza e funzione della città di Tebe nella cultura greca. Atti del Convegno Internazionale*, pp. 345–366. Pisa and Roma: Instituti Editoriali e Poligrafici Internazionali.

Kraay, C. M. 1956. The Archaic owls of Athens: classification and chronology. *Numismatic Chronicle* 16: 43–68.

———. 1976. *Archaic and Classical Greek coins.* Berkeley: University of California Press.

———. 1984. Greek coinage and war. In: W. Heckel and R. Sullivan, eds., *Ancient coins of the Graeco-Roman world: the Nickle numismatic papers,* pp. 3–18. Waterloo, Ont.: Wilfrid Laurier University Press.

———, and M. Hirmer. 1966. *Greek coins.* London.

Kroll, J. H. 1981. From Wappenmünzen to gorgoneia to owls. *American Numismatic Society Museum Notes* 26: 1–32.

———. 2001. Review of Le Rider 2001. *Schweizerische numismatische Rundschau (Revue suisse de numismatique)* 80: 199–206.

———. 2002. Review of K. Shipton and A. Meadows, eds. *Money and its uses in the ancient Greek world. Bryn Mawr Classical Review* 2002.07.24.

Lambros, P. 1891. ΑΝΑΓΡΑΦΗ ΤΩΝ ΝΟΜΙΣΜΑΤΩΝ ΤΗΣ ΚΥΡΙΩΣ ΕΛΛΑΔΟΣ. Athens.

Le Rider, G. 1966. Monnaies crétoises du Ve au Ier siècle av. J.-C. École Française d'Athènes. *Études crétoises* 15. Paris: P. Geuthner.

———. 1971. Sur le monnayage de Byzance au IVᵉ siècle. *Revue Numismatique* 13: 143–153.

———. 1989. À propos d'un passage des *Poroi* de Xénophon: la question du change et les monnaies incuses d'Italie du sud. In: G. Le Rider, K. Jenkins, et al., eds., *Kraay-Mørkholm essays. Numismatic studies in memory of C. M. Kraay and O. Mørkholm*, pp. 159–172. Louvain-la-Neuve: Institut Súperieur d'archéologie et d'histoire de l'art.

———. 2001. *La naissance de la monnaie: pratiques monétaires de l'Orient ancien.* Paris: Presses universitaires de France.

Lewis, D. M. et al., eds. 1992. *The Cambridge ancient history*, vol. 5: *The fifth century BC.* Cambridge: Cambridge University Press.

Liampi, K. 1996. Das Corpus der Obolen und Hemiobolen des thessalischen Bundes und die politische Geschichte Thessaliens im 2. Viertel des 5. Jahrhunderts v. Chr. In: W. Leschhorn, A. V. B. Miron, and A. Miron, eds., *Hellas und der griechische Osten: Studien zur Geschichte und Numismatik der griechischen Welt. Festschrift für Peter Robert Franke zum 70. Geburtstag*, pp. 99–126. Saarbrücken: SDV Saarbrücker Druckerei und Verlag.

MacDonald, D. 1987–88. The significance of the 'Boiotian League/Chalkis' silver issue. *Jahrbuch für Numismatik und Geldgeschichte* 37/38: 23–29.

Mackil, E. 2004. Wandering cities: alternatives to catastrophe in the Greek polis. *American Journal of Archaeology* 100.4: 493–516.

Mann, M. 1986. *The sources of social power*, vol. 1: *A history of power from the beginning to AD 1760.* Cambridge: Cambridge University Press.

Martin, T. R. 1985. *Sovereignty and coinage in Classical Greece.* Princeton: Princeton University Press.

Matzke, M. 2000. Die frühe Münzprägung von Teos in Ionien: chronologische und metrologische Untersuchungen um die Frühzeit der Silbermünzprägung. *Jahrbuch für Numismatik und Geldgeschichte* 50: 21–53.

May, J. M. F. 1966. *The coinage of Abdera (540–345 BC)*, edited by C. M. Kraay and G. K. Jenkins. London: The Royal Numismatic Society.

Melville Jones, J. R. 1998. The value of electrum in Greece and Asia. In: R. Ashton and S. Hurter, eds., *Studies in Greek numismatics in memory of Martin Jessop Price*, pp. 259–268. London: Spink.

———. 1999. Ancient Greek gold coinage up to the time of Philip of Macedon. In: M. Amandry and S. Hurter, eds., *Travaux de numismatique grècque offerts à Georges Le Rider*, pp. 257–275. London: Spink.

Migeotte, L. 1984. *L' emprunt public dans les cités grecques. Recueil des documents et analyse critique.* Québec: Éditions du Sphinx.

———. 1994. Ressources financières des cités béotiennes. In: J. M. Fossey, ed., *Boeotia antiqua IV. Proceedings of the 7th international congress on Boiotian antiquities, Boiotian (and other) epigraphy*, pp. 3–15. Amsterdam: J. C. Gieben.

Milne, J. G. 1931. The coinage of the Eleians. *Numismatic Chronicle* 11: 171–180.

Morgan, C. 2003. *Early Greek states beyond the polis.* London: Routledge.

Mossman, P. L. 1993. *Money of the American colonies and Confederation: a numismatic, economic and historical correlation.* Numismatic Studies 20. New York: American Numismatic Society.

Newell, E. T. 1923. *The Andritsaena hoard.* Numismatic Notes and Monographs 21. New York: American Numismatic Society.

Osborne, R. 1985. The land-leases from Hellenistic Thespiai: a re-examination. In: G. Argoud and P. Roesch, eds., *La Béotie antique. Lyon-Saint-Étienne 16-20 mai 1983,* pp. 317–323. Paris: Editions du CNRS.

Papadopoulos, J. K. 2002. Minting identity: coinage, ideology and the economics of colonization in Akhaian Magna Graecia. *Cambridge Archaeological Journal* 12.1: 21–55.

Papageorgiadou-Banis, Ch. 1993. Koinon of the Keians? The numismatic evidence. *Revue belge de numismatique et de sigillographie* 139: 9–16.

Perdrizet, P. 1899. Inscriptions d'Acraephiae. *Bulletin de correspondance hellénique* 23: 90–96.

Picard, O., and S. Gjongecaj. 1998. Trésor d'Apollonia 1941. *Revue numismatique* 153: 103–105.

Plassart, A. 1935. Locations de domaines sacrés à Thespies. In: G. Doumergue, ed., *Mélanges offerts à M. Octave Navarre par ses élèves et ses amis,* pp. 339–360. Toulouse: E. Privat.

Price, M. J., and N. M. Waggoner. 1975. *Archaic Greek coinage: the Asyut hoard.* London: V. C. Vecchi.

Psoma, S. 1999. Ἀρκαδικόν. *Ὅρος* 13: 81–96.

———, and D. Tsangari. 2003. Monnaie commune et états fédéraux. La circulation des monnayages frappés par les états fédéraux du monde grec. In: K. Buraselis and K. Zoumboulakis, eds., *The idea of European community in history,* vol. 2: *Aspects of connecting poleis and ethne in ancient Greece,* pp. 111–142. Athens: National and Capodistrian University of Athens.

Purcell, N. 2005. The ancient Mediterranean: the view from the customs house. In: W. V. Harris, ed., *Rethinking the Mediterranean,* pp. 200–234. Oxford: Oxford University Press.

Raven, E. J. P. 1950. The Amphictionic coinage of Delphi. *Numismatic Chronicle* 10: 1–22.

Raymond, D. 1953. *Macedonian regal coinage to 413 BC.* Numismatic Notes and Monographs 126. New York: American Numismatic Society.

Reinach, T. 1911. L'Anarchie monétaire et ses remèdes chez les anciens grecs. Mémoires de l'Institut National de France. *Académie des Inscriptions et Belles-Lettres.* 38.2: 351–364.

Rhodes, P. J., and R. Osborne. 2003. *Greek historical inscriptions, 404-323 BC.* Oxford: Oxford University Press.

Rizakis, A. D. 1990. La politeia dans les cités de la confédération achéenne. *Tyche* 5: 109–134.

Roesch, P. 1973. Pouvoir fédéral et vie économique des cités dans la Béotie hellénistique. In: *Akten des VI. Internationalen Kongresses für Griechische und Lateinische Epigraphik, München 1972*, pp. 259–270. München: C.H. Beck.

———. 1982. Études béotiennes. Paris: Boccard.

Rutter, N. K. 1997. *The Greek coinages of southern Italy and Sicily.* London: Spink and Son.

———. et al., eds. 2001. *Historia numorum.* Italy. London: British Museum Press.

Salmon, J. 1993. Trade and Corinthian coins in the west. In: *Convegno del Centro Internazionale di Studi Numismatici. La monetazione corinzia in Occidente: atti del IX Convegno del Centro internazionale di studi numismatici, Napoli, 27–28 ottobre 1986*, pp. 3–17. Roma: Istituto italiano di numismatica.

Schachter, A. 1981–94. *Cults of Boiotia.* London: Institute of Classical Studies.

Schaps, D. M. 2004. *The invention of coinage and the monetization of ancient Greece.* Ann Arbor: University of Michigan Press.

SEG: Supplementum epigraphicum graecum. 1984–. Amsterdam: J. C. Gieben.

Seaford, R. 2004. *Money and the early Greek mind: Homer, philosophy, tragedy.* Cambridge: Cambridge University Press.

Seltman, C. T. 1975 [1921]. *The temple coins of Olympia.* New York: Attic Books.

SNG ANS 7: Sylloge nummorum graecorum (United States). The collection of the American Numismatic Society, part 7: *Macedonia* vol. I: *cities, Thraco-Macedonian tribes, Paeonian kings.* New York: American Numismatic Society. 1987.

SNG Cop. Philasia-Laconia: Sylloge nummorum graecorum (Denmark). The royal collection of coins and medals, Danish National Museum, vol. 3, *Greece: Thessaly to Aegean Islands.* West Milford, NJ: Sunrise Publications. 1982.

SNG Delep.: Sylloge nummorum graecorum (France). Bibliothèque Nationale: Cabinet des Médailles Collection Jean et Marie Delepierre. Paris: Bibliothèque Nationale. 1983.

SNG Fitzwilliam: Sylloge nummorum graecorum (Great Britain), vol. 4: *Fitzwilliam Museum: Leake and General collections,* part 4: *Arcnania-Phliasia.* 1956.

SNG Lockett: Sylloge nummorum graecorum (Great Britain), vol. 3: *The Lockett collection.* part IV: *Peloponnese - Aeolis (gold and silver).* 1945.

SNG Manchester: J. F. Healy. 1986. *Sylloge nummorum graecorum (Great Britain),* vol. 7: *Manchester University Museum: the Raby and Güterbock collections.* Oxford and London: Oxford University Press and Spink and Son.

Spier, J. 1987. Lycian coins in the Decadrachm hoard. In: I. Carradice, ed., *Coinage and administration in the Athenian and Persian Empires,* pp. 29–37. Oxford: British Archaeological Reports.

Stazio, A. 1983. Moneta e scambi in Magna Grecia. In: *Megale Hellas: storia e civiltà della Magna Grecia,* pp. 105–169. Milano: Libri Schweiwiller.

Syll.³: W. Dittenberger. 1915–24. *Sylloge inscriptionum graecarum.* 3rd edition. Leipzig: S. Hirzelium.

Talbert, R. J. A. 1971. Corinthian silver coinage and the Sicilian economy, c. 340 to c. 299 BC. *Numismatic Chronicle* 11: 53–66.

Taxay, D. 1966. *The U. S. Mint and coinage: an illustrated history from 1776 to the present.* New York: Arco Publishing Co.

Thompson, M. 1968. *The Agrinion hoard.* Numismatic Notes and Monographs 159. New York: American Numismatic Society.

Tod, M. N. 1948. *A selection of Greek historical inscriptions.* 2 vols. Oxford: Clarendon Press.

Trevett, J. 2001. Coinage and democracy at Athens. In: A. Meadows and K. Shipton, eds. *Money and its uses in the ancient Greek world,* pp. 23–34. Oxford: Oxford University Press.

Troxell, H. 1982. *The coinage of the Lycian League.* Numismatic Notes and Monographs 162. New York: American Numismatic Society.

Trundle, M. 2004. *Greek mercenaries from the late Archaic period to Alexander.* London: Routledge.

van Alfen, P. G. 2005. Problems in ancient imitative and counterfeit coinage. In: Z. H. Archibald, J. K. Davies, and V. Gabrielsen, eds., *Making, moving and managing: the new world of ancient economies, 323–31 BC,* pp. 322–354. Oxford: Oxbow.

Vollgraff, W. 1901. Inscriptions de Béotie. *Bulletin de correspondance hellénique* 25: 359–378.

Walker, A. 2004. The coinage of the Eleans for Olympia. In: *Leu Numismatics, Auction 90, 10 May 2004.* Coins of Olympia. The BCD collection.

———. 2006. Coins of Peloponnesos. The BCD collection. *LHS Numismatics, Auction 96, 8–9 May 2006.*

Wallace, R. W. 1987. The origin of electrum coinage. *American Journal of Archaeology* 91.3: 385–397.

Wallace, W. P. 1956. *The Euboian League and its coinage.* Numismatic Notes and Monographs 134. New York: American Numismatic Society.

Warren, J. L. 1863. *Greek federal coinage.* London.

Warren, J. 1989. The 1980 Kato Klitoria hoard. In: G. Le Rider, K. Jenkins, et al., eds., *Kraay-Mørkholm essays. Numismatic studies in memory of C. M. Kraay and O. Mørkholm,* pp. 291–300. Louvain-la-Neuve: Institut Súperieur d'archéologie et d'histoire de l'art.

Wartenberg, U. 1997. The Alexander-Eagle hoard: Thessaly 1992. *Numismatic Chronicle* 157: 179–188.

Willem, J. M. 1965. *The United States trade dollar: America's only unwanted, unhonored coin.* Racine, Wis.: Whitman Publishing Co.

Williams, R. T. 1965. *The confederate coinage of the Arcadians in the fifth century BC.* Numismatic Notes and Monographs 155. New York: American Numismatic Society.

———. 1972. *The silver coinage of the Phokians.* London: Royal Numismatic Society.

Wroth, W. 1894. *Catalogue of the Greek coins of Troas, Aeolis, and Lesbos. A catalogue of the Greek coins in the British Museum*. London: British Museum.

———. 1902. Greek coins acquired by the British Museum in 1901. *Numismatic Chronicle* 2: 313–344.

Index Locorum

Hoard Index

Other

General Index

Inconsistencies inevitably appear in the spelling of ancient names. In general, the spelling in the index reflects that used in the body of the text.

reasons for striking, 191, 204–205,
  214–215
  See also Alexander-type coinage,
    posthumous; bronze coinage;
    cooperative coinage; electrum
    coinage; fractional coinage;
    fiduciarity; Kleuchares coinage
    of Side; large denomination
    coinage
Coinage Decree, Athenian, *see* Athenian Coinage Decree (*IG* I³ 1453)
coin types,
  See cistophoroi; Croesids; drachms,
    pseudo-Rhodian of Mylasa;
    fractional coinage; large de-
    nomination coinage; pegasi;
    "Phokaic staters;" *plinthopho-
    roi*; small denomination
    coinage
coins,
  archaeological publication of,
    177–180, 181, 187–188, 192
  as bullion, 53
  hoarding of, 218
colony, 54–55, 57, 70, 75, 76–8, 207,
  207 nn.18, 20, 208
commodification,
  of electrum coins, 215, 218
"common benefactors",
  epithet of the Romans, 131, 133
cooperative coinage, 201–235,
  commercial motives for, 212–219,
    213 n.41
  economic motives for, 203–205,
    210, 220–221, 225, 228,
    230–231, 235
  production of at Phokaia and
    Mytilene, 210–219
  purposes of, 202–205, 203 n.8,
    208–210, 212, 219–220,
    223–225, 227, 234–235
  types and inscriptions of, 205–209,
    213 n.39, 221, 225, 226–227,
    229, 231–232, 233–234
Corinth, *see* Korinth
Corcyra, 207 n.20
Corycean cave, 179, 180, 188, 197
credit, 88, 88 n.4, 94 n.43
  social, 27, 29
  "credit money," 88
Croesids, 45, 57
Croesus, 39, 39 n.10, 43, 44, 45
Curium, 188, 197
Cyrene, 179, 180, 181, 182, 184, 185,
  188, 197
Cyzicus, *see* Kyzikos

Datos, 62, 70, 70 n.43, 73, 75

Datos-Crenides area,
  as metal-producing district, 67–68
Delos, 179, 180, 184, 185, 188, 190,
  191, 192, 192, 197
Demeter,
  important deity on Paros and
    Thasos, 78
Demetrius of Phalerum, 120
Demetrius Poliorcetes, 113, 120, 121
Demochares of Leukonoe, 120, 121
Dicaea by Abdera, *see* Dikaia
Dikaia, 63, 68, 202
Dionysios Chalkous, 99
Dionysios son of Melas, 134, 135
Dionysos,
  important deity in Thrace, 62,
    63, 75,
  important on Paros and Thasos, 78
  worshipped in Mylasa, 145,
  important at Thebes 229
dokimasia, 117, 119
"downdating" of hoards, 55
drachms,
  pseudo-Rhodian of Mylasa,
    125–133, 137–146
Dura Europos, 179, 180, 188, 198
Dyme, 225, 231
Dyrrhakion, 202, 207 n.20

economy, economies, 203
  closed monetary, 185
  of early Hellenistic Athens, 110,
    121–122
  of *koina*, 220, 222–225, 230–231,
    234–235
  modernizing vs. primitivizing
    views of, 88, 88 n.4, 94, 94 n.41
  multi-centered, in Homer, 26, 30
  of non-Greek world, 30
  ancient Greek vocabulary of, 24
Edonoi, 79
Eion, 62, 70, 73, 77
"Eion", 63, 64, 65, 68
eikostē, 101
eisphora,
  at Athens, 101
  levied by Boiotian *koinon*, 224, 225
  levied by Akhaian *koinon*, 234
enktesis, 222, 235
electrum coinage,
  early Anatolian, 37–46, 216, 217,
    217 n.55, 218
  of Kyzikos, 214–219
  of Mytilene and Phokaia, 211–219
  production of, 216–218, 216 n.52,
    219
  See also "lion paw fractions",
    KUKALIM, WALWET

Eleusis, 103
Elis, 202, 228, 231
Ennea Odoi, 63, 63–64 n.12
epigamia, 222
eppasis, 222 n.65, 235
Eretria, 202
ethnos, 219
ethnē,
  Thraco-Macedonian, 68, 100, 202,
    207 n.17
Euboia, 202
Euromos, 130, 131
exchange,
  in Homer, 17, 24–25, 27–30, 31,
    32–33
  development of in Archaic Greece,
    24, 30–34
  vocabulary of, 24–27
  See also spheres of exchange
exetastēs, 113

Failaka, 179, 180, 188, 198
fiduciarity, 53–54, 100, 104
Finley, M.I., 21, 34
fractional coinage, 213, 214, 228 n.80
  early Abderite, 49, 52, 53
  of Akhaian *koinon*, 232
  Athenian, 103, 104
  of Boiotian *koinon*, 228
  of Greek cities in Thrace, 64, 65,
    68, 70, 76 n.63
  Milesian, 57
  of Orkhomenos, 227
  See also "lion paw" fractions

Galatia, 152–153
Galepsos, 62, 64, 67, 68, 70, 72, 73, 75,
  76 n.62, 77–78
Gazoros, 71
Gela, 209 n.25
gifts,
  in Homer, 5–6, 25, 27, 33
gold,
  in Homeric exchange, 17, 28–29, 31
  mined in Thrace, 67–68
gold:silver ratio, 217–218
Gortyn, 202, 207 n.17
Greek law, 87, 87 n.2
Greek Law of Sale, 87, 88, 93, 93 n.38
Gyges,
  name not on early electrum coin-
    age, 38–39

Haliartos, 229 n.83, 230
Halikarnassos, 130
Helike, 231, 232
Herakleia by Latmos, 130, 132
Herakles,
  important deity in Thrace, 62,

Plates

Plate 1

1   2   3

4   5   6

All coins on this plate are enlarged

KUKALIṂ, WALWET, and the Artemision Deposit

Plate 2

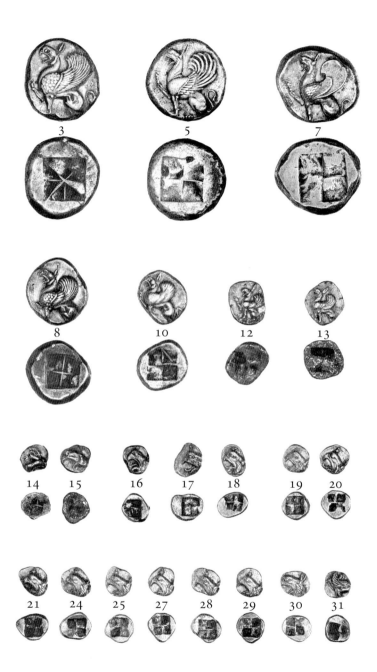

3 5 7

8 10 12 13

14 15 16 17 18 19 20

21 24 25 27 28 29 30 31

Small Change and the Beginning of Coinage at Abdera

Plate 3

The "Lete" Coinage Reconsidered

Plate 4

The "Lete" Coinage Reconsidered

Plate 5

57 61 63 65 66 81 92 93 96

110 113 114 115 116 133 137 139 142

144 145 147 148 149 150 156 161 169

170 172 178 182 185 186 188 190

1992:83

200

The Pseudo-Rhodian Drachms of Mylasa Revisited

Plate 7

Group I

Group II

Group III

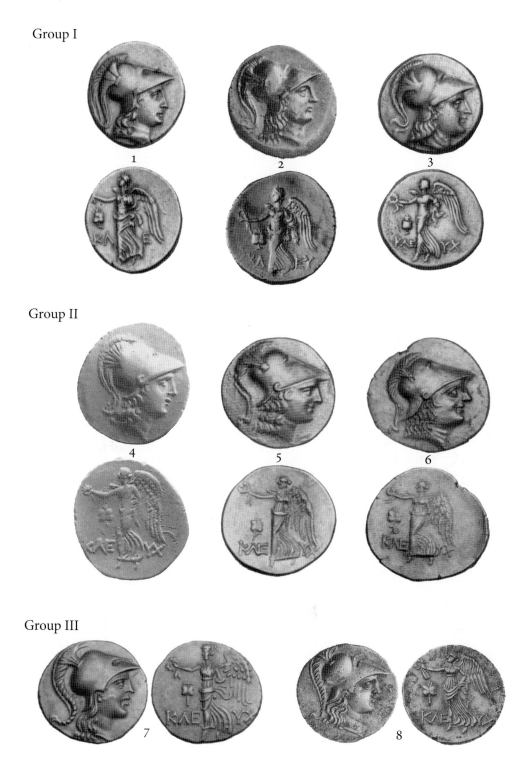

Amyntas, Side, and Pamphylian Plain

Plate 8

Group IV   Amyntas

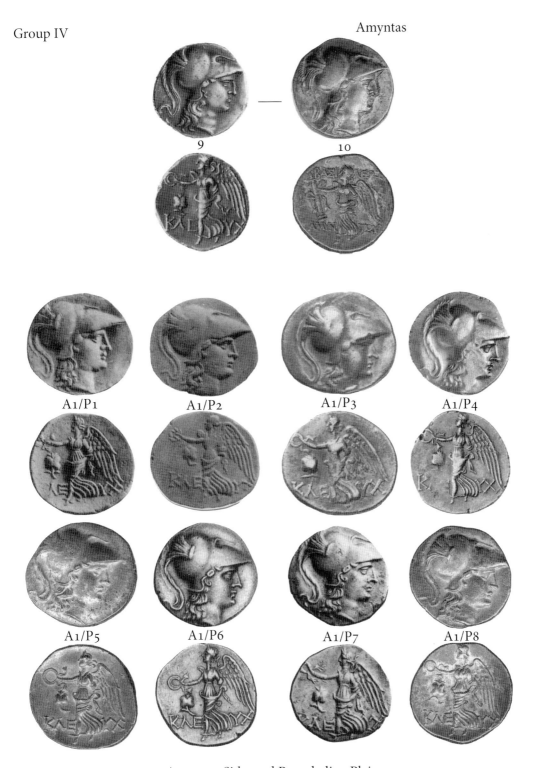

9 — 10

A1/P1   A1/P2   A1/P3   A1/P4

A1/P5   A1/P6   A1/P7   A1/P8

Amyntas, Side, and Pamphylian Plain

Plate 9

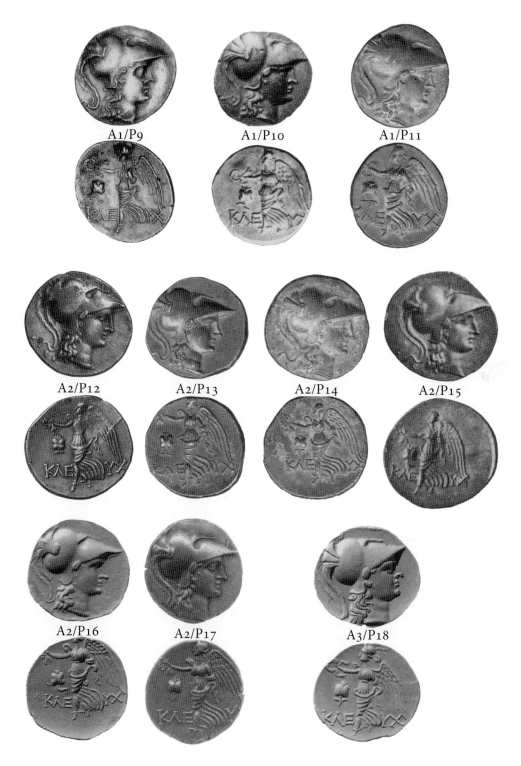

A1/P9　　　　A1/P10　　　　A1/P11

A2/P12　　　A2/P13　　　A2/P14　　　A2/P15

A2/P16　　　A2/P17　　　A3/P18

Amyntas, Side, and Pamphylian Plain

Plate 10

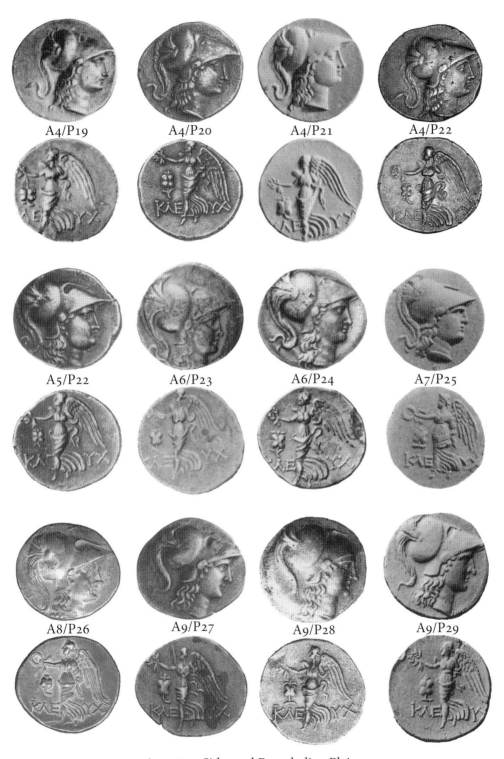

A4/P19   A4/P20   A4/P21   A4/P22

A5/P22   A6/P23   A6/P24   A7/P25

A8/P26   A9/P27   A9/P28   A9/P29

Amyntas, Side, and Pamphylian Plain

Plate 11

A9/P30   A9/P31   A9/P32

A10/P33   A10/P34   A10/P35

BMC 44   *BMC* 39   *BMC* 45   *BMC* 41

Amyntas, Side, and Pamphylian Plain

Plate 12

BMC 46   *BMC* 42   *BMC* 40   *BMC* 38

BMC 7   *BMC* 6   *BMC* 3   *BMC* 1

BMC 2   *BMC* 5   *BMC* 4

Amyntas, Side, and Pamphylian Plain

Plate 13

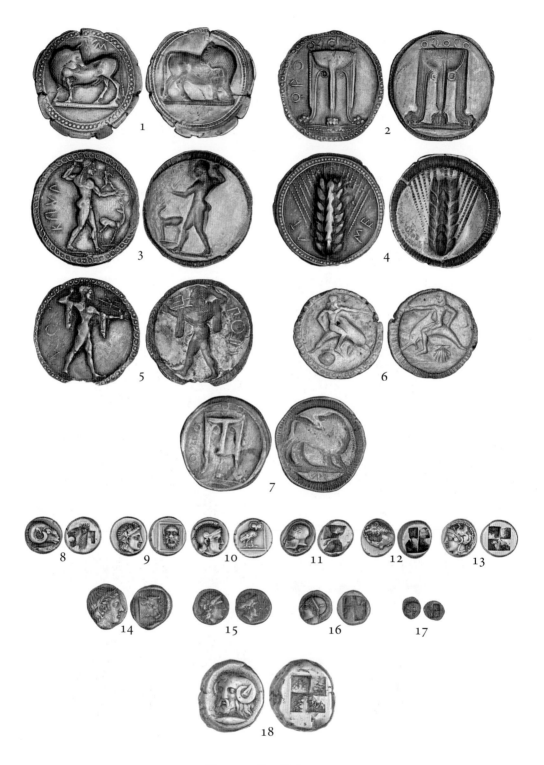

Cooperative Coinage

Plate 14

Cooperative Coinage